BOSCH
Invented for life

 CAMBERLEY AUTO FACTORS
www.camberleyautofactors.com

 C000182536

 THE CARAVAN CLUB

 JAGUAR

 KONI

 JAGUAR • DAIMLER
Heritage Trust

 QH

 RO

 UNIPART AUTOMOTIVE

THE BRITISH AT
Le Mans
85 YEARS OF ENDEAVOUR

IAN WAGSTAFF

THE **BRITISH** AT

Le Mans

85 YEARS OF ENDEAVOUR

FOREWORD BY
DEREK BELL MBE

MRP PUBLISHING LTD for MOTOR RACING PUBLICATIONS
PO Box 1318, Croydon CR9 5YP, England
www.mrpbooks.co.uk

Distributed by Vine House Distribution Ltd
Mullany Business Park, Deanland Road, Golden Cross, East Sussex BN27 3RP
Email: sales@vinehouseuk.co.uk
www.vinehouseuk.co.uk

North American distribution by
MBI Publishing Company
St Paul, Minnesota 55101-3885, USA

First published 2006
Copyright © 2006 Ian Wagstaff and MRP Publishing Ltd

Ian Wagstaff has asserted his right to be identified as the author of this work

British Library Cataloguing in Publication Data
A catalogue record for this book is available from the British Library.

ISBN 1-899870-80-6
EAN 9781899870806

Printed and bound in Great Britain by The Amadeus Press, Cleckheaton, West Yorkshire

Design by Jack Andrews Design, Westerham, Kent – www.jackandrews.co.uk

CONTENTS

Introducing BEN

by Gerard Barclay, Chief Executive

Through the publication of this book, the author Ian Wagstaff has expertly laid out the rich history of the British at Le Mans and highlighted the contribution we as a nation have made to the event. In doing so he has also created an opportunity through which he can support his chosen charity, BEN, the Motor and Allied Trades Benevolent Fund. Sales of this book will raise significant funds that will enable us to continue our much-needed work and therefore we are extremely grateful to both Ian, and the publisher John Blunsden, who have kindly donated their services to the project.

I am sure that many of you reading this Foreword will have never heard of BEN and so I thought it appropriate to outline what we do.

BEN – the Motor and Allied Trades Benevolent Fund – is the automotive and related industries' own charity and the very heart of the industries we encompass.

The Fund was founded in 1905 by A. J. Wilson, then an advertising agent for Dunlop, because he recognised that a number of his colleagues were facing terrible hardship, and rather than continue the ad hoc collections he was being asked to contribute to, he wanted to offer them an organised body that could help solve the issues they were facing. Today, over one hundred years later, Wilson's caring vision is as much needed as it was then, and reaches out to more than 15,000 people, over 50 per cent of whom are of working age. BEN is not cause specific, and our only defining factor is that we exist to help and support the people who work or have worked in the industries we serve. BEN helps men, women and children connected to the motor, motorcycle, cycle, commercial vehicle and agricultural engineering industries plus all their associated trades who are facing times of need, hardship or crisis. For the last 20 years this has meant that we have

had a strong involvement with the Motorsport industry, working with the British Racing Drivers' Club, the Motorsport Industry Association and the Grand Prix Mechanics Benevolent Fund, who over the years have made a number of financial contributions to BEN in support of our work in this sector.

So how does BEN Help? The work we undertake is split into two main areas. Our team of professional Welfare Officers and network of over 90 trained welfare volunteers provide vital support to people in the community. Help is given in many ways including advice, support and friendship for those facing distress. We also provide financial and emotional support to people facing severe hardship.

In addition, BEN has four residential and nursing centres, which provide a home to over 350 people of differing needs and ages. At BEN's newest centre, Town Thorns, near Coventry, there is a 'Young Physically Disabled Unit' and at Alexandra House, in Southport, a 'Palliative Care Unit'. Residential, nursing and specialised 'Elderly Mentally Infirm' care plus sheltered housing are also offered.

As well as the nursing and residential centres, the Fund operates a workplace daycare centre in Coventry. This was the first of its kind to be opened in the UK, offering a safe and comfortable environment where anyone with a connection to the automotive and related industries can leave an elderly parent or relative to be cared for during the working day, leaving them free to concentrate on the job that provides their livelihood.

We hope you'll agree it's a worthy cause, and accept our heartfelt thanks, as by purchasing this book you are providing support for thousands of people in need.

FOREWORD

by Derek Bell MBE

When one considers the British influence at Le Mans since the early part of the last century, it's long overdue that someone should write about it.

Le Mans would not have become the world's greatest race had it not been for the Brits! In many different ways we have supplied a major part of the grid and filled the circuit with up to 50 per cent of the fans, who have drunk most of the beer and injected vast amounts of cash into the local coffers.

Of course, we must not overlook the fact that it was the French who gave us such an amazing event in order to do this, or that despite the rest of the world wishing to change the format of their race, the ACO have done a magnificent job in religiously sticking to their rules and always governing with a rod of steel.

Ian Wagstaff writes at length about the men, the machines and the teams that have graced the eight-mile circuit of Le Mans, but from a personal angle I would like to record how much Le Mans has done for we the drivers in providing us with a unique stage on which to perform and a setting for the many tales we can tell for the rest of our lives of our experiences on that challenging circuit.

Imagine those moments at night on the demanding Mulsanne straight, before it was neutered, holding the throttle to the floor in top gear for a full minute. That unique sense of loneliness, almost a tranquility, sitting in the greatest cars ever, in a capsule surrounded by the finest engineering in the world; the howl of the engine becoming a purr as we glance at the instruments, checking that the left bank of the engine is the same temperature as the right, maybe the oil temperature has decreased as the cool night air assists the turbos in creating more power, watching the rev-counter jostle between 8100 and 8200, and considering that maybe we had achieved 245mph that time.

Then peering out of the screen as the miles thunder by and the tops of the trees are silhouetted by the full moon; just miniscule adjustments on the wheel keep the car straight on that narrow trace that has become so revered until we have to balance the car flat through the fastest corner in the world, down into the braking area for Mulsanne corner.

I am so fortunate to be one of the few drivers to have had this almost surreal experience; we are so privileged. Driving into the night and into the dawn are very difficult but special times, but to me the time around midnight is the most spectacular of all.

One cannot mention Le Mans without relating to the fans, so many of whom make the pilgrimage each year from all over the world. My first win was with the John Wyer Gulf Mirage team in 1975; this was my first with Jacky Ickx. Following that I won with Porsche, and I have to say that although, quite understandably, I did not receive the same level of support from the crowd that I had enjoyed in the Mirage years, it was very interesting to witness the fans after dawn on Sunday, after many cars had fallen out and they realized that there was a Brit in front, albeit in a Porsche. Gradually the Union Jacks started appearing, particularly over the brow at the Dunlop bridge and down into the Esses; this is when their enthusiasm really pumps you up, when exhaustion is beginning to creep in.

I shall never forget the time when, following victory with Jacky, we went to the once famous Restaurant des Hunaudières on the Mulsanne straight for dinner with M. Chandon. As we parked outside, hundreds of fans both inside and outside the restaurant stood on the tables to cheer us and clap. It was a truly memorable moment, and it made me realize that someone had appreciated our efforts!

I suppose my one regret was that I never won for a famous British manufacturer like Bentley, Aston Martin or Jaguar, but I will never complain about driving for Porsche, to my mind the greatest team of all; thanks to their brilliant engineers and crew we had unparalleled success. And of course I had the greatest drivers of the time as my team-mates; Ickx, Stuck and Holbert.

As Jacky once wrote to me: "We need the best designers, engineers and mechanics to build the best car, and then we need luck." I had all of those from time to time, but my lifetime memory will be standing on the winners' rostrum with Andy Wallace and Justin, my eldest son, having driven the McLaren into third place in 1995 on Father's Day; it was so nearly a British victory!

What more can one say about a race that has given so much pleasure to so many people for so many years?

INTRODUCTION

*This book is dedicated to the memory of Len Seldon and Roy Wagstaff,
both of whom spent their working lives in the British motor industry.*

Writing in *The Times*, Michael Sissons pointed out that Britishness was a 19th century invention, designed to enable the British Empire to function. There is something about the Empire behind the rationale for this book. Politically correct it will not be, it may even stoop to jingoism, but it is written, and is to be read, in the firm belief that the British truly do rule over La Sarthe, even if the results sheets of the past couple of decades would indicate otherwise.

I confess that initially I did not really grasp the full significance of the subject myself despite the privilege of having been there to witness the historic victories of 1988 and 2003. It took a telephone conversation with Alain de Cadenet halfway through the writing to really get to grips with the concept. I can trace my family in England at least back to the mid-16th century; I do not think any of them even travelled out of the country until young, fated Harry Wagstaff left with the Bedfordshire Regiment for the Western Front. However, it took a man whose father was French to make me truly understand the ethos behind this book. I cannot begin to describe it in the few short words of this introduction. You have to be there to feel it, but perhaps you will have at least some small inclination of the concept by the time you have finished reading the following pages.

Patriotism is a strange thing. Indeed, in the wrong hands it can lead to an Isandhlwana or a Heysel. One has to have a certain sympathy with the pre-war students of the Oxford Union for their views on the subject. When it comes to sport it can, though, be a thing of joy, which is why I find something missing in the almost non-nationalistic world of current Formula One. It can also bring you down; the slog from Twickenham to Richmond Station, when France has just snatched the Grand Slam away in the last quarter of the match, is the longest walk you can make. But you bounce back; Jonny Wilkinson kicks a winning drop goal and suddenly the world is a wonderful place. The British at Le Mans seem to follow their compatriots, whether they be in a Bentley EXP Speed 8 or a Morgan Aero 8, with a passion that they rarely show in Grand Prix racing. I suppose you can understand this to a point. The current World Champion's car was built in my native county of Oxfordshire...but it is French, isn't it?

However, there is more to being British at Le Mans that just

waving flags at a Jaguar, Aston Martin or Bentley as it goes past the grandstands. There is all the activity that surrounds the race and the many British aspects of that. I have to use a French expression for it; it is a certain *je ne sais quoi*.

I cannot claim the idea as mine own. It came first from Gordon Creese, special events manager for BEN, the Automotive and Related Industries Own Charity. We had both noticed that the only book specializing on a British aspect of Le Mans was one on the British cars...and that a Frenchman wrote it. It gives but one sentence on the Lagonda victory of 1935, but to criticize would be to run the risk of heaving breezeblocks around in my greenhouse. The complete book of the British, the following cannot be. Indeed, I flee from any volume that describes itself as "the complete book" of anything; usually they are pretty thin. Instead this can only be seen as a celebration of the British at Le Mans, a hymn to every Brit involved, not just the cars and the drivers, but an endless flow from Vernon Pugh to Matthew Woodward, although what Mr and Miss Pugh would have thought of the beer mountains I shudder to think.

Tom Kristensen receives scant mention in this book, and that only because he was Guy Smith's co-driver in a Bentley. Jacky Ickx appears more than the Dane, but only because most of his wins were shared with British drivers. This work has strict, and I hope unique, parameters and there are plenty of other books on Le Mans – Amazon currently lists 106 – that will give you a wider picture.

A time-frame of 85 years has been chosen, which might puzzle those who are thinking strictly of the 24-hour race. This year is the 100th anniversary of the first ever Grand Prix, a lengthy affair in itself that was won by Ferenc Szicz in a Renault. This race is of no interest to us because, although Herbert Austin may have been in the crowd, no British drivers or cars were involved. It would be another two years before Austin's own cars were entered for a Grand Prix, and that race would be held in Dieppe. The Grand Prix did, though, return on a few occasions to Le Mans, and in 1921 Segrave and Guinness entered with works-prepared Sunbeams: the British presence at Le Mans had begun. It is from this moment, therefore, that the book takes its subtitle.

This book is structured more as a series of essays rather than providing a single flowing story. Arbitrarily, I have divided the years into eight separate eras. In order that the chapters can be placed into context, each era begins with an overview of how the British performed during the period in question. This is followed by chapters pinpointing a marque, or specific cars, relevant to that period, and then a driver who, I feel, personified that era. Not all were outright winners and none have been great Grand Prix drivers, but they represent either the times or a specific aspect of the period. Perhaps inevitably, there will be some who will disagree with my choice, and I hope that they will at least find their favourites lurking in the text or in one of the many sidebars that are a feature of the book. Those drivers chosen for the latter treatment are there because they have a tale to tell. In results terms they may not necessarily have been successful, they may not even have raced very much at Le Mans, but their collective stories help to build a picture. There is a serendipity about the fourth chapter in each section. These are eight subjects that do not really fall into the above categories; sometimes they are relevant to the period in hand, sometimes not. They enable me to bring in just a few of the many who help to make Le Mans the British event it is.

The nearer I came to finishing the book the more I began to dread the question, "have you spoken to…?" To all those who were met with a sheepish look to their question, I apologise. *Tempus* did indeed *fugit* and, as my elder son asked when I first said I was about to write this book, "how many volumes are you doing?" There are many to whom I have spoken over the years who in some way have helped me understand the British at Le Mans. It would be impossible to list them all here, so I will confine myself to those who have assisted during the nine months since I first looked at a blank Apple Mac screen and thought about John Duff. Some have been subjected to lengthy interviews; others have helped during brief telephone conversations. To those who have contributed their thoughts specifically for the book I must add those who recently I have interviewed for articles on endurance racing for *Racecar Engineering* magazine. There are times when the information that they gave me has spilled over into this work.

There are a few people who I really must single out for special mention. Interviewing the two nonagenarians, Marcus Chambers and Michael Burn, was a great privilege, while Adrian Hamilton, when I arrived to interview him, said that the car was warmed up and would I like to take it out for a while. The car in question was the 1953 winning Jaguar C-type; for the next hour, responsibility weighed heavily upon my shoulders. I risk the sin of omission in publishing the following list of those who I must also thank for their help; to any others I may inadvertently have missed, I offer my apologies.

Bill Allen, Charles Armstrong-Wilson, Richard and Veronica Attwood, James Bailey, Nick Bailey, Clive Baker, Ian Bamsey, Stuart Barnes, Derek Bell, Jeff Bloxham, Nigel Bonnett, Karine Bordeau, Martin Borland, Gordon Bruce, Martin Brundle, Tony Bushe, George Byford, Hugh Chamberlain, Clive Chapman, Sam Collins, Martin Colvill, Ray Cook, Trevor Cook, Chris Cooke, Julian Cooper, Michael Cotton, Shaun Cronin, Simon Cronin, Gordon Cruickshank, Bob Curl, Ted Cutting, Ian Dawson, Alain de Cadenet, Peter Dumbreck, Sarah Durose, Guy Edwards, Roger Ellis, Nick Ferguson-Gow, Patrick Fitz-Gibbon, Trevor Foster, Graham Gauld, Graham Godfrey, David Greenwood, Sir Malcolm Guthrie, Angela Hamilton, Peter Hardman, Michael and Sally Harrison, Cliff Hawkins, Neville Hay, Alan Hearn, Jason Hill, John Hindhaugh, Tim Holloway, Paddy Hopkirk, John Horsman, George Howard-Chappel, Jill Howes, Nicola Howlett, Miles Hutton, David Ingram, Maurice Jobson, Glyn Jones, Richard Jones, Roger Lane-Nott, Bob Leggett, Martin Lee, Martin Lewis, Robin Liddell, Calum Lockie, Ian Ludgate, Peter Lumsden, Stuart McCrudden, John McCullogh, Michael MacDowel, John McNeil, Allan McNish, Ray Mallock, John Manchester, Rupert Manwaring, Tony Marsh, Bob Marshall, Graham and Wendy Marshall, Simon Maurice, Fiona Miller, Janice Minton, Ed Morris, Graham Morris, Dave Morrison, Gordon Murray, David Northey, Jackie Oliver, Martyn Pass, Patrick Peal, Graham Prince, Ken Rider, Mark Rider, Stuart Rolt, Tony Rolt, Mike Salmon, Roy and Susan Salvadori, Ben Sayer, Roland Schedel, Noel Scholey, Martin Short, Michell Seaman, Adam Sharpe, Ian Skailes, Barrie Smith, Guy and Alicia Smith, Sam Smith, Richard Shepherd-Barron, Stephen Slater, Tony Southgate, Gordon Spice, Quentin Spurring, Dr Stephen Stamp, Sir Jackie Stewart, Steve Tarrant, Michael Taylor, Simon Taylor, Phil Tiller, Ian Titchmarsh, Tony Tobias, Jonathan Tubb, Harry Turner, John Wagstaff (no relation), Chris Wakley, Andy Wallace, Jonathan Ward, David Warnock, Derek Warwick, Gordon Wingrove, Matthew Woodward, Alexander Yelland and the ladies of Chinnor Library.

Many of the photographs in this book come from private collections and are therefore individually credited. However, I must also thank Zoe Mayo (LAT Photographic), Dave Hill (Ford Photographic) and Lynda Clark (BMIHT) for their assistance in sourcing pictures, Stuart Rolt and Adrian Hamilton for allowing me access to their fathers' photographic files, as well as David Rolfe, John Nutter and Alan Shaw of the Bentley Drivers Club for guiding me through the W.O. Bentley Foundation archives including Woolf Barnato's own cuttings books. Nic Waller kindly sent me some of his father Derek's photos from the early 1950s. It is, I believe, Nic's intention eventually to use this never-been-seen-before collection as a basis for a book.

To the above must, of course, be added my publisher John Blunsden, whose patience and calm were inspirational. And the family; we read authors thanking their wives for putting up with the writing of a book. It is only when you actually pen one that you understand what is really meant. Thank you, Gill, and my apologies for this obsession of mine. Thanks too to my elder son Tim for buying the annual 2.00am hot dog at Tertre Rouge; it is probably a good thing it's too dark to see what we are eating. Also apologies to his younger brother Richard for still not having taken him to Le Mans.

Finally, alright, it is not British and there are times in this book when I have patriotically taken a swipe at its treatment of some British entries, but all of us who believe Le Mans to be the greatest motorsporting event on the planet must thank *L'Automobile Club de l'Ouest*, without whom we would have to think of somewhere else to go in mid-June.

Ian Wagstaff
Chinnor, 2006

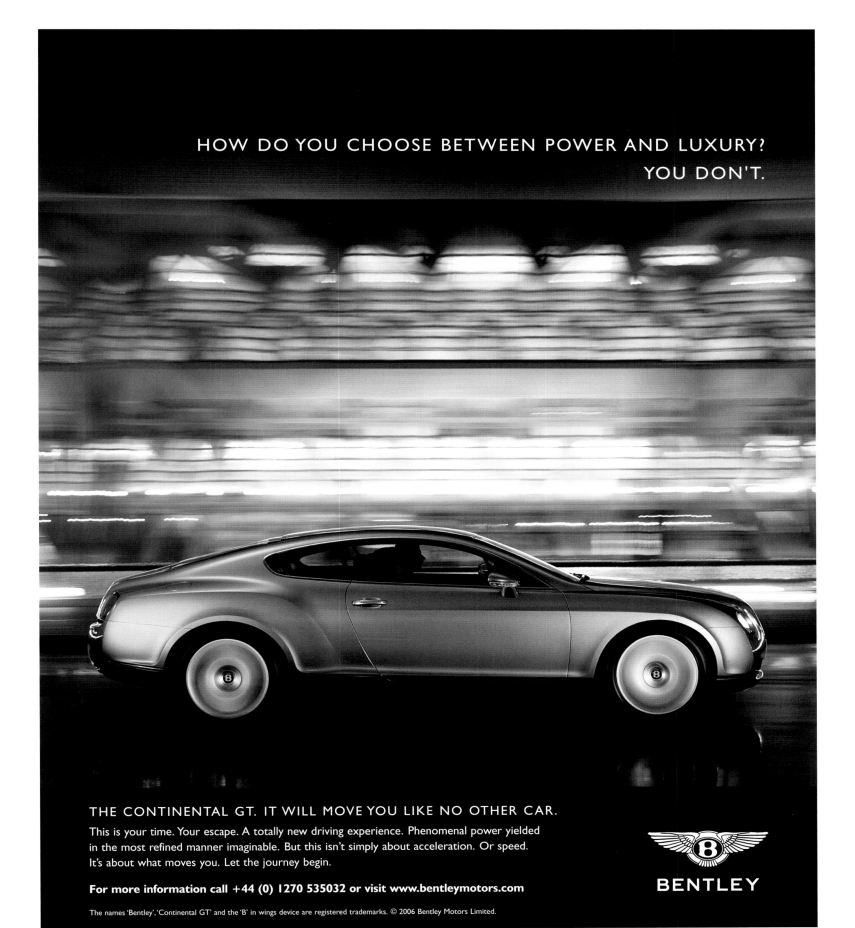

HOW DO YOU CHOOSE BETWEEN POWER AND LUXURY?
YOU DON'T.

THE CONTINENTAL GT. IT WILL MOVE YOU LIKE NO OTHER CAR.

This is your time. Your escape. A totally new driving experience. Phenomenal power yielded in the most refined manner imaginable. But this isn't simply about acceleration. Or speed. It's about what moves you. Let the journey begin.

For more information call +44 (0) 1270 535032 or visit www.bentleymotors.com

BENTLEY

The Bentley Boys

"It has been a very wonderful weekend." So said *The Motor* report of the 1930 Le Mans 24-hour race. Those wonderful weekends had begun at La Sarthe in 1923 and have continued to this day. By 1930 the pioneering marque of Bentley, represented here by the Speed Six that Clive Dunfee has run into the sand at Pontlieue, had been joined by a number of other British makes. The sixth-place Lea-Francis of Sammy Newsome and Keith Peacock passes the stranded Bentley. *(W.O. Bentley Foundation)*

CHAPTER I

THE BRITISH AT LE MANS
1923-1930

"There is nothing so bad or so good that you will not find Englishmen doing it."
(George Bernard Shaw, *The Man of Destiny*)

Blame must be laid at the door of Captain John Duff, proprietor of Duff & Aldington, 10 Upper St Martin's Lane, London WC2, the sole representative in the Long Acre area for the Bentley motorcar. If we are to be pedantic, the wiry Captain Duff was a Canadian and was born in Central China. However, it was he who metaphorically dropped the flag to start the British love affair with *Les Vingt-Quatre Heures du Mans*, that most delightfully absurd of sporting events that so captivates the minds of its aficionados that they annually swarm across the channel in their droves to become a part of it and to soak in its unique atmosphere.

Quite how the race came about is essentially a tale of Frenchmen and so has little place in this book. Also, it has been well recorded elsewhere. Suffice to say that strictly speaking this was not, at first, a 24-hour race, but a far more complicated affair than that, the initial 24 hours of competition being just part of a 72-hour trial to be spread over three years in order to test the speed and endurance of the finest sporting road cars. All but the smallest of them had to have four seats; the concept of the sportscar was still to be defined – and perhaps it never truly has been.

What we now regard as the 1923 race was, in fact, the first qualifying round for a Triennial Cup, donated by one of the aforementioned Frenchmen, Emile Coquille. He was the French agent for the Rudge-Whitworth detachable wire wheel, and it was after this Coventry-based company that the Cup was to be named. Perhaps it is appropriate that those early awards were named after a British firm.

Yet the Triennial Cup was awarded only once, in 1925, and it went not to a British team, but to a French Chenard-Walcker. But in 1924 a Rudge-Whitworth Cup, a biennial award based on an Index of Performance, was also introduced and this continued to be awarded until 1960. An annual overall winner of the endurance race was not officially recognized until 1928, when the Bentley of Woolf 'Babe' Barnato and Bernard Rubin won the 'Special Rudge-Whitworth Cup for greatest mileage in 24 hours'.

If the above three paragraphs have confused you, worry not. Even *The Autocar* wrote that first year: "He would have been a clever man who could have indicated what constituted the basis of the Rudge-Whitworth Cup." But as far as most people are concerned, *Les Vingt-Quatre Heures* began in 1923…and it was not won by a British car. Not yet, anyway.

The proverbial writing, though, was on the wall and a British car, the 3-litre Bentley entered by Duff and co-driven by Frank Clement, from the Cricklewood car maker's experimental department, was the quickest at the track that inaugural year. Clement made the fastest lap, averaging 66.69mph around what was then a 10.73-mile circuit.

Of course, one has to thank the French for laying on the race. It is, after all, the august *Automobile Club de l'Ouest* that has run *Les Vingt-Quatre Heures* from the start. Le Mans may once, in the days of the Plantagenet kings, have been under English rule, but it is now quintessentially a French town. The French car makers, whose products run almost every day on some of the roads that make up the race track, have

John Duff and Frank Clement flew the flag for Britain alone in 1923 and 1924, finishing fourth the first year and winning the next, although such overall placings were unofficial. *(W.O. Bentley Memorial Foundation)*

In 1924 Duff's team established a signalling base at Mulsanne that was linked by landline to the pits. *(W.O. Bentley Memorial Foundation)*

Frank Clement was head of Bentley's experimental department and its one professional driver. W.O. described him as "an irrepressible optimist." *(W.O. Bentley Memorial Foundation)*

had success here from time to time. Peugeot, for example, has won the race twice and Renault once; sometimes their drivers had names like Didier and Jean-Pierre and at others, such as Derek and Mark. In all, cars from the host nation have won at Le Mans 14 times. German machinery, it must be said, has come out on top on 22 occasions, all but one of them from 1970 onwards. One nation, though, has consistently provided winners from 1924 to 2003, missing out only in the 1960s. (Even then, the 1968 and 1969 winner was assembled in Slough, but being a Ford these tend to be claimed as US wins; certainly the organizer's records state that they were so.) The same nation has provided 32 winning drivers, five more than its nearest rival. It can even lay claim to one of its tyre companies (although Dunlop has latterly become US-owned) having shod 34 race winners, 20 more than the next up. That nation is, of course, the United Kingdom of Great Britain and Northern Ireland.

Its first representative, the Captain Duff-entered Bentley 3-litre of 1923, proved a fine precursor of what was to come. Duff, like so many at the time a Great War veteran, was keen on the idea of the Rudge-Whitworth Cup. Indeed, he is thought to have been one of the first to enter for it. However, W.O. Bentley, founding father of the marque that still carries his name, thought it a "ridiculous" idea, suggesting that no car would survive it, and only with "massive reservations" did he agree to the idea and to lending Clement as one of the car's drivers. Arthur Saunders and Jack Bezzant were the mechanics, the pair travelling in the car to the track from Dieppe with Clement at the wheel and everything that was needed stowed on board. At the last minute Bentley agreed to supervise Duff's pit which, he recalled later, was little more than a tent. It was an idea he was not to regret; a few hours into the race and he had changed his mind. In his autobiography Bentley said that he "began to realise that this as a race might have been instituted especially for our benefit." The D139, as it went past the pits, may be said to have been his road to Damascus.

It rained a lot that first year and the road broke up very early in the race. Duff, finding himself four laps behind the leader on that first Sunday morning, and with the weather having improved, started chasing hard, almost catching up before his brakes failed for a second time and he sailed up the escape road at the Mulsanne corner. At this stage of the race he was regularly breaking the lap record, but then he ran out of fuel at midday some three miles from the pits. His co-driver, Clement, borrowed a soldier's bicycle and set off from there with cans of petrol. However, the reason for the loss of fuel was that the tank had been holed by a stone, and over two hours were to be taken up in repairing it.

The Frenchman whose bicycle Clement had taken – without permission, it has to be admitted – was reported to have "heaved an immense sigh of relief" when the Bentley eventually pulled into the pits with his property in the tonneau.

The incident at Mulsanne had not been the first problem with the Bentley's two-wheel brakes. Earlier in the race these had been shown to be inadequate. *The Autocar*, while praising the car's "low build and racing equipment," called the absence of front-wheel braking "a most serious disadvantage." Of all the faster competitors, the Bentley was the only one to be so-handicapped. Duff nearly rammed another car that had braked sharply with a burst tyre. A headlamp was also damaged by a stone, causing further problems. The following year the car would be fitted with brakes on all wheels and a headlamp stone guard. Fifth place was a poor reward for all the effort in 1923, but Bentley had shown what it could do at Le Mans. *The Autocar's* report said that the duel between the English car and the French Chenard-Walcker had been the outstanding feature of the race. It also pointed out that Duff and Clement had driven during the rain that fell during the early part of the race without either headgear or goggles. "The French spectators were certain they would catch cold." One thing was certain: they would be back.

The number of British cars should have doubled in 1924, but the Sunbeam to be driven by Kenelm Lee Guinness and Dario Resta was withdrawn. Duff, back again with Clement and with a new 3-litre chassis, was reported to have appeared resplendent in blue beret and brown plus-fours. *The Motor* praised the speed in which he both raised and lowered his Bentley's hood; a new rule had been introduced that year mandating the erection of the hood for two laps. It has to be said, though, that the brave Canadian made a poor start and that his car was to suffer from a jammed gear-change and broken shock absorbers, but on the Sunday morning it took the lead from a La Lorraine. In the last hour Duff decided to change the rear wheels as a precaution and found the locking ring to be seized. The rules then dictated an average speed for a five-lap period which included wheel changing, something the driver did not realize. The team was therefore credited with a total of 1290 miles rather than the 1380 that were actually covered; it was to be the slowest ever Le Mans victory. Nevertheless, it was enough to give Britain its first victory at Le Mans, officially just 10 miles ahead of the La Lorraine, but as Bentley was to point out, in reality nearly 100 miles to the good.

The following year was the first for which the British arrived in any numbers. There were two Bentleys this time, which were regarded as the favourites; even the French were said to have thought they would win the Triennial Cup. Joining them were two 3-litre Sunbeams and even a 747cc Austin Seven, although the latter – the smallest car in the race – would only last eight laps before retiring with a holed radiator. The famed Le Mans start, in which the drivers had to run across the road to their cars, was introduced that year and in those days they had to erect their hood and side curtains before proceeding. Duff was again the most successful at this, but Henry Segrave, the only Briton to win a Grand Prix during that era, was in front by the end of the first lap in his Sunbeam. H. 'Bertie' Kensington-Moir, in the second Bentley that he was sharing with Dr J. Dudley Benjafield, caught Segrave after two hours and the pair scrapped for the next three laps. The British were taking Le Mans seriously. However, it was another two years before they were to begin domination. Both Bentleys retired, the previous year's winner following an under-bonnet fire caused when the float chamber of a carburettor broke. The other ran out of fuel due to a miscalculation caused by testing the car with the hood up. The Sunbeam that S.C.H. 'Sammy' Davis shared with French driver Jean Chassagne finished second, but the Segrave/Duller car was eliminated with clutch trouble.

The Bentley attack had grown to three cars for 1926, but their time was yet to come and all three retired. 'W.O.' reckoned that preoccupation with record

breaking at Montlhéry might have had something to do with it. No other British cars were entered in either this or the following year.

The Bentleys nearly did not win in 1927 either, but lack of preparation had nothing to do with it. We are now into the realms of comic book adventure and a story that still resounds today. That the fine journalist Sammy Davis was at the wheel of the star of the tale has helped subsequent generations to marvel at the events. "Written in cold print as part of some book, the whole thing would be deemed fantastic and impossible," recalled Davis in anything but cold print in his book 'W.O'.

Clements and Leslie Callingham were down to drive a 4½-litre, while George Duller with Baron d'Erlanger and Benjafield with Davis were at the wheels of the 3-litres, the Benjafield/Davis car being known as 'Old Number Seven' despite the fact that this time it was carrying the number '3'.

In the twilight hours when, as Davis recorded, distances were difficult to judge, disaster befell. The three Bentleys were out in the lead with Davis having fallen back from Duller to prevent him from being bothered by his headlights. As he approached White House, Davis noticed some splintered wood and a scattering of earth, enough to ring an alarm bell. Nevertheless, he was still not quite prepared for what he found as he rounded the corner. The 4½-litre was on its side with the other 3-litre atop of it. Two French cars, one of which had started the melee by skidding off the road before bouncing back in the path of Callingham, were also part of what Davis described as "an appalling mass of smashed cars." Davis recalled

Following an eventful Great War, John Duff was to purchase two Fiats to race at Brooklands, including the monstrous 'Mephistopheles', which cost him £100. His first Bentley followed and then the partnership with William Aldington as a dealer in that marque. In 1923 he entered Bentley chassis No 141 for Le Mans, also racing the car in the San Sebastian touring car Grand Prix and the George Boillot Cup at Boulogne. The chassis for his 1924 winning car was a new one in which he and Woolf Barnato were also to secure the 24-hour record at the French track, Montlhéry. (W.O. Bentley Memorial Foundation)

that he "slid right into the mass."

He dismounted to search for Duller, shouting "George! George!" On finding that both Duller and Callingham had survived more or less intact ("Are you hurt, George?" to which came the strange reply, presumably referring to the car, "No, but this one's very dead."), he returned to his Bentley and backed out of the tangle of broken cars. As he limped away

with a bent front wheel so another French car crashed into the wreckage. At the pits Davis found the stub-axle was all right and a replacement wheel ran true. One of the headlamps was restored to health and a sidelamp was tied down with tape. Davis "pulled and tugged and pushed" the mudguard roughly back into place. All the time Sammy was working on the car W.O. kept saying: "The axle, look at the axle." But

GRANDS PRIX AT LE MANS

In celebrating 85 years of the British at Le Mans we actually have to go back two years before the inauguration of the 24-hour event. The *Automobile Club de l'Ouest* was asked to run the first post-war *Grand Prix de L'ACF* – colloquially thought of as the French Grand Prix – at Le Mans.

The city had been the site of the first ever Grand Prix back in 1906, when there had been no British presence, although Herbert Austin is reported to have been among the spectators. For the 1921 Grand Prix, a 10.7-mile circuit, which had been chosen the previous year for a *voiturette* (light car) race, was used and the same layout was to be in place for the first six of the 24-hour races and, with one very minor modification, for the following three.

Among the drivers for the 1921 Grand Prix were a young Henry Segrave, taking part in his first major race, and Kenelm Lee Guinness. Both were members of the Anglo-French STD (Sunbeam-Talbot-Darracq) squad. They were said to have displayed great steadiness, although Segrave finished over an hour behind the victor. When asked about the race, Segrave remarked that he was "never likely to forget it." He was to compete just once in the 24-Hours, leading in the early stages of the 1925 race before falling back with clutch trouble, his Sunbeam retiring just before midnight. 'KLG', who gave his initials

to a brand of spark plug, returned to Le Mans in 1922 to win a *voiturette* race.

In 1923 the Grand Prix had moved on to Tours, where the Sunbeams dominated and Segrave came first. Only one other Englishman was to win a French Grand Prix in the inter-war period: William Grover Williams, who raced as 'Williams', took the first Monaco Grand Prix in 1929 and was also the victor when the French *grande epreuve* returned to Le Mans the same year. Reports describe that event as "a dismal affair." Invariably described as enigmatic and recently made the subject of a novel, 'Williams' died while in German custody shortly before the end of the Second World War, having been arrested by the Gestapo two years earlier.

There remained just one more Grand Prix at Le Mans. In 1967, use was made of the Bugatti circuit, a 'Mickey Mouse' affair utilizing the start/finish straight and the pit lane complex, running under the Dunlop bridge and then doubling back through a series of curves and sharp bends behind the paddock. It was in the days when everything seemed green: 14 of the 15 cars – and all of the finishers – were made in the UK, nine of them being painted in the national hue. Six of the drivers were also British, but they didn't fare so well: Jackie Stewart and Chris Irwin were the best of the survivors in their BRMs, being classified third and fifth, respectively, although the latter's H16 engine had cried enough four laps before the end.

The year 2006 sees the 100th anniversary of the inaugural Grand Prix, which took place at Le Mans. However, the first occasion on which British drivers took part in a major event there was the French Grand Prix in July, 1921. Here one of them, Sunbeam-mounted Henry Segrave, avoids the Duesenbergs of eventual winner Jimmy Murphy and André Dubonnet. *(LAT Photographic)*

16

Davis didn't want to look at the axle; it was bent and well back on the right-hand spring. The frame was also bent and the front cross-tube bowed. He drove off "purposely deaf to W.O.'s entreaties."

Despite its sad state, the Bentley continued on in second place. Starter motor trouble for the leading Aries meant that the British car overcame a four-lap deficit to put itself on the lead lap. Then the French car pulled away again. Late on the Sunday morning W.O. thought he heard a change in the engine noise of the leader. Benjafield, now at the wheel of the Bentley, was aghast to see a 'faster' signal as he passed the pits. With an hour and a half to go before the end of the race W.O. was proved right as the Aries stopped at Mulsanne corner and 'Old Number Seven' limped on to a famous victory. Amazingly it is in the record books as the easiest win, the Bentley finishing 217 miles ahead of the second-placed Salmson.

It was the beginning of a run of four wins for the marque, with Woolf Barnato, heir to the interests of the Kimberley diamond company, about to put himself in the record books with three victories from just three starts. The nationality of the opposition changed over these years, the most formidable being Germany with the 7.1-litre Mercedes SS that took on the Bentleys in 1930. That this race, at least up until 2.30 on the Sunday morning, was inspirational can be seen in the theory that Ian Fleming based an incident in his book *Moonraker* on it. Forget what the film and toy car industries say about Aston Martin, the true James Bond chase features 007 at the wheel of a Bentley, his adversary Hugo Drax, driving a Mercedes.

Five Bentleys – three works Speed Sixes and the two supercharged 4½-litres of the Hon Dorothy Paget – took on the sole Mercedes of Rudolf Caracciola and Christian Werner. Davis recalled that the team was worried because "as W.O. pointed out, we had 'got' to win."

For over half the race the Bentleys harried the

German car, sometimes leading, sometimes not. Sir Henry 'Tim' Birkin in one of the fast Paget cars was – as had already been agreed – particularly aggressive in the opening stages, but as the race progressed so it fell to Barnato and Glen Kidston to be the Mercedes' main thorn. Once the Mercedes failed to restart following a night-time pit stop, the claim being that its dynamo had burnt out, the Bentleys could settle down to take first and second places, the Barnato/Kidston car finishing ahead of another of the Speed Sixes. It was the second win for the car known as 'Old Number One', the third for Barnato and the fifth for Bentley. "It was a notable triumph for British cars," Davis wrote two years later. The Bentley marque, though, was not to win again for 73 years.

The number of British cars in the race increased during these early years. French entrants, which had been represented by all but one of the cars in 1923, dropped to below half and in 1928 and 1929 it had been the Americans who had challenged the Bentleys. In 1928 a Stutz threatened, and eventual winners Barnato and Rubin only won by eight miles. The battle had been close until 2.30 on the Sunday afternoon

By the turn of the decade the Le Mans pits were more sophisticated than they had been in 1923. Here the Birkin/Chassagne supercharged car makes one of its night-time pit stops during the 1930 race. *(W.O. Bentley Memorial Foundation)*

W.O. reckoned that in 1927, "for the price of three damaged cars," his company scooped the headlines of the press, putting the Bentley marque firmly on the map. The White House crash, reported Sammy Davis as he returned to the pits, was "a most unholy mess!" *(W.O. Bentley Memorial Foundation)*

Davis and Benjafield pressed on after the 1927 White House crash despite a twisted chassis. The car waves a defiant offside front wing on its way to ultimate victory. (W.O. Bentley Memorial Foundation)

Two Talbots designed by the Swiss-born Georges Roesch were entered for the 1930 race. The John Hindmarsh and Tim Rose-Richards car, seen here at Mulsanne, finished fourth behind the sister car of Brian Lewis and Hugh Eaton. Nine competitors qualified that year for the next season's Rudge-Whitworth Cup, five of the first six being British. (W.O. Bentley Memorial Foundation)

Benjafield (left) and Davis, winners of one of the most remarkable of all Le Mans races. The good doctor pulled into the pits with a quarter of an hour left to allow journalist Davis to carry out the final laps. (W.O. Bentley Memorial Foundation)

when the Stutz lost top gear. Then Barnato also had to slow the Bentley with a cracked chassis and a leaking radiator, enabling the American car to close up, but not by enough. The following year he and Birkin in 'Old Number One' led home three other Bentleys; it was the marque's easiest pre-war victory. In addition to outright victory, the car was also the first to take the Biennial Cup and the Index of Performance as well. Only two other entries were ever able to repeat this feat.

The above would indicate that it was Bentley that dominated the British entry in the early years. But while this is true, others were also lining up. An AC should have run in 1925 but for the last-minute discovery of a fractured radiator holding-down plate; Lagonda, Aston Martin and Alvis all entered the fray in 1928, and Lea-Francis a year later. The front-wheel-drive Alvises did well on their debut, finishing sixth and ninth. The MG name appeared for the first time in 1930. Where Bentley had initially trod, others were now following. It says something for the way in which the British had come to love Le Mans that of these makes, Bentley, MG and Aston Martin have all been back to La Sarthe in the 21st century.

By 1930 the British were beginning to look as if they owned Le Mans, with the 'Roesch' Talbots of Brian Lewis/Hugh Eaton and John Hindmarsh/Tim Rose-Richards following home the two Bentleys and Earl Howe/Callingham in an Alfa Romeo being chased home by the sixth-placed Lea-Francis of Keith Peacock/Sammy Newsome. However, that lone Alfa may have been an indication that things were not going to last that way for long.

CHANGING FACE OF A PUBLIC ROAD CIRCUIT

In 1923 the circuit for *Les Vingt-Quatre Heures* ran as far north as the Le Mans suburb of Pontlieue before heading south down the long N138 towards Mulsanne village, a stretch of road that was to become the most famous straight line in motor racing, the *ligne droit des Hunaudières*, or Mulsanne straight. John Surtees, on his first visit to Le Mans, observed that "it seemed to go on and on everlastingly." At the edge of the village, the course turned sharp right, even if the N138 continued straight on. Stirling Moss recorded how grateful he was for this latter fact when his brakes failed in 1954. The race track ran on through the Indianapolis (slightly banked like its American namesake) and Arnage bends that are still in use today, then ran alongside a building, the White House, creating a deadly blind bend, though seemingly innocent in appearance, that was to become part of Le Mans folklore, and finally on past the pits and up again to the acute hairpin at Pontlieue.

Since 1932, that long drag up to Pontlieue has been omitted, having been replaced by a series of bends that start just after the pits complex and join the N138 at Tertre Rouge corner, thereby reducing the lap distance from over 10 to a little under 8.5 miles. In recent years a regrettable chicane has appeared just after the first long right-hander and before the now familiar Dunlop bridge. Until very recently the road then ran downhill to the Esses, but in the last few years this has been replaced by sweeping curves. From the Esses it is but a short sprint to Tertre Rouge and then along the tree-lined start of the Mulsanne straight.

Two chicanes have now emasculated this long road, the one place where the drivers said they could relax. Relax, at speeds of ultimately up to 250mph? Some terms are relative. Richard Attwood, the 1971 winner, quips that he would no longer like to race at Le Mans "because it's much harder work. We used to have almost a minute of stargazing!"

The White House is now bypassed and another series of curves and bends named after car manufacturers Porsche and Ford ensure that speeds alongside the pits and main grandstands and terraces no longer have the lethal potential of the 1950s. The section from the White House area to Tertre Rouge is now a conventional racetrack such as might be found hosting any common or garden Formula One Grand Prix. There are those who have raced at Le Mans in the past who decry this stretch of the circuit and will pour scorn on the two Mulsanne chicanes, but the demands of modern motorsport mean that the changes probably had to be made. "This track is dangerous," said novelist Nevil Shute, a racing driver himself, on a visit in 1958.

The chicanes apart, the run from Tertre Rouge to the White House is much as it was in 1923, although obviously no longer the rutted track that it was capable of becoming. To stand, in the middle of the night, alongside the Mulsanne kink that before the construction of the chicanes was the most fearsome feature of an otherwise interminable straight, is to participate in a timeless event. Strictly speaking, authority forbids you to be there, but many British fans do appear, and no doubt will continue to find their way through the forest to such vantage points.

Around this section of the track, dotted lines in the centre of the road and signs that point to towns like Angers and Alençon are a reminder that this is the public highway along which any Frenchman can motor sedately in his Renault or Peugeot. But for a few short days and one long weekend in June it becomes the *Circuit Permanent de la Sarthe*, named after the Département and the river that passes by to the west of the circuit.

DICK SEAMAN

In the inter-war period the British Le Mans winners were arguably better known in this country than their Grand Prix counterparts. Of the three Englishmen who did win GPs during this period only Segrave competed in the 24-Hours. However, Chris Nixon, the most recent biographer of Dick Seaman, recorded that the 1938 German Grand Prix winner was an enthusiastic spectator at Le Mans in 1933. Seaman, who was at the start of his own career, drove a 2-litre Bugatti, which he had just persuaded his parent to buy for him, down to La Sarthe with former school friend Tony Cliff.

Cliff remembered the black Bugatti as being a "ghastly little car" that was a trial in which to travel. No arrangement had been made for accommodation, so the pair wandered around the track for a long time before returning exhausted to the car. They then laid down in the car park with their suitcases propped up to protect them from the wind, if not the stumbling French spectators. They had been lying down for about four hours before Seaman was up and off again to see who was leading the race.

Just being at Le Mans can be an exhausting experience, and on the way home a tired Seaman crashed into the back of a bus outside Victoria Station. The car was little damaged and he went on to race it at both Donington and Brooklands later in the year.

Having raced a Lagonda at the Spa 24-Hours in 1936, Seaman was approached to race the marque at Le Mans in 1939. At first he was undecided, feeling, as recorded by his original biographer Prince Chula, that the race was both "dull and dangerous" for a driver, but that he should take the opportunity if waving the flag for Britain. By then he was a winning member of the works Mercedes-Benz team, so he wrote to his employers for permission to race at Le Mans. Director Max Sailer pointed out that not only was June right in the midst of the team's racing season, but that Le Mans event was also a "very dangerous" event. It is, therefore, ironic to record that the greatest British driver of the immediate pre-war period was killed at Spa that June whilst leading the Belgian Grand Prix.

Dick Seaman – a promising life cut short. *(MNF collection)*

"England, My England," wrote Sir Henry Birkin. Jim Dugdale's painting of Birkin, specially commissioned for this book, captures a corner of the double Le Mans winner's "England", the Arnage right-hander at Le Mans. Birkin's first victory at the circuit came in 1929 when he shared this six-cylinder Bentley with Woolf Barnato. *(Original painting by Jim Dugdale – reproduced by kind permission of Bodyshop Magazine)*

CHAPTER 2

'W.O.' AND
THE BENTLEYS

"These are the things that make England." (Stanley Baldwin)

If there is one man who personifies the British at Le Mans in the early days it is, despite his initial lack of enthusiasm for the event, W.O. (Wilfred Owen) Bentley. His step-grandsons, David Northey and Miles Hutton, remember him as a very modest man. "He could never understand what all the fuss was about. His way of being enthusiastic about anything was to say 'good'."

Despite the fact that he seems not to have liked children, they remember him with affection, "never vindictive" and always speaking "in a very ponderous manner." The family recall him being far from amused when his second wife, Margaret, wanted to be taken to see her newborn grandson, David, in the middle of the blitz. Northey talks of a time when his grandmother took him to a stream to catch sticklebacks. W.O., pipe clamped in mouth, asked him what he was doing. "I'm catching 'stickybacks'," replied the small boy. "He corrected me without humour," says Northey. His grandson also remembers him quietly sitting in the corner of a morning rolling up his cigarettes for the rest of the day.

Such was Bentley's shyness that it could make him appear austere, although he could be "quite a joker." He was so nervous when he first drove Margaret in a car that he kept crashing the gears. When he was invited back to Le Mans many years after his cars' victories there, it was she who had to make the speech. Nevertheless, the French hold him in high regard; there is a Place W.O. Bentley in Mulsanne village. In 2003 the city of Le Mans paid its own tribute to the return of the marque by producing a brochure specifically on Bentley.

Born in 1888, the youngest of nine children, Bentley had started work as an apprentice to the Great Northern Railway Company in Doncaster. He moved to London initially working for the railways and then for the National Cab Company. His own introduction to racing appears to have been in 1909 when he rode a 5hp Rex motorcycle at Brooklands. He was to compete in both the two- and four-wheeled Isle of Man Tourist Trophies, driving a DFP in the latter, a French make with which he had made his racing car debut at the Aston Clinton hill-climb in 1912. He was also famously stopped on Wimbledon Common for speeding, but the magistrate threw out the case claiming that it was impossible to do 60mph. He thought nothing of driving from Cricklewood to Norwich and back before breakfast to see how an engine would perform.

With his brother 'H.M.', Bentley acted as the UK concessionaire for DFP. Wishing to use aluminium pistons for the DFP, he had visited the French foundry Corbin, with Bentley & Bentley subsequently becoming the UK agent for Corbin pistons. These he was to supply to the Admiralty for use in aircraft engines.

In May 1917 a prototype Sopwith Camel fighter specifically built for the Navy was tested at Martlesham Heath. Its 150hp rotary engine was of particular

Initially reluctant to become involved in the Le Mans 24-Hours, W.O. Bentley was to become a regular in the pits. *(W.O. Bentley Memorial Foundation)*

interest, being the first of a new design by the now RNAS engineering liaison officer Bentley. Initially titled the AR1 (Admiralty Rotary No1), it soon became the BR1 (Bentley Rotary No1). It was, in effect, a superior copy of the French-designed Clerget engine but with steel-lined aluminium cylinders. It would not be long before squadrons in France were being issued with BR1-engined Camels; a second aero-engine, the BR2, followed. Bentley himself was occasionally to fly with pilots over the trenches. He was to say that the "genesis" of his cars was the engine of the DFP and the rotary BR1.

The initial Bentley car, the 3-litre, in theory appeared in 1919 at the Motor Show, having been built in New Street Mews, off Baker Street. Bentley recorded how Harry Varley and draughtsman F.T. Burgess worked under his supervision for "nine hectic and anxious months." Bentley admitted that much of the car was a mock-up, although by January 1920 *The Autocar* had been able to test the first complete vehicle. A factory was established in Cricklewood and an early team

John Duff established a record time of 41 seconds in raising the hood of his Bentley in 1924. *(Bentley Motors)*

The Bentley team being prepared before the 1927 race. Following the infamous White House crash only one of them was to finish, albeit in first place. *(LAT Photographic)*

built up, many of whom were to become well-known in their own right, men like Frank Clement, 'Nobby' Clarke, Wally Hassan and Clive Gallop. At one point you could buy a 3-litre Speed Model, an open touring, sporting four-seater, from £1125.

The 3-litre was the car that agent John Duff was to take to Le Mans a few years later. However, the first to appear at a major race meeting, chassis Ex 2, did so at Brooklands in 1921 with the experienced and optimistic Clement winning his third race with the car, one of the spring sprints, the '90 Short', at 87.13mph. In the light of what was to happen to the marque, perhaps it should be recorded that a Rolls-Royce took part in the same race, spinning on the Finishing Straight and striking a fence, after which one of its back tyres fell off. From the beginning it had been Bentley's intention to publicize his car by entering it for what he called "suitable" races.

In 1922 Bentleys started to appear in races abroad including, as W.O. said, "of all places" Indianapolis, an event that proved a costly exercise, Douglas Hawkes' car being unable to stay with the Miller-engined Indy racers. Three cars were also entered for the Isle of Man TT, driven by Clement, Hawkes and, in his last major race, Bentley himself. Finishing in second, fourth and fifth places, the Bentleys took the team prize.

The early Bentley victories at La Sarthe have been recorded in the previous chapter, but it is interesting to note that, having questioned the value of competing in 1923, W.O. described the next year's contest as "a most important race for us." He was to become involved in "an almost non-stop contest" with his Board about racing. However, he was to believe that he and his team became a little too pleased with themselves. "It would have been better for our souls if we had not been so successful so early." Even Woolf Barnato, who by that time had become chairman of Bentley Motors Ltd, told the editor of *Sporting Life and Sportsman*: "I will readily admit that this racing business can be overdone."

Barnato went on to point out "the Bentley Company's object in racing at all is to 'improve the breed' and that is why we specialize in such races as the Le Mans 24-Hours race, where cars must to all intents and purposes be standard models, whereby any knowledge we gain as to modification can always be incorporated in our 'dead standard' design."

Racing was expensive, and the formidable Barnato had stepped in to save the under-capitalized company from falling into the hands of the Receiver in 1926. "He was an engineer," says David Northey of his grandfather. "He never professed to be a business man."

Five years later the firm became a victim of the Wall Street crash and, with millionaire sportsman Barnato no longer prepared to keep it in business, the Receiver did move in and Bentley was sold to Rolls-Royce. Perhaps at this point it should be recorded that according to his daughter, Diana Barnato Walker, during his time as chairman 'Babe' "did as he was told by W.O. Bentley and didn't commandeer the best car by virtue of his position in the company."

The majority of cars built during W.O.'s time were

3-litres. These were followed by a 6.6-litre, six-cylinder car, the four-cylinder 4½-litre and then the Speed Six, a more powerful version of the six-cylinder with higher-compression engine and twin SU carburettors. Bentley's swansong for his eponymous company was an 8-litre, of which only 100 chassis were built. Towards the end the directors sanctioned the building of 50 supercharged 4½-litres in order to homologate the Hon Dorothy Paget's team for Le Mans. "The one car he really disapproved of was the 'blower'," says Northey, underlining a well-known fact.

The Paget cars were operated from Welwyn Garden City, with Amherst Villiers providing the supercharging expertise and, as Bentley himself pointed out, "Clive Gallop (the) engineering talent (and) 'Bertie' Kensington-Moir (the) race management experience." Birkin was the driving force. Bentley mused on how much the team must have cost Miss Paget. He was annoyed that work on the production 'blowers' detracted from the development of his 8-litre. Over 30 years later, Bentley wrote that photos of the "Paget-Birkin set-up," as he called it, filled him with "sadness."

The decision to stop racing had come before Rolls-Royce took over. Much was made in the London daily papers regarding the decision of the Bentley Company to withdraw from the sport, it having been decided before the 1930 Le Mans race that, if successful, the marque would not return the following year. Bentley and Barnato retired from the sport at the same time. "The reasons for the withdrawal of Bentley and myself dovetailed," said the latter. "Captain Barnato believes the time has come for younger men to uphold the racing prestige that he and others have helped to gain for Britain in the eyes of the world," said one of his fellow Bentley directors.

Production of the cars was moved from Cricklewood to Derby and then, in 1946, to Crewe. In recent years its ownership has gone abroad and the Volkswagen Group now owns the marque. W.O. Bentley, who died in 1971, stayed on for a while at Rolls-Royce in what appears to have been far from ideal circumstances. Bentley, as will be seen in Chapter 6, had not, though, finished with Le Mans. Moving on to become chief designer at Lagonda, he was not happy that two cars of that marque should be entered for the 1939 race. Nevertheless they were, and they performed surprisingly well. Could this be a case of *déjà vu*?

BARNATO THE CRICKETER

The 'all-round sportsman' may sound something of a cliché, but there seems to be no doubt that Woolf Barnato was one such. He raced motor boats, winning the 1925 Duke of York's Trophy, and horses as well as cars and tried his hand at pugilism, it being reported that he fought against "'Terry', the boxing barman of the Bat Club."

Wisden, the famed cricketing almanac, records that he also played six first-class matches for the Surrey County Cricket Club, keeping wicket against both the Varsity teams (coming up against the future India captain, the Nawab of Pataudi), Hampshire and Lancashire. Indeed, in 1930 he played for the Second XI just days before winning at Le Mans. It was suggested at the time that he might be the richest man in county cricket. The *Daily Mirror* reported that he was certainly the first amateur to act behind the stumps for Surrey since the start of the 1909 season.

Playing against Hampshire in 1928 he came to the notice of the press. According to the *Southern Echo*, "Captain Barnato failed to hold a catch when standing well back. The ball came plumb into his hands, though rather to the right side, and the wicket-keeper started to appeal 'How's – but the 'that' was not uttered, as before he could finish the call, the ball had popped out of his gloves and fallen to the ground." He scored six not out in his only innings of the match. Against Lancashire his wicket fell twice to bowler Macdonald for one and two runs respectively. In the first innings he was the final victim as Macdonald took three wickets in four balls. Clearly, Barnato was rather more successful at motor racing.

In total, 35 entries have been accepted by the ACO for Bentleys at Le Mans, the vast majority between 1923 and 1930. Initially, use was made of the 3-litre, a type which won in 1924 and 1927. In the second of these years one 4½-litre model was included in the three-car team and it was this car that took the initial lead, Frank Clement breaking the lap record on the second lap, only for his co-driver, George Duller, later to become involved in the famous White House crash. "Every time he went round the course

A tradition was started in 1927 when victory was celebrated at the *Savoy Hotel*. The winning car was squeezed through the front doors of the establishment. *(W.O. Bentley Memorial Foundation)*

History was repeated in 2003 when the winning EXP Speed 8 was shoehorned into the *Savoy*. *(Bentley Motors)*

THE 'BENTLEY BOYS'

Between 1923 and 1930 there was a total of 23 Bentley entries for Le Mans, two of them being the Hon Dorothy Paget's 1930 'blower' cars. The pioneering John Duff was joined in 1925 by the first official works car, driven by 'Bertie' Kensington-Moir, head of Bentley's service department, and Dr Dudley Benjafield.

Twenty different drivers were called upon to become a 'Bentley Boy' at Le Mans, the most prolific being Benjafield, who raced Bentleys there on six occasions, the last being for Paget, and Frank Clement, who took part five times for the marque. The others were Duff, Kensington-Moir, 'Sammy' Davis, George Duller, Clive Gallop, 'Scrap' Thistlethwayte, Leslie Callingham, 'Tim' Birkin, Bernard Rubin, Woolf Barnato, Glen Kidston, Jack and Clive Dunfee, the Earl Howe, Richard Watney, Baron Andre d'Erlanger, Jean Chassagne and Giulio Ramponi. All but the last three can be said to be British.

They varied from amateur 'playboys' to the one professional driver, the experienced Clement. Bentley himself called them "sporting men of independent means" and they drove for no financial remuneration. Benjafield was a Harley Street surgeon, Duller was a champion jockey and the colourful d'Erlanger an international banker. Some, like the formidable Barnato and his friend Rubin, were immensely wealthy. Both Rubin and Kidston were subsequently to lose their lives in flying accidents.

Although history remembers them as the 'Bentley Boys', strictly speaking this was the term used by the other teams for the early mechanics such as 'Nobby' Clarke, Walter Hassan, Leslie Pennal and Stan Ivermee. However, after a while the newspapers started to use the term for the drivers. In London, the south-east corner of Grosvenor Square even came to be known as 'Bentley Corner' thanks to the adjoining flats of Barnato, Birkin, Kidston and Rubin.

As far as Le Mans was concerned, the high-living Barnato was the most successful of them all, winning on each of his three appearances on the track. Immensely wealthy thanks to his father's time in the South African diamond fields, Barnato saved Bentley Motors from receivership in 1926, his fortune giving the company at least short-term security. Although by now chairman of the company, he did not expect favourable terms as a driver. Being an excellent all-round sportsman, he didn't need them.

various things kept coming loose as a result of the 'crash'," said the *Evening News* of the 3-litre that was eventually to win. The *Sheffield Telegraph* recorded the victory celebrations that year: "Into the midst of a group of diners at the Savoy London, last night, there

drove a motor car." Said the *Daily Mail*: "The victory represents a great British triumph."

The following year all three cars were 4½-litres; although now, in the words of Bentley himself, "getting short of breath," four of these appeared in 1929, with

A flying pit stop for the Clement/Chassagne Speed Six in 1929. Unlike the other team cars this one was fitted with an ML magneto and KLG spark plugs. *(W.O. Bentley Memorial Foundation)*

Frank Clement and Dick Watney's Bentley makes a night-time pit stop during 1930. This particular team was drawn together at the last minute. *(LAT Photographic)*

Glen Kidston shared the 1930 winning drive with Barnato. The following May he was killed when his aircraft crashed among the mountains in Africa. Birkin wrote: "In him England lost a man who should be an example to all young Englishmen of how to live." *(LAT Photographic)*

GLEN KIDSTON

The early Le Mans drivers had some enthralling stories to tell, and not just of their racing exploits, perhaps none more so than Glen Kidston. His father, an army captain, had died in 1913 and left a fortune, made by the family in Scottish industry, to be inherited by Kidston when he came of age.

The following year he enrolled as a cadet at the Britannia Royal Naval College, Dartmouth. With the outbreak of war the cadets were sent to sea, in Kidston's case to the ageing armoured cruiser HMS *Hogue*.

On September 22, *Hogue* was on patrol in the North Sea with two other obsolete cruisers. In the early morning the German submarine U9 struck, sinking at first HMS *Aboukir*. Midshipman Kidston stood on the bridge taking photographs of the tragedy when he was hit by the spray from a torpedo that had found his own ship. He dived into the water, where he spent 40 minutes before

he could reach a rescue boat, aboard which he is said to have wrung out his shorts and trousers, dried them off and redressed. Meanwhile, U9 had hit again and sunk the third ship, HMS *Cressy*, creating an unparelleled disaster. The U-boat commander, Otto Weddigen, was hailed as a hero in Germany.

In 1917, Kidston himself transferred to submarines and at one point was trapped on the seabed. He subsequently joined the aircraft carrier HMS *Courageous*, aboard which he acquired a love of flying.

After the war Kidston also took up motorcycle racing and speedboating, continuing to lead a charmed life as he escaped relatively unhurt from a number of crashes. However, his luck turned in 1931 when flying a De Havilland Puss Moth to Cape Town. The plane crashed in Natal and this time Kidston did not survive; he was 32. In 1939 the Admiralty was to commission a trawler, the HMS *Glen Kidston*, for wartime service.

W.O. Bentley in the late 1960s. *(Patrick Fitz-Gibbon collection)*

Barnato and 'Tim' Birkin – who regarded W.O. as the finest team manager that he drove for – given a new, short-chassis Speed Six model. Following the latter's victory, ("One of the finest fillips that has ever been given to the British motor industry," according to *The Times of Malaya*), all three factory cars were Speed Sixes in 1930. Dorothy Paget's two 'blower' cars completed the Bentley line-up.

The papers were thrilled with Birkin's performance as the 'hare' in one of the latter, although Harold Pemberton in the *Daily Express* observed that the driver was "a sick man" at the time, recovering from an operation for appendicitis. "The Bentley triumphed according to plan," said A.G. Throssell in the *Daily Telegraph*, although adding "whether Birkin's tactics affected the final result is difficult to say." The *Daily Sketch* recorded "the delight of the British spectators."

While Birkin was the hero, it was the Speed Six of Barnato and Kidston that won, and it has to be said that Bentley reckoned 'Babe' to be "the best British driver of his day." ("He drove so smoothly, with no apparent rush or hurry," recorded his daughter.) One contemporary report stated: "The English motor industry largely benefited by the success of these two amateur champions." Their car was the same that had

won the previous year, chassis LB2332. In 1929 it had competed with the race number '1' and it was as 'Old Number One' that the car became known, whatever number it carried on its flanks. Indeed, in 1930 it carried the number '4'. (There was nothing unusual in this, the 1927 winning 3-litre was known as 'Old Number Seven', despite carrying the number '3' in its victory year.) Having come first at Le Mans in 1929, 'Old Number One' repeated the feat in the Brooklands Six-Hours race the same year. It also finished second in the Brooklands 500. The car was then rebuilt over the winter to win at Le Mans for a second time.

Barnato kept 'Old Number One' as his personal car, and in 1931 it was again entered for the Brooklands 500 handicap race, this time driven by Jack Dunfee and Cyril Paul, and winning at a speed in excess of 118mph. Crashed in 1932, it was rebuilt several times and, in 1990, became the subject of a court case as to its provenance.

In contrast with what had gone before, Anthony Bevan's Bentley 4½-litre, which he shared with William Mike Couper, went almost unnoticed in 1931. There followed a couple of unfortunate years for Jean Trevoux's ex-Birkin 'blower' car. Post-war saw three appearances for Jack Hay's closed Bentley Corniche. Hay was one of the first to enter when it

was announced that *Les Vingt-Quatre Heures* was to be run again. Initially he selected his wife as co-driver, but in the event it was Tommy Wisdom who shared the car with him; sixth place overall was an admirable result. By the time the car reappeared in 1950 it was said that it had already covered around 125,000 miles. Every year it finished, although by 1951 it was back in 22nd place.

A second Bentley was entered during this time, the TT of Eddie Hall that came eighth in 1950. This was the same 4.3-litre car, now with coupe body, that Hall had originally hoped to run at the cancelled 1936 race. His 1950 co-driver was Tom Clarke, who transferred his allegiance to Hay's Corniche the following year. And that, for a very long time, was that. The Hay Bentley crossed the line having averaged 71.6mph. But up front there was a new name for the victory rostrum: Jaguar. The victorious C-type of Peter Walker and Peter Whitehead had averaged 93.5mph.

It was to be half a century before we were to see a Bentley entered for Le Mans again. The race, though, as W.O. was to write, had been "a great blessing." Bentley had been in racing for business, not for amusement. When it was stated that the Bentley EXP Speed 8s would not be raced again following their 2003 win, it could be seen that the brand's current owner, the Volkswagen Group, had the same approach.

Almost three-quarters of a century later and Bentley returned to win at Le Mans again. The victorious car sweeps past the Esses on its way to Tertre Rouge. *(Bentley Motors)*

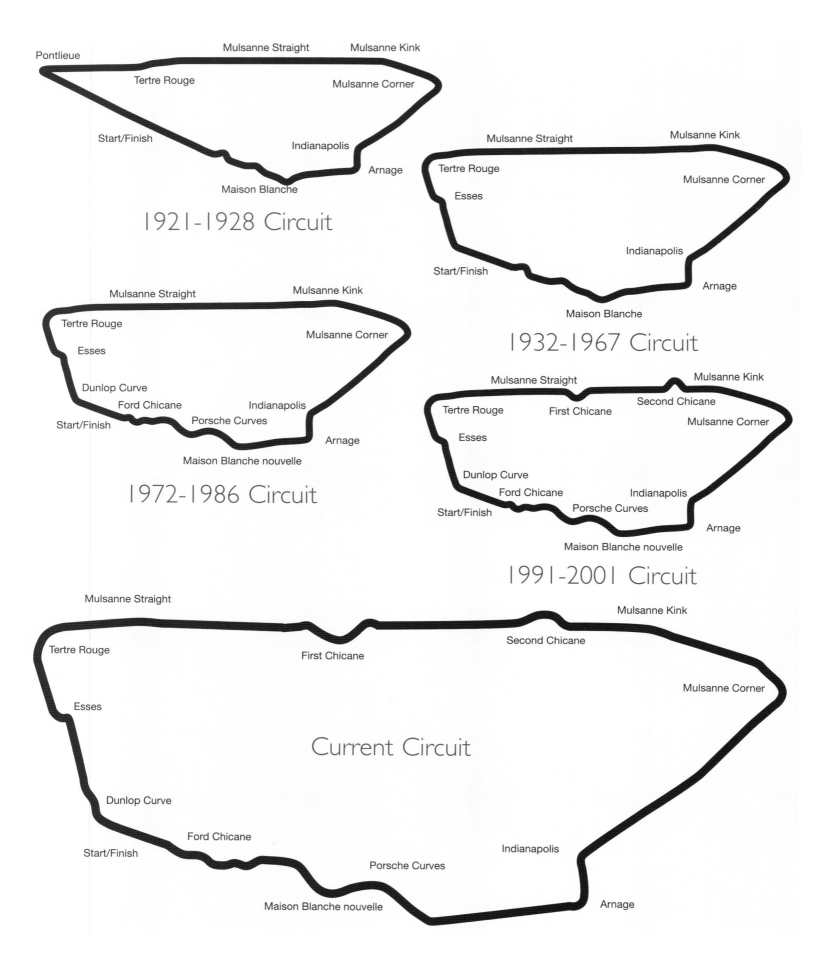

Pontlieue

Mulsanne Straight Mulsanne Kink

Tertre Rouge

Mulsanne Corner

Start/Finish

Indianapolis

Arnage

Maison Blanche

1921-1928 Circuit

Mulsanne Straight Mulsanne Kink

Tertre Rouge

Mulsanne Corner

Esses

Start/Finish

Indianapolis

Arnage

Maison Blanche

1932-1967 Circuit

Mulsanne Straight Mulsanne Kink

Tertre Rouge

Mulsanne Corner

Esses

Dunlop Curve

Ford Chicane

Indianapolis

Start/Finish

Porsche Curves

Arnage

Maison Blanche nouvelle

1972-1986 Circuit

Mulsanne Straight Mulsanne Kink

Second Chicane

Tertre Rouge First Chicane

Mulsanne Corner

Esses

Dunlop Curve

Ford Chicane

Indianapolis

Start/Finish

Porsche Curves

Arnage

Maison Blanche nouvelle

1991-2001 Circuit

Mulsanne Straight

Mulsanne Kink

Second Chicane

Tertre Rouge First Chicane

Mulsanne Corner

Esses

Current Circuit

Dunlop Curve

Ford Chicane

Indianapolis

Start/Finish

Porsche Curves

Maison Blanche nouvelle

Arnage

CHAPTER 3

SIR HENRY 'TIM' BIRKIN

"A knyght ther was, and that a worthy man." (**Geoffrey Chaucer**, *The Canterbury Tales*)

Racing drivers in the immediate post-war years, after both 1918 and 1945, must be seen in a different light to those who have only known peace. The attitude of men like 1953 Le Mans winners Tony Rolt and Duncan Hamilton can surely never be compared to that of those who have travelled the clinical modern route of kart racing, racing school and lesser formulae into the now relatively safe sport of international racing. That is not to criticize today's racing drivers, but theirs must be a different perspective. One man for whom the Great War must have clouded the way he viewed his own existence was Sir Henry Ralph Stanley Birkin, known to his friends as 'Tim', and from April 1931 until his death two year later, the 3rd Baronet Birkin, of Ruddington Grange, Nottinghamshire. For Birkin, the subtitle of Sapper's novel *Bulldog Drummond* – "the adventures of a demobilised officer who found peace dull" – would appear to be appropriate.

There is no doubt that Birkin became very single-minded about his motor racing. In his autobiography, *Full Throttle*, he admitted just how much his father, Sir Thomas Stanley Birkin, the former High Sheriff of Nottinghamshire, wished him not to race. It is hardly surprising that he suffered every time Tim competed. Both his other sons had been killed at the age of 22, the elder Thomas, a lieutenant in the 25th Squadron, RFC in France during 1917, and the youngest, Archie, avoiding a fish cart during practice for the motorcycle TT race in the Isle of Man 10 years later. Birkin's Bend on the TT course between Barregarrow and Rhencullen is named after him. Archie and Tim had shared a Bentley in the 1927 Brooklands Six-Hours, the track's historian, William Boddy noting that the latter "drove unduly wildly."

Sir Thomas, who died in 1931, was at least spared the news of his middle son's early death. However,

The No 1 car of Birkin and Barnato took the lead at the start of the 1929 race and proceeded to dominate the next 24 hours. The Pontlieue hairpin was cut off that year by an alternative road. Here the Bentley Speed Six takes one of the newly created corners. *(Bentley Motors)*

A DAMNED DULL SUBJECT

Michael Burn, writer, journalist, commando and the ghost writer of *Full Throttle* at his Portmeirion home in 2005. *(Author)*

'Tim' Birkin's autobiography, *Full Throttle*, written not long before his death, was to inspire future racing drivers. Grand Prix winner Innes Ireland, who was to finish just once in his seven starts at Le Mans, mentioned in his own autobiography, *All Arms and Elbows*, that when a teenager he was given a copy by an old lady who owned a 3-litre Bentley. "It inspired my dreams and I imagined myself doing the things Tim Birkin had done."

Duncan Wiltshire says that *Full Throttle* also inspired his father, Ray, as a schoolboy. Many years later, as will be seen, he was to become responsible for bringing early Bentleys back to Le Mans.

The book was ghost-written by a young dropout from Oxford University. Michael Burn had found himself in the summer of 1932 in the fashionable French resort of Le Touquet, favourite location of "rich and fashionable people" (his grandfather had been instrumental in creating the resort). He admits to having been captivated by the guests of Syrie Maugham, former wife of author Somerset Maugham. One of these was Birkin, "in love," says Burn, with another guest, the well-known socialite Sylvia Ashley, whose five husbands included Douglas Fairbanks Senior, Clark Gable, two lords and the Georgian noble Prince Djordjadze, who won the 1931 Spa 24-Hours driving a Mercedes-Benz SSK with Goffredo Zehender.

Burn was meant to be returning to New College for a second year, but had not done any work and was "beginning got get scared." He recalls: "I was 19 and wanted to be a writer."

Birkin confessed that he had been asked to write his autobiography and, even though he had only just met Burn, and despite the fact that the young man knew nothing about cars, he asked him if he would like to compile it. So far, so good. Then Birkin rang his publisher, G.T. Foulis, to be told that it was too late. If the book was to be ready for Christmas it had to be written in the next three weeks. At this point it should be noted that Burn, a sprightly and hospitable gentleman now in his nineties, still confesses to know nothing about cars, notwithstanding that his second book was a history of Brooklands entitled *Wheels Take Wings*. Since then he has written about 20 volumes (as well as having been *The Times*' youngest foreign editor) and none of them have had anything to do with cars, let alone motor racing.

Perhaps ignorance really is bliss, for Burn and Birkin took up the three-week challenge when others, more experienced in writing, would have baulked at the thought. Most of the work was carried out at Burn's parent's home in London with Birkin "striding up and down and dictating" and Burn furiously taking notes. Looking back, Burn is amused that anyone should think that the very literary style, certainly of the early part of *Full Throttle*, could have been written by Birkin.

His father, writing about his son in a letter dated November 17, 1932, said: "I think it is an amusing effort for a boy of 19 and holds your attention upon a damned dull subject."

In 1995, the BBC ran an hour-long play, part of its 'Heroes and Villains' series, based on these three weeks, although relocated to Birkin's Norfolk home. It starred the comedian Rowan Atkinson as Birkin, perhaps a strange choice for such a character, but Burn reckons he gave a plausible interpretation of Birkin's persona. "I thought he was adequate, nothing jarred." But other actors were well off the mark. Burn is portrayed as a nervous young man, frightened by Birkin's driving to the point of digging his finger nails so hard into his hands that they bled, and totally in awe of the great man. Burn points out "I was never frightened of Tim." He certainly never scared him with his driving; indeed, he chastised a friend of Burn's for cornering too fast. The Bentley character was equally inaccurate. His grandson, David Northey, is still incensed at the way the shy W.O. could be portrayed as being "like a bookmaker." Burn was originally asked to do the voice-over. "At first they couldn't believe I was still alive." Later, "they rang apologetically and said my voice did not sound old enough."

Burn recalls that Birkin took him to Brooklands and drove him round the track. He thinks that it may have been in the Single-Seater, but "that can't have been, can it?" He also carried out an interview with Sir Malcolm Campbell, whom he confesses neither he nor Birkin liked.

He was destined to have a career every bit as filled as that of Birkin. The son of Sir Clive Burn, who played cricket for Oxford University, bowling out both W.G. Grace and C.B. Fry and who became secretary of the Duchy of Cornwall, Burn joined *The Times* and was sent to cover the visit of the King and Queen to North America before the Second World War. He confesses to some not particularly savoury acquaintances before the war, including the spy Guy Burgess. He also met Hitler while on holiday, having he admits initially been taken in by the way in which the Nazi government had reduced Germany's unemployment problem. But he was not fooled for long, indeed his politics swung in the opposite direction, and with the coming of war he found himself initially in Norway and then taking part in the daring commando raid on St Nazaire, where he was captured.

By 1943 Burn was incarcerated in Colditz along with, as will be seen, some future Le Mans racers. He certainly remembers 1953 winner Tony Rolt as "tall, handsome and always trying to escape." If he found himself in Colditz, surely he must have been a would-be escaper, too? "No," he says; he did his bit listening to the wireless and looking out for guards, but he never made a bid for freedom. He was never quite sure whether it was because the Germans realized he had met Hitler, or because a spy in one of his previous camps had told them he was giving lectures on communism to his fellow prisoners that he ended up in the famous castle.

Burn returned to *The Times* after the war, working in Vienna and Budapest before leaving the paper in the early 1950s to become a full-time writer.

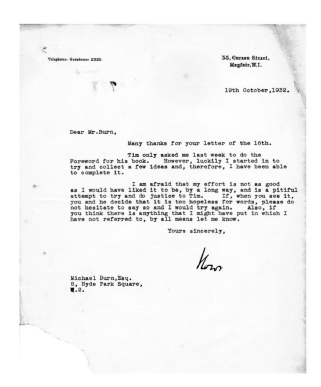

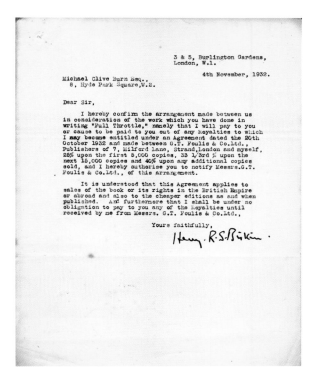

he insisted that Birkin's secretary send him telegrams every half-hour when he was racing, often an almost impossible task. Until these were received he would, his son said, "see nobody, speak to nobody and take no food." He did not, though, go to the length of forbidding his son to race; had he done so, the younger Birkin still reckoned that "it would not have destroyed, nor yet cooled, a passion that so dominated me."

Michael Burn, who ghost wrote *Full Throttle*, says that Birkin could be very determined. He also recalls him as "very extravagant, generous…and fond of women. He wasn't at all a respectable person; he was anything but stuffy. He was very good company and marvellous for a young man to admire." He was interested in other people. His politics were right-wing, even for his time and place, and Burn believes that he would have been appalled to learn that the person whom he allowed to write his story would get into trouble with the Germans during the forthcoming war for giving lectures on communism to fellow prison camp inmates.

Burn describes Birkin as "very lithe, larger in build, but still like a ballet dancer." He was athletic, but still smoked a lot. His attitude to racing can be gleaned from a contemporary press quote following the 1930 race: "Exciting, yes, but really one must not exaggerate. Three tyres burst during the time I was at the wheel, but they all burst in the right way at the right place.

"I always think if your time is to come it will come just as surely on the top of a bus or anywhere else as on the motorcar racing circuit."

Tim Birkin first appears in the lists as a racing driver at Brooklands in 1921 at the wheel of a 2-litre DFP that had been taxed for the road. Woolf Barnato made his debut at the track at the same time. The DFP featured a strange mahogany-planked body and a narrow cowled radiator from W.O. Bentley's own

pre-war DFP. He was placed third in a '100 Long' handicap race, but only recorded in *Full Throttle* an occasion when he stopped for a trivial problem only to find that the shackle pins that held the springs to the frame were also about to collapse. In this he thought he possibly saw "the working of Providence."

Could this be the thinking of a man who has just been in the Great War, initially with the 108th (Norfolk and Suffolk Yeoman) Field Brigade, and then as a lieutenant in the Royal Flying Corps flying out in Mesopotamia? As the locals said of that place: "When Allah made hell it found it was not bad enough, so he created Mesopotamia and added flies." The British forces suffered in the region and Birkin was invalided home with malaria. The Air Force List records him as an Aeroplane and Seaplane Officer, seniority of Lieutenant, as of April 1, 1918. Burn recalls that Birkin did not talk about his war service. "He was very English and it was not done to talk about yourself if you were English."

Birkin was to say that he did not race between 1921 and 1927 for business reasons. However, there may be some significance in that this gap in his racing career coincided with the period of his marriage to Audrey Latham, the daughter of Sir Thomas Latham, a director of Courtaulds. The pair wed in July 1921 but divorced in 1928, an unusual occurrence for those days. Two daughters were born to the couple during this time. In 1927 Birkin reappeared at Brooklands sharing a 4½-litre Bentley with his brother in the Essex Motor Club's Six-Hours race. He had divided the driving of the DFP with his friend Clive Gallop, another former RFC pilot, who was responsible for the camshaft design of the 3-litre Bentley, and it may have been through his influence that Birkin first became involved with the legendary marque.

All the Bentleys in the 1927 Brooklands Six-

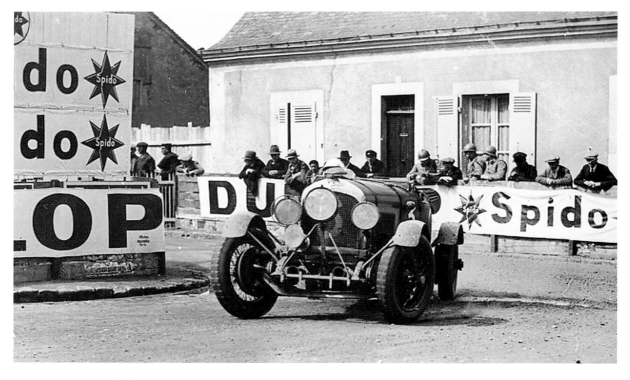

The year is 1928, and the Pontlieue hairpin was still in use. Birkin and Chassagne drove a superb race, but Bentley's reluctance to allow his cars to carry wheel jacks created a drama out of a punctured tyre. *The Motor* described Birkin's final lap as "the finest performance in the whole race." *(W.O. Bentley Memorial Foundation)*

Birkin (left) said that when he finally stumbled into the pits in 1928, only one man had "all his wits about him." The 47-year old Chassagne (centre) quietly observed, *"Maintentant, c'est à moi,"* picked up a couple of jacks and ran back to their car. The puncture and the subsequent collapsed wheel were to cost the pair three hours. *(W.O. Bentley Memorial Foundation)*

Hours, except that of the Birkins, had experimental duralumin valve rockers, which broke up; only the brothers' version had steel rockers. Birkin was to record his disgust that, following a fuel stop, he was replaced in the car by one of the other Bentley drivers whose car had already retired; he omitted to say that it was the experienced Frank Clement. Problems with all the gears except third, which was engaged by means of a hammer, meant that the car was only placed third. The following year, and beneath a threatening sky, Birkin was to come home first in the Six-Hours, although an Alfa Romeo driver was to take the main prize on handicap.

Because of the preference at Brooklands for handicap racing, it is perhaps unfair to judge a driver's career by his results there. However, Birkin received his 120mph badge (for lapping the banked track in excess of that speed) in 1929, the 14th driver to do so. He also won a BRDC Gold Star for Track Racing the following year. The fame of the man with the spotted blue-and-white silk scarf must, though, be based on his two Le Mans wins and his remarkable performance in the Pau Grand Prix. He led for the first 20 laps of his first race at La Sarthe, returning to win the next year with Barnato. His debut was notable for the incident of the jack. In an effort to lighten his cars as much as possible, Bentley had instructed that none of them should carry a jack. (As will be seen in an incident some years later, fellow team member Dr Benjafield would not have known what to do with a jack even if he had carried one.) In the lead, and approaching the top of the hill after Pontlieue, the Bentley ran over a horseshoe nail, and before Birkin could pull up, the tyre had disintegrated and the canvas jammed itself between the wheel and the brake drum. "So there I was," Birkin was to say, "six miles from the pits" and with no jack, "the only implement of which I was really in need." Using the jackknife, a hammer and a pair of pliers – tools that "were in my pockets" – Birkin set about the offending tyre.

Having eventually got it free, he carried on, getting as far as Arnage before the rim collapsed and the car slid into a ditch. Only three miles to go now…Birkin ran for the pits, but the hero of the next part of the saga is a Frenchman, Birkin's 47-year-old co-driver Jean Chassagne. As, with "joints aching," Birkin arrived at the pits, so Chassagne grabbed a couple of jacks and ran all the way back to the Bentley. Once the car had been returned to the race both drove it like madmen. It will be remembered that this was still in the days of the Rudge-Whitworth competitions, and such were their rules that the Bentley would have to finish within a certain time if it was to qualify for the second half of the competition the following year. As the race drew to a close, pit signals informed Birkin that he must break the lap record on the final tour if he was to be back 12 months later. The crew in the Bentley pit thought the feat highly unlikely. However, when Birkin's mechanic Chevrollier was to hear the unmistakable sound of the engine of an approaching Bentley, even though it was still a long way off, he realized that he was about to achieve it. "He's done it!" he yelled, dancing up and down.

It was the first of a hat-trick of fastest laps for Birkin. The following year, though, was a much easier affair for him, and the car that he shared with Barnato led home the "slow and solemn procession" of Bentleys that were the feature of the race's final 15 minutes. "Like a squadron of battleships," reported *The Motor*.

Birkin then became responsible for the famous 'blower' Bentleys, the 4½-litre supercharged cars of which Bentley himself was never convinced. "To supercharge a Bentley was to pervert its design and corrupt its performance," he said in his autobiography. But Birkin persuaded the Hon Dorothy Paget, a wealthy socialite more used to horse racing, to provide the funding to develop the 242bhp cars, using the supercharger expertise of Amherst Villiers. The first appearance of a 'blower' Bentley was at that race which seems to punctuate Birkin's career, the Brooklands Six-Hours, in 1929, the race then being run by the Brooklands Automobile Racing Club, the Essex MC having disbanded. Two of these supercharged cars were entered for Le Mans the following year, both of them retiring – Birkin's having been used as the 'hare' to break Carraciola's Mercedes-Benz – leaving victory to the much less powerful Speed Sixes.

The year 1930 also saw Birkin and the 'blower's finest hour. It was an unusual situation. The mudguards and the headlights were removed and the four-seater car was entered in the *Formule Libre* French Grand Prix, up against some of the finest Grand Prix machines that France could offer. True, a change in the date of the event had meant that the top Italian teams were not present, but imagine, let us say, a Zytek 04S, with its lights removed, up against a grid of mid-field Grand Prix runners such as Toyota and Red Bull…and coming second. The incongruity of it all was underlined when Birkin used his horn to persuade top Bugatti driver Louis Chiron to move over in practice. Only one Bugatti remained ahead of the Bentley at the end of the race; nothing should detract from this performance. However, because of the tight confines of the very different street track that came

The 'blower' Bentley's finest hour came in a Grand Prix. Birkin's car towered over the other contenders as he sped to a remarkable second place at Pau behind Etancelin's purpose-built Bugatti. "The crowd laugh at your Bentley, *capitaine* Birkin," said Charles Faroux, one of the founders of the 24-hour race, "but I tell them not to laugh. I have seen the Bentleys at Le Mans and I know. I am Faroux. I am not a.......fool." *(W.O. Bentley Memorial Foundation)*

There are those who want to stare at the camera but there are others intent on Birkin's face. The Pau circuit may have been one of the fastest in France, and not the round-the-houses affair of more recent years, but the Englishman has still obviously had to work hard for his second place. *(W.O. Bentley Memorial Foundation)*

33

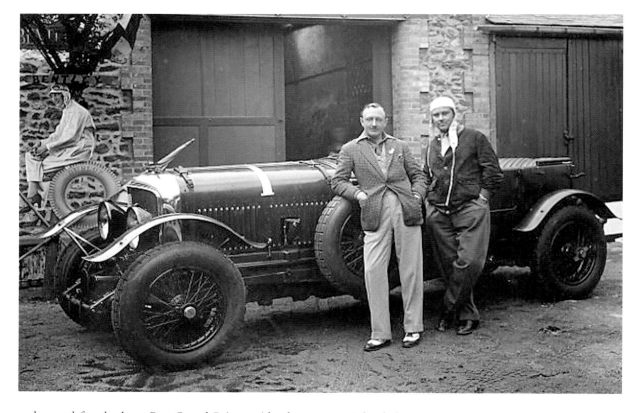

to be used for the later Pau Grand Prix, an idea has grown up that Birkin had wrestled a most unsuitable machine (Ettore Bugatti had described the Bentleys as "trucks") around a twisting track. But that used for the 1930 race was outside the city and could have been described as almost Le Mans-like in character. Certainly, its long straights assisted the supercharged sportscar. However, a photograph taken of Birkin in the car just after the race shows the strain he must have been under.

One of Dorothy Paget's 'blower' Bentleys, 'No1', was converted into a single-seater during the winter of 1929/30 and this became a famous sight at Brooklands. Birkin took the Outer Circuit lap record with the car, which at one point was off the ground for around 70 feet. Although Paget withdrew her support from the sportscar operation towards the end of 1930, she still kept the single-seater and Birkin continued to race it, again raising the Brooklands lap record, this time to 137.96mph, a record that stood for two years.

With the Rolls-Royce takeover of Bentley in 1931, all racing came to a stop, and Birkin was forced to go outside the country for his next winning mount for Le Mans. It was obvious that he felt very keenly the criticism that he and Earl Howe were to receive that year for using an Alfa Romeo, but the pair had little choice if they wanted to win outright. Birkin, in turn, fiercely moaned at the UK car industry for failing to provide drivers like himself, Howe and Sir Malcolm Campbell with suitable contenders. The industry, he said, had shut itself up "in a high tower like the Lady of Shalott." He also wanted to see road racing on the British mainland, a futile but rather wonderful hope. While British cars would again win Le Mans, genuine open-road racing has never taken place on the UK

mainland, the nearest attempt occurring many decades later when, in October 1985, Royal Assent was given for a Formula 3000 street race in Birmingham, which was staged from 1986 to 1990. When plans, never to be brought to fruition, were announced in 1933 for a road racing track between Ivinghoe and Tring, the media remarked on how this would meet some of the demands made by Birkin in what was then his recently published autobiography. But it was not to be.

Having won Le Mans in an Alfa Romeo in 1931, it was at the wheel of another Italian car, a new Grand Prix Maserati 8C/3000, that he led the first five laps of the 1933 Tripoli Grand Prix, an event that was to descend into farce for most, but tragedy for Birkin. For an Englishman to lead such a race was indeed a rare event. At half-distance he was still running second to the great Tazio Nuvolari, but poor pit work put him back to third before the finish. It was to be Birkin's last race. Exactly why he died is now open to conjecture. He burnt his arm on the exhaust pipe during one of the pit stops and the wound turned septic. It is also thought that the malaria from which he had suffered since the war was a contributing factor. Initially it proved impossible to diagnose the complaint, but eventually blood poisoning was diagnosed and so began a three-week fight for his life during which his former Bentley team-mate Benjafield, a medical doctor, was reported rarely to have left his side. Two blood transfusions were performed, but Birkin's temperature continued to range between 101 and 103 degrees. The newspapers of the day reported how, in his delirium, he believed himself to be back on the racetrack. The News Chronicle stated "three times recovery seemed possible." However, Birkin passed away in the Countess Canarvon Nursing Home, in

Birkin wrote of his "first year in exile." He appears to have been embittered by the fact that he had to drive an Italian car to victory in 1931. Nevertheless, *The Motor* stated that the race had shown "what British drivers could do." Birkin and Francis Howe set a new record speed for the race in the latter's Alfa Romeo. *(LAT Photographic)*

By 1931 Birkin was also forced to use an Italian car in Grand Prix racing. He shared his Maserati with the scientific George Eyston (left) to come fourth in the gruelling and tedious French Grand Prix at Montlhéry. The track became particularly slippery and the cars' seats most uncomfortable. Birkin got away with losing a large patch of skin, Eyston, by contrast, lost the seat of his trousers to the delight of the French in the grandstands. *(LAT) Photographic*

London, on June 22. Michael Burn recalls: "It seemed even then odd that he should have died."

He was buried at the churchyard in Blakeney, the site of his country home on the north Norfolk coast. Burn, who was present that day, remembers the funeral as a well-attended event. Birkin's final resting place was a suitable location for a man who, in addition to his racing, loved his wild fowling. His title passed on to a 72-year-old uncle.

Perhaps it is ironic that Birkin died in pursuit of glory in a race that turned out to be anything but glorious. The Tripoli Grand Prix was a lottery event, with the 'winners' drawing the names of the 29 entrants. In theory the money would go to the person who had drawn the winning driver. But as the draw was carried out some time before the race, contestants and drivers had the chance to conspire. Quite what happened and just how corrupt the race turned out to be has been the stuff of conjecture and conflicting stories ever since.

One story was that Birkin was offered 70,000 or 100,000 lire should he win by the man who had drawn his name. However, Giovanni Canestrini, the editor of La Gazetta dello Sport, is said to have reckoned Birkin was one of those drivers who were determined to win the race in order to upset the plans of those who wanted to rig it. His opening laps would appear to bear that out.

While the facts of the race may now appear clouded, it is perhaps worthwhile recalling the story as the News Chronicle saw it for the obituary that it published on June 23:

"Just before the race he found himself bereft of useful mechanics. He had decided to give up against hopeless odds of no replenishment pit staff when he heard that a nearby village could win at least £15,000 if he ran, as they had drawn him in a State lottery.

"In the truest spirit of sportsmanship Birkin changed his mind and decided to give the villagers a run for their money against the Italian champions, handicapped as he was.

"He was standing third in the race with a fair chance of winning when he had to stop at the replenishment pits for an engine adjustment. He had to do all the work himself. With £15,000 for the villagers hanging on every second he lost, he, in a hurry, caught his forearm on a red-hot exhaust pipe.

"Rather than waste time and let down his village champions, with a laugh he refused a dressing, jumped into the car and finished third. The villagers entertained him royally afterwards.

"But that neglect of the burn, acting on a system impaired by war wounds, created the toxic state which proved fatal."

It is poignant to think that Birkin, who was to include a chapter in his autobiography entitled 'England, My England', was to die as a result of what may have happened in Africa and that his last race was in an Italian car. The fact that another chapter, one dealing with the immediate post-Bentley period, is entitled 'First Year in Exile', shows how he felt about such matters. How it must have hurt when Mussolini sent him a telegram congratulating Birkin and Earl Howe on winning Le Mans "for Italy."

CHAPTER 4

WHAT MAKES
IT SO BRITISH?

"Britain, formerly known as Albion, is an island in the ocean, lying…at a considerable distance from Germany, Gaul and Spain." **(Bede, A *History of the English Church and People*)**

Changes to any racing circuit, however necessary for safety, will always be met with cries of it not being like it used to be. This is particularly true of the Mulsanne straight, now emasculated by two well-meaning but uninspiring chicanes. British spectators of a certain age will wax lyrical about sitting in the old *Café de L'Hippodrome* at Les Hunaudières, watching cars go past at speeds that, in Derek Bell's case the year he drove the Gulf Porsche 917, rose to 247mph. Presumably those who bemoaned the loss of the run up to Pontlieue in 1932 sounded off in a similar vein.

The same may also be said of the long right-hander just after the start. Prior to the chicane being installed just before the Dunlop bridge one could watch, say, an early Group C car appearing to go light as it emerged from under the bridge and wonder at the utter commitment of its driver. Change, though, is not necessarily always for the worse. Although, as Calum Lockie – who drove a diesel Lola in 2004 – points out, the series of sweeping curves that have replaced the former downhill straight that led from the bridge to the Esses have moved the cars further away from the spectator – and certainly, the crowds are no longer as close to the action as they once were – it is still possible to witness a modern prototype barrelling through this complex on the limit, and to do so is to watch mechanical poetry.

This was no more so than with the two Bentleys in 2003. Paradoxically, the EXP Speed 8 can appear both a thing of beauty and a misshapen monster; it depends upon the angle from which you view the car. However, sweeping through the curves towards the Esses, the numbers '7' and '8' coupes appeared in their element; there was fluidity about their movement that appeared almost organic. And, dammit, they were British.

This is where the cynic steps in and claims that they were really green Audis. Looking at it one way, it is certainly difficult to distinguish between the nationality of the 1999 winning BMW V12 LMR and that of the 2003 victor. Both were entered by a German-owned company and both had a German engine. The cars themselves were built in Britain, the BMW at the Grove, Oxfordshire, headquarters of Formula One constructor Williams and using composites supplied by Lola, and the Bentley by Audi-owned, but Norfolk-based company rtn (*the lower case is intentional*). However, one was decidedly Teutonic, the other definitely British, and the best way one can explain this is to say that it was a spiritual thing. One observer has also said that whether a car is British or not can be gauged by the reactions of the British spectators. Given that, at the end of the 2003 race there was no doubt about the 'Britishness' of the Bentleys as Englishman Guy Smith, who drove the last stint in the winning car, found out.

There was a time when a car's nationality was never in question. It has been suggested that in the early days W.O. Bentley ensured that all his component suppliers were British, although this insistence went by the board as he strived for yet another win. Perhaps the

"British spectators of a certain age will wax lyrical about sitting in the old *Café de L'Hippodrome* at Les Hunaudières." In 1983 it was still possible to thrust a camera out of the window and record the cars racing past at well over 200mph, unfettered by any impending chicanes while enjoying a relaxing meal with colleagues – see evidence on page 39. *(Author)*

And dammit, they were British. The second place Bentley of Johnny Herbert, Mark Blundell (not to mention Australian David Brabham) in 2003. (Bentley Motors)

Very Teutonic, but the chassis of the 1999 winning BMW V12 LMR, seen here lining up for the Mulsanne corner, was built in Oxfordshire by Williams. (Author)

It can be very confusing. The Chrysler Viper, one of whose drivers was Brit Justin Bell, is definitely from the USA, but what of the Nissan heading it at the end of the Mulsanne Straight? One of the two works Nissans in 1999 was actually a Courage C52, while the other was constructed in England by G-Force with help from Nigel Stroud. Visually there was little difference although this is the French-built car. (Author)

first confusion comes with the Anglo-French Talbot marque, although the success that this had in the early 1930s was undoubtedly British. Lagonda, Jaguar, Aston Martin – all were truly British in their time, but all three are owned by the USA's Ford. Still, we live in a world where the England football manager could be Swedish so we must take our Britishness where we can find it.

Perhaps in this Formula One television-dominated world in which we now live, attitudes have changed. However, writing in the 1950s, Stirling Moss, admittedly no lover of the race, said that when an Englishman thought of French motor racing circuits it was not Reims or Rouen that came to mind, classic tracks though they were, it was Le Mans. Moss believed this to be natural as, he observed at the time, British cars had "achieved some their most glamorous feats outside the old cathedral town." He continued to wax lyrical: "Year by year, each June, British drivers and cars trek to the town to do battle for twenty-four hours against the best opposition that the rest of the world can produce in the way of sports cars." At the time he wrote that the Vanwalls were only just beginning to show that it really was possible for a green car to win a Formula One race. Until then, for a Briton to enjoy major success he really had to trek to Le Mans.

British drivers and cars had, of course, won races abroad before the 'Bentley Boys' made it a habit…but not often. Driving a Sunbeam, Henry Segrave won the French and San Sebastian Grands Prix in 1923 and 1924 respectively, while S.F. Edge and Charles Jarrott had started the whole business off way back in 1902, Edge winning the Gordon Bennett Trophy at the wheel of a Napier and Jarrott the Circuit des Ardennes. "Frenchmen, Belgians and Englishmen who had come over to see the race vied with one another in congratulating me on the run," said the latter in his 1906 book *Ten Years of Motors and Motor Racing*. Congratulating their fellow countrymen on winning at this level was not something the British had much chance of doing until they started to race at Le Mans; there is no doubt that the 24-hour event was the first to put British drivers on the metaphorical world map.

As with the cars, it is not always obvious which drivers can be claimed for the British camp, particularly as the British Empire still had over a couple of decades to go when the first Le Mans endurance race was run. One could also say that Bentley's most successful driver, Woolf Barnato, was born in South Africa, but it would be churlish to exclude him from a story such as this. Barnato was the grandson of Isaac Isaacs, an East End of London shopkeeper whose son Barnett ('Barney') changed his name to Barnato and went to South Africa at the age of 25 with just £25. There he competed with Cecil Rhodes and went on to make his fortune in the Kimberley diamond mines. Barnett sailed to England with his two-year-old son Woolf in 1897, but is said to have committed suicide during the journey, a verdict that granddaughter Diana Barnato Walker questions in her autobiography *Spreading my Wings*.

As mentioned, the man who paved the way for the British at Le Mans, John Duff, was actually Canadian, his grandparents having emigrated from Scotland in the mid-1850s. The son of missionaries, he was born in Kiukiang, China and sent to Canada only to return having been expelled from school. With the coming of the Great War, aged 19, he travelled via the Trans-Siberian railway to enlist in the British Army, becoming a lieutenant in the Royal Berkshire Rifles. When he died in 1958 the *Bentley Drivers Club Review* said that he "had been the first British Entrant and Driver to win Le Mans and thereby clearing the way to other famous victories. What greater epitaph could a man have than that?"

Duncan Hamilton was actually born in Cork and lived in Ireland until the age of six. Indeed, he told the writer F. Wilson McComb that he regarded himself as "a Southern Irishman." Still there was no-one more British than Hamilton, and after all, the history of 19th century Britain is populated by great generals – Wellington, Kitchener, Wolseley – who were Englishmen born in Ireland.

There are some, though, whom we must omit. For example, despite the fact that he was born in England, current sporting rivalry means that, even though he has been regarded as an 'honorary Brit' when driving for Bentley and Aston Martin, David Brabham must be firmly placed in the Australian camp. While Brabham's World Champion father Sir Jack was never claimed to be anything other than antipodean, Ken Miles' parents were British and he was born and brought up in the UK. However, he spent most of his adult life in the USA, so where does this leave us? Suffice to say that he was one of the drivers of the second-placed Ford that featured in the memorable, if controversial 1966 finish.

British, indeed any nationality's, motor racing by its very nature does not need to borrow its sports representatives from other countries. There is no need

for a Zola Budd, a Mike Catt, a Graham Hick or a Kevin Pietersen. At least there was not until the A1 Grand Prix series commenced in 2005, and Norwich-born Ralph Firman, himself a Le Mans contestant in 2004, became an honorary Irishman, but that is outside the remit of this story. Still, it was sad to see a correspondent for the magazine *Autosport* comment that he originally did not think that A1 GP would work because teams and manufacturers in other formulae had become international, certainly European, and that national identities were things of the past. Given the euphoria when Johnny Wilkinson kicked the winning drop goal in the 2003 Rugby Union World Cup, or the awakening of national consciousness during the 2005 Ashes, sport at the highest levels still inflames patriotic passions and nowhere can this be more so than in the grandstands opposite the pits at Le Mans.

Guy Smith recalls that the British spectators facing the Bentley pits would take it in turns to wave their flags, these 'stints' coinciding with those of their heroes opposite. Yet even this dedication pales before the efforts of such as the Japanese Nissan supporter who appeared to be waving his very large flag for the whole of the 1999 race, even standing alone in the small hours of the morning. The British are not the only ones to take their Le Mans seriously, although it has to be said that they are the only ones to have done so consistently over the years.

With the demise of the original Bentley campaign in 1930, British drivers had to look elsewhere for their mounts. The first of the post-Bentley years, 1931, may have seen an Alfa Romeo victory, but the drivers were the Englishmen Earl Howe and 'Tim' Birkin. In the immediate post-war period the British were more likely to return to the cockpits of British-built cars, but by the mid-1960s it was becoming difficult to decide just what was British. The 7-litre Fords were definitely American, but the Ford GT40 Group 4 cars were built in Slough, England. However, if we are to call them British then we must include such as the Lola and TWR-built Nissans and the 1999 BMWs. With the 1990s, and a car that was first designed by TWR to be a Jaguar and ended up winning twice as a Porsche, the picture become most confused. No, if the reader will forgive, Ford must be seen as an American vehicle manufacturer although its GT40 looms large in this book through the exploits of British entrant

The British front runners at Le Mans have tended to be English or Scottish although Ulsterman Eddie Irvine finished second in 1994 for Toyota having led until the last couple of hours. He seems to have enjoyed the race in contrast to his fellow countryman John Watson who will tell you how he hated it. "It's 22 hours too long." He points out how dangerous the track was in the 1970s and 1980s. His final appearance from seven starts was in 1990, the only time that he finished the race – in 11th place, so perhaps you can forgive his jaundiced attitude. Watson (right) is seen here with fellow Jaguar driver, Australian Larry Perkins. *(Simon Maurice)*

American Briggs Cunningham used a very British team gathered from the Bentley Drivers Club and led by Stanley Sedgwick to carry out time keeping duties in the 1950s. *(Derek Waller)*

S.F. Edge with his mechanic Cecil Edge at Champigny before the start of the 1902 Gordon Bennett Trophy. There are those who have traced the use of British Racing Green back to his Napier although it was probably first used on Charles Jarrott's Paris-Berlin Panhard the year before. *(LAT Photographic)*

John Wyer and British drivers like 1969 winner Jackie Oliver.

We can no longer identify the British by their green war paint. Indeed, colour was never a guarantee of nationality. The 1935 winning Lagonda, the early works Aston Martins or the Frazer-Nash that was placed third in 1949 were among those who looked as if they bore allegiance to Italy. The 1908 Austin, the first ever British Grand Prix car, now displayed at the Heritage Museum at Gaydon, is currently red. It is perhaps difficult for those new to motor racing to realize just how significant national colours – relevant to the entrant, not the driver or manufacturer – once were. Ian Skailes, who ran a Chevron B16 at Le Mans in 1970, says his was "a very British effort." Accordingly the car was in British Racing Green with Union Jacks on its flanks. "There was only one colour I could have a racing car and that was BRG." Those who ran the Bentleys from 2001 to 2003 understood this, although perhaps there was a need to distance the cars as much as possible from their German ownership. Jaguar did, at least, first run its Group C cars in green in 1985, but this soon (and before Le Mans) gave way to the gaudy livery of the cigarette brand Silk Cut.

It is generally felt that BRG is a deep Brunswick Green, although in truth there have been many shades of green used by British entrants over the years. Sometimes, like the hue revived by Aston Martin in 2005, they are particularly associated with a specific marque. It has been said that the colour was introduced in 1903, the year that the Gordon Bennett Trophy was held in Ireland, in honour of the host country. However, this flies in the face of why the race was held in Ireland that year. In 1902 the Gordon Bennett Trophy had been won by S.F. Edge for Britain and it fell to the winning nation to organize the following year's race. Given that racing was banned on the main roads of mainland Britain, the event was held in Ireland, then 'British territory.' An eyewitness, Henry Knox, stated that Edge's Napier was already a shade of olive green when it raced to victory on its way from Paris to Innsbruck in 1902. It is said that this was the same paint as was used for the doors and window frames of Napier's factory.

Charles Jarrott recorded an even earlier example of racing a green car. The Englishman's first ever car race was the 1901 Paris-Berlin in which he was entered on a Panhard. On arriving in Paris to pick this up he found that it had been painted green, "a beautiful rich, dark

colour." He was puzzled as to why only his mount was this shade, but the French explained that it was because he had been allotted the number 13. As this was considered unlucky they had decided to nullify it by painting the car green, which in France was regarded as the lucky colour. Napier historian David Venables believes that Edge may have been persuaded by his friend Jarrott that his car should also be painted this propitious colour, thus starting a tradition.

Today there is a feeling that the British national colours might just be those of the Union Jack. The UK team competing in the A1 GP single-seater series was originally to have red, white and blue Lola-Zyteks. Then it was said that they might be green, but when the car appeared at Brands Hatch in 2005 it was, indeed, finished in red, white and blue. The fact that as it sped past at racing speeds it was virtually indistinguishable from the other predominantly white cars in the field may have proved a point. When the dark green Bentleys raced past on their way to victory in 2003 there was surely a certain frisson caused by their very British appearance.

A very British scene in the middle of France. Prince Michael of Kent (bearded, behind car) shows an interest in the works Jaguars on the grid. *(George Byford)*

THE CLASSIC BRITISH WELCOME

At the beginning of the 2000s, the mayor of Saint Saturnin, a village to the north-west of Le Mans, became worried that the new bypass would mean a dearth of British fans visiting whilst on their way to the track. He thus instituted the 'Classic British Welcome,' a Friday morning event that he hoped would attract them back.

It has to be said that the first year not many turned up. Undeterred, the mayor asked a local British 'expat' to contact the car clubs in this country. The result was that now as many as 300 classic British cars arrive in the village on the Friday before the race. Saint Saturnin is dressed with Union Jacks and a garden party atmosphere prevails. Sir Stirling Moss, Derek Bell and Johnny Herbert are among those to have dropped in.

Each year there is a featured marque, one of the earliest having been Jaguar. The Jaguar Enthusiasts Club became a sponsor of the event, the club having sent a party to Le Mans every year for the last 18 under the leadership of committee member Simon Cronin. He first went to the race in 1975 and has not missed a year since, now travelling down in his Jaguar Mk2 and looking after a party of some 60 enthusiasts, organizing campsites, ferries and grandstand seats. He has sat in the same seat since 1988. Like so many others in this book, his first trip was with Page & Moy, the result of having heard an advertisement on Radio Luxembourg. His interest in the race had already been formed as a boy to the extent that he had built his own wireless set in order to catch the BBC Light Service broadcasts from the track.

The nearby village of Saint Saturnin now holds an annual Classic British Welcome. The Jaguar Enthusiasts' Club has been one of the sponsors of the event; president Natalie Rosine and committee member Simon Cronin were among those present in 2003. *(Simon Cronin collection)*

Patrick Peal (second from left) worked at Le Mans in the early 1990s on the publicity for the Lotus Esprit GT cars. In 2004 he found himself back at the track for the second Le Mans Classic event, team managing a Lotus Eleven S2 Le Mans that, as he says, had been "lurking unloved" in Scotland for 30 years. Despite being run by perhaps the only all-amateur team on its grid, the Lotus was classified 20th after the three races as well as 10th in the Index of Performance. *(Patrick Peal)*

Unlike the highly successful R8C roadster, the 1999 LM GTP R8C was a very British Audi. It was designed by Tony Southgate and built by rtn in Norfolk. Audi Sport UK undertook its running. Three of the six drivers, including (seen here) Perry McCarthy, were British. Both cars retired with transmission failure. *(Original painting by James Dugdale – reproduced by kind permission of Zurich Financial Services and Bodyshop Magazine)*

CLASSIC LE MANS

No account of the British at Le Mans should fail to mention the Classic Le Mans, another excuse for natives of this country to flock to France to witness endurance racing cars, in this case ones that may have featured in past 24-hour events. "Where else," asks former Lotus PR man Patrick Peal, who team managed a Lotus Eleven S2 in the 2004 event, "can you enjoy upwards of 350 sports-racing cars spanning the 1920s to the 1970s being campaigned with panache, flair, enthusiasm and determination despite their age and value?"

The event takes place biennially, the third one happening in July 2006. Peal reckons: "The organizers have come up with a great format that retains the challenge and spirit of the famed 24-hour endurance race, yet reduces the demands on rare and ancient racers – cars and teams." The entry is split into grids by decade. Each grid has three 45-minute races in the 24-hour period – a couple of day races and one at night time. To make it even more true to the history of the race, the first race sets off with a Le Mans start with the drivers running across the track to their cars.

PART TWO
1931–1939

Lone Victory

"Happy and glorious." The British were involved at all levels during the early 1930s, chasing both class wins and overall victory. Here in 1934 the 10th place Aston Martin Ulster of Maurice Faulkner and Reggie Tongue leads the Alfa Romeo 8C 2300 of Earl Howe and Tim Rose-Richards that was involved in the lead battle before retiring with clutch failure. *(LAT Photographic)*

CHAPTER 5

THE BRITISH AT LE MANS
1931-1939

"You've got to savour it, haven't you?"
(Lawrence Dallaglio, member of the England Rugby World Cup winning team)

After the flurry of Bentley wins, there was to be only one more outright victory for a British car in the years up to the Second World War. There was also the first, indeed only, win for a British pairing in a foreign car. Against this there occurred a period during which the British dominated in terms of sheer numbers; in just over a decade they went from providing the sole non-French entry to accounting for two-thirds of the field.

The year 1935 is the one to truly celebrate. The 2.3-litre supercharged Alfa Romeos were favourites for a fifth successive victory, a trend started in 1931 when Sir Henry Birkin and Earl Howe won in the latter's 8C-2300. However, the majority of cars were British including nine Singers, seven Aston Martins and MGs and six Rileys. Interestingly, despite the widespread use of national racing colours, not all of these were painted green, the works Astons, for example, being coloured red. Also in an unpatriotic red were the two Lagonda Rapides entered by motor trader Fox and Nicholl. The three works MG PAs all had lady drivers known collectively as 'George Eyston's young ladies', or more popularly as his 'dancing daughters'. *The Motor* reported that "with one or two exceptions, the British cars looked very much the smartest and best-turned-out of the whole entry. Each British marque seemed to have been on its mettle to produce glistening, clean cars."

First to his car, the blue Alfa Romeo that he was sharing with Earl Howe, was the Hon Brian Lewis (later Lord Essendon). It was said that minutes before he had seemed the least interested person at the track. Now he was on the move before anyone else and, although a Duesenberg that had been placed further up the grid briefly led him out of the first bend, by the Mulsanne straight he was in the lead followed by two more Alfas. Six laps later Lewis pitted to change a distributor and at about this time the Lagonda of John Hindmarsh moved up to second place.

By the eighth hour the car, co-driven by Anglo-Portuguese Luis Fontès, was in the lead. The second Lagonda of Dr Benjafield and Sir Ronald Gunther

was then fifth behind the Lewis/Howe Alfa, although having lost all but top gear it fell back to an eventual 13th place. During the night the lead changed places several times, a Bugatti and two of the Alfas, including the Lewis/Howe car, taking turns to lead the field. At 5.30am the latter went out with a holed piston, and by 10.00am the Hindmarsh/Fontès car was back up front. And there it was to stay, despite frequent pit stops with falling oil pressure.

However, the Alfa driver Pierre-Louis Dreyfus had at, one point, thought differently. The Frenchman, who raced under the name of 'Heldé', had passed the by now cruising Lagonda with 20 minutes to go and, believing himself to be in the lead, relaxed his own speed. Indeed, the loudspeakers proclaimed him to be in first place. "A groan of sympathy went up for Fontès' bitter luck," reported *The Motor*. But in truth Dreyfus had merely put himself onto the lead lap. By the time he discovered this – the voice on the loudspeaker corrected itself with just two minutes to

The MG Midget of Francis Samuelson and Freddy Kindell was not classified in 1931 as it completed its last lap in 31 minutes 28 seconds rather than in under the maximum permitted 30 minutes. *(LAT Photographic)*

The Aston Martin, chassis LM5, of 'Bert' Bertelli and Pat Driscoll secured the Rudge-Whitworth Cup in 1932, finishing seventh in that year's race. *(LAT Photographic)*

go – it was too late to do anything about it.

It was not just the Lagonda's victory that made this a year for the British to savour. Twenty-two of the cars that finished came from this country and most of the classes were won by British cars. Charles Martin and Charles Brackenbury's Aston Martin Ulster took the Rudge-Whitworth Biennial Cup as well as the Index of Performance and the 1½-litre class; the class lap record set by them was to stand until 1950. All but one of the other Astons finished. The 2-litre class fell to the supercharged MG Magnette of Frenchmen Phillippe Maillard-Brune and Charles Druck, while Stanley Barnes and Archie Langley won the 1-litre category in their Singer. The three MG lady team cars crossed the line together, and bringing up the tail of the field were two 748cc Austins. Then, as now, just to finish Le Mans was an achievement worthy of laurels.

The British Minister of Transport, Leslie Hore-Belisha, sent a telegram to France stating: "This is really splendid. My congratulations to all concerned."

The beginning of this period – the year 1931 – saw a significant shift in the balance of power, but at least there was a win for a British driver pairing. This time there was just one Bentley, and a private entry at that; there would be no works cars again until 2001. With the British motor industry intent on economic survival, only Aston Martin sent a full works team from these shores. The Italians, in the shape of the Alfa Romeos, were expected to win, and they duly did so. By midnight, as others fell by the wayside, the 8C-2300 of Earl Howe and Tim Birkin had moved up to second place. On the 84th lap it passed into the lead and then its main rival crashed. By morning it was seven laps ahead of the 7.1-litre Mercedes-Benz now in second place. The German car was reported by *The Motor* to have been throwing tyre treads in the early stages of the race, only regaining its lost speed after ditching its Engelbert tyres and fitting Dunlops,

"tyres of a British make." However, the Mercedes was unable to gain on the Italian car and Birkin/Howe took the chequered flag, the first pairing to pass 3000 kilometres in the history of the race. They also took both the Rudge-Whitworth Biennial Cup and the Index of Performance. *The Motor* proudly said that they had "showed what British drivers could do," also pointing out that it was one of the finest drives of Birkin's career.

Interestingly, Howe's Alfa had only been readied at 5.30am on the day of the race. A last-minute decision to run all the Alfas on pure benzole, instead of a troublesome 70-30 mixture, had meant raising the compressions ratios and changing the pistons. The head of Alfa Romeo's racing department had to rush off to Paris in Birkin's Bentley Speed Six saloon to make arrangements and *The Motor*'s aeroplane (the magazine used a 'plane in those days to get its report back to London) was requisitioned to fly to the French capital to collect the pistons. It could be said, therefore, that Bentley also had a hand in the 1931 victory. (An 8-litre Bentley tourer with Barnato and Birkin aboard was also used to open the circuit.)

Only six cars finished that year from a total of 26 starters, and two were British. The London-built Talbot model 105s took third place each year from 1930 to 1932. In 1931 it was the pairing of Owen Saunders-Davies and Tim Rose-Richards that achieved this after the quickest of the Talbots, weary it would seem after competing in a gruelling Brooklands Double-Twelve race, retired. Its drivers, Hindmarsh and Lewis, had been running second at the time. In fifth place was the sole surviving Aston Martin LM6 of Aston director Auguste Cesar 'Bert' Bertelli and Maurice Harvey. The three-car team, which had also had little time to prepare after the Brooklands race, had suffered light and wing bracket failures (rope was used to keep the wings in place) and the car of Humphrey Cook and Jack Bezzant had to retire after it had run over its own nearside front wing.

Francis Samuelson, at the wheel of his MG Midget, is reported to have come "tuff-tuffing by" towards the end of the race, the car belching out smoke. Thinking himself to have sufficient time, he ran the last lap at reduced speed only to be disqualified for taking two minutes too long. Samuelson had been sharing the car with Freddy Kindell, a mechanic from MG's racing department at Abingdon. A second Midget, driven by the Hon Mrs Chetwynd and H.H. Stisted, retired with a sheared key in the timing gear. The Hon A.D. Chewtynd had become worried during the evening that his wife's car was 20 minutes overdue and he could find no information as to what had happened. Eventually Stisted limped into view "inordinately cheerful" but "perspiring of brow." The car had been abandoned as, whatever was done to it, it would only give "two bangs and a whoof." The Midgets, said *Light Car*, had "created a wonderful impression among the French, who had never seen anything quite so small move so fast."

Aston Martin, with former winner Sammy Davis as team manager, again entered a full team in 1932, the only other make to do so being Alfa Romeo. This year there was just seven British cars. One of the Astons, that of Bertelli and 'Pat' Driscoll, took the ninth Biennial Cup (as well as the 1½-litre class) at the last minute when the Caban, which had seemed a likely winner, was forced to crawl to the finish. It is said to have been the fulfilment of Bertelli's greatest ambition. A week later the team was given the honour of opening the Shelsley Walsh hill-climb, an important event on the British motorsport calendar in the 1930s.

Again a British Talbot, that of Lewis and Rose-Richards, came in third. W.F. Bradley, continental correspondent of *The Autocar* (and whose son Bill was to race at Le Mans) referred to the pair as "those two fine English sportsmen who so closely resemble each other." They were to come third again in 1933, this time at the wheel of an Alfa Romeo. Both Astons and Talbots suffered from plug trouble in 1932 which, said Bradley, "seriously jeopardized the chance of British success in the race." Indeed, the Astons, misfiring badly, had all been forced to pit at the end of the first lap. It was felt that the excessively hot weather and the use of unsuitable fuel were the cause of the problem.

The previous year's winners, Howe and Birkin, moved into the lead after six hours in their Alfa, but had lost it again by midnight, then regained it in the early hours only to retire with a blown cylinder head gasket. A plug change just before midnight had been indicative of the trouble ahead. Finally, it should be reported that a couple of Frenchmen entered Birkin's old supercharged Bentley, but one of them, Trevoux, turned it over at White House on the very first lap, where it remained an obstruction for several hours.

The gap between first and second in 1933 was to be matched only by the finish in 1969, with just 10 seconds splitting the leaders as they crossed the finishing line. However, there was no British involvement in that earlier last-minute struggle, although the third car home was an Alfa Romeo crewed in fine style by Lewis – who had led the Alfa team away at the start – and Rose-Richards, matching their 1932 performance in the Talbot. Two Brooklands Rileys, one of them the 1932 Tourist Trophy-winning car, made their Le Mans debut among the 10 British cars entered for the 1933 race, and Alex von der Becke and Keith 'Kim' Peacock drove theirs into fourth place behind the Alfas to take the Index of Performance. *The Motor* reported that it "more than upheld the reputation of the manufacturers and the prestige of the British light car." Two of the three Astons finished that year, as did a standard Singer Nine Sports four-seater, "which it can truly be said gave a great account of itself." First of the Astons, the fifth-placed Ulster, was crewed by Pat Driscoll and Clifton Penn-Hughes, while sharing the seventh-placed car with Bertelli was none other than Sammy Davis, who was making a comeback to driving; his participation had been kept quiet until the last moment. Shades of the previous year, the nearside front wing of this car broke off, but Bertelli was driving at the time and by now he was adept at roping them back on. After the race he was presented with a model mudguard made by the Earl of March.

The MG Midget of John Ludovic Ford and Maurice Baumer was said to have won everyone's admiration in finishing sixth that year. Indeed, "it more than surprised the spectators," said the report. What was described as "a popular British entry" but also a "rather decrepit" Austin Seven was among those that failed to get to the flag, while the ex-Birkin Bentley was crashed again. The latter had been in clutch trouble during practice and was only on the grid thanks to help from one of the former 'Bentley Boys', Jean Chassagne, by now a Castrol representative in France.

The weather was glorious for the 1934 race, in fact it was almost too hot. The field this time was considerably larger thanks to the British; over half of the 44 starters came from this country. But again, no one expected a British-built car to win, although two of the much fancied Alfa Romeos were British-entered. Unfortunately, the only Alfa to survive and to win the race was not one of the British entries, but the next seven cars to finish all originated in the UK. Heading them was the Riley of Frenchmen Jean Sebilleaué and Georges Delaroche. The Rileys also took a clean sweep of the Index of Performance, led again by von der Becke and Peacock, who also won the Rudge-Whitworth Biennial Cup ahead of two Singers, the first of which was driven by Lewis and Hindmarsh. For some time von der Becke and Peacock had fought neck-and-neck with the Charles Martin/Robert Lindsay Eccles MG Magnette for the handicap award, but while the latter were to finish fourth overall, they fell back in the competition for the Index.

Earl Howe's Alfa had led again at one point on the Saturday only to lose over an hour with lighting problems and then to retire with a faulty clutch. Aston Martin's result was not one to remember either

George Eyston's three MGs were not the only female-crewed cars at Le Mans in 1935. Elsie 'Bill' Wisdom and Kay Petre retired after 35 laps in their Riley MPH. Wisdom's husband Tommy competed in the same race in a Singer but also retired. *(LAT Photographic)*

although the car of Mortimer 'Mort' Morris-Goodall, driving brilliantly, and John Elwes ran as high as second for eight hours before its retirement in the 19th hour, a magnificent achievement for an unblown 1½-litre car. But sadly, matters went simultaneously pear-shaped for the Aston team. First the car of Thomas Fotheringham and John Appleton went missing, then Morris-Goodall was late and, to cap it all, the privately entered Aston of Reggie Tongue (who was racing under the name 'Vincent') disappeared at the same time. There was talk of the Bentley disaster of 1927. Then Tongue hobbled in with a flat tyre, telling sad tales of the other Astons round the track. Morris-Goodall had serious engine trouble and Appleton was thought to have a broken oil pipe, but at least the driver was working on it. It was to no avail, though, and both cars were out of the race. Another car to have run as high as second, "travelling at an astonishing pace," was, remarkably, the 1.1-litre MG Magnette of Ford and Baumer, two of the heroes of 1933. A punctured fuel tank during the 10th hour put a stop to their moment of glory.

Following the British victory of 1935, the 1936 race was cancelled due to civic unrest in France. The entry for that year, though, had indicated another possible shift in the balance of power. French manufacturer interest had increased and the short era when the entry was dominated by British cars and the race usually won by Italian ones was over. The proverbial writing on the wall proved correct when the race returned in 1937 and future Land Speed Record holder John Cobb was nominated as the official race starter. French cars were to win the three remaining events in the run up to the Second World War. There was a reasonably strong UK entry in 1937, particularly in that British preserve, the 1½-litre class. However, half the total number of cars entered that year were French, and the following year France provided an even larger percentage of the field and the British challenge was the poorest for a long time.

Of the major prizes during these three years the only one to fall to a British car was the 1937 Biennial Cup, which went to Morris-Goodall/Robert Hitchens' particularly sick 2-litre Aston Martin. At one point towards the end of the race Morris-Goodall was thought to have retired the car, but this proved not to be so. A great shout was said to have gone up as the car limped out of the pits.

The only other car surviving that could still win the Cup was the MG Midget then being driven by newcomer Dorothy Stanley Turner, and according to *The Motor*, "lapping merrily." However, the Aston staggered to the finishing line to win the award, with Miss Turner, who shared the car with Joan Riddell, having the consolation of an ovation as she crossed the line. Elsewhere, there had been drama connected to the following year's Biennial Cup. In order to qualify, the Archie Scott/Ted Halford HRG had to complete 164 laps. With just three minutes to go it had done 163 and then, on the far side of the track, it stopped. Scott managed to get it going again and with seconds to go he crossed the line "to thunderous applause." The Hon J.M. Skeffingham and R.C. Murton-Neale were reported to have "quietly" taken fifth place overall, as well as the 1½-litre class, in their two-year-old, privately entered Aston Martin Ulster. The car had been prepared at Murton-Neale's Speed Models in Notting Hill.

The ultimately third-placed Lagonda of Dr John Benjafield and Ronald Gunther leads Charles Martin/Charles Brackenbury and John Elwes/'Mort' Morris-Goodall (both in Aston Martin Ulsters) in 1935. *(LAT Photographic)*

It is 1935, and the winning Lagonda of Hindmarsh and Fontès is bearing down on the little 750cc works Austin of Charles Dodson and R.G. Richardson which came home a valiant 28th. *(Sally Harrison collection)*

Sadly, 1937 saw what was described as one of the worst motor racing crashes to date. A French amateur driver was killed and Liverpool-born South African Pat Fairfield, who had been driving a Frazer-Nash-BMW, succumbed to his injuries early on the Monday morning.

The following year the highest placed British crew was that of Peter Clark and Marcus Chambers in another HRG, who finished back in 10th place. The pair would win the 1½-litre class 12 months later. Plucky Miss Prudence Fawcett and Geoffrey White were also reported to have distinguished themselves in 1938, finishing 13th and surviving a bout of misfiring in their Morgan. Having said that, the highest placed British-built car that year was a French-entered Singer. *The Autocar* observed a particular incident that could provide ammunition to anyone reckoning a woman's place is not in the pits: "The Morgan's *commissaire*, pondering, no doubt, on that car's fair driver, fell through into the MG pit complete with a door, felling six bewildered people in the process." By contrast, the Morgan of White and Geoffrey Anthony that finished 15th in 1939 was described as "unobtrusive" and "quite monotonously consistent."

The final year before the war did see a British challenge with two Bentley-designed Lagonda V12s entered, to W.O.'s disgust; he felt that they were not yet sufficiently developed. Arthur Dobson and Charles Brackenbury were paired in one, their Lordships Selsdon (who was to win 10 years later when the race returned) and Waleran in the other. Selsdon was reported as dazzling everybody at Gruber's restaurant, the 'in-place' for the Le Mans crowd, with his cap, shirt and tie in three shades of red and his trousers of bright blue.

The two Lagondas came in a worthy but unsensational third and fourth and were predicted to do better in 1940. *Motor Sport* magazine, in particular,

The Talbot 105s performed well during the early 1930s and were still racing at Le Mans over 70 years later, John Rushton's 1934 model being entered for the Legends race in 2005. *(Author)*

was enthused by their potential. "Britains (*sic*) Great Come Back at Le Mans" ran the headline to its leader. It was pointed out that the Lagondas were making their racing debut and would have done well had they finished "fifth and sixth or even seventh and eighth." Not only did they finish higher than this but they also averaged a higher speed than the previous year's winner. "Big green British cars thundered round the course with the utmost regularity, as in days of old." *Motor Sport* also reminded its readers that the designer had already been responsible for five Le Mans winners. "The workmanlike green cars" had "represented Britain so worthily in the race," said the magazine, obviously looking forward to an even better result the following year. Herr Adolf Hitler, however, had other ideas.

Jim Campbell's Aston Martin Ulster follows a couple of Talbots and the rest of the field at the start of the 2005 Legends race. *(Author)*

THE LEGENDS

It is the morning of the Le Mans 24-Hours. Out on the track history is being recalled thanks in the main to a Briton with a passion both for the race and, in particular, for Bentleys. Every other year a 'Legends' race takes place before the main event, a recent feature initially masterminded by the late Ray Wiltshire, a one-time president of the Bentley Drivers' Club and the only ever non-French director of the ACO.

Ray's son Duncan recalls that the ACO seemed oblivious of its heritage. However, in the early 1980s Wiltshire Senior plus Dennis Miller-Williams and Tom Northey, the public relations managers of Rolls-Royce and Pirelli, respectively, organized a race-day cavalcade of British contenders from the past. The ACO was amazed to find out just how popular the event was and what was intended as a one-off became a regular feature.

In 2001 Motor Racing Legends, as the Wiltshires' organizing company is now known, was given permission by the ACO to hold a 40-minute historic race on the Saturday morning. This now runs every other year, is now an hour long, and is exclusively for cars of a type that have competed in the 24-Hours. The initial race was for cars that competed between 1949 and 1965. In 2003 the years were 1959 to 1971 and in 2005 from 1935 to 1955. As Duncan Wiltshire points out, it is important to keep varying the eras. About half of the entries tend to be from genuine Le Mans contenders.

In 2001 David Piper drove home first in his Ferrari 250LM ahead of the actual 1959 winner, the Aston Martin DBR1/2 of Peter Hardman. The 2003 victor, a Ligier JS3, was a little less charismatic; it was not even British, even if its driver Willie Green was. The 2005 race was a British triumph dominated by Jaguars, with Johnny Herbert and Green putting on a show in D-types, Herbert eventually pulling away in Nigel Webb's 1955 car. Webb himself shared the fifth-place C-type with one Sir Stirling Moss. A spontaneous applause broke out as the latter drove round on his initial lap.

In 2004 Motor Racing Legends also ran an hour-long race for 34 Group C and GTP cars. Gary Pearson's Jaguar XJR-11 headed the field until differential failure, handing victory to Charlie Agg's Nissan R90CK, which was said to be topping 214mph on the Mulsanne straight.

Johnny Herbert waves a wheel of Nigel Webb's Jaguar D-type during his entertaining drive to first place in the 2005 Legends race. *(Author)*

CHAPTER 6

HINDMARSH AND THE LAGONDAS

"An idea that is not dangerous is unworthy of being called an idea at all." (Oscar Wilde)

There is nothing very British in the name of the 1935 winning car. 'Lagonda' is, in fact, the Shawnee Indian word for a place in Ohio, home of the company's founder Wilbur Gunn. In the late 19th century, Gunn, although an engineer, travelled to the UK as an opera singer. By the turn of the century he was manufacturing motorcycles and soon one of his creations represented Great Britain in an International Cup race. But despite its name and the fact that its Le Mans-winning car was not even painted green, Lagonda is truly a British make.

The first year that Lagondas were entered for *Les Vingt-Quatre Heures* was 1928, so the marque was among the initial British entries to follow Bentley's pioneering efforts. A meticulously prepared team of three cars was subscribed to by 16 of the leading British Lagonda agents. "The Lagonda cars have given very good accounts of themselves in practising and are well-finished attractive looking cars closely resembling the standard speed model," said *The Motor* in its preview of the race. Baron d'Erlanger and Clive Gallop, who had raced for Bentley the previous year, were included in the team, as were Douglas Hawkes, Frank King, Lagonda's sales manager, Francis Samuelson and Major E.J. Hays. (Hawkes, who was to race a SARA the following year, had twice driven in the Indianapolis 500, finishing 13th in 1922 in an almost standard 3-litre Bentley with DFP-derived body and retiring an Eldridge in 1926.) The team was "splendidly managed" by the calm 'Bertie' Kensington-Moir, who had raced for Bentley in 1925. The 2-litre cars were the fastest in their class – reaching 95mph at a point between Pontlieue and Mulsanne.

As the cars roared away at the start, d'Erlanger was left behind. The Baron stepped out of his car and, in measured fashion, lifted the bonnet first on one side and then on the other before finding that the spark plugs were wet with petrol. Eventually he got going to cheers from the British supporters. However, the team was to become involved in the incident that reminded observers of the Bentley team's crash at White House the previous year. Samuelson had been

cornering wildly and ignoring the pit signals to slow down. D'Erlanger came round the Mulsanne corner to find his team-mate coming back off the sandbank and straight at his Lagonda. It is said that the Baron's reactions reduced the effects of the accident. Nevertheless, both front dumb-irons, a spring leaf, a tyre and other components on his car were affected. He was grazed about the eyebrow and the bridge of the nose. Gallop, who was about 400 yards behind him, noticed spectators running towards the corner and, correctly assuming that something was amiss, slowed to walking pace to get past.

D'Erlanger returned to the pits and handed over to Hawkes, who took the car out for an exploratory lap only to find the nearside front Hartford shock absorber to be dangling. This had to be removed and, to equalize matters, the other one slackened right off. The springs were then no longer considered adequate to take the full power of front-wheel brake

The privately run Lagonda of Tim Rose-Richards and Brian Lewis in 1929. After just 28 laps the former pitted because the car's floorboards had been on fire. This was traced to an escape through the cylinder head gasket. As water could not be taken on for another 12 laps that effectively meant the end for the team. *(LAT Photographic)*

In 1934 John Hindmarsh shared a Singer with Brian Lewis, the pair finishing in seventh place, as well as second in the Rudge-Whitworth Cup competition. *(Sally Harrison collection)*

application. Consider how well the car did to then average 65mph without front brakes or dampers. Samuelson, meanwhile, was firmly embedded in the dreaded Mulsanne corner sand. It took two hours of frenzied digging to extract the car, only to find that the gearbox had been damaged.

At around midnight, d'Erlanger shot into the pits complaining that he could not see a thing; one headlamp bulb had burnt out and the lamp brackets were loose. Kensington-Moir, said *The Motor*, dealt with the problems "speaking in a quiet, distinct voice that would soothe the most troubled or excited." At the end of the race the Baron's car was in 10th place.

Single Lagonda entries took part in 1929 and 1934, and in the first year the car of Rose-Richards and Lewis was said to have "gone down with flying colours." Five years later Lord de Clifford and Charles Brackenbury came 16th in the former's Rapier Special. The car had been reduced in size to be eligible for the 1100cc class. It was catalogued as the De Clifford Special, having been modified by Dobsons of Staines with the co-operation of the factory. His Lordship was particularly tall, requiring a heightened windscreen for the car. It is also recounted that he took two caravans to the track, one for himself, the other for his butler.

When Lagonda launched its 4½-litre M45 Rapide it was the firm's largest-engined car to date. De Clifford made a highly publicized run to Brindisi in one, beating the train by 14 hours. Arthur Fox, of race preparation specialist Fox and Nicholl, could see the potential of the car and bought three black competition chassis with 10ft 3in wheelbases as opposed to the 10ft 9in of the standard car. Fox and Nicholl had already been successful as an entrant of the Georges Roesch designed Talbots. Other modifications to the Rapides included uprated Girling rod brakes, negative-camber road springs, a combination of Luvax hydraulic and Andre-Hartford friction dampers, a specially braced Bishop steering box, a close-ratio gearbox and a 3.14:1 final-drive ratio. Fox was also given free access to Lagonda's own test beds, which allowed him to uprate the Meadows 6ESC engines that were fitted. The initial idea was to take advantage of the fact that a ban on superchargers would keep the Alfa Romeos away from the 1934 Tourist Trophy. The three cars came home fourth, fifth and eighth.

The trio was still at Fox and Nicholl's premises in Tolworth when Lagonda went into receivership in April 1935, but despite this, Fox went ahead and entered two of them for Le Mans. One was to be driven by John Hindmarsh, who had finished fifth in the 1934 Tourist Trophy, and Luis Fontès, while the other was originally to have been piloted by Dr Dudley Benjafield and Geoff Manby-Colegrave. However, Sir

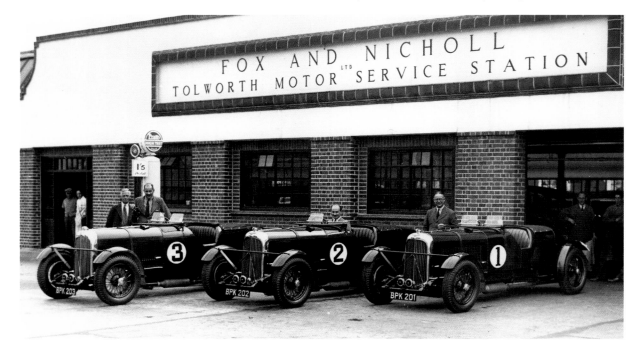

Fox and Nicholl saw the potential of the Lagonda M45 Rapide and purchased three competition chassis, initially to run in the Tourist Trophy. The trio, two of which were entered for Le Mans, was still at the company's premises when Lagonda went into receivership. *(Sally Harrison collection)*

Fox and Nicholl had earlier entered Talbots at Le Mans. In 1930 Hindmarsh and Rose-Richards finished fourth overall behind the Biennial Cup-winning sister car of Eaton and Lewis. Here they lead the Bugatti of Marguerite Mareuse and Odette Siko *(LAT Photographic)*

Ronald Gunther eventually took the latter's seat. The cars, which were fitted for the TT with bright red, lightweight, doorless, dual-cockpit bodies, were now equipped with full lighting, a secondary bonnet strap, scuttle-mounted cooling vents and specially curved handbrake levers to prevent problems with the frantic Le Mans start. It has been said that offset bonnet bulges indicated some engine fettling, but the details of this have not been recorded. For the earlier TT the 122bhp engines had been given unique crankcases made from high-tensile RR50 alloy, larger diameter crankshaft big-end journals, redesigned con-rods, a higher compression ratio, slot-free valves held by split cotters and oversize studs to hold the block to the crankcase. The nearside coil and distributor of the production car had been replaced by a Scintilla Vertex magneto with a horizontal Scintella magneto replacing the normal BTH fitting on the offside. The twin SU carburettors were linked to four SU fuel pumps in case of failure.

Although they had a power disadvantage over the Alfa Romeos that had won the previous four Le Mans, the Lagondas proved competitive thanks to their torque. As recorded in the last chapter, the Hindmarsh/Fontès car, registered and known as BPK 202, went on to victory at 77.86mph despite a lengthy dawn pit stop to repair some offside front damage and the last-minute confusion over Heldé's Alfa. A contemporary report had it running "like a train" during the race. However, it is also said that there was virtually nothing left in its sump as it crossed the line. At one point a Lagonda first and second looked on the cards, but at noon Benjafield, in BPK 203, found himself stranded, said *The Motor*, "on the by-pass" with locked transmission. He had been in third place with the second-placed Heldé temporarily stranded in the pits.

A mechanic was sent out to the good doctor, whose mechanical knowledge was somewhat limited. The frustrated mechanic had to stand behind the fence shouting out instructions. The first difficulty was to identify the jack, with Benjafield pulling out various tools from the box until it was located. Perhaps Bentley had been right not to give his drivers jacks back in 1928. Finally, by rocking the car back and forth, Benjafield freed the cogs and was able to lock the transmission into fourth gear. The Meadows engine was capable of coping with this and he returned to the race, his speed now reduced by about 30mph.

A couple of stories, probably worth ignoring, arose about the two Lagondas. One said that their identities had been switched during the race. Another came from Frenchman Just Emile Vernet, who was driving a La Lorraine that year. He wrote that it had been Fontès, not Benjafield, who had been given a lesson in gearbox repair. *The Motor* report, let alone the actual result, should indicate that this was highly unlikely. Eyewitness accounts from the Fox and Nicholl team have since shown it just did not happen.

One thing that one can be sure about is that Benjafield purchased BPK 203. After passing through a number of hands since, it came up for auction in 2005 and fetched the highest price to date – £430,000

One of BPK 202's former possessors, David Johnson recalls buying the 1935 Le Mans winner from a Princes Risborough hardware shop owner in the late 1960s, beating the then BPK 203 owner Robbie Hewitt to the sale. He also managed to rescue the original brown logbook, which showed the car to be registered in the name of Fox and Nicholl. Johnson admits that the car's life during his ownership was "unadventurous" but he did take it to Le Mans for a couple of anniversary runs. He had work carried out on the car by another former owner, Douglas Hull. The Finmere garage owner had run the Lagonda into the back of an unlit lorry during the blackout, which had resulted in his losing the sight of one eye. *(Sally Harrison collection)*

The great artist Gordon Crosby catches the moment, around 10am on Sunday, June 16, 1935, when John Hindmarsh overtook Heldé to take his Lagonda into the lead of the 24-hours race. *(By kind permission of the Harrison family)*

To the victor the spoils. John Hindmarsh accepts the winners' garland in 1935. *(Sally Harrison collection)*

including buyer's premium – for a car at one of H&H Classic Auctions' sales. Such was the atmosphere at the sale that many of those present are said to have been on their feet by the time auctioneer Simon Hope's hammer fell. The eventual price was 54 per cent over estimate, so perhaps it was no surprise that applause broke out in the room. The car also returned to Le Mans to be the star of a parade to mark the 70th anniversary of the 1935 win, while BPK 202 now resides in a museum in Holland. Ten years previously both cars had been present at a celebratory function on the site of the old Lagonda factory, now a branch of Sainsbury, before setting off again for Le Mans. Hindmarsh's younger daughter, Sally Harrison, drove the winning car onto the site, while her son, also called John, travelled in it down to Southampton.

Hindmarsh returned to Le Mans in 1937, but he was to die in an aircraft accident in September the following year. In addition to being a talented racing driver he also acted as a senior test pilot for Hawker-Siddeley and flew the prototype of the Hurricane fighter. He was trying out one of the first 500 production Hurricanes when he crashed on St George's Hill, on the outskirts of Brooklands. The Hurricane had canvas-covered wings, but an aluminium flap over the fuel tanks just next to the fuselage. According to fellow pilot Maurice Summers, brother of the legendary Vickers and Supermarine chief test pilot 'Mutt' Summers, this flap blew off as Hindmarsh was in a power dive. The airflow over the wing was disrupted and, in an attempt to make the elevator work, Hindmarsh engaged full throttle. Sadly, it was not enough.

A serving officer in the RAF, having transferred from the Tanks Corps, Hindmarsh drove five times at

Le Mans, always for Arthur Fox. He and 'Tim' Rose-Richards brought their Talbot home in fourth place in 1930, scoring the best figure of merit for the first leg of the seventh Biennial Cup. The following year he took his Talbot into the pits late in the race with the fuel tank wobbling behind, thanks to a cracked chassis-frame. Efforts were made with straps and rope and the use of tommy bars as tourniquets to overcome the problem, but after another couple of laps Fox decided to retire the car. In 1934 Fox entered a Singer that Hindmarsh was to share with his 1931 co-driver Brian Lewis. They finished seventh, securing for the car second place in the 10th Biennial Cup behind the

There was no doubting what Maurice Jobson's employers manufactured. The Trico PR man is here observed at Le Mans in 1982. *(Author)*

It took over 40 years for Maurice Jobson to rebuild his Lagonda 16/80 tourer, a labour of love that was rewarded when the car took part in the 70th anniversary victory parade in 2005. *(Maurice Jobson collection)*

THE WIPERS MAN

From the late 1960s through to the 1980s, a succession of British journalists owed their first visit to Le Mans to one man, Maurice Jobson, publicity manager of the Trico wiper blade concern. The company used to run an engineering exercise – checking on the efficiency of the teams' wipers and wiper motors – at Le Mans, which was led by development engineer Geoff Smithers. The young Jobson, who remembers how Trico overcame the wipers lifting on the early Ford GT40s, was taken along to observe. He became enamoured with the place, his enthusiasm

being such that he even travelled there one year on a Lambretta scooter. It was a passion that he was able to pass on following his elevation to the publicity department. A trip to Le Mans, he rightfully concluded, was an excellent PR exercise. Thus a cross-section of automotive consumer, technical and trade press followed him, like the children behind the pied piper, across the channel.

Such was the efficient and gentlemanly way that Jobson organized these trips that there are grown men who still go misty-eyed about them. Chris Wakley was one of the lucky ones to accompany him in 1969. Accommodation was always at the *Boule d'Or* in Brulon, where Madame Fautrat provided just the right Gallic ambience. Each year she would send the party off to the track with magnificent hampers. Dinner, on both the Friday and Saturday nights, would be at the restaurant on the Mulsanne straight, the second evening a leisurely one, occasionally pointing the camera out of the window as cars travelled past at possibly over 240mph.

In 2005 Jobson returned to Le Mans for the first time for many years. In 1961 he had inherited from his father a 1932 Lagonda 16/80 tourer, which was in a sorry state. Over the next 43 years he slowly rebuilt the car, it always being his ambition to take it to Le Mans. The work was finished just in time for the 70th anniversary of the Lagonda victory in the 24-Hours and the parade of some 60 cars that the Lagonda Owners Club took to the track. In the early hours of race morning Jobson "had the honour" of joining the other club members on a lap of the circuit. "It was quite something."

On his return, he detoured to Brulon and asked the current patron of the *Boule d'Or* about Madame Fautrat. Although long retired, it seemed that Madame still lived in the village. Jobson was directed to her house where he met with the typical French embrace of a long established friend.

Riley of Alex von der Beck and 'Kim' Peacock.

One of Fox and Nicholls' 'tea boys' recalled that Hindmarsh used to give him sixpence for cleaning his car, a vast sum of money in those days. The tall 'Johnny Quickmarsh', in fact, was remembered as being very friendly and approachable, as well as "breezy." In his large tweed overcoat, with belt tied rather than fastened, he appeared dashing and very much in the film star mould. He had two daughters, of whom Susan, the elder, was to marry 1959 Le Mans winner Roy Salvadori. Her sister Sally was born in 1935, her mother being unable to travel to watch her husband's greatest race through being pregnant at the time. Hindmarsh's wife, Violette Cordery, whom he had married in 1931, was also a notable motorist, being the first woman to drive round the world. Her prowess in motorsport – she was twice winner of the Royal Automobile Club's Dewar Trophy – was such that one year she was the only lady present among the 200 people attending the Brooklands Automotive Racing Club's annual dinner.

By a sad coincidence, the rich and enigmatic Luis Fontès, like Hindmarsh, died in an aeroplane. Born in Hampstead of Anglo-Portuguese origin, Fontès had a 100 per cent success record at Le Mans simply because

he raced there just the once. Shortly afterwards, while under the influence of alcohol, he was involved in a fatal road accident and was jailed for manslaughter. Then during the early months of the Second World War he flew for the Air Transport Auxiliary, and in 1940 he crashed fatally in a Vickers Wellington bomber in Wales. It is said that Hindmarsh and Fontès had made a good pairing to cope with the varying demands of Le Mans, the former being particularly steady, the other very fast.

Despite the 1935 win, Lagonda was in financial problems; the receiver had been brought in and the company was revived as LG Motors. All the models had been dropped apart from the LG45, which used a revised version of the M45 chassis and virtually the same engine.

The facelift was the work of one W.O. Bentley, whom LG Motors boss Alan Good had brought in as chief designer. Fox and Nicholl built up four special Lagonda LG45s, two of them two-seaters, the others four-seaters. With no Le Mans race in 1936, the two-seaters ran in the French Grand Prix (staged that year for sportscars), the four-seaters in the Spa 24-Hours, the TT and the Brooklands 500-mile race. Just one LG45 was entered by Arthur Fox for Le Mans the following year, driven by Charles Brackenbury and 1935 winner Hindmarsh. It retired during the night with a stretched valve, a problem that it had been suffering from since the 11th lap.

As already related, Lagonda made one more visit to Le Mans before the war, the two V12s, perhaps to W.O.'s surprise, finishing well in third and fourth places in 1939 without setting the track alight.

After the war the company was acquired by David Brown, who merged it with Aston Martin in 1948. As such, the marque was to reappear twice at Le Mans in one of the less successful chapters of Aston Martin racing history. The 1954 Lagonda V12 was larger than the Aston Martin DB3S, but used a chassis that was virtually the same. However, it suffered from a fundamental design deficiency in that the crankcase and the diaphragms carrying the main bearings expanded at the same rate, being made of the same metal. Because of the cost, a redesign was out of the question, and the engines were built with minimum

bearing clearance, which led to a reluctance to fire up on cold days. The Lagonda V12 was little loved at Aston Martin, but it took two trips to Le Mans before it was shelved.

Two cars were entered the first year, but only one was ready. However, Eric Thompson, who shared the car with 1950 British Hill Climb Champion Dennis Poore, went off the road at the Esses with terminal rear-end damage. Again two cars were entered in 1955, but just one was raced, a new chassis having been developed with a narrow multi-tubular spaceframe forming a rigid central backbone structure. Poore shared the car with Reg Parnell this time. Luck was definitely not with Lagonda on this, its final outing at Le Mans. The *plombeur* had failed to correctly attach the fuel filler, the fuel splashed out and the car ground to a halt after 93 laps. It was not a dignified end to the Le Mans story of what, after all, was one of just four British production car manufacturers to have won the 24-Hours.

Ever the dapper RAF pilot, John Hindmarsh. *(Sally Harrison collection)*

The number '4' Lagonda of Hindmarsh and Fontès leads three other cars, including two of the soon-to-be-vanquished Alfa Romeos, through the Esses. *(Sally Harrison collection)*

As so many of his generation, Hindmarsh also raced at Brooklands. Here, in 1934, his Singer (nearest the camera) is seen in close combat with the Hamilton/Black Alfa Romeo during the BRDC 500-Mile race. *(LAT Photographic)*

58

CHAPTER 7

MARCUS CHAMBERS

"May God Almighty give us success over these fellows." (Lord Nelson)

The story of British success at Le Mans in the immediate pre-war years is not, with the exception of 1935, one of outright victories. Instead, it is a tale of class wins and of fields often packed with English cars. It is an era for such as Aston Martins, MGs and HRGs, and it was when driving one of the latter that Marcus Chambers and Peter Clark took the 1½-litre class in 1939. It was not Chambers' first involvement with the race; that came in 1937 "when I somehow managed to get myself selected as second mechanic" for the HRG of Ted Halford and bookmaker Archie Scott. Nor was it to be his last. Chambers went on to become the legendary competitions manager, first of BMC and later of Rootes, posts that were to bring him back to La Sarthe in 1955 and 1964, although most of his motorsport fame during this period lies in the rallying successes that he masterminded.

The son of a Royal Navy Admiral, Chambers had started his own tuning business in 1936. Work on Clark's HRG – which was then being used in trials competitions – brought him into contact with the car company's directors, Halford, Robins and Godfrey, and the job in the pit crew at Le Mans. A special car was prepared for the event by the factory, with Halford driving it to the circuit.

There is something to be said about an endurance event for which drivers make their own way to the circuit in the very cars that they are to race. Many of the competing cars would still be driven to Le Mans well after the war, although by then their nominated racing drivers were unlikely to have been seen at the wheel on the way there and back. Photos exist showing the returning 1953 Jaguar team in the car park of a typically British roadside café, Coronation bunting round the building underlining the significance of the year.

But such practices have long been consigned to the pages of history. Darren Turner would not have got as far as the first traffic lights out of the Prodrive factory, let alone Junction 11 of the M40, had he tried to take an Aston Martin DBR9 from Banbury to Le Mans. Having said that, designer Gordon Murray now rues the fact that he did not drive the 1995 winning McLaren to the track; the F1 GTR was the only Le Mans victor of recent times that really *could* be driven on the road. More recently, muses Murray, he found himself at the wheel of another McLaren, driving through the early morning streets of London and following the actual car that had finished third at Le Mans. "Surreal," he describes the experience.

It has to be said, though, that even in 1937 there was something against the idea of driving competing cars to the race. On his way to the track, Halford managed to sail though a hedge at about 90mph. The excuse for what he described as "an incident" was a faulty front shock absorber…

Chambers, who because of work was unable to get himself to the track until the Friday night, recalls his surprise that Halford should have been driving at that speed, whatever the state of the car. Luckily, Imperial Airways was able to deliver a new front axle on time.

Marcus Chambers, who raced an HRG at Le Mans in 1938 and 1939, poses before a fine Michael Turner painting showing his class-winning drive the second year. *(Author)*

Marcus Chambers and Peter Clark won the 1500cc class in 1939 despite having to reduce their speed in the final two hours because of minor engine troubles. *(Ludvigsen Library)*

Halford was not the only Briton to crash a racecar on the way to Le Mans. In 1950, Reg Parnell had an accident near Brionne in a works Aston Martin. His pregnant wife, Marion, who was in the car with him, suffered a broken back, and a reserve DB2 had to be pressed into service for the race. Team manager John Wyer was typically unamused when Parnell wondered if Aston boss David Brown would sell him the wreck.

The 1937 race itself was also incident-filled for the HRG team. A weeping radiator was found that morning and had to be re-soldered. Then, after just three laps, Halford had to stop near Indianapolis to investigate a case of bad clutch slip. A temporary cure was achieved by what Chambers recalls as a "liberal use" of the fire extinguisher; an excess of oil in the sump had caused a leak out of the rear main bearing of the Meadows engine. Halford then narrowly missed being involved in the sad accident that took the life of the popular Pat Fairfield. Having just been overtaken by a Bugatti pilot, whose driving had concerned him, Halford felt that he ought to slow down going into White House. As a result he avoided the crash by just a few seconds.

Chambers was involved in the next incident when Scott brought the car into the pits with no oil pressure. To meet the regulations of the time and to avoid disqualification, Chambers and chief mechanic Fred Mead had to drop the sump onto the track; the pipe from the oil pump to the centre main bearing was broken. The good news was that a spare pipe was being carried in the car; the bad news was that the on-board tool kit did not have a spanner of the correct size to do the job. Not for the last time Chambers got his picture in the press, although he was never again to be photographed for quite the same reason. The shot showed him filing the jaws of a larger spanner down to size, using a windscreen bracket as a vice. The next untoward occurrence saw the petrol tank spring a leak and the frantic chewing of gum by the pit crew. Chambers reckons the tank had been strained during

its *en-route* trip through the hedge. And so the saga goes on; next Halford was black-flagged and chastised by the Clerk of the Course for not having put his lights on. Finally, 20 minutes before the end of the race, the oil pressure went again, this time on the Mulsanne straight. Scott stopped to allow the engine to cool and carefully retimed his return to the race to enable him to reach the finishing line just as the chequered flag was brought out. It was an eventful start to Chambers' Le Mans career.

We now move on to his two years as a driver, a tale in which we bring in 'Puffed Wheat', a well-known cereal on British breakfast tables for many years, and a stuffed turtle. The ways in which gentlemen racers have found the means to compete at Le Mans have been many and varied. Tim Birkin's money came from lace, Nick Mason's was to come from pop music. Peter Clark worked for the family business of George Clark and Sons, who produced the aforementioned cereal. He also owned an HRG which he asked Chambers to drive at Le Mans the following year. The team was christened *l'Ecurie du Lapin Blanc*, which those with schoolboy French will recognize has nothing to do with turtles, but was painted on the back of a stuffed turtle that hung over the team's pit. The creature had been brought back by Clark from a holiday in the West Indies to become the team's mascot, while the team name came from an Austin Seven single-seater that had been sprinted and raced by Chambers and Clark and was known as the 'White Rabbit'.

If Chambers was right to have been surprised by the speeds that Halford had been attaining on the way to the previous year's race, then perhaps we should now raise an eyebrow about his own pre-race contretemps. Chambers was driving the HRG through the streets of Le Mans when a young cyclist ran across his bow. The bicycle's front wheel was buckled and the rider was distressed that he couldn't continue his work. However, it seems that the cyclist was not looking where he was going, a fact agreed upon by the gathering crowd, so having slipped the lad a few francs, Chambers drove off to applause from the throng. Perhaps there is a lesson here; maybe it is a good idea that, in theory at least, Le Mans cars are no longer driven on the road. It is a lesson Bentley should have listened to in 2003, but that is a story for later.

In an age of precise and practiced pit drills, it is difficult to imagine just how carefree matters could be in the late 1930s. It was only on the morning of the race that the team, checking over the car in a mews near the Place de la Theatre, was approached by a gentleman with a hooked nose, a Basque beret and a Sherlock Holmes pipe. He urged them to practice their pit drill, and as he was none other than the 1927 winner Sammy Davis, they thought it a good idea to take his advice. Skilled pit work was important to Davis. As editor of the Lonsdale Library's 1957 volume on *Motor Racing* he devoted an eight-page chapter to the subject, also observing that the workmanlike organization of the British teams caused favourable comment at Le Mans. "The team chief is wise who listens attentively to any opinion before the race and gives it full consideration," he wrote. Chambers and

Marcus Chambers describes Mortimer 'Mort' Morris-Goodall as "a fine sporting gentleman" and with good reason. During the 1939 race Chambers, concerned that the oil supply was not working properly, had stopped just after Tertre Rouge to investigate the valve gear of his HRG. Morris-Goodall pulled his Aston Martin up in front of Chambers and asked if he needed a message taking to his pit. Chambers thanked him but felt he had probably found the trouble and would soon be going again. It was, says Chambers, "a very sporting gesture."

Morris-Goodall drove in every Le Mans 24-Hours between 1933 and 1952 and again in 1995, when he returned at the wheel of a works Triumph TR2. His first six appearances were all in Aston Martins, as were the 1951 and 1952 races, when he drove a DB2. Born in 1907, he started racing Astons at the age of 22, competing at Brooklands every year until the advent of war. Like Chambers he served an apprenticeship at Sunbeam, where he had contact with such as Segrave.

In 1932 he was invited by 'Bert' Bertelli to join the works Aston team and, three years later, he was one of the founders of the Aston Martin Owners Club. Half of his six pre-war drives at Le Mans were shared with Robert Hitchens, who was killed in action after a brilliant period commanding a Motor Gun Boat in Coastal Forces. After the war, Morris-Goodall returned to Le Mans, initially as a member of Peter Clark's HRG team.

company listened; and they saved 13 minutes with their newly developed pit drill.

Davis was to reappear in Chambers' life in 1954, when the latter applied for a position with MG, which was about to restart its competition department. On hearing that Davis was technical advisor for the BMC Motor Sport Committee, he sought out the former 'Bentley Boy', who recommended him for the job. It was the start of a significant seven years in Chambers' life.

Meanwhile, for Chambers and Clark, the 1938 race was far less eventful than that of Scott and Halford the previous year. However, an hour before the finish the oil supply to the rocker gear dried up and Chambers was forced to carry on at a reduced speed. The pair finished 10th overall and second in class.

For the following year they made various changes to the HRG's engine to ensure that the oil feed problem did not repeat itself. Other modifications included a rushed improvement to the cooling system. A local Le Mans plumber reworked the system for them, and Chambers recalls that after the race the pair went to his house to thank him and have "a little something to drink to the *Entente Cordiale.*"

Other changes made to the HRG included a shorter tail and slightly larger rear wheels and tyres. This gave the car a maximum speed at Le Mans of just under 100mph; the fastest cars that year were doing about 140mph down the Mulsanne straight. Chambers says that the cornering of the HRG was much better than that of most of the field and he and Clark planned to restrict themselves to a maximum of 90mph.

Once again all went well in the race until near the end. Chambers had planned to check the rocker shaft feed when Clark handed over to him two hours before the finish, but he forgot to do so. This, he now believes, was perhaps because somebody had just stolen his Leica camera; Chambers has always been a keen photographer. Almost immediately he felt the engine going off tune, so he pulled onto the grass and stopped to check. He found that the bronze bushes in the rockers were wearing away and the tappet clearances were about an eighth of an inch. He restored the oil flow by unscrewing the release valve spring and reset the tappets.

Fortunately, the engine held together until the end of the race and Chambers and Clark were rewarded with first place in the 1½-litre class. The HRG had spent a total of 24 minutes in the pits during the 24 hours, but Chambers observed that Lord Selsdon's Lagonda had only been in the pits for 15 minutes that year. "Better room for improvement," he says.

The Aston Martin Ulster of 'Mort' Morris-Goodall and John Elwes, which was in second place before its retirement during the 19th hour of the 1934 race, follows a Tracta and a BNC. *(LAT Photographic)*

In 1938, the front-runners were all French, although there was still a strong British presence in the smaller classes with the Chambers/Clark HRG and the Fawcett/White Morgan being singled out that year as distinguishing themselves. Here, at what in those days was referred to as the New Esses, the HRG follows three other entrants including a pair of French cars, Comotti's Delahaye and the Talbot of Etancelin and Chinetti. *(LAT Photographic)*

Chambers himself was not to race again at Le Mans. War was declared that September, and being on the Royal Navy Volunteer Reserve list, he wrote to Earl Howe to see if he could get him into Coastal Forces. The letter must have worked as Chambers soon found himself under instructions to report to HMS *King Alfred* at Hove for training. By 1942 he had joined the Engineering branch of the RNVR, probably because the RN Engineering Commander had a Frazer-Nash with the same type of Meadows engine as the Le Mans HRG; Chambers' interview was spent mainly discussing possible modifications to it. Towards the end of the war Chambers rebuilt the HRG, which Clark was to swap for a Bugatti Type 44 and then buy it back a decade later. A further 10 years on he sold it again, since when, says Chambers, it has had "a troubled history." Last heard of, it was in France.

In 1954, as previously mentioned, Chambers joined MG and was told that the factory had entered three cars of a new type for Le Mans the following year; there had been no works cars at the race since 1935, but now Chambers and MG were on their way back to La Sarthe. After an absence of 20 years, the MGs, said one contemporary report, "were a welcome sight." The three EX 182 cars were truly described as prototypes, a term that has since become much abused. In this case, they were the forerunners of the soon to be announced MGA. In fact the cars were originally entered as production models, but a delay with the body pressings meant that the announcement of the new car had to be delayed by three months. Chambers believes that Sammy Davis, who acted as team manager, with Chambers as his assistant, may have put in a word with the ACO to enable the change in entry to be made. Shades of Davis' pre-war advice to the young HRG team, pit stop drill was an important part of the pre-race preparations in the grounds of the *Chateau Chêne du Coeur*, where the team was staying. Chambers recalls that initially some of the drivers were flippant about this idea, but they were soon shown up

by the veteran Davis. Chocks left under the wheel and bonnet straps left undone would be pointed out in a quiet voice.

Detailed reports of the 1955 Le Mans tragedy which occurred opposite the pits recount how another column of smoke was noticed shortly afterwards from the area of White House. Dick Jacobs had crashed one of the MGs – he had probably been distracted by the smoke from the grandstand area – and had been seriously injured. Chambers believes that with the local hospitals understandably crowded, Jacobs' treatment was probably delayed. However, the team had its own doctor, an MG owner from Stow-on-the-Wold, who was able to see Jacobs. Then BMC flew over a medical team including a thoracic specialist and brought Jacobs home. He was to spend four months in hospital in Oxford and was never to race again.

The other two MGs ran well through the night. Chambers describes Davis as sitting on his stool on the pit counter "looking like a bedraggled old eagle," and by then all enthusiasm had gone from the team, which even had to move its transporter to make room for a pumping wagon, rushed in to alleviate matters after the toilets behind the pit had overflowed. The two remaining MGs finished the race, that of Johnny Lockett and the British-born American Ken Miles taking a creditable 12th place. Chambers was not too pleased that the British public address announcer seemed to ignore the fact.

We now jump forward to 1964, by which time Chambers had joined the Rootes Group as competitions manager. Not that he had been idle during the intervening period, but the sporting history of BMC is mainly concerned with rallying, and Marcus Chambers had been the person who had taken the works team to the forefront of this discipline before parting to face his next challenge.

Rootes had entered three production Sunbeam Tigers for Le Mans, and he was not happy about it. He has since said that there were so many faults in

In 1938 Chambers and Clark finished 10th overall and second in class. Even better was to come. *(LAT Photographic)*

the Sunbeam Le Mans programme that it was destined to be "something between failure and farce from the start." Brian Lister, who built the cars, would have liked them to have used spaceframes rather than production frames, and to have been clad in an aluminium, Tiger-like body that could accommodate a 4.7-litre Ford V8 engine such as was found in the Shelby Cobras and was well developed and reliable. However, the management insisted on a more standard car, which meant it had to be raced with the compact 4.2-litre engine installed in the standard body and frame. Chambers feels that the project was started too late, also that there seemed to have been a political agenda that worked against any chance of competitiveness. Rootes was returning to Le Mans in the wake of its 1961 success when it had won the Index of Thermal

The Chambers/Clark HRG passes the 1938 winning Delahaye of Chaboud and Tremoulet, which pauses at Arnage for a minor adjustment to be made. *(LAT Photographic)*

63

Efficiency with a Sunbeam Alpine. However, the Tiger programme had not really been worked out with any understanding. The fact that Rootes was no longer competing in the Alpine class was, says Chambers, something that the management failed to realize, even following the race.

So Chambers found himself taking over a project that had many flaws, and they did not exclusively concern the cars. A very expensive hotel, the *Hotel Ricordeau*, had been booked for the test weekend by his predecessor, Norman Garrad. The cost was just one aspect that appalled him. "The presentation of the meals took no account of the fact that time might be needed for urgent work," he says. The result was "considerable disagreement" with the owners.

Matters on the track did not look good, either.

During the trials, former Rootes driver Michael Parkes, by then with Ferrari, took one of the Tigers out for three laps. "He inferred that we had a lot more to do to become even slightly competitive." The engine was running hot, the roadholding was poor, and the brakes were worse. The team went home.

During the period between the trials and the race, the roadholding and the brakes were improved, but low oil pressure was a problem on all of the team's four Shelby engines. After a troublesome pre-race practice, which underlined the team's lack of competitiveness, Chambers could only console himself on race day in that at least the cars looked to be well turned out. And that was about it: one car retired with piston failure after three hours, another with a broken crankshaft. The engine of the first of these blew up in spectacular fashion at Tertre Rouge, pumping what was described at the time as "a pall of oily brown smoke" over the circuit. The second engine let go as the car was level with the beginning of the pits. Driver Peter Procter remembered a flash of fire from under the bonnet. The engine had blown up in such a mighty way that its bits locked the steering solid, Procter having to stop the car by rubbing it along the pit counter. It was lucky, as he was to say, that no other car was being refuelled at that point. It was discovered later that the Shelby test-bed had been out of action during the time that the Tigers' engines were being prepared. A refund was eventually received from the American company.

So ended Marcus Chambers' relationship with *Les Vingt-Quatre Heures du Mans*. The years 1937 to 1939, 1955 and 1964 cover a period in the race's history during which much changed. Chambers' own story well illustrates the involvement of many of the participants who have not been concerned with outright victory, but who nevertheless have helped to make Le Mans such a fascinating event. La Sarthe is one of the few places where it cannot be said that history only remembers those who came first.

CHAPTER 8

THE ENTHUSIASTS

"They'll drink every hour of the daylight and poach every hour of the dark."
(Rudyard Kipling, *Norman and Saxon*)

Crowd statistics at any circuit should be taken with the proverbial pinch of salt. However, every year between 50,000 and 80,000 British enthusiasts are thought to cross the channel and head for the Le Mans 24-Hours contest. In the years when a British car is likely to win, such as 2003, this may rise to around 100,000. The only other circuit races to be able to match these figures are the British Grand Prix and the Goodwood Revival meeting, and even then this is to match a British-only total for Le Mans against all nationalities for the other two meetings. To this must be added the obvious fact that the British have to leave their own country to attend Le Mans.

When one considers that outside Formula One motor racing has to be ranked as a minority sport in the UK, these figures are impressive and make this race in France one of Britain's major sporting events. Sadly, this fact seems regularly to be missed by the national media, although *The Times* did manage to highlight the 2003 Bentley win on its front page. The days when the BBC Light Programme featured on-the-hour bulletins are long over.

The Brits have been streaming south in June for many years. Former *Autocar* editor Peter Garnier described it as "a British public holiday held in France." The magazine he was to head, in its first ever Le Mans report, observed that Mr Vernon Pugh and Miss Pugh had "motored down on (*sic*) an Alvis car" while Mr T.P. Searight "had the misfortune to sprain his ankle when walking at the back of the pits in darkness." The following year there were still only a few British onlookers, but the numbers were to grow. Before long they would be reserving the best hotels, strolling around the Place de la République and meeting at Grubers Restaurant. The city's own communications department admits that it was "the English alone (who) created a sort of festive atmosphere in Le Mans."

Writing in the mid-1950s of the advertisers' pits, Frenchman Georges Fraichard said: "Sometimes an Englishman (and goodness knows there are plenty of them at Le Mans) amazes everyone by his capacity for drink."

That festivity continues to this day. At the end of the 2001 race, when Bentley returned, a party of suitably clad British gentlemen set up their table, complete with candelabra and champagne glasses, in front of the podium. "It's a beautiful place to go to watch the very best of British eccentricity," says Radio Le Mans presenter John Hindhaugh. He cites a group in the Camping Du Houx site called the Chateau de Piste Artistes who, every year, hold a themed dinner on the Friday night; it might be black tie, or Christmas, or a curry (with appropriate Indian dress). There are also such as the Porsche Curve Pirates and more. These groups sometimes have their own websites, like the famed Beermountain.com. "There is skill in building a beer mountain!" quips Hindhaugh, adding: "Part of the point of Le Mans is the campsites." He recalls some chaps in an aged Talbot van with a huge sound

The British still congregate around the *Hotel de France*, made famous by John Wyer's frequent residence. *(Stuart Barnes)*

65

Perhaps it never gets as bad as Glastonbury, but there are times when the British do have to grin and bear some squalid conditions. *(David Ingram)*

The return of Bentley brought out the best in British eccentricity. Just finishing the race was cause for a celebratory drink on the main straight. *(Martin Lee)*

George Byford brought British organization to the Le Mans scrutineering. *(George Byford collection)*

A British entry comes under the eye of the Le Mans scrutineers. This is the Richard Lloyd Racing Porsche 956 in 1983. *(David Ingram)*

system thumping away on Radio Le Mans next to an oldtimer in a vintage Bentley with a little frame tent. "Fantastic, it's what it's all about," said the latter.

It is perhaps an obvious thing to say, but the Le Mans 24-Hours is more than just a motor race, and it is the British who are the most passionate about the event. Those who make the annual pilgrimage are either true motor racing enthusiasts or that unique breed of what can only be called Le Mansophiles, who may only go to this one race. Allan McNish points out that these are not the average F1 fans. They are often knowledgeable and, as a former winner, McNish is well placed to observe, "respectful." At Le Mans the fans can get closer to the drivers, but at the same time, says the Scot, they also "respect the space of the driver."

Many will be happy to put up with what may be squalid conditions. Whatever, they are very different from those who rise from their Sunday afternoon television couches once a year to go to Silverstone and call themselves motor racing fans. McNish says: "You get a better class of spectator at Le Mans." Or, as John Hindhaugh observes, there are two kinds of people in motor racing, those who understand 24-hour events and those that do not.

THE SCRUTINEER

Some areas of British influence at Le Mans are more obvious that others. Scutineeering is one where this country's expertise has been called upon in the past. There was a time when the cars would be passed round from station to station while chief scrutineer Jean-Louis Foucherant sat in his office and passed out paperwork. If any one team was found to have a problem everyone seemed to descend upon it, and work on all the other stations seemed to stop. "I didn't think this a good idea," says George Byford, who from 1974 to 1983 was chief scrutineer for the British Racing Drivers Club. He also recalls that "niggly faults" tended to be found in many of the British cars.

In 1984 Byford was invited by the ACO, at the suggestion of Alain Bertout, editor of *L'Action Automobile*, to become international scrutineer for the Le Mans 24-Hours. "I'd done French at school before the war and had forgotten most of it," he admits. Silverstone, the home circuit of the BRDC, had been running its own, admittedly much shorter, endurance race since the mid-1970s and the team there was becoming experienced in examining long-distance sportscars. Byford was joined at Le Mans by his deputy Mike Garton. From then until 1990, when a permanent FIA technical delegate was brought in, Byford endeavoured to bring scrutineering at Le Mans up to the standard found at Silverstone. The French scrutineers had a habit of all halting at the same time for a long lunch. "I did not think this good enough, so I made them go in shifts." He also recalls incidents such as that of the Ecosse footwell. The home scrutineers were all for checking this with "a bit of wire." Foreseeing that this could lead to days of wrangling over perhaps one quarter of an inch, Byford made a gauge to do the job. It was just one of many changes that he made to ensure a transparent fairness.

"It's not just a race, it's a festival," says McNish. "The British subscribe to this more than any other nation. They turn up in their thousands. You meet them when you are driving down on the Sunday before the race. The traffic is just full of British-registered cars and French policemen trying to book them. The French actually treat it very well. They realize that there is a British invasion and they are going to have to learn the Queen's English for a weekend."

McNish also tells the story of the British tabloid journalist who telephoned the Le Mans police. The 1998 World Cup was on and the story was of English football fans being arrested in their droves. The writer, pointing out that there were about 80,000 British fans at Le Mans, wanted to know how many arrests had been made. The answer was just one.

There is also a fierce loyalty and it is nothing to hear of a British spectator who has been to the race over 30 times. Nick Ferguson-Gow, a claims director at Seascope Insurance Services, has attended on 34 consecutive occasions. His friends reckon this must be a record, but he is dubious. Ken Rider first went in 1966 on a £25 Page & Moy trip and has only missed three races since – 1968, 1969 and 1970. Ferguson-Gow nearly did not attend in 1999 when his wife was heavily pregnant, but as he says, she held on until June 20 when their daughter Alexandra was born. He describes the Porsche 917 and Ferrari 512 years as "quite unforgettable." Martin Lee has not missed a race since 1978, and that includes 1986, when the ACO thoughtlessly brought forward the race to May 31-June 1, which just happened to coincide with his wedding anniversary.

Traditions die hard. David Greenwood and his sons Douglas and Duncan have been attending the race regularly since 1983. They still take the same tin opener that they had that year, not to mention a tin of ham. David has also managed to preserve, and annually wear, the yellow-and-blue beanie hat that was given away with the programme in 1983 – no mean feat.

Former Nottingham garage owner Trevor Cook went for the first time in 1971 and has not missed a year since. He quickly became involved with Page & Moy and for many years has been responsible for organizing the camping for the tour company's coach drivers and couriers. This involves taking around five tons of tenting equipment to the Camping Du Houx at the track a couple of days before the event. In the heyday of such tours he could be looking after about 120 people. The Internet and ease of travel have meant that not so many go to Le Mans this way now; the days when Page & Moy chartered two boats from Newhaven to Dieppe are long gone. It used to be that Cook also had to collect all the fans' tickets from the circuit a few weeks before the event. There were times when this involved flying there in a friend's Piper aircraft with a suitcase in which to hold around 2000 passes. One year an over-enthusiastic customs official asked to see the contents of the case and demanded some £65,000 in VAT. It took quite a few days to sort that one out.

Some just turn up; others like Trevor Cook may become involved in logistical nightmares. Caterer Paul

Nick Ferguson-Gow (right) has attended 34 consecutive Le Mans 24-Hours. During one of them he took the opportunity to pose with Jacky Ickx, whose six victories could be said to pale beside this figure. *(Nick Ferguson-Gow collection)*

'Henny' Collins was responsible for the catering of the Richard Lloyd Racing squad during the Group C era. *(David Ingram)*

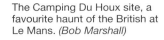

There is doubt as to whether Tony Southgate was involved in the design of this particular 'Silk Cut' car. *(Martin Lee)*

The Camping Du Houx site, a favourite haunt of the British at Le Mans. *(Bob Marshall)*

THE BEERMOUNTAIN

Beermountain.com was originally set up to advise Brits on how to get to Le Mans, what to bring and where to camp. In fact, it was originally known as 'The Le Mans Camping Survival Guide' to help out those who arrived at the circuit with nothing in the boot of the car other than some old French francs and a sleeping bag. What grew out of it was a kind of leadership of irreverent British humour and enjoyment of all things non-PC (and sometimes non-

Twenty-four hours is a long race. One has to do something… *(Matthew Woodward)*

'Mr Toad' leads a flypast of the intrepid 'Wild Choppers' squadron through the trade section of the paddock. *(Matthew Woodward collection)*

motorsport related) at the race. As a result, says its 'CEO', Matthew Woodward, (known simply to his companions as 'Mr Toad') it is now perhaps best known for its advice on building 'beer mountains,' the latest camping techniques ("very Heath Robinson stuff," says Woodward) and, more recently, 'The Wild Choppers,' a display team of slightly unfit, modern day, would-be 'Bentley Boys' on original Mark 2 Raleigh Chopper bikes, who entertain the crowds in the build-up to the race. 'The Wild Choppers' are appropriate at Le Mans, says Woodward, as not only do they add to the humour, but they also act as a tribute to the RAF Hurricane pilots who were briefly stationed at the circuit during the Second World War.

"Le Mans is so much more than just the best motorsport event in the world. The camaraderie is fantastic, especially on the camp sites – at Le Mans all the Brits are the best of friends and nothing is too much trouble if you find yourself in need of any help. The atmosphere is incredible and the many events and parties all around the circuit make the event simply unique. So much so that I think it's fair to say that not all of today's visitors go just for the race. In fact, some of them probably don't see too much beyond the start and finish!

"From humble roots, we have grown massively, and as the race approaches each year, we now have thousands of visitors to our website each day and hundreds of 'beer mountaineers' in our forums," says Woodward. "Radio Le Mans has been a great supporter and we are thus in touch with 'Little Britain' whilst it is camping at Sarthe. Last year even the ACO recognized us by letting us bring the 'Wild Choppers' into the 'Village' for a display, which I hope even W.O himself would have approved of!

"Beermountain seems to have evolved into a support service for the visitor which everyone can be a part of. Best of all, through the cold winter months we can share our experiences and plan how to make the next year's trip even more memorable than the last one."

Edwards told *Autosport* in 1992 that his organization was having to feed up to 70 people from just one team, not to mention another 15 to 20 from Radio Le Mans. That meant having to work from a 10ft x 8ft trailer kitchen and a refrigerated truck of provisions; £5000 worth of the food was driven out from the UK. 'Henny' Collins is another example of a British caterer who has become a regular at Le Mans. David Ingram recalls her looking after the Richard Lloyd Racing team back in 1983. Perhaps not surprisingly, she was also responsible for the culinary needs of the Bentley squad 20 years later.

The Page & Moy trip has been the initial experience for many Le Mans enthusiasts. Roger Lane-Nott, now Secretary of the British Racing Drivers' Club, remembers visiting the race for the first time in the late 1980s with a fellow Royal Navy lieutenant. These two responsible defenders of our shores, on leave from their submarine, made their slightly the worse for wear way to what they thought was their bus for a sleep and woke to find themselves on the way to Barcelona. They were dropped off at Lyon to make their own way back to the track, arriving to find the race over.

Shaun Cronin first attended in 1975 as an 11-year-old. He recalls the Camping Du Houx as being pretty basic, something that has not changed to this day. What was different, though, was that he did not meet many British people then. Like David Greenwood, he wonders how they used to cope without Radio Le Mans. "Things have changed almost beyond recognition since those times," says Cronin. "During the early years it was a bit difficult to work out who was winning and all the other race positions," adds Greenwood, "and it was not unusual to see a little knot of English-speaking people heading towards a loudspeaker every hour to try and hear an English version of what was happening."

It was at Camping Du Houx that a TVR with RAF roundels on the door was recently observed by another Brit, Bob Marshall…but to continue with this story would be to offend national sensibilities. One hopes that the 'Silk Cut'-liveried Triumph Spitfire spotted by Martin Lee during the TWR Jaguar era did not live up to its name. As Lee remarks, the national rivalries in the campsites are taken in good part, even the year when an England versus Denmark soccer match was on television. (England won the football, but then Tom Kristensen won the race.)

Retired sales manager Graham Godfrey, whose consecutive run of Le Mans is a mere 24, observes how, once a particular British marque is entered for the race, hoards of enthusiasts descend on the camping sites in

similar cars; he took his early Marcos when that make returned in the mid-1990s. John McCullogh, who travels down every year with Godfrey, took his TVR in 2003 and 2004 to celebrate that marque's return. Godfrey has also taken a TVR Griffith, but not, he confesses, when the TVRs have been present; he now admits unpatriotically to having a "red Italian car." He is also one of those who illustrate how this business of the annual pilgrimage to Le Mans is handed down through the generations; both his sons, Robert and

One of Ray Cooke's French colleagues at Tertre Rouge signals as a pair of British-built Lolas passes by in 2005. *(Author)*

THE BRITISH MARSHALS

Those enthusiasts who choose to become the most involved must be the marshals. British marshals are regarded, quite rightly, as being among the best in the world. Around 100 each year are invited to officiate at tracks overseas. Marshalling at Le Mans is an international affair and the British can be found scattered around the track, some at that "corner of a foreign field" that remains British, Post 70, others with their French and other colleagues.

The current *chef de post* of the British national post is expatriate Tony Bushe. There has been an official British station since the early 1980s, and nearly always on the Mulsanne straight. Bushe recalls that it was the British post that had to deal with the tragic Jo Gartner accident there in 1986. Originally the Brits were at Post 35, near the Antares, but the desire to keep fresh has meant a succession of moves over the year, including a brief while at the Indianapolis corner. Now they reside at Post 70, near the rise towards the end of the Mulsanne and on the golf course side. This post even has its own website.

Each post is allowed 30 marshals and three *chefs* who work in three teams of 10. It would be impossible to list them all, but Philip Steward must be mentioned as one of the original team. Other loyal regulars at Post 70 include Bob Rae, Margaret O'Malley, Stuart Hamilton and Peter Goodbody. Michel Pomies is the assistant *chef* to Bushe.

Ray Cooke, who is to be found elsewhere, at the Tertre Rouge post, explains how British course and incident grade marshals apply through the MSA (Motor Sports Association) by the end of March, this application then being passed on to the ACO. The form that is then sent to them enables them to request a specific post. Cooke, who first marshalled at Le Mans in 1999, chooses to enjoy the

"camaraderie" of the French. Post 19 is mainly manned by volunteers from Pau, although there are now around half a dozen Brits there. Cooke prefers the way in which the marshals eat communally on a predominately French post. Others of his fellow countrymen can also be found at the first and second Mulsanne chicanes, at Indianapolis, while some, particularly Tony Appleton and Tony Coates, seem to have been near the Esses at Post 14 "for years." The dedication of marshals is the essential ingredient of all races, which simply couldn't even happen without them.

The assembled company of the British national marshals' post. *(Tony Bushe collection)*

Steve Tarrant was understandably thrilled to hear from the ACO's Daniel Poissenot that, following a year's operations and convalescence, he was again authorized to marshal at Le Mans in 2006. *(Steve Tarrant collection)*

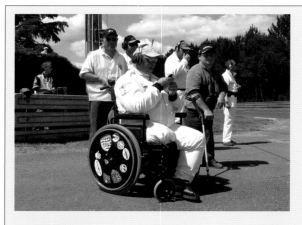

STEVE TARRANT

Steve Tarrant first travelled to Le Mans "a naïve 22-year old" on the obligatory Page & Moy coach. He had never been abroad before and recalls suffering from the innocence of youth and the need to reduce the weight of a crate of beer that he had acquired at the hypermarket on the way to the track. The sight of a Porsche hurtling out of control into the gravel trap at the Esses made him, in his alcoholic haze, forget the safety of his position behind the 15-foot debris fence and, he says, "make a fool of myself". On the way back the coach stopped in Paris. The lad from deepest Dorset had never seen sights such as those that assailed his eyes that evening outside the Moulin Rouge.

The two following years, 1984 and 1985, saw maturity setting in, with Tarrant admitting that he was "much more there for the racing". Clad in his New Man livery, he was rewarded with back-to-back victories for his favourite Porsche. In his defence in those days there was little to support in the way of British cars. By now marriage was beckoning, so priorities changed and the annual trip to Le Mans became a thing of the past.

In the 1990s Tarrant started marshalling in the UK, and in 1999 he found he was able to combine a holiday in South Africa with helping to man a post at Kyalami. He was now beginning to harbour ideas of going back to Le Mans as a marshal. It was not going to happen in 2000, but a week after that year's race he found himself marshalling at the Goodwood Festival of Speed. Here he "buddied up" with an experienced marshal, Andy Carpenter. The pair had never met before, but Carpenter was a Le Mans veteran. Indeed, he was even wearing his white Le Mans

marshal's overalls that day. Tarrant remembers constantly questioning him about the 24-hour race. What was about to happen has inexorably linked their names.

The pair stood at the top of the Goodwood hill, Tarrant with the chequered flag, Carpenter as his fire cover. Heading in their direction was the four-wheel-drive Lotus 63 of John Dawson-Damer. The driver lost control, left the track and slammed into the two marshals. Dawson-Damer was killed instantly, while Tarrant and Carpenter required resuscitation at the scene. Tragically, Carpenter was to die on the operating table. Tarrant, whose right leg had already been taken off by the force of the car, was in hospital for 16 weeks. It was to be two years before he could return to work and even in 2005 he had to spend time in hospital.

Towards the end of 2002 Tarrant received a surprise e-mail from Bernard Nirrengarten, chief of marshal's Post 106. Carpenter had marshalled there in 1999 and 2000 (prior to that he had seen service on Post 35) and Nirrengarten was seeking for information on his former colleague. Following this contact it was arranged, with the help of the MSA and ACO, that Tarrant's then wife, a marshal herself, would work at Post 106 the following year with Tarrant as a spectator. This post – between Arnage and the Porsche Curves – is unique in that all the others tend to be biased towards one nationality or another while this one is truly international, with seven or eight countries represented. It is here that Andy Carpenter's ashes are buried and a plaque mounted on the barrier.

Tarrant enjoyed the experience in 2003, but something was missing. It was not really marshalling. Now divorced, he wanted something more for 2004, and with Nirrengarten's help he achieved his goal of becoming a genuine Le Mans marshal. Given that Tarrant operates from a wheelchair, this must be noted as some achievement. Understandably he was not allowed what is referred to as 'trackside'. However, he was able to act as an observer and, from behind the barrier, as a flag marshal when the others were out on the track. "I may have been behind the Armco, but I was wearing the white of a Le Mans marshal." He is proud to have been included in the 2004 team photo taken of the Post 106 marshals. During 2005, hospitalization prevented him from returning. The photo for that year shows an empty chair in the middle with Tarrant's name on it. There was little doubt that the marshals of Post 106 wanted him back for 2006.

Steve Tarrant's colleagues at Post 106 made it clear they were looking forward to his return. *(Steve Tarrant collection)*

Simon, have become regulars. Everybody has their tales about Le Mans; one of Godfrey's is how he put himself and all his friends on the wrong ferry. "Then we were bumped out of our hotel…and Mercedes beat Jaguar."

The drive to and from the English Channel is regarded by most as part of the experience, although the newly completed motorway from Rouen to Le Mans may dampen the ambiance. If they choose, though, Brits can still take in the classic, no longer in use, French tracks en route, particularly through Rouen.

Even before the chosen port, one can become embroiled in the happening, such as finding oneself at a service station alongside a Jaguar C-type. The experience heightens when one arrives at Portsmouth, as in 2003, to find not one, but around a dozen C-types on their way to celebrate the 50th anniversary of the Rolt/Hamilton win, all lined up for the hydrofoil. The Ferrari Testarossa in the next line paled into insignificance. Could it have been the Testarossa that, in 2000, had been seen in company with a Porsche 911, returning home on the Sunday night at a steady 40mph and holding up a 1700cc Renault Trafic-based motorhome for mile after mile?

For those on the Portsmouth-Le Havre ferry, it starts as the boat crawls past a major proportion of what remains of the Royal Navy and, perhaps significantly if there are French cars to beat, that archetypical symbol of British greatness, HMS *Victory*. No wonder patriotic fervour will cause a cheer even for the Morgan trailing some way behind the rest of the field.

Leading automotive PR man Gordon Bruce, himself no mean club racer in his day, recalls setting off after the race one year in his Ford Capri 2.8i. In the traffic jam leaving the circuit, Bruce found himself immediately behind a Morris Marina. A former road test editor for *Motor* magazine, he regarded Marinas as anathemas. As the traffic cleared Bruce set off for the port at an appropriate speed – "well, we all raced home in those days, didn't we?" Arriving at the Channel by what he thought was the quickest route, he joined the queue for the ferry…and found himself again just behind the self same Morris Marina. It was, he recalls, a demeaning experience.

John Hindhaugh remembers driving away from the circuit in an Audi-loaned estate in 2005 and, on the far side of Alençon, seeing a phalanx of red Ferraris in his rear-view mirror. "This is going to be fun," he thought. In the middle of all these red cars was another dark blue Audi estate car with fellow RLM presenter Joe Bradley at the wheel. He muses not on how annoyed the Ferrari owners must have been at having an Audi in their midst, but on how much more fed up they were when it went past them and they saw it was a diesel.

Of course, it helps when there is a chance of British victory. When, for the first time since the 1950s, factory Jaguars were entered in 1986, it was reckoned that the British fan contingent was higher than ever. There was certainly an increase in bookings that year, helped no doubt by an 8 per cent reduction in admission charges. "The autoroutes were packed with GB plates," reported *Autosport*. The French police enjoyed themselves handing out 900-franc speeding fines on-the-spot. As start time approached, much noise was to be heard opposite the Jaguar pits; in marked contrast, opposite the Sauber-Mercedes team all was quiet. Then Le Mans' equivalent of "the barmy army" broke out into a chorus of "Ere we go" as the pace car set off.

The old saying about it not being necessary to be mad, but it helps, must surely apply to the British legions at Le Mans. The conditions may be far from opulent, yet for some, at least, that is no cause not to bring out the candelabra and don the dinner jacket before sitting down to dinner in the campsite. At arguably the opposite end of the scale, there was the

Jaguar C-types, on their way to celebrate the 50th anniversary of the Rolt/Hamilton victory, wait to catch the high-speed crossing from Portsmouth. *(Author)*

Nowhere in world motorsport is the level of British patriotism as high as at Le Mans. *(Martin Lee)*

character, recalled by Martin Brundle, who in 1988 stood in the grandstand clad only by a Union Jack around his waist. Lap after lap, every time a Jaguar passed by, he peeled off the national flag to reveal his nakedness. Ray Mallock pays tribute to the army of Union Jack wavers, something he first really became aware of when he drove a Nimrod-Aston Martin in 1982. "They were still around in the morning, helping us out."

Brundle also says that as evening comes at Le

cars parked outside. It is an excuse for a lot of tired and emotional people. As Derek Warwick points out, you remember "how many people were p****d and sleeping everywhere and anywhere."

Nigel Bonnett (his first visit a Page & Moy trip in 1979 at which he became "besotted with the event") and his mates had what they thought was a unique way of making an early recovery from the campsite squalor. With everybody else heading for the ports on the Sunday evening they used to take themselves to the municipal swimming baths in the town. "We never saw anyone else from the race there." After a number of years of this, to their disgust they found that it was shut in 2005.

While some are content to spectate, others like to become involved. It took Colin Cooke 12 trips to Le Mans before he found himself in a pivotal role. He first went in 1978, a last-minute decision to go on, yes, a Page & Moy trip. He blames the lack of sleep that weekend for his failure to pass his 'A' levels; perhaps such things are preordained. His alternative career route took him into motorsport, and in 2004 he found himself working at Le Mans for the first time – as chief mechanic for the works Zytek. "I saved myself a special moment," he says. "At 3.00am, I stood outside the garage for about five minutes, just soaked up the atmosphere and put myself back in the tribunes,

Mans, the aroma of the campsite barbecues make their way into the drivers' cockpits. In similar fashion Derek Warwick recalls the smell of bacon while driving through the morning "and thinking you lucky b******s."

The tented encampments, often very obviously British territory, are a vital ingredient of Le Mans. When TVR returned there in 2003 (Peter Bolton and Ninian Sanderson had driven a lone Grantura there in 1962, which had retired in the first hour) it seemed as if every tent had one of the Blackpool-built

JEFF BLOXHAM

One group of Brits who can be found inside the debris fencing are, of course, the media. Interest in Le Mans has been shown by the British press right from the beginning. *The Autocar* was there at the start, heading its report "1,372.5 Miles in 24 Hours at Le Mans". Bentley enjoys its first mention in the second paragraph. In these days of computers it is difficult to remember just how hard journalists had to work to get their copy back. *The Motor* was known to use a private aeroplane. In 1927, for instance, it reported that a De Havilland DH9 had been supplied for its use by Messrs A.D.C Aircraft Ltd. Its pilot, Captain T. Neville Stack, covered the 320 miles between Le Mans and Croydon in 310 minutes. "This enabled us to publish in *The Motor*, on sale everywhere last Tuesday, a seven-page report, illustrated from sketches as well as photographs of an event finishing on Sunday at 4.30pm 300 miles away."

The British media are among the most loyal. The Italians lost interest once the Ferraris stopped winning, the Japanese swarmed in the 1990s but have since shrunk in numbers, while the Germans never seem to have had quite the same passion despite the success of their cars. Over the years it has been the British and the French press who have remained the most loyal.

Arguably the most steadfast wordsmith has been Michael Cotton, whose story is recounted elsewhere. Jeff Bloxham perhaps best personifies the British photographer, having attended 28 Le Mans races, almost 20 years having been as *Autosport*'s chief lens man. He reckons he may have spent as much as five months of his life at the track. He observes how every track improvement has been detrimental to photography. At one time superb pictures could be taken on the exit from the Mulsanne corner; the great shot one could once take of a car coming under the Dunlop bridge was ruined when the track was realigned and, says Bloxham, the debris fencing always seems to be in the wrong place. Photographers used to be able to drive themselves from corner to corner but, he points out, now they have to use shuttle buses that can never be relied upon to get them back at the right time.

Of course, the track is not the only thing that has changed in Bloxham's time. In his early days he shot black-and-white film that he had to take back to England on the overnight boat. During the course of the event he could use about 40 films, that is around 12,000 to 15,000 images. The move to colour meant that someone had to take the film back on the Sunday, but now everything is digital with pictures being sent back every hour. But one thing has not changed for Bloxham: he used a Nikon camera when he first went to Le Mans. He still uses a Nikon.

The British journalists are amongst the most attentive at the race…well, usually. In 1974 Noel Scholey was covering Le Mans for the US radio station CBS as well as doing a favour for *Motor* in the days when the press box was in the tribune on the outside of the track. The magazine's team was working shifts, with Scholey helping out with a night-time slot and keeping himself awake with coffee and Scotch whisky. It was, he recalls, "a truly boring race." He duly dropped off to sleep. When Eric Dymock came to relieve Scholey, he asked if anything significant had happened. As far as he was concerned, no, nothing had occurred. A small matter of John Nicholson losing control of his De Cadenet and smashing into the side of the track right below the press box had not been enough to disturb his slumbers. It seems a strange place to have an accident, but a rod-end had snapped and the car had turned straight into the barrier.

Race engine wizard Nicholson had only been down as reserve driver. However, in the weeks preceding the race Alain de Cadenet had been collecting a Hewland DG300 gearbox from Paddington Station when a belligerent taxi driver had knocked him from his Honda ST70 motorcycle. By the time of the race he thought that the resulting broken left collarbone had mended. However, in practice, while de Cadenet was negotiating a right-hand bend, the collarbone "snapped like a carrot." As the car went off, its newly installed aluminium front splitter sliced the tops off the ACO's nice new submerged runway-style lights.

Nicholson accordingly stepped in to drive with Chris Craft. Unfortunately, a change from Dunlop to Firestone tyres set up an unfriendly harmonic resonance in the car, causing the rod-end failure. Craft had already had to change a broken rear left radius arm bolt by himself as it had broken in the pit lane, but only after he had left his own pit, which meant the mechanics were unable to work on the car themselves. Nicholson also made a couple of stops to check out the still worrying rear end. Then, as he was travelling past the pits, the car turned sharp right, slammed into the barrier and spun down the track, finally coming to a halt 200 yards further down. Nicholson jumped out while Scholey remained firmly asleep.

looking back in."

As Cooke and the team sat around at Calais on the return trip they were approached by a couple of men who asked if they had been to Le Mans. It seemed that this pair, too, had been to the race and wanted to know if they were part of a team.

Cooke recalls the conversation. "'Yes', we said proudly, 'the Zytek team.' They looked at us blankly, so we continued. 'The little black car that was third on the grid.' 'I don't remember that one,' said one of them. 'Who won the race anyway? Was it an Audi?'"

As Cooks says, "Le Mans means a lot of different things to a lot of different people."

The true enthusiast camps on site and never leaves the circuit. *(David Ingram)*

One just has to stop on the Mulsanne straight. *(David Ingram)*

Media interest is not confined to journalists and photographers. Motorsport Industry Association award winner Tony Tobias climbed his first tree at the beginning of the Mulsanne straight in the late 1960s. By 1973 he was attending in an official capacity as advertisement manager of the British Racing and Sports Car Club. Now business development manager of *Racecar Engineering*, his enthusiasm has not dimmed. *(Stuart Barnes)*

Combine the cross of St George with the cross saltires of St Andrew and St Patrick and you have a rallying point for the British at Le Mans. *(Simon Maurice)*

75

Green and Blue

"Fair is our lot – O goodly is our heritage!" The 1950s was arguably the greatest decade at Le Mans for the British. Stirling Moss and Jaguar were firmly in the national consciousness and even if England's favourite motor racing son neither won nor even seems to have liked Le Mans, he put up some typically stirring performances there. *(Original painting by Richard Wheatland – reproduced by kind permission of BEN)*

CHAPTER 9

THE BRITISH AT LE MANS 1949-1958

"The maxim of the British people is 'business as usual'." (Winston Churchill)

The year 1953 was one of 'those' years, the kind that sporting enthusiasts later go misty-eyed about. It was the time of the Coronation and the country was basking in the reflected glory of the conquest of Everest by a British-led party (cue Sir William Walton's *Orb and Sceptre* march, for effect). At the Oval that magical pairing of Surrey spin bowlers, Tony Lock and Jim Laker, destroyed the Australian cricket team's second innings between them. It was said that the Aussies were over the hill, but whatever, it meant that the Ashes were back in England's hands for the first time since the infamous 'Bodyline' tour of 19 years earlier.

Elsewhere, footballer Stanley Matthews laid on three goals in the final minutes of the FA Cup Final between Blackpool and Bolton to earn for the match the sobriquet of 'The Matthews Final', and jockey Gordon Richards rode his only Derby winner, *Pinza*. Both men were to become Knights of the Realm. Golfers will also tell you of the significance of the British Open that year, even if it was an American who won it.

Jaguar had come first at Le Mans two years previously, but 1953 was the scene of one of its most significant victories. Today it is not always easy to prove the saying that racing improves the breed. That year, however, provided one of the most obvious of examples as the Dunlop-Girling disc-braked C-types were able, for lap after lap, to dive far deeper into the Mulsanne corner than the more powerful Ferraris. This was during a heady time when the vast majority of teams were works-entered. They included Jaguar with three of its lightweight C-types, or more correctly XK 120Cs, plus assistance for a Belgian-entered car. Aston Martin had a trio of new DB3S models, while Bristol and Austin-Healey also flew the flag for Great Britain.

Jaguars had first been seen at La Sarthe three years previously when two XK 120s were placed 12th and 15th. A third XK 120, driven by Leslie Johnson and Bert Hadley, had been running as high as second during the early hours of the morning, but was to retire in the last hour after having fallen back to seventh. This car

It is 1949 and night has fallen on the first post-war Le Mans. Despite a predominance of French entries there is still much British interest including six Aston Martins and three HRGs. Also included are representatives of the Bentley, Healey, Frazer-Nash, Alvis, Riley, MG and Singer marques. There is also to be a British driver, Lord Selsdon, in the winning Ferrari, although he will have been at the wheel for less than two hours. *(Tony Rolt collection)*

In 1951 Tony Rolt and Duncan Hamilton found themselves in a coupe for the only time at Le Mans. Their Nash-Healey leads the class-winning Jowett Jupiter of Gordon Wilkins and Frenchman Marcel Becquart. A Jowett, that of Tommy Wisdom and Tommy Wise, also took the 1½-litre category the previous year. *(Duncan Hamilton collection)*

Jones that he really did not like the Le Mans 24-Hours: "Being that long in a car is too long." Nevertheless, he set a new lap record that year, and at midnight the car that he shared with Jack Fairman was still in the lead. But 92 laps into the race, and in the region of Arnage, the car's oil pressure suddenly plummeted and a connecting rod went through the side of the crankcase. The surviving C-type of farmers Peter Walker and Peter Whitehead moved into a lead that it was not to lose. The tall and usually smiling Walker also became one of the few drivers to have won Le Mans at their first attempt. With Aston Martins in third, fifth and seventh places and a Nash-Healey in sixth, the British were truly back. As *Autosport* reported: "The green cars of Great Britain made a grand show as they lined up in front of the pits."

"Whether or not Britain can build a Grand Prix winner remains to be seen, but today a British car in its first race ran clean away with the Le Mans 24-hour sports car *Grand Prix d'Endurance*," said Rodney Walkerley in *The Motor* under his byline *Grande Vitesse*.

Any hope of a repeat performance the following year was dashed by the streamlined new bodies of the works C-Types; prior to the trials Jaguar had been unable to test the cars at sustained speeds of anything over 120mph. Modifications were made in an attempt to overcome the overheating problems that had resulted from the drooped noses, but to no avail, and all three cars retired with cooling difficulties within the first couple of hours.

And so to 1953. It was a significant year for endurance racing as the International Sporting Commission (CSI) of the *Fédération Internationale de l'Automobile* (FIA) had announced a World Sports

was not painted green but white, Johnson saying that as a Scot he had been economizing on the paint.

The following year saw the first appearance of the Jaguar XK 120C, one of the great Le Mans cars. Stirling Moss, so early in his career that he still had a full head of hair, set off, perhaps not the lure of legend, but even so at an arranged speed that saw him 20 seconds ahead at the end of the first hour. Fifty-four years later, and now the official starter of the first ever 24-hour race at Silverstone, Moss admitted to commentator Brian

The Union flags are waving over the pits as Jack Hay's Bentley Corniche makes a stop in 1951. The car took part in three Le Mans races, Tom Clarke being Hay's co-driver in the final year when the Corniche came 22nd. In the previous years it had been placed sixth and then 14th. *(Derek Waller)*

Car Championship for manufacturers. However, this was not something that was to attract Jaguar, which saw far more mileage in winning Le Mans, and built and entered cars accordingly. Indeed, it was not until 1959 that a British make, Aston Martin, was to win the championship. In retrospect, and given Jaguar's domination of Le Mans during the 1950s, this might appear strange, but it was not so, bearing in mind that the series never really seemed to appear on the Coventry marque's radar. As William Heynes, chief engineer of Jaguar Cars, said: "It will probably not come as news to anyone that the C-type Jaguar and also the D-type Jaguar were designed specifically for the 24-hour race at Le Mans."

One thing the championship did, though, was to heighten interest in endurance racing. The entry was packed with works teams and with Grand Prix-winning drivers, four of whom had either taken already, or were destined to take the World Championship.

Now lightened and equipped with disc brakes, the C-types were to prove the class of a very fine field, Duncan Hamilton and Tony Rolt winning at an average of over 100mph, the first time that this milestone had been achieved. Moss did his usual 'hare' act until fuel starvation dropped him and Peter Walker back to 23rd place. Rolt snatched the lead from one of the Ferraris that had been challenging Moss during the opening 'Grand Prix'. Throughout the night he and Hamilton were dogged by three Italians, occasionally losing the lead to the Ferrari only to regain it. The two Alfa Romeos dropped out, but the Ferrari remained until retirement during the 19th hour; a clutch, much abused as the Ferrari drivers tried to save their brakes, had failed. Moss and Walker moved back up from 23rd to second while another Jaguar finished fourth.

Jaguar Cars sent a telegram to the Queen's secretary: "The Jaguar team humbly present their loyal duty to Her Majesty and advise her that in her Coronation year they have won for Britain the world's greatest international car race at Le Mans, France, yesterday." The Fleet Street press reckoned that the win could be worth as much as £1 million to the British motor industry in extra orders over the next few years. It had already been estimated that Jaguar's 1951 win had resulted in US$12,000,000 worth of Jaguars being sold in North America. "The victory bonus will be shared by the entire industry," said journalist Courtenay Edwards.

It was a good job that the Jaguars *did* perform well. All four Aston Martins dropped out, both Bristols caught fire – Tommy Wisdom was trapped for a short while and received cuts and burns – and the two Allards fell out, the first after just three-quarters of an hour. Two Austin-Healey 100s, though, lapped steadily and both finished "in good form" in 12th and 14th places; Edwards reckoned their performance had been an outstanding feature of the race. Donald Healey was inundated with orders as he stood in the pits assisting the refuelling and lap charting. Each of the Austin-Healeys had one British driver, Johnny Lockett sharing with Maurice Gatsonides, the Dutchman who brought us the speed camera, and journalist Gordon Wilkins, who first raced at Le Mans before the war

in a Singer, partnering Frenchman Marcel Becquart. The Austin-Healey 100 was the only car at Le Mans that year that was available to the public in the form in which it was raced, priced £850. Also successful was the Frazer-Nash of Ken Wharton and Lawrence Mitchell which won the 2-litre category. Sadly, 1953 was also the year in which the British-born American Tom Cole was killed, thrown from his Ferrari when it careered off the track at White House.

The next year Jaguar was back with a new car, the beautiful D-type. Again the battle was with Ferrari, again Moss pulled away first, and again there were times when it could have gone either way. In the end the D-type was unable to emulate the C-type by winning its first Le Mans – its glory was still to come. Nevertheless, the outcome could have been different if William Lyons has been a more ruthless and less sporting man, as will be related. However, the British surely do not win by protesting, and Ferrari, despite using too many mechanics when the leading car proved reluctant to start, came home about two and a half miles ahead of the 1953 winners.

So much has been said and written about the 1955

Scrutineering in 1950. Number 24 is the Ferrari 195S of Luigi Chinetti, who had carried out most of the driving duties the year before when he had shared the winning car with Lord Selsdon. *(Duncan Hamilton collection)*

John Cooper (to right of bonnet) takes an interest in the Bristol 450/C of Tommy Wisdom and Jack Fairman prior to the start of the 1955 race. The team award-winning Bristols finished in seventh, eighth and ninth places, with the Wisdom/Fairman car leading the formation finish across the line even though it had completed fewer laps than its stablemates. *(L.J.K. Setright)*

The start of the 1954 race with Tony Rolt and Stirling Moss making a dash for their Jaguars (14 and 12 respectively). Jack Fairman already lags slightly behind as he runs to his Aston Martin (8). *(LAT Photographic)*

For many years the road from Tertre Rouge to the Mulsanne corner was the most awe-inspiring straight-line stretch in all motor racing. Speeds of over 240mph were eventually reached, the highest of all time, 251mph, being set in 1988, albeit not by a British car or driver. This was the view from the air in 1955. *(LAT Photographic)*

Le Mans. It proved to be the first of the D-type's three victories, but there was little to celebrate that year. The early stages of the race were a classic with – shades of 1931 – Mercedes-Benz versus the top British marque. Mike Hawthorn, who was to set the fastest lap every year including this until his final appearance at Le Mans in 1958, battled with Juan Manuel Fangio's Mercedes until about the time of the first routine pit stops. Even after the terrible accident that then took the lives of over 80 spectators, the fight continued, with Moss and the inexperienced Ivor Bueb battling in their Mercedes and Jaguar, respectively. Like Moss during his Jaguar days, Hawthorn had been sent out to break the opposition. He was up against two of the greatest drivers of all time with a Le Mans novice as his co-driver. However, just after 2.00am the Mercedes team was withdrawn on the orders of senior management at Stuttgart. From then on the Jaguar had an impregnable lead, eventually finishing well ahead of the Aston Martin that Peter Collins shared with the Belgian motoring journalist Paul Frère and a Belgian-driven D-type.

Although the win had been achieved under terribly sad circumstances it has to be seen as the first of a hat-trick for the Jaguar D-type. Five such cars were on the start line for the next year's race, all detuned for economy, but with two entered by a new name to Le Mans, Ecurie Ecosse. Quite how this now famed team came down from the north will be related in another

Much has been written about the catastrophe of 1955, perhaps too much. It is the nadir of the Le Mans tale, perhaps of all motor racing history. In its wake the sport would never be the same again. Two of the three drivers involved were English and there were British spectators among those who lost their lives. The *Daily Telegraph* recorded two of their names the next day, 23-year-old Jack Diamond from Edgware and 24-year-old Robert John Loxley of Worcester.

Quite how many of their compatriots were either side of the start/finish straight that day will never be known, but all will have been affected by the grim tragedy, from the two representatives of Hammersmith Hospital, Duncan McDermott and Geoffrey Dickinson, who had been sitting in the grandstand and who assisted the rescue workers, to the *Daily Mirror* reporter Pat Mennem, who rushed to Paris with a film that he had acquired from a photographer of the *South Wales Argus*. "The moment the disaster occurred I hurried to the scene and was pleased to see two English doctors with their coats off working hard. They were ordinary spectators and they must have contributed to the saving of many lives," observed a Swedish doctor.

There were many witnesses from the other side of the track, some of whom feature elsewhere in this book like Duncan Hamilton and John Wyer, who reckoned the accident took place opposite the Aston Martin pits. Aston designer Ted Cutting was looking down the track for Roy Salvadori at the time. He observed a Mercedes-Benz coming towards him with the driver's hand in the air. Suddenly he was aware of being able to see the underside of the car with all four wheels off the ground. He also saw the driver's body lying on the ground. However, "I didn't really realize what I had seen." The wreck seemed to be perched on the banking and it was impossible to see from the pits that the engine and front suspension had scythed through the crowd. Wyer, too, said he did not see what had happened to the Mercedes as he was concentrating on another, spinning car.

The Aston drivers, like so many at the track, were also unaware of the true nature of the tragedy. Salvadori and Peter Collins continued the scrap they had been having, slowing down past the pits where there had obviously been an accident of some kind and then dicing round the rest of the track. It was not until midnight that someone told Cutting what really had happened. Aston team manager Reg Parnell sent him back to the *Hotel de France* at La Chartre with instructions to take a treble brandy and then to go to bed.

Duncan Hamilton was also in the pits at the time of the accident. He had just waved to four French lads over the other side of the track to whom he had spoken at an earlier race in Rouen. Then a Mercedes was flying through the air and a *gendarme* was lying dead at his feet, hit by debris. He recalled being too horrified to think, but Tony Rolt suddenly arrived and, telling his co-driver to look after their wives, Hamilton joined the race.

The British drivers involved were both Grand Prix people, one of them, Mike Hawthorn, among the best of his day. For almost two and a half hours he had been trying to break the lead Mercedes-Benz, its German nationality said by some to have been the proverbial red rag to the Englishman. As the time came for his first stop he overtook the far slower Austin-Healey of fellow-countryman Lance Macklin and then pulled over, slowing down and heading for the pits. Macklin, who had drum brakes, unlike Hawthorn whose Jaguar was disc brake-equipped, was suddenly faced with a D-type immediately ahead of him and slowing far quicker than he ever could. In order not to run into Hawthorn, Macklin braked, his wheels locked; he swerved to the left and, in his own words, "began to skid." Two Mercedes were hurtling towards him at around 150mph, the first driven by a Frenchman who competed under the name of 'Pierre Levegh'. Two years earlier he had come achingly close to winning the 24-hour race single-handed and, in doing so, sufficiently impressed Mercedes team manager Alfred Neubauer for him to give him a drive for 1955. 'Levegh' hit the Austin-Healey and his Mercedes was catapulted into the air. The engine and parts of the disintegrating car ploughed through the crowd; 'Levegh' and over 80 other people were killed. Cutting says that a number of people from La Chartre had loyally positioned themselves opposite the Aston Martin pit and, distressingly, some were among those who died.

Immediately after the event Macklin blamed Hawthorn, Hawthorn blamed himself and then the French press also blamed the young Jaguar driver. However, when it came to the official inquiry Macklin refused to implicate anyone, and the inquiry exonerated Hawthorn. Among the British eye-witnesses, former winner Lord Selsdon said: "In my opinion no blame can be attached to anyone." Spectator L.F. Ward stated: "Mike Hawthorn did not, in any way, do anything that he should not have done."

The aftermath of the tragic 1955 accident, which involved British drivers Mike Hawthorn and Lance Macklin. The latter's Austin-Healey 100S was badly damaged in the incident, although it was the Mercedes of the Frenchman who raced under the name 'Pierre Levegh" that wreaked havoc among the crowd. *(LAT Photographic)*

Jaguar's victory in 1955 was a sombre one in the light of the horrendous accident earlier in the race. Loïs Rolt recalled how she forcibly had to persuade Mike Hawthorn to return to the race, which he was then to win with Ivor Bueb. The latter had to take over the wheel in the aftermath of the crash; it was his first ever stint in a race at Le Mans. *(Rodolfo Mailander/ Ludvigsen Library)*

Lotus founder Colin Chapman drove in two Le Mans, the first being in 1955 when he shared a Lotus Mark 9 with Ron Flockhart, the car being disqualified at about half-distance. *(Clive Chapman collection)*

chapter. However, here it must be recorded that it was to enter the dark blue winning car in both 1956 and 1957, first with the all-Scottish pairing of Ron Flockhart and Ninian Sanderson, then with Flockhart being joined by 1955 winner Bueb. The first of these years produced mainly a two-way battle between the D-type and the Aston Martin of Peter Collins and Stirling Moss, who had joined the Feltham-based team. It may have been a race that he professed to dislike, but Britain's most famous racing driver was still twice a runner-up at Le Mans. The works Jaguars that year had the shortest of races. Two were out on the second lap when Frère spun at the Esses and Fairman also spun in avoiding him, only to be collected by a Ferrari. Then a pit stop just two laps later put Hawthorn's D-type so far back that it was effectively out of the race.

There were no official works Jaguars in 1957, but five D-types nevertheless started the race. Ecurie Ecosse improved on its previous year's result with

TEAM LOTUS ON A TIGHT BUDGET

Michael Taylor drove at Le Mans with Innes Ireland in 1958. On the way to the circuit, with the three Lotus team cars on Ireland's own transporter, they broke down at the *Chateaux de Montreuil,* a few miles from Calais. "We repaired to the bar," recalls Taylor, "and asked the owner, who was an old friend of my father from before the war, to see if he could summon up some help." However, it was early evening and no assistance was likely to be available until the morning. "This was no good for us as practice was the next day and the lighting and various other items still had to be installed – typical Chapman, last-minute stuff in those days.

"We decided to unload the cars and Innes and I, and one of the two mechanics, drove through the night. We had no lights at all, no tax and no insurance, but it was our only way to get the cars there on time. We left the other mechanic to follow the next day after repairs.

"The first *gendarmes* we encountered stopped all other traffic and, whistling like crazy, sped us on our way. This occurred five times along the route. We had taken it in turns to lead as driving so low down with no lights proved quite tiring. We were glad to reach the circuit in one piece."

The question of who was actually to drive the cars in the race had been troubling Lotus boss Colin Chapman. Michael Parkes, Taylor and Ireland were all down to drive one car and this was long before the days when three drivers could be used. Taylor recalls that Parkes' father was chairman of Alvis at the time and Chapman was "trying to get close to the company for commercial reasons." He refused to nominate the drivers.

"On race day I told Innes to come down to breakfast in his racing overalls and I did the same. The race didn't start until 4.00pm so it looked rather odd to the other drivers. When Mike came downstairs we both said what bad luck that he had not been chosen, and off he went, leaving us to share the car…"

Taylor and Ireland had been driving for about 10 hours in the pouring rain. "Water was sloshing about in the car and Colin decided on a modification. At the next stop he had about eight holes drilled in the floor of the car. I took it out again and water poured in through the new holes." Taylor's feet were soon under water.

What was even worse, "on every corner the car gave a great lurch sideways, which wasn't what Lotuses were designed to do. Eventually, having to swerve to miss another driver lying in the road, I lurched into the sand. Colin's economies became apparent as there was no sand shovel, so I had to unscrew a headlamp cover and dig out with that. Very tiring."

Taylor got going again, but the car finally expired not far from the pits with a sheared distributor. "I got word to the pits and they sent out a replacement part. The difficulty was it was against the rules to replace such spare parts so he could hardly hand it to me. I indicated a spot in the grass a little way away and said to him 'drop it there.' I went over to take 'a call of nature' when three marshals surrounded me. Lying in the grass in front of me lay the spare part for all to see – a Mexican standoff. There was nothing more I could do and our race was run."

The Stirling Moss/Peter Collins Aston DB3S leads the Ninian Sanderson/Ron Flockhart Jaguar D-type in 1956. The pair finished second and first respectively. *(LAT Photographic)*

second as well as first place, the runner-up car being driven by Sanderson and John Lawrence. Furthermore, a French-entered Jaguar was third, a Belgian Jaguar fifth and Duncan Hamilton's own D-type sixth. Five private D-types, with factory-prepared engines, were again entered in 1958, but it was to be another three decades before a Jaguar was again to win at Le Mans.

Of course, these immediate post-war years were not just about Jaguar. British cars and drivers were a prominent feature of the 1950s; one of the latter, Eddie Hall, drove for the whole 24 hours on his own in 1950 to finish eighth overall in his Rolls-Royce-modified 1934 Tourist Trophy Bentley.

Aston Martin continued to be a regular participant, the marque continuing as it had left off before the war with no fewer than six cars starting the 1949 race. Other British makes such as HRG, MG, Bentley, Lagonda, Riley and Singer also survived into this period as Le Mans racers. The records mention that one of the drivers of the 1949 winning Ferrari was British; the car was certainly entered by Lord Selsdon, but it would be fair to say that he only relieved co-driver Luigi Chinetti for a few laps on the Sunday morning. There were only six British-built finishers, but they included the third-placed Frazer Nash of Norman Culpan and Harold Aldington and the sixth, seventh and eighth Bentley, Aston Martin and HRG.

The first year of the new decade saw the British in third to sixth places with Sydney Allard's own 5.4-litre device heading the Rolt/Hamilton Nash-Healey and two Aston Martins coupes. The Aston of George Abecassis and Lance Macklin won both the 3-litre class and the Index of Performance, while a new Jowett Jupiter driven by Wisdom and Wise took the 1½-litre class, beating by 14 miles a record set by Aston Martin back in 1935. Fourteen of the 16 British cars finished that year.

The Aston influence on the race continued in 1951 with third (Macklin/Thompson), fifth (Abecassis/Shawe-Taylor), seventh, 10th and 13th places. A Jowett Jupiter again won the 1½-litre class, this time driven by Becquart and Wilkins. Aston Martin's DB3s were considered among the favourites for the 1952 race,

but the only representative of that marque to finish was the Clark/Keen car back in seventh. Britain's highest placed finisher was the Johnson/Wisdom Nash-Healey, a far distant third behind the Mercedes-Benz. While the following year was an all-Jaguar story, Bristol came good in 1954 with the first three places in the 2-litre class for its distinctive 450 coupes. The marque was to take the class again in 1955.

This was the year that Donald Healey became disillusioned by the way that prototypes were being allowed into the race and so he withdrew his team of Austin-Healeys. Healey was stung by an accusation in the French journal *L'Equipe* that his cars were also prototypes. "I can only repeat that the Austin-Healeys are basically production cars," he said. He also criticized the Society of Motor Manufacturers and Traders, which seemed content that its members were entering cars described as 'prototypes of cars you intend to put into production'; Healey knew that such vehicles would *never* go into series production. The hypocrisy was rife, but was eventually to be accepted as the norm; today's Lolas and Zyteks are referred to as 'prototypes', but who believes that either of them will ever see the M6 motorway, let alone the A40?

Peter Jopp and Dickie Stoop were forced to retire their Frazer-Nash Sebring in the closing stages of the 1957 race. *(LAT Photographic)*

Healey pointed out that in order to make his cars competitive he would have to introduce "special high-compression cylinder heads and multiple non-British carburettors, multi-pad-type disc brakes with a complicated servo system and special wheels to suit close-ratio gearboxes and ratios quite unsuitable for normal use. The bodies would have to be converted to virtually single-seater shells. The resulting car would bear no resemblance to our production model with its expensive specification – brakes alone would cost more than a complete production car." (This in a letter from Donald Healey to *Autosport*.) Healey wanted to sell sportscars that their owners could use on both road and track without being frightened off by large manufacturers running race-only specification cars.

By the mid to late 1950s new British names were coming into the race, cars from such specialist racing car manufacturers as Cooper (first seen in 1955 with Jaguar and Coventry Climax-engined cars), Connaught, Kieft, Tojeiro, Lister (still a contestant in the 21st century) and Lotus. Among the mass-production car makers, Triumph entered the fray with its TR2, while MG also returned in 1955 with three prototypes that were based on the soon to be introduced MGA.

A little 1.1-litre Lotus Eleven, driven by Reg Bicknell and Peter Jopp, was to come seventh overall and win its class in 1956. A year later a 750cc Lotus-Climax provided the biggest form-upset of the race with Cliff Allison and Keith Hall winning the Index of Performance, much it was said to the chagrin of the French, ahead of the 1100cc version of Mackay Fraser and Jay Chamberlain. It was described as the biggest

success yet for Colin Chapman's operation. AC did not do too badly either in 1957 with Peter Bolton's Ace-Bristol, which he shared with Ken Rudd, coming 10th overall. The little North London manufacturer Arnott had an aluminium-panelled, Coventry Climax-engined entry that year for racing school pioneer Jim Russell and Dennis Taylor, which failed in the sixth hour.

Lotus was back in 1958 with six cars, but most of them retired, with the Eleven of Alan Stacey and Tom Dickson coming last after the latter had spent two hours digging the little car out of the Mulsanne sand. Both Listers also retired, but AC now had two entries, which came eighth and ninth overall. There was also the only Le Mans entry for the Slough-built, Triumph TR-based Peerless driven by Percy Crabb and Peter Jopp. Triumph sent two engineers to help prepare the engines and the car finished 16th overall, and established a record of only seven minutes for pit stops.

That year Aston Martin was felt to have its best ever chance of an outright win with its three DBR1/300s, but there were still 12 months to go before that dream became reality. Stirling Moss certainly dominated the early stages of the race, establishing almost a minute's lead in his Aston, then dropping out with a broken con-rod before three hours were up. Six British cars finished that year of the 20 that had started, but three of these failed to complete the required distance. Apart from the second-placed privately entered Aston Martin of the Whitehead brothers up front it was not a year for the British to remember, but Aston's day would come soon.

MOSS AND THE 'MON AMI, MATES'

Three of the most talented of all English racing drivers came to the fore in the early part of the 1950s. It was a time when a Grand Prix driver thought nothing of competing in endurance races, with Le Mans as much a part of his calendar as any Formula One race. Of the three, Mike Hawthorn and Peter Collins have become inextricably linked as "mon ami, mates", the title historian Chris Nixon chose for his fine biography of the pair, while the other, Stirling Moss, was described by Nixon as "the third man."

As recorded in these pages, Hawthorn was the only one of the trio to win at Le Mans, also setting the fastest lap in four consecutive years from 1955 to 1958. Although exonerated by many, his involvement in the serious 1955 crash left a shadow over his victory year. Moss scored the fastest lap in 1951 in one of the debuting Jaguar C-types, but otherwise his record is similar to that of Collins; they only finished twice at la Sarthe, both times in second place, and retired on all their other appearances. Unlike Hawthorn, neither was to win the World Championship, although both might well have done so had it not been for selfless acts which benefited other drivers, by Collins in 1956 and Moss two years later.

Between them they won 22 Grands Prix, Moss with 15 and one shared victory, Hawthorn and Collins with

three apiece. By modern standards these may appear modest totals, but those were years with many fewer World Championship rounds and a considerably higher mortality rate. These 22 races include some of the classics of all time, including Hawthorn's narrow victory over Fangio at Reims in 1953 and Moss' domination of the theoretically quicker Ferrari at both Monaco and the Nürburgring in 1961. If one is forced to single out any one event to laud Moss then it must surely be the Mille Miglia of 1955 in which, assisted by passenger Denis Jenkinson, he drove his Mercedes-Benz 300SLR to an epic victory in a race that the Italians considered their own. "He worked as I have never seen anyone work before in my life," wrote 'Jenks'.

Cars brought both joy and grief to all three drivers. Collins was killed when his Ferrari went off the road at the Nürburgring in 1958; his great friend Hawthorn retired as World Champion at the end of the year only to die in a road accident shortly afterwards, while Moss' international career was effectively ended in 1962 by an inexplicable crash during a minor Formula One race at Goodwood. These days, Sir Stirling still competes in historic racing, and in 2005 he could be seen in the Le Mans Legends race at the wheel of a Jaguar C-type, the same model of car in which he had made his debut there over half a century before.

CHAPTER 10

THE C-TYPE AND D-TYPE JAGUARS

"It had all the evidence of an absolute victory obtained by the Lord's blessing upon the godly party principally." (Oliver Cromwell)

Occasionally, very occasionally, an inanimate, man-made object can be described as a thing of beauty. R. J. Mitchell achieved this with the Supermarine Spitfire. Jaguar has arguably, perhaps uniquely among car manufacturers, done it twice with the D-type and the E-type. One was an outright racer, the other a road car, but both competed at Le Mans. By contrast, the Jaguar C-type, or more correctly XK120C, was an arguably simpler looking machine, not a thing of beauty but of purpose. Together the C- and D-types created a legend at Le Mans. (Of course, beauty is a subjective matter. Martin Brundle believes the much later, slab-like Group C Jaguars to have been "beautiful". Having driven one to victory at Le Mans he is perhaps entitled to this view.)

The Jaguar XK120 was one of the sensations of the 1948 Motor Show in London. Both its flowing lines and its twin-overhead-camshaft, six-cylinder 3.4-litre engine stamped it as one of the classic sportscars of all time. Three were privately entered for Le Mans in 1950, with one factory mechanic loaned to each team. Two of Jaguar's most senior personnel, Raymond 'Lofty' England and designer Bill Heynes, were also present to assess the race. The former was to be described, along with John Wyer and Mercedes-Benz's Alfred Neubauer, as arguably one of the three greatest team managers in motor racing. Certainly, as far as 1950s endurance racing was concerned, they were peerless. England and Heynes came to the conclusion that if they incorporated standard parts into a lightweight frame and used a "properly designed" aerodynamic body, they could win this race.

The next year four Jaguars were entered for Le Mans, each under the name of one of their drivers: Leslie Johnson, Robert Lawrie, Stirling Moss and Peter Walker. There was no indication of their being factory entries or being anything other than conventional XK120s. What appeared was described by Basil Cardew in the *Daily Express* as "an experimental model which was held back in secret for the last two months." Jaguar founder William Lyons described it thus at the time: "It is a prototype of a new 3½-litre

sports model which we hope to build for sport. Our engineers worked for six months on the design and started work on the prototype two months ago." It was the Jaguar XK120C, known to history as the C-type. Despite never having raced in anger before, and although two of the three cars that made the startline retired, the third scored a famous victory driven by Peter Walker and Peter Whitehead. "Both are at an ideal age for the game," said Cardew. They were in their late-thirties.

The win, England was to say, put Jaguar "on the map." It was only after the 1951 Le Mans that the Americans could really identify the brand. By the end of the following year, Jaguar Cars had become the largest dollar earner among all the imported makes in the United States of America.

Much has been written about these iconic cars and their successors, the D-types, notably by that painstaking Jaguar historian Andrew Whyte. Over 50 were built between 1951 and 1953, a number of which

Turning back the clock. Spontaneous applause broke out as Sir Stirling Moss took over Nigel Webb's Jaguar C-type during the 2005 Legends race. *(Author)*

Jaguar's first Le Mans victory came in 1951 with Peter Whitehead and Peter Walker. The former, a wealthy Yorkshireman, had been the first ever privateer to run a Ferrari Formula One car two years previously. In winning the 1949 Czech Grand Prix he became the first British driver since Dick Seaman to win a major international race outside his native country. In addition to Le Mans he twice won the Reims 12-hour race, but was killed competing in the Tour de France in 1958 when his Jaguar 3.4 saloon plunged off a bridge. Walker was a gentleman farmer who, during the same year as his Le Mans win, finished seventh in the British Grand Prix for BRM, an heroic feat in a desperately hot cockpit. He retired after the 1955 Le Mans race, but sadly died an alcoholic down-and-out in 1984. *(Jaguar)*

can still be seen in historic racing. As *The Autocar* pointed out, the month after Le Mans the C-type was "a fresh version of the famous XK120, intended purely for competition and racing purposes." Unlike the XK120 there was no intention that this should be a dual-purpose car. It consisted of production XK components in a short and rigid triangulated steel-tube frame. The engine was the familiar 3.4-litre, six-cylinder with 'tuning modifications' that included an 8:1 or 9:1 compression ratio. Harry Weslake had been involved in increasing its power output. Looking at the car now it seems the personification of a straightforward 1950s sports-racing car, but at the time, *The Autocar* reckoned that the structure was of "a very interesting design." The opportunity to get away with just one small door gave Jaguar the ability to increase vertical height just at the point where rigidity tended to be lacking. The Malcolm Sayer-designed bodywork was, said *The Autocar*, "in accordance with the modern ideas of fairing, or streamlining." It is only when you see it alongside the cycle-mudguarded sports-racers that competed alongside it do you realize just how modern the C-type must have appeared in 1951.

In 1952 you could buy a production one for £1495 plus purchase tax, making a total of £2327 1s 1d. For

that you would get a car capable of a top speed of 143.7mph and which would deliver around 16mpg. Having observed the Mercedes-Benz 300SLs on the Mille Miglia, Stirling Moss, perhaps erroneously, reported that the C-type's top speed was not high enough if Jaguar wanted to win Le Mans again. Instructed by Lyons, Sayer designed a new streamlined nose and tail. England, away at the Monaco Grand Prix, which that year was for sportscars, was unaware of what was happening. Testing was limited; in practice the C-types showed just how prone they were going to be to overheating, and before the race was very old all three factory C-types were out, although in the case of Moss' car this was nothing to do with the constrictive nature of the nose. It was all, said England, "the greatest mistake."

Following the 1952 debacle, Lyons was determined that the team was going to win again in 1953. All the panels on the car were lightened, an innovative rubber fuel tank fitted, a new Borg & Beck clutch installed and the engine performance was increased to 220bhp. Three-choke Weber carburettors and a new induction system that gave the cars an exhaust note "like a whiplash" were fitted. The modification that has gone down in history, though, was the fitting of disc brakes designed and developed by the Dunlop Aviation Division. The company's managing director Joe Wright and development engineer Harold Hodgkinson were on hand at Le Mans to see the brakes perform. Remarked Hodgkinson, "these brakes will bring the Jaguar down from 150 to 30mph in under 300 yards and they do not wear out." The drivers were said to have thought them "terrific" and before the race the team was reckoning that they could save around six seconds a lap. For all these modifications, the C-types looked more like 1951 cars than those of the previous year. The team was also well prepared, having been given the use of Gaydon airfield for testing.

'Mort' Morris-Goodall, now Jaguar's competitions manager (although he was only with the firm for just over a year), test driver Norman Dewis and Len Hayden, who with Gordon Gardner was to be the mechanic for the Tony Rolt/Duncan Hamilton car, took the three factory C-types, XKC 051, 052 and 053, to the race. There was also a privately entered car for *Ecurie Francorchamps*. Arriving at Le Mans, the three works cars gave very little away, little other than the minimal practice being required; England was convinced that they were ready to race. It has already been said in this book, but it is worth repeating, that the C-types finished first, second, fourth and ninth. Given the international flavour of any team these days, it will forever be remembered as one of Britain's finest hours at Le Mans. Only a Cunningham C5R got in the way of a perfect finish for the factory.

Like the C-type, the existence of its successor, the D-type, was kept a secret until just before the race for which it was mainly intended, Le Mans. Early in May the press was told that three new cars were to be entered for the event. These would embody "many new features, some of which will remain secret until the day of the race." What the firm was prepared to release was the fact that the car was to use monocoque

The Jaguar team assembles for a talk from William Lyons. The couple to the left of the picture are Aileen and Alfred Moss, parents of the bobble-hatted Stirling. *(Derek Waller)*

construction, with the streamlined body and chassis to be built as one unit using special magnesium alloy. The thus rigid and lighter car was to be only 32 inches high, six inches lower than the C-type, and the engine again the 3.4-litre, twin-overhead-camshaft XK unit, now with horsepower increased to over 250bhp. Disc brakes, naturally, were to be used, but the wire-spoked wheels of the previous year were replaced with light-alloy ventilated disc wheels. A prototype car had already been testing on the Jabbeke highway in Belgium, reaching 178mph. As in the previous year, the works team would be accompanied by the C-type of *Ecurie Francorchamps*, the car now up to factory specification with disc brakes and triple Webers.

The D-type was built to win Le Mans, period. John Wyer, then team manager of the rival Aston Martins, believed that if there had been a little less emphasis on this and on using production components it could have been "a world beater on any circuit." However, a win at Le Mans was more likely to result in the increased sales of road cars rather than victory anywhere else or in the World Sports Car Championship, a series that Jaguar was not to win during this era. Jaguar's attitude to the championship was made perfectly clear during 1953, its inaugural year. With one race to go, the five-day Carrera Panamerica in Mexico, it was a single point ahead of its rival Ferrari. Given that only the best four results could be counted, Jaguar had 27, Ferrari 26. 'Lofty' England and Stirling Moss went out to reconnoitre the course, but that was it. In vain, John A. Cooper, the sports editor of *The Autocar*, pleaded: "It is hoped, for the prestige of this country, that the Coventry firm will be able to see its way clear to entering a works team in this event…What about it, Mr Lyons?" But Lyons was unmoved. Victory at Le Mans was sufficient.

A famous victory. Duncan Hamilton presses on in 1953. *(Duncan Hamilton collection)*

The victorious 1953 team stops off for a cup of tea and a greasy fry-up on its way home from Le Mans. The cafe is adorned with bunting to celebrate the Coronation. *(Duncan Hamilton collection)*

Work being carried out on C-types and, nearest the camera, a prototype D-type, at the Browns Lane, Coventry factory in 1954. *(LAT Photographic)*

87

DRIVING THE C-TYPE

Gary Pearson understandably describes being able to race the 1953 Le Mans-winning Jaguar C-type, XKC 051, as "a great privilege." Pearson was brought up surrounded by Jaguars while the factory's team manager Lofty England was a good friend to his father, John, a noted Jaguar restorer. Pearson Engineering had already been maintaining the car for owner Adrian Hamilton when Gary was asked to drive it at the first Goodwood Revival meeting. (Only two drivers now enjoy this honour, the other being Sir Stirling Moss.) He has since won the Freddie March Memorial Trophy for 1952 to 1955 sports-racers twice with XKC 051 and once with his father's 1954 Cooper-Jaguar.

Pearson points out that the C-type has been restored

Gary Pearson drives the 1953 winning C-type as it should be driven. The car has been restored to its original condition, but is still raced at Goodwood in a genuinely competitive manner. *(Author)*

to period specification, unlike many of those that it is up against. "That makes it so much sweeter to run at the front." Its characteristics are the same today as they were in 1953. It may not have a particularly high straight-line speed, but it does have those disc brakes, making it so much easier to stop than any other car of the early 1950s. Pearson describes it as having "a very nice balance" and being "a very neutral handling car," which makes it easy for him to carry the speed into the corners. It has, he says, "absolutely no vices." Those who have driven it testify to what a tractable car it is, easy to drive even through the country lanes.

Pearson has also raced Ben Cousins' XKC 027, but describes XKC 051 as his favourite. He should have driven the latter in the 2005 Le Mans Legends race. He led the first of these events back in 2001 and was ahead until two laps before the end when his Lister-Jaguar's fuel pump switch failed. In 2003 he shared a lightweight Jaguar E-type with David Franklin, while in the Group C/GTP race of 2004, he again led tantalizingly until one and a half laps before the finish when the crownwheel and pinion broke on his Jaguar XJR-11. Unfortunately he had to withdraw his entry for the 2005 race due to a back operation. However, Pearsons Engineering was responsible for looking after Nigel Webb's two cars, including the winning Jaguar D-type that uses the chassis from 1955 24-Hours winner XKD 505 and the C-type driven by Stirling Moss. The company also maintained the third-placed D-type recreation of Ben Eastick.

Mike Hawthorn, who was to become Britain's first Formula One World Champion in 1958, scored his only victory at Le Mans three years earlier. However, he set fastest lap at the track on four consecutive appearances. *(Rodolfo Mailander/Ludvigsen Library)*

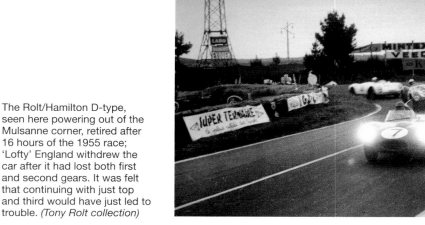

The Rolt/Hamilton D-type, seen here powering out of the Mulsanne corner, retired after 16 hours of the 1955 race; 'Lofty' England withdrew the car after it had lost both first and second gears. It was felt that continuing with just top and third would have just led to trouble. *(Tony Rolt collection)*

The D-type's gestation period was somewhat longer than that of the C-type, but it was not to share its predecessor's first-time-out winning ability. Having said that, the car was to win at Le Mans three times, from 1955 to 1957. The second year of its use saw the only real shake-up in driver line-up made by Jaguar in the 1950s. The 1951 winners Walker and Whitehead were now out, while Moss had joined Mercedes-Benz. In his place came Mike Hawthorn, whom England believed could, on his day, be quicker than his compatriot. The car was also improved. The original magnesium-alloy tub at the front was replaced with a steel frame, "for ease of repair," said England. Changes were made in the engine, and a Malcolm Sayer-developed long nose further improved the purposeful beauty of the machine. The bonnet itself was now 7.5 inches longer. The cockpit had a higher windscreen, behind it being

a more streamlined one-piece headrest and tail fin. Was there ever a better looking Le Mans car?

Three works cars were entered, as usual joined by *Ecurie Francorchamps*, which now had a D-type at its disposal, and the American, Briggs Cunningham. The following year – during which William Lyons was knighted – was to be the last appearance for the D-types in factory guise. The three works cars again had Belgian companionship with the *L'Equipe Nationale Belge* version and, for the first time at Le Mans, a Scottish entry from Ecurie Ecosse. Interestingly, they were joined by a Jaguar XK140 entered by Robert Walshaw and driven by Walshaw and Peter Bolton. However, this car was disqualified at midday on the Sunday for refuelling a lap early, despite which it continued to circulate for another hour and a quarter.

As England, who took over the reins of the company from Sir William in 1972, pointed out, Jaguar was a company that took homologation regulation seriously. Andrew Whyte believed that 87 D-types were made in all, 67 of them 'production' cars; 16 D-types were converted to the road-going XKSS version. Such has been the appeal of the car that some excellent replicas have been produced, some of them true reproductions. Unfortunately, the way in which the front frame could be detached from the monocoque centre section has led to confusion as to the current identity of some cars. Major components from perhaps one car can now be found as part of two separate vehicles. This has led to serious debate among the purists, but for those in the grandstands, the fact that so many D-types can still be raced in such as the Le Mans Legends events has to be a plus. The car that Johnny Herbert drove to victory in the 2005 race appears to be the 1955 winner XKD 505 to the casual spectator, and part of it almost certainly is, even if there was never any record of it being sold by the factory as an entity.

From 1957 Jaguar was to be represented by independent entries until the arrival on the scene of the TWR Group C cars three decades later. Ecurie Ecosse, Duncan Hamilton, *Equipe National Belge* and

Los Amigos, the team associated with Jaguar's Lyon agent Henri Peignaux, flew the flag in 1957. The result was described by Andrew Whyte as "Britain's most crushing victory of all time." All four squads – now with 3-litre engines – were back a year later to be joined by Maurice Charles with an ex-Ecurie Ecosse car. *ENB*, however, had transferred its allegiance to Lister, two of that marque being entered in 1958 with Jaguar engines. Sadly, Jean Brussin, the owner of the *Los Amigos* entry, was killed in an accident at Tertre Rouge. Brussin was the only Jaguar driver to lose his life in the Le Mans 24-Hours.

The Scots kept going, entering a D-type in 1959 and 1960. That final year also saw a development of the D-type, a 3-litre prototype known as the E2A. An entry was made by Briggs Cunningham, the factory emphatically denying that it was a works car. "The news that Mr Briggs Cunningham, millionaire American sportsman, had entered two Jaguar cars for this year's Le Mans 24-hours race has given the impression, in

some quarters, that this indicates a return of the Jaguar Company to the racing scene. This is incorrect…" said a company statement. The sole car to start showed promise in practice, but had to stop with a fuel leak after a mere three laps. Various incidents followed and it was retired in the 10th hour. Two years later another Jaguar appeared in Cunningham's white-and-blue colours. Peter Sargent had a similar car entered for himself and Peter Lumsden, as did Maurice Charles, who shared with John Coundley. They were true GT cars. The Cunningham car came third in that category, with the Sargent car, which had been leading it until the last hour before gearbox trouble (fifth) intervened, that showed more than a passing resemblance to the E2A; they were in fact E-types.

The E-types would be back in 1963 and 1964, Peter Lindner Racing and Peter Sargent entering dramatic looking lightweight versions in the second of these years, but the era of the true Jaguar sports-racing roadster was over. Indeed, a two-decade gap was now to occur before any other car was entered bearing this charismatic name.

Ted Cutting was an essential member of the Aston Martin team during the 1950s and 1960s, designing the 1959 winning DBR1. *(Author)*

TED CUTTING

In early 1949 Ted Cutting was working for Sydney Allard, but planning to get married and live in Richmond. Hearing that Aston Martin was based at nearby Feltham he applied for a job "and I got it." He was put to work on a new chassis-frame for the DB2, the bodywork of which was designed by Frank Feeley, whom Cutting describes as "a genius."

Cutting remained with Aston until 1964; perhaps the most significant part of the company's racing history. During that time, "I had two successive terms of contract with three months notice. That was quite something. I was also quite well paid by Yorkshire standards!" After the 1955 Le Mans race he was appointed chief racecar designer, replacing 'Willie' Watson. "The first car I did was the DBR1," he says.

That is some statement for it was the DBR1 that won Le Mans for Aston Martin in 1959. The prototype car, DBR1/1, was built for the race in 1956, the works entering it with a 2.5-litre engine alongside two DB3S models. Driven by Tony Brooks and Reg Parnell it ran as high as fourth during the night, but retired in the final hour. Four other cars were built, DBR1/2, which was constructed for the 1957 season with a 3-litre engine, being the actual Le Mans winner. Three of them were in the 1959 Le Mans team, all having benefited from considerable development work and modified rear bodywork.

Cutting used a multi-tubular spaceframe design which, as he says, was "typically modern then." However, Aston Martin "had all sorts of troubles with the (David Brown CG537) gearbox" of the DBR1, but, as Cutting points out, that was one part of the car for which he was not responsible. He had hoped to be able to use a new gearbox design and, if necessary, have an independent rear suspension based on the Mercedes-Benz 300 SLR, and he recalls being "slightly annoyed" at being unable to do so.

Cutting was also responsible for the Aston Martin project cars, the DP212, 214 and 215, recalling that "I walked round the parts bin" when first told by John Wyer that the first of these had to be 'different'. "I decided that I would build the 212 with DB4 front suspension and steering gear and a mixture of Lagonda Rapide and DBR2 rear suspension. The chassis-frame was a 'cut and shut' version of the DB4 chassis with aluminium instead of steel used wherever possible. The car was finished 10 days before Le Mans. "That was fairly typical of the time," says Cutting.

The aerodynamics of the 212 proved a problem, the car suffering from lift at Le Mans. Indeed, Cutting admits "we didn't know anything about aerodynamics." It did, though, get away first. It was in the days of the famed Le Mans start, when the drivers ran across the road to their cars. Cutting confesses to having left the Aston in gear with the handbrake off, which was against the regulations. Driver Graham Hill jumped in, put his foot on the clutch before pressing the starter motor and shot away first to the great delight of Raymond Baxter on the broadcast system.

Although the 212 retired at Le Mans with piston failure, Aston Martin owner David Brown was sufficiently encouraged to sanction two GT cars, the 214s that were known as DB4GTs and a prototype, the 215, for the following year. All used the same chassis, which in theory was contrary to the regulations although no problem ever arose. The 215 was effectively a development of the 212. Lack of aero testing the previous year was made up for with use of the Motor Industry Research Association's proving ground. Cutting recalls Mike Salmon testing the car at MIRA on a "typically cold and damp" day. During the race Phil Hill was timed on the Mulsanne straight at over 198mph.

CHAPTER 11

ROLT AND HAMILTON

"I make no doubt but that I shall be able to amuse you with many anecdotes about him."
(Private William Wheeler, 51st Light Infantry Regiment, 1809)

Some time in the late 1960s a young student was using his vacation to earn enough to keep his Austin-Healey Sprite on the road by working as a porter at Oxford's Radcliffe Infirmary. That particular day he had been sent to assist the X-Ray department, ferrying patients to and fro. Those who were reasonably fit were collected in a wheelchair; those less able were transported by trolley. The name on the next slip said 'Mr D. Hamilton', and the instruction for the porter was to take a trolley.

On arriving at the ward the student was directed to a private room. The patient, a James Robertson Justice-like figure, interpreted the look on the porter's face as one of concern. That certainly came into it because there was no way in which he could have lifted this rather large gentleman onto the stretcher. However, there was more to it than that.

"Don't worry, porter," said the patient, "I can jump on the trolley." As he did so, the student revealed the real reason behind his expression. "Are you," he asked,

"*the* Duncan Hamilton, the 1953 Le Mans winner?"

The patient seemed delighted to have been recognized, and as the student had recently finished reading *Touch Wood!*, Hamilton's entertaining autobiography, the pair chatted about his career. Stories they reminisced about included the time that Hamilton had found himself on an operating table in Portugal just one weekend after his famous victory. At the X-Ray desk, the receptionist asked Hamilton about any previous hospital experience. "You had better ask the porter," he replied. "He knows more about that than me."

Such was Duncan Hamilton, arguably the most ebullient of all British Le Mans winners and a man whose exploits at La Sarthe are inextricably linked with those of the dapper Major Tony Rolt, the man who introduced him to the race and who was the lead driver of the 1953 winning car. Rolt's career, in fact, had begun before Hamilton's and he was already making progress as a front-running racing driver when

Duncan Hamilton quite understandably described the last few yards of the 1953 race as an unforgettable experience.
(Duncan Hamilton collection)

The Rolts and the Hamiltons became firm family friends. (Left to right) Angela and Duncan Hamilton, Loïs and Tony Rolt are seen together on vacation at Klosters. *(Tony Rolt collection)*

war intervened. His career can be traced back to being a member of an Eton team in an inter-public schools trial, a type of motorsport that reached its zenith between the wars. An indulgent, widowed mother then agreed to buy him a racing car after he had declined a horse. His first race was the Spa 24-Hours in a Triumph Southern Cross. In 1938 he purchased the famous ERA R5B known as 'Remus' from Prince Birabongse of Thailand, who raced under the name 'B.Bira'. This was modified by Freddie Dixon, and in 1939 Rolt showed his prowess by winning the British Empire Trophy at Donington Park. He was still only 19 years old.

What follows shows the mettle of many of those who raced in the immediate post-war period. For many of them, every day must have seemed a bonus. Hamilton's wife Angela told *Reveille* magazine that there would be no point in trying to persuade him to give up racing as he would only take up some equally dangerous pastime. He was to state that motorsport was far safer than being in an Artic convoy heading for Russia. *Touch Wood!* is full of wartime tales, including his being sunk on both aircraft carrier HMS *Glorious* and the cruiser HMS *Curlew* in the same action. Rolt's

Tony Rolt was also an excellent single-seater driver. After the war he purchased the Alfa-Aitken seen here at the 1947 Grand Prix de Frontières at Chimay in which he was placed eighth. The car started life as the Alfa Romeo Bimotore; one owner, Peter Aitken, who was killed during the war, had the rear engine removed while further modifications were made by Freddie Dixon during Rolt's ownership. *(Tony Rolt collection)*

wartime career was such that it would be written about in books even if he had never been to Le Mans.

Both Rolt and his wife Loïs came from military backgrounds. His father had been a Brigadier and Rolt was actually a serving officer in the Rifle Brigade when racing in the late 1930s. The Brigade was heavily involved in the fighting around Calais during the time of the retreat to Dunkirk and Rolt was captured. What followed was the stuff of legend, the type of tale that would serve to revive people's spirits in the austere post-war years *(see side bar)*. Hamilton told historian F. Wilson McComb that he was also captured, in his case during the Norwegian campaign, and along with seven others was sentenced to the firing squad; only two of them escaped. It was a story that he did not recount in *Touch Wood!*.

Hamilton and Rolt first teamed up at Le Mans for the 1950 race, the latter having invited Hamilton to share Donald Healey's 3.4-litre Nash-engined Healey. "They were huge personal friends and evenly matched behind the wheel. They were both from an engineering background and were kind to their cars," says Hamilton's son Adrian.

Hamilton was an imposing figure, "a great character, fun to be around" and at times "a tremendous liability," recalls Adrian affectionately. He was also "a very kind man, always happy to talk to anyone." Mike Salmon, whose own Le Mans career started shortly after Hamilton's had finished, confirms that beneath the bluff exterior "he really was a gentle man." Ian Skailes, who competed at Le Mans in 1970, remembers how Hamilton rang him after the race to congratulate him on "a splendid effort"; that meant a lot to the young Chevron driver. "He was a lovely man, most entertaining, but not given to compliments," he says.

During his early career Hamilton raced a variety of single-seaters, including a much loved Lago-Talbot that seemed to suit his personality, a Bugatti 35B, a Maserati 6CM, a works HWM and, like Rolt, 'Remus', but increasingly he became a sportscar specialist. He was the first private owner of a Jaguar C-type and was to intersperse his works drives for Jaguar with races in his own C- and D-types. Rolt, too, drove a variety of single-seaters post-war including the Alfa Romeo Bimotore, by then with just one engine, and Rob Walker's Connaught and Delage-ERA. Eager for a drive with Jaguar, he kept in touch with the works' team manager 'Lofty' England. A hint that if he went to Dundrod at his own expense it might lead to his becoming the reserve driver was taken up. Halfway through the race Leslie Johnson became ill and Rolt took his place. An excellent performance in Ireland secured him a permanent place in the team and a chance to drive a Jaguar the following year at Le Mans. When asked whom he would like as co-driver he replied "Hamilton."

Hamilton's life was recalled, not always with complete accuracy, in *Touch Wood!*. Adrian provides an example that his father chose to miss from his autobiography. In 1957 his mother, Angela, was to perform the opening ceremony for a new swimming pool at his Old Woking prep school. His father had been asked to sponsor the pool and a deal was struck, remembers Adrian, that also had something to do with his school fees. To the headmaster's delight, Hamilton turned up in the long-nose Jaguar D-type that he was to drive at Le Mans in 1957 and 1958. However, said worthy was slightly less pleased when, just as he had finished his welcoming speech, the Le Mans winner pushed him into the deep end and drove away.

Hamilton, who died in 1994, "just loved Le Mans." Indeed, he even built his own gigantic caravan to travel to the race. After his retirement he still used this to attend the event until eventually "it fell apart."

Tales have been told, often by Hamilton himself, of the copious amounts of 'fuel' that he personally consumed. However, a much-repeated story of how he and Rolt won the 1953 race "courtesy of Martell" has been denied by Rolt and refuted by 'Lofty' England. Rolt's son Stuart, the current chairman of the British Racing Drivers' Club, says that the pair would have simply gone out to dinner on the Friday evening with their wives, but there is no way that they would have been drunk the night before the race. There was a misunderstanding, caused by the fact that both the Rolt/Hamilton and the team's reserve cars were out at the same time during practice, both carrying the number '18'. However, talking on camera to Neville Hay, England stated that Hamilton's story of a 25,000 franc fine having to be paid by William Lyons was "a load of rubbish." It seems that the matter was settled amicably by England himself, with talk of a mere 100 franc fine to keep the ACO committee happy. The problem had been resolved by the Friday afternoon, "but don't tell Duncan that," said England with a grin, "it would spoil a good story."

By contrast, the meticulous Rolt is not one for broadcasting his undoubted achievements. That he was a remarkably quick driver there is no doubt, despite his what is now called 'gentleman amateur' status. The pre-war results had stamped him as one of the brightest talents of his generation. Indeed, an Auto Union official, noticing him flat-out on greasy cobbles at Berne and assuming him to be 'Bira', was ready to offer him a test drive. Post-war his was the fastest British driver/car combination in the 1953 and 1955 British Grands Prix. In the latter race, driving the underpowered Connaught, he was a mere 1.2 seconds slower than Mike Hawthorn and Maurice Trintignant in their works Ferraris. In the 1953 Mille Miglia he averaged 100mph for the first 400 miles before his C-type retired. Occasionally Rolt even had the measure of Jaguar team-mate Stirling Moss, arguably the greatest of all English racing drivers.

Driving the Nash-Healey, Rolt and Hamilton finished fourth overall in their first year together at Le Mans, the latter recalling: "we…found we enjoyed this kind of classical endurance racing." A master plan was employed to drive quickly when the rest of the field was easing up, such as in the rain or at night. "The old man was very good in the rain," remembers Adrian (second place in the abandoned 1951 Silverstone International Trophy, two places ahead of Juan Manuel Fangio, was to confirm that). There was also a determination, wrote his father, not to become involved in the usual "unholy dice" at the beginning of the Le Mans race.

Adrian also says that his father reckoned that Le Mans was won and lost at night. "That was the time to wind the pressure up. He had very good night vision, having been in the Fleet Air Arm during the war."

Sydney Allard was third in 1950 with his mighty 5.4-litre Allard, and Hamilton reckoned that had it not been for a wrong arrangement at one of the pit stops, he and Rolt could so easily have kept their compatriot back in fourth place. However, towards the end Rolt had to nurse their car with failing brakes and a suspect rear axle, the result of a shove in the rear by a French car many hours earlier, and with half-an-hour left, Allard's fast running co-driver, American Tom Cole, moved ahead of him.

Healey invited Rolt and Hamilton to drive for him again the next year. This time the car, now with a 3.8-litre engine, was to be a saloon, the only occasion that they would drive such a car at Le Mans. It was felt that

Tony Rolt's first year at Le Mans was 1949, when he shared Rob Walker's Delahaye 135CS with Guy Jason-Henry. Bearing trouble brought a halt to the car after 126 laps. *(Tony Rolt collection)*

The year 1950 brought Rolt and Hamilton together for the first time at Le Mans. The latter was to write that they found they rather enjoyed endurance racing. *(Duncan Hamilton collection)*

the bodywork would offer less wind resistance than an open car, an important factor given they were using what was basically a touring car's engine. One benefit of the closed car was that the drivers were able to fill it with, in Rolt's case, sweets and, in Hamilton's, fruit. There is still an orange, well past its sell-by date, on display at the Hampshire-based classic car business now run by Adrian Hamilton. The story is that this was found hidden away in the depths of the 1953 winning Jaguar C-type and has now been preserved for posterity. The Nash-Healey never missed a beat during the 1951 race, eventually finishing sixth.

Rolt and Hamilton joined the official Jaguar works team for 1952, the year when all their C-types retired with overheating as a result of the newly designed sloping nose. At the very end of that year Hamilton had an accident driving through Cobham, during which he knocked over a police box and demolished a bus stop sign. Reports of the event got out of hand: "*La morte di Hamilton*", headlined one Italian paper. Messages of condolence flooded in from around the world. A Swiss journalist rang the Hamilton household to be answered by the man himself, who had not even been detained in hospital. "It's impossible," said the newsman. "You're dead. I heard it on the radio."

The following year the Jaguars, as already noted, were fitted with Girling-Dunlop disc brakes and were considerably lighter. Rolt took the lead just after 5.00am and so began the battle with the Villoresi/Ascari Ferrari, sheer power versus braking ability. Victory was only assured for the Jaguar once the Ferrari's clutch had begun to slip. Hamilton had "achieved my dearest sporting ambition."

"He was immensely proud of winning that race," says Adrian. He was also to come close on two more occasions, the first again with Rolt. It might be said that in 1954 the conditions were ideal, for Hamilton

(Left to right) Hamilton and Rolt enjoy the result of their first Le Mans together with wives Loïs and Angela. They had come fourth overall as well as third in the 5-litre class. *(Tony Rolt collection)*

The 1953 victory was not all plain sailing. A bird hit the C-type as it was doing about 150mph on the Mulsanne straight, breaking both windscreen and Hamilton's nose. *(Duncan Hamilton collection)*

Streamlined noses brought disaster for the Jaguar team in 1952. Here Hamilton clings to the inside of Tertre Rouge in his smoking C-type followed by a Lancia sandwiched between a couple of Cunninghams. *(MNF collection)*

at least, because it rained. But a fuel filter problem lost the pair about 10 minutes, while Rolt was forced off the road during the morning by a Talbot, causing the handling of the car to change. Again it was a battle between Ferrari and Jaguar, the D-type having replaced the XKC. When five mechanics, rather than the legal two, descended on the leading but troubled Ferrari, Hamilton was all for protesting, but William Lyons would have none of it. He wanted to win the race, as he said, "the British way."

Towards the end of the nail-biting race Rolt needed to come in to replace his goggles with a visor; every car was sending up clouds of spray in the rain. To save time Hamilton jumped into the car instead and took up the chase after Gonzalez, whose Ferrari had at last started. Initially just 90 seconds adrift of the red car, Hamilton admitted to "frightening myself to death," reaching 173mph on the Mulsanne straight when the storm was at its worst. "I had driven with a total disregard for the consequences." But unfortunately for the pair, the rain stopped with a quarter of an hour to go and Gonzalez was able to slightly increase his lead. It had been a classic battle. Ironically the nearest Hamilton had to an accident occurred almost on the finishing line, where three Bristols had lined up for a formation finish, oblivious of the fast closing Jaguar.

Rolt was driving at the time of the tragic 1955 Le Mans accident, arriving at the pits in its aftermath for Hamilton to take over. Both men witnessed the terrible events, Rolt having been not far behind 'Levegh', while Hamilton was waiting for the Jaguar to come in. It was Loïs Rolt who sat Mike Hawthorn down in a caravan to try and calm him, eventually persuading him, by hitting him she was to admit, to return to his car. The crash, says Rolt, "was no one's fault. It was a racing accident." One doubts that their own car's eventual retirement with lost gears would have troubled Rolt and Hamilton that day.

After fulfilling his commitments to Rob Walker's Connaught, Rolt retired at the end of that season. It was not a result of the 'Levegh' crash, just that he felt it was time to move on. By then he was collaborating with Harry Ferguson on the development of the Ferguson four-wheel drive system and needed to work on the project full-time. From this came FF Developments and the Ferguson P99 four-wheel-drive Formula One car that won the Oulton Park Gold Cup in 1961 with Stirling Moss at the wheel. The company became a particularly successful transmissions innovator. Gearboxes and differentials were supplied to many top vehicle manufacturers; the McLaren F1 and Jaguar XJ220, both of which raced at Le Mans, used product from the company. Son Stuart joined his father in 1981, becoming chief executive five years later. In 1994 FF Developments was sold to Ricardo, which brings the story neatly back to Le Mans. The Audi R8s

In 1955 "tall, good looking" Tony Rolt, now 37, told the *Daily Express* that he could no longer spare time for regular racing and that the famous sportscar partnership had ended. "I just dare not commit myself to another season of racing with all the travelling and practising and preparation it involves. But I hope I shall get a drive occasionally." Together Rolt and Hamilton had competed in six Le Mans together, covering around 12,500 miles at about 100mph. *(Tony Rolt collection)*

THE INVETERATE ESCAPER

Tony Rolt, then a serving officer in the Rifle Brigade, was captured in the early days of the Second World War during the fighting around Calais, although not before earning the first of two Military Crosses. There was never any clear order to cease fire, but his platoon found itself the opposite side of a concrete wall to a host of Germans with large numbers of British soldiers surrendering around them.

On the march from Calais to a camp on the Austrian border he made the first of a number of attempts for freedom, jumping into a ditch with two others, one of whom was an airman. They eventually found a Fiesler Storch plane, but could not get near it and the RAF type wandered off, not to be seen again. Rolt and his remaining companion eventually walked into a German outpost and were recaptured.

A year later Rolt found himself in Biberach, 60 kilometres from the Swiss border. In the August he and a Royal Engineer walked out of the camp dressed as workmen. Always thirsty, and in conditions that changed from very hot in the day to cold at night, they made their way to very near Switzerland before walking into a German border guard with an Alsatian dog. They were taken to the border post where they could actually see over to Switzerland. The result was solitary confinement for a fortnight.

Nine months followed in a "ghastly old fort" at Posen, in Poland. There, he and his companions tried bribing a sentry and also carried out a diversionary action during which they hid under the castle's bridge, but they were found, the resulting punishment being more solitary confinement. At his next camp, Warburg, he and a colleague tried dressing as plumbers with the idea of walking through the gate. Unfortunately, Rolt's lack of German saw that attempt foiled.

His next try met with more success. A team of five dressed as members of a Swiss Red Cross commission. They watched the genuine group arrive at the camp and, after waiting a suitable length of time, walked out, two of them as civilians, the others as German soldiers. Rolt, clad in mackintosh and slouch hat, was one of the former. For two days they walked and then, helped by the fact that two of their number were fluent German speakers, caught a train. Seeing an "officious looking bunch" of police on the train, they decided to bail out and were caught trying to head out of the town in daylight.

Another attempt at disguise involved a party escorting a 'German general' (actually a Sapper colonel, 'Tubby' Broomhall) from the Eichstadt camp in Bavaria. Rolt admits that the idea, which was quickly foiled, was not the best that they had.

In February 1944 he was transferred to that home for persistent escapers, *Oflag IVC* – Colditz Castle. It was here that he had the idea that arguably made him as famous as the 1953 Le Mans win. It was Rolt who thought of the plan to build a glider and actually fly out of the castle. Aerodynamicist Bill Goldfinch (RAF) designed the contraption and the team of Rolt, Jack Best (RAF) and 'Stooge' Wardle (Royal Navy) built it behind a false wall in the attic. The idea was that the four should draw lots when the time came to find the pair who would escape this way, but in the winter of 1944 they were ordered not to use it; the climate had changed and escapees were now being shot. The massacre of the *Stalag Luft III* airmen, following 'the Great Escape', had shocked all.

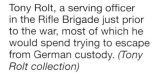

Tony Rolt, a serving officer in the Rifle Brigade just prior to the war, most of which he would spend trying to escape from German custody. *(Tony Rolt collection)*

Mechanic Frank Rainbow holds the wheel chock, Tony Rolt stands to the right, now with a visor in his hand and Lofty England just behind him, as Duncan Hamilton prepares to set off after the final pit stop of 1954. Rolt had been driving brilliantly considering that, wearing goggles, his vision was seriously impaired by the torrential rain. *(Duncan Hamilton collection)*

The 1954 race was a dramatic one, held in sometimes appalling conditions. Rolt and Hamilton put up an impressive fight, the former, who said Hamilton was "on terrific form" taking a trip into the Arnage sandbank when carved up by a Talbot driver. Misfiring and controversial pit stops also worked against the team and at the end they were still about 2.5 miles behind the winning Ferrari. *(Duncan Hamilton collection)*

that won five times from 2000 to 2005 all used Ricardo gearboxes.

Hamilton raced on after 1955, but the following year he was sacked by England for winning the Reims 12-hour race. Having been 'robbed' of certain victory there the year before, he was in no mood to slow down for one of his team-mates as instructed. England told him he would not be driving for Jaguar at Le Mans; within two hours Enzo Ferrari had asked him to join his team and he had accepted. He was teamed with the Spanish aristocrat Alfonso de Portago. The pair was fastest in practice for Le Mans, but de Portago was involved in a second-lap crash that also wrecked two works Jaguars. The Spaniard remarked that it was as well that it had been he who had had the accident, otherwise Hamilton might have been accused of writing off his former team's cars on purpose. As it was, the crash meant that he did not get to drive in the race that year.

A letter is still in existence from 'Fon' de Portago, dated April 16 the following year, in which the *Marchese* stated that Andre Dubonnet had bought the previous year's Talbots and was looking for drivers for Le Mans. He had recommended Hamilton to Dubonnet and suggested that he write to him. Within less than a month the Spaniard and his co-driver Ed Nelson had been killed in Italy, along with 10 spectators, their accident resulting in the end of the fabled Mille Miglia.

From now on Hamilton was to drive his own cars at Le Mans, sharing his D-type in 1957 with Masten Gregory. During the night he complained to his pit about "pedestrians" on the track – other drivers walking back having abandoned their cars. This was the year that an exhaust pipe fractured, the flames cutting into the monocoque. Asked how the car was, Gregory, who had been driving at the time, said it was fine when it was not on fire. A plate of bulletproof steel was clandestinely cut from a police armoured car and bolted to the floor of the Jaguar; today it sits on the wall in Adrian Hamilton's office. The labour put the car back into last place, but then Hamilton and Gregory worked hard and eventually finished sixth, desperately trying to overtake the fifth-place Ferrari and give Jaguar a clean sweep of the top six.

The other time that Hamilton came close to a second Le Mans victory was in 1958. Recalling that year, Adrian says that his father "really should have won the race." He certainly drove brilliantly. Twenty hours into the event Hamilton and his co-driver Ivor Bueb were just one lap behind the leading Ferrari. The chances were that the drivers of the Italian cars would have to put too much strain on their drum brakes in order to maintain their lead over the disc-braked D-type. Suddenly, there was thunder and lightning. Hamilton should have been in his element, but a Panhard had stopped right in the middle of the road near Arnage. The inside of the French car had misted up and the driver, vision totally gone, had ground to a halt. Even today, Hamilton's son Adrian has things to say about that Frenchman. One of the Jaguar's wheels got onto the grass and the car spun off the track backwards, hitting a bank before somersaulting and landing across a drainage ditch. Hamilton fell from the car into the water, to be saved by a couple of sheltering spectators. He believed that if the cockpit of the car had not fallen across the ditch he would have been killed.

The magazines of the day made light of Hamilton's wounds, and it is true that his legs were not broken. However, the ligaments were damaged and the pain was real. "The legs weren't exactly up to Olympic running standards," recalls Adrian. John Coombs, his entrant in saloon car racing, was the first to see him in hospital and was appalled to find that he was "steaming", for no-one had removed his sodden clothes. It could have been worse: Hamilton said that earlier in the race an unknown spectator had thrown his hat in front of his car to warn him of impending trouble. A privately entered Jaguar D-type had crashed, its driver, the Frenchman Pierre Brousselet, who raced under the pseudonym 'Mary', having been fatally injured. "If I had not braked I could not have avoided two cars in an accident round the bend," Hamilton told the press.

Hamilton was to drive in one last major race, the 1958 Tourist Trophy at Goodwood, using his own D-type; he was still walking with crutches. In the months

Hamilton ran his own entry during his last two years at Le Mans. The team personnel list for 1957 makes fascinating reading.

In 1957 Alfonso de Portago wrote to Hamilton suggesting a possible Talbot drive for Le Mans. However, the Englishman returned to Jaguar.

Tony Rolt collaborated with former tractor manufacturer Harry Ferguson on four-wheel drive development. One result was the Ferguson P99 Formula One car that came first in the 1961 Oulton Park Gold Cup. Peter Westbury, seen here demonstrating the car at Shelsley Walsh in 2005, also used it to win the RAC British Hill Climb Championship in 1964. (Author)

Duncan Hamilton took son Adrian to his first Le Mans 24-Hours in 1965, travelling down in a Ferrari 250 2+2. One of the drivers of the winning Ferrari 250LM that year was the American Masten Gregory, who had been his father Duncan's co-driver in 1957. Adrian recalls, perhaps not unexpectedly, "it was all rather exciting."

That was the first of 31 Le Mans that he has been to. He has run eight cars himself during that time including Porsche 911S, Chevron and Ford GT40. In 1984 he was team manager for the Paul Vestey/Charles Ivey Racing Porsche 956 driven by Alain de Cadenet, Chris Craft and the Australian Allan Grice. De Cadenet brought the car in for an unscheduled pit stop at about 7.00pm "in a right panic" saying that he had a puncture in the left-hand front tyre. "I went round the car and then came back and told Alain that he had not got a puncture. He hadn't even got a wheel on the car…"

Hamilton also assisted his father's old friend James Tilling in doing the English language commentary during the mid-1970s. At the time he was a hay fever sufferer, which meant that the commentary was interspersed with much sneezing and blowing of the nose. Such was the impression that he made on one spectator that a letter was sent to *Motoring News* referring to "Mr Hamilton's rather inept commentary."

"So I gave up that job." He did, though, retain his commentator's armband from 1973 on which James Tilling's name had been crossed off and his own written on. The give-away legend '73' was subsequently covered with a passport-sized photograph of himself, and this is what Adrian has used to get into and around the Le Mans track on every visit since. "It's never failed!"

The year prior to the acquisition of this rather useful armband, Adrian had attended as a member of the press corps, having applied as a motoring correspondent of *Exchange & Mart*…

The Le Mans 24-Hours has been part of the Hamilton family's life since 1950, yet the appeal does not seem to diminish. "It is a wonderful race," says Adrian. "It's still a magical event. You could have a dozen 24-hour races about the world, but none would be like Le Mans itself."

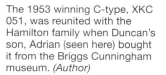

The 1953 winning C-type, XKC 051, was reunited with the Hamilton family when Duncan's son, Adrian (seen here) bought it from the Briggs Cunningham museum. *(Author)*

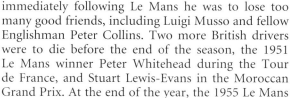

immediately following Le Mans he was to lose too many good friends, including Luigi Musso and fellow Englishman Peter Collins. Two more British drivers were to die before the end of the season, the 1951 Le Mans winner Peter Whitehead during the Tour de France, and Stuart Lewis-Evans in the Moroccan Grand Prix. At the end of the year, the 1955 Le Mans winner and 1958 World Champion Mike Hawthorn was killed in an accident on the Portsmouth road near Guildford; Hamilton went to identify his body at Guildford Mortuary.

The following April he gave a dinner party at the Royal Thames Yacht Club to announce his retirement from racing.

——————————— CHAPTER 12 ———————————

ECURIE ECOSSE

"I have brought you into the ring, now see if you can dance."
(attributed to William Wallace)

There will be those who claim that the most patriotic British assaults made on Le Mans were not by green cars but, until commercialism stepped in, ones that were coloured blue. On their flanks was the cross of St Andrew. The name may have sounded French, but that only served to add to the mystique of Ecurie Ecosse and the Le Mans 24-Hours. Scot Innes Ireland, who first received the call to test for it in 1957, pointed out that the team then "was a magic name in motor racing." He was given his chance to drive for it at Le Mans in 1959.

The majority of British victories at La Sarthe have been by factory-entered cars. Before the Second World War, John Duff and Fox and Nicholl entered winning cars, but since then the only example has been by this charismatic equipe. Where others have – sometimes manfully – failed, the Scots have scored twice.

It is said that Ecurie Ecosse founder David Murray reckoned his team's Jaguar D-type should have won the Goodwood Nine-Hours sportscar race in 1956; it was his belief that a lap scoring error had handed the victory to Aston Martin. The team's biographer Graham Gauld refers to a theory that it was then that Murray threatened to get his own back on Aston and decided to enter for Le Mans.

The team was initially a bunch of Scots often using their own cars brought together under the one banner by Murray, a chartered accountant, who had raced up to Grand Prix level before crashing in practice for the 1950 German Grand Prix. Some say this event was the start of Ecurie Ecosse, Gauld says not, but it was at about this time that he put forward the idea to run a team of young Scottish drivers. Gauld was to be a part of the Ecurie Ecosse story right through, accompanying the team as a young journalist in its early days and reforming it with Hugh McCaig in 1983.

In the beginning, legendary mechanic 'Wilkie' Wilkinson provided the technical expertise and Murray's car repair business in a cobbled Edinburgh backwater, Merchiston Mews, became the team's headquarters. Initially the team consisted of Jaguar XK120 owners Bill Dobson, Sir James Scott Douglas and Ian Stewart, Dobson winning on the team's first outing at its local track Charterhall. In the next decade Ecurie Ecosse notched up around 68 wins. Other drivers joined, and by the time the team's first era ended over 50 top drivers had driven the distinctive cars in their patriotic metallic blue, including two world champions.

The team might have had plenty of experience in the first half of the 1950s racing Jaguar C-types and such as Cooper-Bristol and a Connaught. However, Le Mans 1956 was a major undertaking. Gauld talks of the "dedicated and sometimes inexperienced amateurs" who went forth on its behalf.

Of the two drivers entered for Le Mans, Ninian

Halfway through the 1956 race the Ecurie Ecosse D-type of Flockhart (seen here) and Sanderson was just 19 seconds behind the leading Aston Martin. It moved into first place in the morning and raced on to victory. *(LAT Photographic)*

99

Ninian Sanderson is the focus of attention on the crowded pit balcony as he leaps into the 1956 winning D-type. *(LAT Photographic)*

Sanderson saw it as an excuse for a wild weekend. His team-mate Ron Flockhart, driving down the Mulsanne straight towards the end of the race with no other cars and no spectators in sight, just the occasional *gendarme*, reckoned he was taking "a pleasant drive down a fast stretch of French highway."

Certainly, the intensity of the previous few years was not present. Mercedes-Benz and Maserati were missing, but there were still works Jaguar and Ferrari teams and Ecurie Ecosse's D-type was an unmodified one straight from the sales catalogue. Sanderson and Flockhart drove consistently throughout, for much of the race battling with the Aston Martin of Stirling Moss and Peter Collins. *Autocar* said "there could have been no more popular winner." The trackside loudspeakers played pipe music and, perhaps predictably, *Autocar*'s headline ran "Flying Scotsmen".

The Le Mans win – the first by a private team for some years – meant that Ecurie Ecosse was definitely in Jaguar's good books and the team was offered three D-types under very favourable terms. In return it had to enter for all the races in the World Sports Car Championship.

Although Ecurie Ecosse had won in 1956, David Murray discounted hopes of victory before the 1957 race, such was the quality of the opposition. However, from having been a surprise winner, his team was now seen in a very different light when it returned to La Sarthe with two of the D-types. The winning pairing had been split up, with Flockhart sharing with 1955 victor Ivor Bueb and Sanderson with Jock Lawrence. One nearly failed to make the race when team manager 'Wilkie' Wilkinson, doing about 180mph, narrowly avoided an old Citroen, the driver of which was quite entitled to be on what was, at that point, an open road.

The race proved to be highly competitive with a fantastic pace being set from the start. In the early stages Flockhart and Bueb held back in fifth place with the leading Jaguar, but the pace took its inevitable toll and the Jaguars moved magnificently to the front, led by the two Scottish cars. "A 'three-hour Grand Prix', then Britannia took over," said *Road & Track* magazine.

Gauld records that when his two cars crossed the finishing line – the Flockhart/Bueb car having covered a new record distance – Murray could not believe it. Certainly his team had proved that the previous year had not been, as some had dared to say, a fluke. There was to be no hat-trick though and both the team's Jaguars retired with holed pistons during the first hour of the 1958 race. Wilkinson believed that the fuel supplied might have been causing detonation. One of the D-types was back at Le Mans the following year, to be joined by a Jaguar-engined Tojeiro, but again both cars retired.

The D-type was surely long in the tooth by then, but Innes Ireland recalled it as "a gem," a revelation after the Lotus Eleven he had driven the year before. In practice, having been told by Masten Gregory that he was braking at the 200-yard marker before the Esses, Ireland tried to emulate his co-driver and, crossed up and sideways, frightened himself. Then he discovered that the American had meant another board much further from the bend; indeed, Ireland's own choice of braking point.

Practising for a Stirling Moss-style getaway prior to setting off for France, Ireland had been caught by Ecurie Ecosse's burly chief mechanic, who asked "what the hell" he was doing. There was no way his fellow Scot was going to allow Ireland to risk breaking the screen by trying to jump over it.

Fearing to admit that he had gone off the road during the race, but faced with a list of lap times that showed one to be much longer than the rest, Ireland invented a story of slower cars and baulking. The next day a newspaper showed a photo of him pushing the D-type on the escape road. By 11.00am Ireland and Gregory were up to second place and another Le Mans victory for the Scottish team looked a possibility. However, a con-rod decided otherwise.

Ecurie Ecosse continued to race at Le Mans, and the long-nosed car that had won in 1957, XKD 606, reappeared there three years later with Bruce Halford joining Flockhart this time. New regulations meant that it now had a high screen and a boot, ostensibly for carrying luggage. The team's luck had run out, though, and again a retirement was posted, this time when a broken crankshaft caused the car to end its race at Arnage.

There was no way in which the D-type could any longer be made competitive. In the December Ecurie Ecosse sold its last one, the 1957 winner, to another Scot, Jack Wober, thus at least keeping it north of the border for a short while longer. In 1962 it was crashed heavily by Richard Wrottesley. The subsequent rebuild and the fact that the damaged front frame was removed led to a confusing situation whereby two XKD 606s eventually emerged.

The Ecurie Ecosse entries for 1961 were for very different machines, one of them the Cooper Monaco for Halford and Tommy Dickson that the team had already raced seemingly everywhere from Charterhall to Watkins Glen. An Austin-Healey Sprite was also entered, which understandably came as a considerable surprise when it was announced; Sanderson and Bill Mackay were down to drive it. Scrutineering was a nightmare that year and much had to be done to both cars in order to placate the officials.

In the race the Cooper was doing fairly well when it started to rain. The six-feet tall Halford, having problems with the high regulation screen, hit a patch of resurfaced track just after the pits. He crashed into the banking and was thrown out, badly damaging his leg. Shortly afterwards Mackay had a major accident in the Sprite at White House, and again the driver was seriously injured. His father, a surgeon, flew out to France and, although not allowed to operate, supervised the necessary operation. Mackay subsequently recovered but he never raced again, going on instead to become a very successful yachtsman.

In 1962 Ecurie Ecosse entered a new Tojeiro-Climax, only for the car to retire after eight hours when the gearbox seized. The team returned to Scotland in its battered transporter, calling in on a club meeting at Charterhall on the way. It was the last Le Mans for Ecurie Ecosse in the David Murray era. Six years later Murray was summoned to court, accused of non-payment of Income Tax. His answer was to flee to the Canary Islands. Ecurie Ecosse staggered on until 1971. Four years later Murray died of a heart attack following what had seemed a minor road accident.

That might have been the end of the story of Ecurie Ecosse and Le Mans if it had not been for a man whom Graham Gauld describes as having been cast in the "David Murray mould," the "ebullient" Hugh McCaig, who had made his money in open-cast mining. He had become involved in the running of the Scottish race circuit Ingliston and in 1983 he came up with the thought that Ecurie Ecosse ought to be revived. The title was now held by a body known as the Friends of Scotland. Gauld, a fellow Ingliston director, arranged a meeting between its representative, the Earl of Elgin, Harry Ballantine, one of the team's later managers, and McCaig, and by the end of the meal Ecurie Ecosse was on its way back to the race tracks in, it was pleasing

The following year Ivor Bueb was Ron Flockhart's partner in the first-placed Jaguar, and is seen here accelerating away from Tertre Rouge and passing the upturned Aston Martin DBR1 of Tony Brooks. (LAT Photographic)

Ron Flockhart drove the last stint of the 1956 race. One of his D-type's hub caps has since become a trophy which has been presented to up-and-coming Scottish drivers, including 1998 Le Mans winner Allan McNish. *(MNF collection)*

to see, an extrovert fashion. Also involved was Ray Mallock, who took on the task of creating a suitable car for the reborn set-up. "I first met Hugh McCaig in Macau in 1981 when he was supporting David Duffield in Formula Atlantic," recalls Mallock. He helped bring their car up to the specification of his own.

Four Ecosse cars were to be built, all conforming to the then current Group C2 'second division' regulations. Apart from the first one they were affectionately known as 'Henry', 'Reggie' and 'Pat', the first of these after its Ford engine, the second because at one stage it had an Austin Rover engine, and the third, well, that was something different. That one was sponsored by Post Office Swiftair, bringing visions of the children's comic character Postman Pat and his little red van…

While the three 'named' Ecosses were built from scratch, the first car was based on the Cosworth DFV-powered De Cadenet that had competed at Le Mans in 1981 under the Dorset Racing banner. The 'new' bodywork was actually from the Nimrod Aston Martin project, in which Mallock was also involved, which had been chopped and channelled to fit. Mallock describes it as simply "a scaled-down Nimrod. If you put the two cars side-by-side you could see the family resemblance." It was a very effective car for Le Mans with very low frontal area and small wheels and tyres. Sitting in the slipstream of a Porsche 956, Mallock was to reach about 220mph, "which was exceptionally fast for 13-inch wheels."

It was an inexpensive way of going international motor racing. After outings at Monza, where the car came second in class, and Silverstone, the car was entered for Le Mans driven by Scots David Leslie and David Duffield and Englishman Mike Wilds. Gauld records that McCaig set off for France in his Bentley Mulsanne Turbo, buying tapes of Andy Stewart along the way to leave Le Mans in no doubt that the Scots were back.

Some things had not changed. Ecurie Ecosse had difficulty in navigating its way through scrutineering again, mainly because the rules regarding the dimension of the pedal box had changed since the De Cadenet was first made. The car was allowed to start, but at the end of the warm-up lap Wilds drove it back into the pits with an electrical fault. Problem traced, it was sent out again only for David Leslie to stop on the Mulsanne straight with a broken washer in the fuel pump – an item worth a mere 20p. Team members set off apace through the Le Mans countryside in search of the car. However, the only work that could be done away from the pits had to be carried out by the driver with tools that were in the car. There were a few basic items taped under the seat but the problem was the washer. In theory a new one could not legally be fitted and there were at least five marshals closely watching the proceedings. Their attention was taken by the sight of two of the mechanics strolling out to the barrier some way from the car. With cars passing by an about 230mph, this was obviously not on and the marshals were looking in their direction as a spare washer was thrown into the cockpit of the Ecosse. However, one of the marshals then marched back towards the car and the team, fearful that the game was up, had to resort to further Scottish cunning. Said marshal was given a bottle of mineral water, which he was asked to give to Leslie. Accompanying this was a plastic cup, which just seemed to have a 100 franc note in it. Problem, in theory, solved. However, fate had the last laugh as the battery was now flat and the engine would not restart.

The car was next entered for a British Grand Prix support race at Brands Hatch, but was written off when a fluid leak caused the rear brakes to fail. A new car, plus spare monocoque, was built that, although visually similar to the original, was in fact a new design by Graham Humphries. Sponsorship came from Bovis Homes, which had backed the Nimrods at Le Mans in 1984. As recounted elsewhere both were crashed and the project was shelved. Bovis transferred its sponsorship to the Ecosse team and when it arrived at Le Mans for the 1985 race it was no longer blue; even the Scots had now lost their racing colours to commercial demands. Richard Williams also moved from being team manager at Nimrod to take a similar position with Ecurie Ecosse, running the team until 1989. Following a C2 class win at Silverstone expectations must have been high for Le Mans, and certainly the car was leading the C2 class at one point. However, a sheared oil pump drive, when all seemed to be going well, put an end to that. A two-car team was planned for the following year, and although Bovis Homes pulled out of the sponsorship, it paid Ecurie Ecosse enough compensation to enable the team to keep going.

Austin Rover was also approached about using its V8 engine, essentially the unit used in the Metro 6R4 rally car. But problems with the engine were discovered just before Le Mans, which meant that the decision had to be taken to run the car below its potential. However, driven by Mallock, Leslie and Wilds, it had spent many laps in the lead of the C2 class by the ninth

IVOR BUEB

In the history of the Le Mans race only five British drivers have won it more than once. Of these Ivor Bueb is arguably the least heralded and it perhaps comes as something of a surprise to learn just how inexperienced he was when he shared the winning Jaguar in 1955 with Mike Hawthorn. Bueb ran a secondhand car business in Cheltenham named after his partner as Ivor Turk Motors. A young Michael MacDowel, who was working in the service department of the nearby Rootes distributor, would often visit the premises and remembers him as "warm-hearted, generous, ready for a laugh" if "overweight" and "quite garrulous."

Bueb started racing in the 500cc Formula Three, becoming a Cooper works driver in 1955 alongside Jim Russell. In September the previous year Jaguar team manager 'Lofty' England had prepared a list of possible drivers for the works D-types with Bueb down as one of four '500cc Types'. He tested at Silverstone, but was told by England that Don Beauman had been chosen instead of him because of his sportscar experience. However, he was called up as a last-minute substitute for Le Mans on the retirement of Jimmy Stewart. The drive to victory with Hawthorn in 1955 was thus his first major race outside Formula Three. However, MacDowel believes that "his

consistency and smoothness" were to make him an ideal driver in the eyes of England.

He also became a mentor to MacDowel, who was racing an 1172cc Lotus Mk 9 at the time, inviting him to share the 1.1-litre class-winning Cooper at the last ever Dundrod Tourist Trophy. For MacDowel this was to lead to a works Cooper drive in the 1957 French Grand Prix and an invitation to be reserve driver for Lister at Le Mans in 1959. Despite the fact that, due to National Service, he had not sat in a racing car for two years, he was sent off at 160mph down the Mulsanne straight with the nose of the car lifting just before the kink. It was at Le Mans that he met Lofty England, the result being that he joined Jaguar in 1960 as, says the company's great historian Andrew Whyte, "chief motor sport wallah." He was also subsequently to become two-time British Hill Climb Champion.

By this time Bueb was a double Le Mans winner having also come first with Ron Flockhart in the Ecurie Ecosse D-type in 1957. However, matters were not going well for him in his private life, and the Formula Two Cooper that he was also racing did not suit his style. Two months later he crashed a Formula One BRP Cooper-Borgward at Clermont-Ferrand and was killed.

hour. Then unfortunately Wilds spun on oil left by a crashed Porsche and was collected by another German machine. Although it took 45 minutes to repair the car, the lead was not lost because the caution flags had gone out following Jo Gartner's tragic accident. Then, at about 200mph, Leslie had a tyre blow at the end of the Mulsanne straight. The resulting crash left the wheel awry and the radiator half torn away, but to David

Leslie such trifles are not reasons to retire. Finding an oil drum of water and a plastic cup, he endeavoured to fill the radiator as full as possible before staggering further down the road. With the temperature rising he stopped again and this time filled the radiator from a standpipe. His third attempt to fill the radiator with water involved raiding a fire engine and eventually he made it back to the pits. However, there was just one

snag. The rules stated that no liquid could be added to a car away from the pits. An ACO official had spied Leslie's efforts, and team manager Williams was told that he should retire. He refused, but it was a futile gesture. The car was disqualified instead.

While all this was going on, the second Ecosse, the previous year's car still with DFV engine and with three American guest drivers, soldiered on to fourth place in the C2 class. It was the first Ecurie Ecosse entry to finish at Le Mans for over two decades, and more was to come that year with Ecurie Ecosse winning the C2 World Championship. It was arguably the best result that the engine – designed for a rally car, remember – ever had, but Austin Rover withdrew its support at the end of the year. That meant the team was back to Cosworth power for the next season, while finance came from the Post Office's Swiftair division. The blue hue was long forgotten; the cars were now red.

Again, one of the cars, driven by Leslie, Mallock and Belgian Marc Duez, took the C2 class lead while two of the previous year's Americans, joined this time by Wilds, ran further back in the field. Once more,

The Ecosse cars were each given nicknames, and here David Leslie kneels beside 'Reggie' before the start of the 1986 race. *(Simon Maurice)*

'Reggie' raced twice in the Le Mans 24-Hours, the first time with the Austin Rover V6 engine, the second with a Cosworth DFL. Mike Wilds (seen here) was the only person to drive it on both occasions. *(Simon Maurice)*

This photo of 'Henry' looks little different to that of 'Reggie' in 1986. The scene is still Le Mans, but the race is the Group C support event of 2004. All three 'named' Ecosses continue to compete in historic racing, 'Henry' and 'Reggie' still using the numbers 78 and 79. *(Author)*

Duncan Hamilton's own D-type sweeps under the Dunlop bridge early in the 1957 race. *(Hamilton collection)*

It may have been relocated and restyled, but the Dunlop bridge continues to be a major feature of the early part of the track. *(Author)*

things seemed to be going well…but this was Le Mans. Exhaust and then clutch problems intervened and drastic methods had to be improvised to get the car out of the pits without a clutch. Then the gears decided that they had had enough, and an hour and a half before the end of the race they had to be changed, which took about 22 minutes.

Yet despite all its problems the car finished second in the C2 class and won the Index of Performance trophy. It was a magnificent attempt, but the cars were now becoming uncompetitive, and it was effectively the last appearance – at least for the time being – for Ecurie Ecosse at Le Mans. There were Ecurie Ecosse stickers on the side of the 1989 C1 Aston Martins, but

the team's involvement in that project has to be seen as minimal.

At the beginning of 2006 a rumour appeared that Ecurie Ecosse might be on its way back to Le Mans with an Aston Martin DBR9. Prodrive boss David Richards was known to have talked to McCaig about the possibility of the team returning to the track a half-century after its famous first victory. At the turn of the year Barry Wood also acquired 'Pat' for his son Tony to race in historic events. It was planned that the car should be run alongside the other two surviving Ecosses – owned by Andrew Smith and McCaig himself – in a squad managed by the latter. One thing seemed certain: Ecurie Ecosse was still very much with us.

The Max Boxstrom-designed Aston Martin AMR1 was originally announced as a joint venture between Aston and Ecurie Ecosse. However, the Scottish team was effectively sidelined and had little say as to what happened during the 1989 season. There were team stickers on the cars, but involvement was minimal. Two AMR1s ran at Le Mans, the Redman/Roe/Los car (seen here) finishing a creditable 11th after suspension damage, the Leslie/Mallock/Sears car retiring with persistent electrical problems. *(Aston Martin)*

Wyer from Aston to Ford

"We could hope only to be respectable." John Wyer did not think there was much chance of another win in 1969. However, by the end of the 24 hours Englishman Jackie Oliver (left with arm raised) had assisted the remarkable Jacky Ickx to victory in the closest contested finish ever seen at Le Mans. With earlier wins in 1959 and 1968 and another to come in the next decade, Wyer was arguably the man of the era. *(LAT Photographic)*

CHAPTER 13

THE BRITISH AT LE MANS 1959-1969

"The old order changeth, yielding place to the new."
(Lord Alfred Tennyson, *The Idylls of the King*)

Motor racing historian David Hodges observed that in winning Le Mans Bentley caught the imagination of the British man in the street. Writing in the mid-1960s, he pointed out that a strong British entry had become almost traditional and, at that stage, one British marque, Aston Martin, had raced at Le Mans more than any other.

In the early 1960s Britain was just at the beginning of its reign as the leading country in world motorsport. The year 1958 was the first that a British driver, Mike Hawthorn, had won the Formula One World Championship. That year was also the first of the Grand Prix Constructors Championship and Vanwall won it, but had it been held in any previous year the British would not have stood a chance. Until then it had only really been the Le Mans wins of Bentley, Lagonda, Jaguar and Aston Martin that had enabled the country to hold its head up in international motor racing.

Now everything was to change. As Cooper, BRM and Lotus spearheaded the British domination of Formula One, so the country's marques began to loosen their grip on Le Mans and there was to be a seismic shift, first to the Italians and then to the Americans. The year 1964 was the last to see entries from Jaguar and Aston Martin for many a long moon. The following year was the last for an MG, although the marque was to reappear many decades later as the badge on what was really a small Lola prototype.

The Ferraris, then the Fords and the Porsches, took over. As the 1970s started so did the period of German domination that has virtually continued to this day. The Aston Martin victory in 1959 would be the last by a truly British, as opposed to just British-built car until that of the Gulf GR8 in 1975, and even that was sponsored by an American oil company. The next time that the name of a British production car manufacturer would be seen on the winner's list would be 1988. The supremacy that British manufacturers enjoyed during the 1920s and 1950s has never really been replicated.

Nevertheless, the 1950s finished well, with Aston Martin coming first and second at Le Mans, which surely, because of the marque's loyalty to Le Mans, was one of the most deserved victories in the history of the event. As usual, Aston Martin did not field the fastest cars. That accolade, Roy Salvadori points out, went to the V12 Ferraris. Speed, though, was not enough. Salvadori credits Stirling Moss as "doing the damage" that caused the Ferrari drivers to over-rev, so laying the foundations of victory for himself and Texan Carroll Shelby. Moss shot off into his customary lead with one of the DBR1/300s. The other two Astons were held back, circulating at a typical John Wyer predetermined speed and, as Salvadori remembers, keeping out of the initial 'Grand Prix'. He and Shelby believed that they had the right mental approach to win such a race and were trying to save the engine and gearbox by late braking and fast cornering. Instead of using up to 5800rpm, they were changing up at about 5400 to 5500rpm. Salvadori was also trying to avoid using first gear, which was not an easy thing to do at the Mulsanne and Arnage corners with a full tank.

After the first hour the Ferraris got into the act and

Roy Salvadori drove for 14 of the 24 hours in 1959, shaking off 'flu on his way to a famous victory. By this time in his career, Salvadori had matured to a consistent driver, second in versatility only, it was claimed, to Stirling Moss. Attention to streamlining that year is said to have given the Aston Martins an additional 10mph on the Mulsanne straight. *(Edward Eves/Ludvigsen Library)*

The traditional 'Le Mans start' was still very much a feature of the race in 1962. Second from the left (car 11) is the Aston Martin P212 in which Graham Hill shot off into the lead. *(Richard Shepherd-Barron collection)*

up front in the early hours of the Sunday morning. The Aston had developed a rear-end vibration and it was a while before this was diagnosed as being caused by a damaged tyre. Team manager Reg Parnell, who discovered the problem, criticized Salvadori for not having identified its cause, which upset the driver and led John Wyer to try to calm him down. Tension was high in the Aston pit.

Wyer was right in his attitude; this was the year that Aston was not to be denied. Late in the morning the Ferrari was retired with overheating and the two DBR1s moved into an impregnable first and second positions. Salvadori recalls being very tired during the event, but nevertheless he drove hard for the maximum 14 hours allowed. (Shelby was suffering from a stomach bug before the race and was worried that he might not last the distance.) Salvadori says the race, in which he continuously feared gearbox trouble, was "good and bad." He still bears the scars on his right foot, which was badly burnt by the heat from the exhaust. As the others celebrated, he fell asleep, exhausted, missing the presentation.

Funnily, Salvadori remembers his earlier times at Le Mans with more clarity. "We had some real tussles." He admits to never having really liked the Le Mans race itself, but he believed that he belonged to "a wonderful team" and he certainly enjoyed the times that the team had at La Chartre.

The win at Le Mans was just one part of a great year for Aston Martin, which also won the World Sports Car Championship, something that Jaguar was not

swapped the lead with the Moss/Fairman car. However, this was to retire with valve failure and, at one point the lone Ecurie Ecosse Jaguar D-type of Innes Ireland and Masten Gregory moved into second place before retiring with a broken con-rod (Salvadori remembers a 'fun' tussle with the Scot). The Ferraris also ran into trouble, and into the lead came the Salvadori/Shelby DBR1.

The Ferraris had not given up, one of them moving

The tail end of the 1962 race gets away including the Sunbeam Alpine (car 33) of Paddy Hopkirk and Peter Jopp. Thomas Harrington Ltd had re-profiled the boot and rear wings of the car so that they were level. Despite having the bearings changed in droll circumstances, the Alpine retired on the Sunday morning leaving Irish rally star Hopkirk with a long walk back to the pits. *(LAT Photographic)*

ROY SALVADORI

The significance of Le Mans 1959 to Roy Salvadori can be seen in the fact that he devoted the whole of the introduction to his autobiography with a description of what it was like that year. Anxiety over the Aston Martin's gearbox, 167mph down the Mulsanne straight, unease over slower cars and the early morning mists, it is all there, on just one page, painting a picture as only a Le Mans winner can. His co-driver Carroll Shelby carried out the final stint with Salvadori sitting in the pits "full of anxiety and hope. The last lap, he said, seemed as if it would never end. Then finally, "anti-climax, the pain of my feet, burned on the DBR1's exhaust, the so-welcome sleep back at La Chartre." John Wyer said that Salvadori drove a textbook race that year, pacing the car to victory.

Salvadori was an archetypal English racing driver of the 1950s, a dashing figure with a flamboyant driving style. He delighted in driving a wide range of cars, seemingly competing in as many races a day as he could possibly manage. Between 1952 and 1962 he raced in 46 Grands Prix, starting at the wheel of Bobbie Baird's Ferrari Tipo 500 and ending his Formula One career with a works Lola-Climax.

He regards one of his best drives as having been in the 1956 British Grand Prix in which he was running second in his Maserati 250F before having to make a pit stop. He was also involved with such as Connaught, Vanwall, BRM and Cooper and became racing manager for the latter on his retirement from race driving.

The first eight of his drives at Le Mans were all with the works Aston Martin team. He retired on six consecutive occasions before finally finishing the race...in the one position that really mattered. A third and fourth were also to follow in subsequent years. Salvadori remained loyal to Aston Martin, his first non-works drive at Le Mans being in 1960 when he drove with Jim Clark for the Border Reivers team at, of course, the wheel of an Aston Martin DBR1. Only in his final two years at La Sarthe did he forsake Aston to drive Jaguar E-types for Briggs Cunningham. Wyer summed up Salvadori's loyalty: "Today…such fidelity may seem a dubious distinction. In the climate of the period, and to me in particular, it had great significance."

As far as Wyer was concerned, Salvadori, despite initially not being a long-distance driver by temperament, became one of the greatest and most intelligent exponents of endurance racing. No man was in a better position to make such an assessment than the Aston Martin team manager.

Wyer was involved in the postscript to Salvadori's Le Mans career. He particularly wanted him to be involved in the development of the Ford GT40. Salvadori accepted, unaware that Wyer was not in overall charge of the project. At the Le Mans test weekend fears gained in earlier trials were confirmed and Salvadori found that the car was both lifting and handling badly. The first day, at 165mph, a door blew off on the Mulsanne straight. The following day the car lifted just before the Mulsanne corner and landed crabwise. Salvadori had to brake hard for the bend and hit the concrete barrier. Unnerved by the whole programme, he sent back his retainer, although Ford did insist on his keeping it.

Wyer felt a sense of loss having to go ahead without Salvadori, but admired him for this decision. "Motor racing", he said, "must be based on mutual confidence between the driver and those responsible for the preparation of the car." Wyer mused on the fact that he and Salvadori perhaps came from a different, less commercial era. Within two years Salvadori had retired, his last race (at Goodwood), perhaps ironically, being at the wheel of the now vastly improved Ford GT40. He finished second, winning the GT class.

Roy Salvadori showed great loyalty to John Wyer, a quality that was rewarded with victory in the 1959 race. In addition to being one of the great sportscar drivers of the period, Salvadori competed in a total of 46 Grands Prix between 1952 and 1962. *(LAT Photographic)*

On the very first lap of the 1963 race Pat Fergusson outbraked himself into the Mulsanne corner and ended up in the sand. However, after much effort he was able to dig out the Lotus Elite he was sharing with John Wagstaff, the pair going on to win the 1300cc class. *(John Wagstaff collection)*

able to achieve until the late 1980s. In addition to Le Mans, the Feltham team also won at the Nürburgring and at Goodwood, three victories from a five-race series. It was observed that the championship was well deserved, and with its "stringent standards" the Aston competition department was being likened to that of Mercedes-Benz.

It also has to be said that there were 19 British cars at the race that year representing seven marques. But apart from the Astons, only the AC Ace of Ted Whiteaway and John Turner and the Lotus Elites of Peter Lumsden/Peter Riley and Jim Clark/Sir John Whitmore finished. This was the first of three consecutive Le Mans races for future World Champion Clark.

We now pass into the age of Ferrari and Ford, although Clark made a great start the next year in the Border Reivers-entered DBR1. By the end of the first lap five cars had passed him, but come 4.00pm on the Sunday the Aston of Clark and Roy Salvadori crossed the line in third place, surrounded by six Ferraris. A notable British success came with first place in the Index of Thermal Efficiency, of which more later, for the Lotus Elite of John Wagstaff and Tony Marsh. There were also class wins for the MGA of Ted Lund and Colin Escott, the French-entered Elite of Roger Masson and Claude Laurent and the Austin-Healey 'Sebring' Sprite of John Dalton and John Colgate.

Clark was first away in 1961 but led only as far as Tertre Rouge. Again he was at the wheel of a Border Reivers DBR1 and again he was partnered by a former winner, in this case Ron Flockhart. Their car was to retire during the 11th hour with clutch failure, but only after Clark had shown why he was to become the best driver of his, perhaps any, era. Former partner Salvadori this year shared with South African Tony Maggs. Their DBR1 also ran a great race, but old age caught up with it in the 19th hour. The year before had been the last for the Jaguar D-type, and now the Aston Martin DBR1 had performed its swansong. The highest placed British car was the ninth-place Triumph of Keith Ballisat/Peter Bolton, the Triumphs

SO NEARLY A LE MANS RACER

This is the story of the man who never raced at Le Mans. Back in 1959 a team could nominate just one reserve driver for all of its cars. Christopher Martyn held that position for Lotus, which had entered a variety of models ranging from the fleet little 750cc Seventeens to a Fifteen Series 3 with a 2½-litre engine. Originally he had been entered to drive a Lotus Elite, which had proved "dreadfully slow" in practice. After the Thursday session, Brit Pearce, who had been mechanic to Mike Hawthorn, went to take the car back to the team's base "and wrote it off completely." Martyn recounts that he was found by the side of the road still sitting in the seat "with bits of fibreglass all over the place."

Martyn confesses that he saw himself as little more than an experienced Lotus Eleven club racer. In practice for Le Mans he did drive the 750cc cars, but not the Fifteen. However, before long into the race all the Lotus entries apart from the Fifteen had dropped out. At the wheel of the surviving car was Grand Prix driver Graham Hill, who at one point had brought it up to seventh place overall.

Come night-time, says Martyn, and Hill's co-driver, the Australian Derek Jolly, was sitting on a folding canvas chair on the pit counter waiting to take over. Now Le Mans, of course, can be a dangerous place, sometimes in unpredictable ways, and all of a sudden Jolly's chair gave way, toppling him over the back of the counter. He split his head on the petrol bowser and was forced to

have stitches in his scalp. For such incidents were reserve drivers invented, so Lotus boss Colin Chapman informed Martyn that eventually he would have to take over the Fifteen from Hill. "I'd never even sat in the car and I said so," says Martyn. "I'd never even raced at Le Mans." Chapman's answer was to tell him not to worry and just to "keep the car on the island."

"I froze, so Chapman told me to go and have a kip in the caravan…which was about 40 yards from the track. Could I sleep? I was s**t scared."

Eventually Martyn dozed off into a fitful sleep only to waken about half an hour before he was due to drive and hear the Tannoy reporting that Hill's Lotus was out of the race. "All I can remember is a sense of tremendous relief."

The following year Martyn was one of those chosen to drive the ill-fated 2-litre Lotus Elite, but following Jonathan Sieff's serious accident in practice that car was withdrawn.

While Martyn may understandably have felt relief in 1959 at not having to drive an unfamiliar car round an unfamiliar track as the early morning mists swirled around, or a year later an unsorted car that the drivers felt to be positively lethal, he now muses on what might have been. He could, perhaps, have been the man who helped the 1962 and 1968 World Champion to his first top-10 position at Le Mans. *Les Vingt-Quatre Heures* is full of buts, as is any motor race, BUT this one concerns a man who never actually raced there…

demonstrating reliability and winning the George Durand team award. The Index of Thermal Efficiency went to Britain for the second time, this year won by the Sunbeam Alpine Harrington of Peter Harper and Peter Procter. The award also came to this country in 1962, returning to Team Elite, its Lotus this time driven by David Hobbs and Frank Gardner.

The year 1962 also saw the debacle of the Lotus 23s, a story that does not reflect well on the ACO. These little cars had already proved incredibly fast and were seen as great favourites to beat the French entries to both the Index of Performance and Index of Thermal Efficiency awards. Two were entered, one using a 997cc Ford Cosworth 105E engine, the other a 750cc Coventry Climax FWMC unit. The scrutineers looked at the cars and decided that they had oversize fuel tanks, their turning circle was too large, their ground clearance was insufficient and, wait for it, their front wheels had four studs while the rears had six. All four wheels, said the ACO, had to have the same number of studs.

Lotus founder Colin Chapman thrived on challenges. The first three problems were solved at the track. Meanwhile, back at the factory in England new four-stud rear hubs were designed and machined and flown to Le Mans to be fitted just before scrutineering came to an end. The head scrutineer now decided that if the car had originally used six studs at the rear, then a mere four must be unsafe. Lotus' Mike Costin pointed out that the six-stud hub had been designed for when a much larger engine was used. There was no real argument so the officials finally decided that the Lotus 23 was "not in the spirit of the race." Chapman was understandably incensed and no works Lotus was ever entered for Le Mans again. Asked recently whether he had ever seen the 24-hour race, Chapman's

The Mike Salmon/Peter Sutcliffe Aston Martin DB4 GT ran strongly in 1964 and was in eighth place in the 19th hour when it was forced to stop for oil before the permitted number of laps had been completed. Disqualification was the unfortunate result. *(Mike Salmon collection)*

son Clive smiled and said: "We Chapmans don't go to Le Mans."

Occasionally the ACO does seem to act in an unfair manner to British entries. Why, for example, was the Mirage M12 really wheeled off the grid in 1982, and why was the works Zytek 04S refused an entry in 2005? One could point out that the latter beat the Pescarolo entry in the Spa 1000kms earlier in the season and that, without the Zytek, the Pescarolos were favourites to win that year. To do so is to run the risk of indulging in idle speculation, but there are those who saw a similarity to 1962.

The start of the 1967 race illustrates a strong British element in that year's driver line-up. The Ford GT40 (car 62) and Lola-Aston Martin SL73 (car 11) featured all-English crews in Mike Salmon/Brian Redman and John Surtees/ David Hobbs respectively. The two Ferrari 330 P4s had one British driver apiece, Peter Sutcliffe in car 19 and Michael Parkes in car 21. David Piper was one of the drivers of the Mirage M1 that is following close behind the Parkes/ Scarfiotti car that finished second overall. *(Mike Salmon collection)*

In the mid-1960s Lotus Elite and Brabham BT8 driver Roger Nathan approached Frank Costin, who had designed bodies for Vanwall, Lister and Lotus, to help him build his own sports-racing cars. In addition to preparing Elites, Nathan ran a business retailing tuning kits for Hillman Imps, so it was not surprising that the results were initially powered by the 1-litre engine from one of the little Rootes Group cars. In 1967 the pair developed an attractive GT version, which was designed primarily to race at Le Mans. Rootes produced a special block for the car and Lucas – this is significant to the story – came up with aircraft-specification wiring especially for the 24-Hours.

The GT was finished only three weeks before the race and Nathan even wondered whether the team should still compete at Le Mans. However, it was decided to go ahead and during 75 laps of testing at Snetterton the car "never missed a beat."

For the race, Nathan was teamed with Mike Beckwith and Frenchman Franck Ruata, and for all three it would be their only Le Mans race. Scrutineering was overcome without difficulty, perhaps to Nathan's surprise. It was his aim to win the Index of Thermal Efficiency and, as it was generally believed that this had been introduced by the ACO to give the French cars something to win, he had studied the regulations meticulously to ensure that there should be no problems at this stage. From then on, though, it was downhill all the way.

During practice the Imp engine started to misfire and just would not run properly, while the hydraulics also began to play up, causing the brakes to bind and the clutch to slip.

Air was being sucked out of the GT cowling and, in an effort to solve the resulting mixture problem, the cowling was converted into a "giant airbox." But the misfiring continued and then a head gasket blew. Eventually the troubles seemed to go away and the Costin-Nathan was qualified in 53rd place.

The car ran for the first four hours of the race, but the puzzling misfire returned and eventually Nathan decided to withdraw the car. The team members returned to their hotel on the Mulsanne straight to find that their rooms had been let to somebody else for the night.

Back in the UK, Nathan found it was the special wiring supplied by Lucas – in theory an improvement over the standard product – that was the main culprit. A tiny spring, worth pennies, had also broken in the needle valve in one of the downdraught Weber carburettors.

The Costin-Nathan cars, which became known as Astras from 1968, had a short but otherwise successful history with over 30 cars being built. A quick glance at the record books would indicate that none were to race at Le Mans again, but in point of fact one did, although it was entered as a Moynet-Simca XS and was powered by a 1.2-litre Simca engine.

By the 1960s British entries were now beginning to look more like GT cars. In 1960 the American Briggs Cunningham had entered the Jaguar E2A, a link between the past and what was to come. A year later there were Aston Martin DB4 GT Zagatos in the race as well as the DBR1s. The DB4s were back in 1962, but now the Jaguar E-types had joined the fray. Salvadori partnered entrant Cunningham in the most successful of these, coming third, one place ahead of another E-type, that of the Peters Sargent and Lumsden.

A works Aston Martin was also entered again that year, one of 16 British cars, and while the 212 was undoubtedly a prototype, it at least looked like a GT. Chased by a hoard of Italian cars, it also led for the first lap, something that looks like a habit for Aston during these years. The driver this time, though, was Jim Clark's great Formula One adversary Graham Hill.

There was plenty of British interest in the smaller classes during these years, but up front Ferrari was having it all its own way. British drivers, if they appeared on the rostrum, did so because they drove the charismatic Italian cars. Thus Michael Parkes was second in 1961, third two years later, then second again in 1967, while World Champions Graham Hill and John Surtees finished second and third respectively in 1964. It was, said Hill after his first experience with the Rover-BRM, pleasant to be back again in a car that could win. Writing in his autobiography in 1969, Hill reckoned it had probably been the best performance he would ever have had at Le Mans. He got that one wrong, as we will see.

In 1963 Cunningham turned up with three lightweight competition Jaguar E-types, while Aston Martin had three works cars, a pair of DB4 GTs and the 215, which was based on the 212 of the year before. One of the Cunningham E-types, that of Cunningham and Grossman, took the 4-litre class. Roy Salvadori in another of the American's Jaguars had to brake hard when the engine of Bruce McLaren's DB4 GT exploded in front of him on the Mulsanne straight and covered the track in oil. The E-type skidded, turned over and caught fire, but Salvadori escaped with just bruised legs; the driver of a following Alpine was less lucky… There was little cause to celebrate at the end of the race, with the Rover-BRM, of which more anon, the best of the British. At least it would have been had it not been running in a race of its own.

While Ford took on Ferrari in the mid-1960s, so the British seemed content to run round looking for class wins. In 1964 this meant just the 1300cc category for a Team Elite Lotus Elite, repeating the team's victory of the previous year. Twelve months later the 1300cc class again fell to a British car, this time a Donald Healey-entered Austin-Healey Sprite, while the 1½-litre category went to the works Triumph Spitfire of Jean-Jacques Thuner and Simo Lampinen. The Sprite, which was driven by Paul Hawkins and John Rhodes, had arrived at the track painted in fluorescent colours, a livery that had to be changed on the orders of the ACO.

In its swansong year MG scored an 11th place overall with the 'droop snoot' MGB of Paddy Hopkirk and Andrew Hedges, the highest place for the marque since the War. Its race was more or less trouble-free, the only drama being when Hopkirk, who competed six times at Le Mans, fell off his Moulton bicycle in the paddock. One minor problem occurred when a *plombeur* broke the car's fuel filler cap; Marcus Chambers, who was running the Sunbeam pit, came up with a replacement. The car, which won for MG the *Motor* Trophy, averaged 99mph. Quoted in the recent biography on him by Bill Price, Hopkirk now says: "That wasn't bad going, but I don't think Le Mans is a great skills challenge. I wouldn't rate it as my proudest achievement. But because of the publicity and the fact that it was racing rather than rallying, and I was known more as a rally driver, then I suppose I took pride in it from that point of view." Many years later another of Britain's favourite rallying sons, 1995 World Champion Colin McRae, raced a Prodrive-prepared Ferrari 550 Maranello at Le Mans, finishing ninth overall with Darren Turner and Rickard Rydell.

In the year 1964 there were 13 British cars; the next season there were but three; the era of strong British entries was over. The final two years of the decade did,

PADDY HOPKIRK

Paddy Hopkirk first went to Le Mans in 1961, then in 1962, for Sunbeam, co-driving with Peter Jopp. The Irishman recounts how one year, as the regulations stated that oil could not be changed, the mechanics dropped the sump and changed one of the bearings, using tights borrowed from Jopp's fiancée, journalist Judith Jackson, to sieve the oil for metal particles. "We all got very excited about that!" The team eventually retired to their hotel and some "wonderful" fireworks that Jopp had bought. At about 4.00pm, "when people were sneaking back to their rooms," they found their doors booby-trapped with these bangers.

Hopkirk, the famed winner of the 1964 Monte Carlo Rally in a Mini, believes that, certainly in his day, 24-hour races came more naturally to rally drivers than circuit racing specialists. "We were used to driving at 4.00am when you are at your lowest ebb." The Rootes team of Hopkirk, Jopp and Peter Harper perhaps personified this more than any other.

Although he was to race 'the big Healey' – the 3000 – elsewhere, his first BMC entry for Le Mans was in an MGB in 1963. For three years he remained loyal to the 'B', sharing initially with Alan Hutcheson, then with Andrew Hedges, finishing on every occasion and, as recorded in this chapter, coming home in the first British car in the GT class to finish in 1965. The cars were "strong and reliable and beautifully prepared." The factory used all its rallying experience to create a car that could race for 24 hours.

Hopkirk claims that the snout-nosed MGB was timed at over 149mph on the Mulsanne. "I must have been having a bit of a tow by somebody!"

The first year Hutcheson put their MGB in the sand at Mulsanne corner, having to resort to using his helmet to try and dig himself out. Hopkirk recalls that when he took over there was "sand coming out of everywhere."

Hopkirk's final year at Le Mans was 1966, when he was again teamed with Hedges, but this time in an Austin-Healey Sprite. Oil leaks caused both this and the sister car of John Rhodes and Clive Baker to retire during the second half of the race.

Paddy Hopkirk (left) and Andrew Hedges were to finish 19th in the 1964 race. Importantly, their MGB was the highest placed British entry, winning the *Motor* award for that year. Their average speed was just a whisker short of 100mph. *(Paddy Hopkirk collection*

Jack Sears and Mike Salmon drove a consistent race in 1963 to finish in fifth place. Their Ferrari 330 LM was entered by Colonel Ronnie Hoare's Maranello Concessionaires. (*Mike Salmon collection*)

though, have something for the British to smile about. The big Fords, although they may have had the origins in the Lola GT, were seen as truly American. However, the smaller 4.9-litre Ford GT40s were, it must be pointed out, built in Slough. In 1968 the capacity of prototype cars was restricted to 3 litres. However, the Group 4 category, which mandated that at least 50 examples of a model had to be produced, still allowed larger engines. The 4.9-litre GT40s fell into this class and so were given a second lease of life. So, too, did the mighty Lola T70 GTs, which were really sprint cars although one of their number was to win the Daytona 24-Hours.

Three of the GT40s in 1968 were entered in the powder blue-and-orange colours of Gulf Oil, a livery that was to become arguably the most charismatic ever to race at La Sarthe. They were run by a certain John Wyer, of whom more later, but just to remind you, he was the man who masterminded Aston's 1959 victory. For two years Wyer's now anachronistic GT40s took on the faster Porsche 908s and, for two years, they beat them.

It was not an easy task. In the early hours of the 1968 race, Porsches held the top four places with the leading Ford back in 10th. But as the Porsches, as well as the Alfa Romeos and Matras, dropped out or ran

PETER SUTCLIFFE

Peter Sutcliffe, who raced four times at Le Mans between 1964 and 1967, retiring on each occasion, points out the "amazing hold" that the race has on people's emotions. As far as he is concerned he was racing in a "golden period." The tracks were "proper circuits" and drivers knew that if they were "foolish or reckless, they would have an accident and end up hurt. You had to temper a sense of immortality with the fact that you might hit a tree." Nevertheless, he recalls, "I always found the whole thing fun."

Sutcliffe made his Le Mans debut partnering Mike Salmon in the Dawnay Racing Aston Martin DP214. The following year saw him at the wheel of an AC Cobra Daytona entered by Scuderia Filipinetti. "It was the most awful car to drive, it didn't handle, it had no sensitivity." Apart from being very fast down the straight "it didn't have a single redeeming feature. I was very glad when it blew up." However, "the Filipinetti set-up was super."

He remained with Filipinetti for 1966, driving a Ford

GT40, having already purchased a similar car himself the year before. Unfortunately, the car's filler cap came open when Dieter Spoerry was driving, causing him to spin on his fuel at the Esses and crash backwards into the bank.

An early entry list shows Sutcliffe still with Filipinetti for 1967, again entered in a Ford. However, a couple of weeks before the 1967 race he received a phone call from Italy.

The same entry list had blanks by the side of the works Ferrari entries, and the once dominant team still had not filled all the seats in its 330 P4s. Sutcliffe went to the factory to meet Enzo Ferrari, the conversation taking place in French despite the latter's knowledge of English. Sutcliffe's co-driver Gunther Klass practically destroyed their car during practice, but the mechanics rebuilt it in six to seven hours with parts flown overnight from Modena. "We were allowed a couple of laps before the race to see if it was all right." Towards the end of the race fuel pump failure brought a halt to the car that, said Gregor Grant in *Autosport*, "Peter Sutcliffe had driven so ably."

114

114

into trouble, so the John Wyer Automotive Ford of Pedro Rodriguez and Lucian Bianchi moved up the field. If ever there was an example of Wyer's mantra that you had to finish to win, this was it. By the end of the 24 hours the GT40 was a clear victor. The only British car to finish that year was the little Austin-Healey Sprite of Roger Enever and Alec Poole, back in 15th and last place having run, it must be said, a superb race. It was not, said contemporary reports, a vintage year. Certainly for British carmakers it was not.

The following year, now that really was vintage as Wyer won again with exactly the same chassis 1075, this time with an Englishman as one of his drivers. Such was the end of that race that a chapter has been devoted to said Englishman, Jackie Oliver. During the final laps Oliver's team-mate Jacky Ickx traded places with one of the Porsches to set up one of the most exciting finishes in Le Mans' long history. Journalist Michael Cotton says that the Belgian was, in fact, playing with Porsche driver Hans Herrmann on the very last lap. He had already worked out that the Porsche's brakes were failing and knew that he could out-brake the German car at the Mulsanne corner and so he actually lifted off to ensure that the Porsche went ahead down the preceding straight. Neither wanted to lead into the tight right-hander; it sounds more like a stage of the bicycle Tour de France than a motor race. An all-English pairing of David Hobbs and Mike Hailwood came third in the second of Wyer's GT40s.

Sadly, 1969 also saw tragedy with the death of John Woolfe. The Englishman's first-lap crash in his privately entered Porsche 917 highlighted the problem constructors faced in building the number of cars required for homologation into the Group 4 class, which enabled them to make larger and faster cars. To construct 25 before even one could race meant that some had to be sold to privateer teams. The works cars were having problems with the 917 that year, so what chance did amateur drivers have? To be fair to Woolfe, he was not as inexperienced as some of the press made out, having been racing for a decade with such cars as Lolas, Shelby Cobras and Ford GT40s.

For two years Wyer had held back the Porsche tide. Now the first of the German manufacturer's many victories was just 12 months away. Wyer was also to transfer his allegiance to Porsche the following year, although his own, magnificent 917s were never to win at La Sarthe.

By the time his Gulf team returned to the top of the rostrum Le Mans would have changed significantly, and not for the better.

Piers Courage, in unfamiliar white helmet, about to leap into his factory Matra 650 at the start of the 1969 race. Sharing with Frenchman Jean-Pierre Beltoise, he was to finish fourth overall. Photographs taken 24 hours later show the talented young Englishman almost unnoticed as the celebrations commence for the most exciting finish in Le Mans' history. (Chris Wakley)

No, not the 1969 winner, but JW Automotive Engineering's other Ford GT40 that year, the third-place car of David Hobbs and Mike Hailwood. Following are a NART Ferrari 250LM and the fastest car in the race, one of the frightening, first-year Porsche 917s. (Ford)

The year 1965 marked the last Le Mans for the BMC works team as well as the final appearance for a genuine MG. The 11th place scored by the well-driven, long-nose MGB was the final chapter in a honourable history that could be traced back to a pair of MG Midgets in 1930. When the MG name reappeared in the 21st century it was to be a branding exercise on what were really Lolas. (BP)

CHAPTER 14

THE ROVER-BRM

"Time is the greatest innovator." (Francis Bacon, *Of Innovations*)

The floor of the Heritage Motor Centre in Gaydon, Warwickshire, is strewn with cars illustrating the history of the British motorcar. It takes something particularly special to have its own dedicated display. One such is reserved for Rover's gas turbine project. Included in this is the unique Rover-BRM Le Mans car, described by the museum's former press officer Jill Howes as "our *piece de resistance.*" It is not the only Le Mans veteran on permanent display; a Group C Aston Martin AMR1 is also in the hall while the Index of Performance trophies won in the 1930s by Alex von der Becke and Keith Peacock are in a display case there. However, it is by far the most fascinating.

The Rover-BRM first appeared at the Le Mans test day in April 1963, an unpainted aluminium, rather ungainly, open-top sports-racer. By the time of the race in June it had acquired its obligatory coat of green. However, when it reappeared two years later it had completely metamorphosed into a low, sharp-nosed coupe. *Motor Sport*'s legendary continental correspondent Denis Jenkinson pointed out in his splendidly pedantic way that it should have been called a BRM-Rover. He was technically correct in that the car had been made by cutting a 1961 Grand Prix BRM P25 chassis in half and fitting a two-seater-width tubular centre section. If that sounds simple then it must be pointed out that the chassis design task that faced BRM's Peter Berthon was a particularly exacting one because of the very different characteristics of the engine. Instead of the 1½-litre V8 BRM unit that would have been found in the rear of the Formula One car, a 150bhp Rover 2S/150 gas-turbine engine had been fitted, driving to a BRM differential unit, the gearbox having just one forward speed and reverse.

There were only two pedals for the drivers – BRM's Grand Prix pairing of Graham Hill and American Richie Ginther – to operate. One controlled the fuel to the turbine, the other was a brake pedal wide enough to be used by either foot. 'Jenks' observed that the turbine being a free-running vertical constant-speed unit running at 35-40,000rpm, it was essential for the pair to drive through the corners with the power on, which meant that the driver had to keep the turbine up to working rpm with his right foot while braking with the left, so that there was no delay once the brakes were released. Unlike a conventional internal combustion engine, which can be speeded up almost instantaneously by use of the throttle pedal, the turbine took time to regain peak revs if allowed to drop low. Hill and Ginther, who being short had to have his own special seat, had plenty to learn during those two test days in April.

Hill, in fact, had first experienced the car at the MIRA (then the Motor Industry Research Association) test track near Nuneaton. His initial impression had been that it sounded like a Boeing 707 airliner when starting up, a stark contrast to its silence when running.

Motor Sport featured the unpainted Rover-BRM on the cover of its May 1963 issue. The car had made its debut at the Le Mans test day. "Its noise will no doubt attract a lot of people to the Sarthe circuit," said the magazine's continental correspondent Denis Jenkinson. *(LAT Photographic)*

Autosport's John Bolster described the Rover-BRM as "easily the most outstanding car technically" at the 1963 race. The applause that it received at the end did, he felt, mean that the crowd believed it to be an important development. (British Motor Industry Heritage Trust)

cover in 1963 but also pictured it being filled with paraffin at what it called "the Esso Blee doolers," a quip that might not have the same resonance 40 years later. During practice a few problems did occur, notably the fact that the body admitted water almost everywhere. The tail also showed a tendency to lift at speed, something that was overcome with a rear spoiler, lowered front wings and changes to the windscreen.

The genesis of the racing project had occurred in 1962 when the Rover T4 experimental gas turbine saloon car had been demonstrated prior to the race. Rover had been the first company to build a gas turbine-powered private car, the P4-based JET 1, back in 1950. A second car, the T3, appeared in 1956. There was even now talk that the front-wheel-drive T4 might be productionized, but this never happened.

The ACO suggested that Rover might like to enter a car to compete for a special award. The idea was not to actually race the car, but to run it alongside all the other competitors in an event of its own. A prize of £1800 awaited it if it could average 93.2mph (a round 150km/h) for the 24 hours. To avoid any confusion about whether the car was in, or just with, the field it was to carry the race number '00'. It was also, being very slow of the line, flagged away last and from a position looking straight down the track as opposed to the traditional angle.

The result was a triumph; Motor was to headline their report "Rover-BRM demonstrates magnificently". This was despite the constraints placed on the drivers that resulted in the quickest lap (113.62mph) being only 6mph faster than their average speed. Had it been in competition with the other entrants the car would

He recorded how the driver had to hold the car on the brake as there was a residual power, even when it was running slowly and permanently in gear. To start off he had to press a foot button to apply the power. Once this was achieved the driver then took his foot off the brake and the car moved forward, accelerating slowly at first.

Motor Sport not only featured the car on its front

During 1964 the Rover-BRM appeared in vastly revised form at the Le Mans test weekend. Graham Hill completed over four hours on the track only to find that the primer grey car was slower than the previous year's project. A press statement was issued saying that "more engine endurance running" was needed and the car was scratched from that year's race. (British Motor Industry Heritage Trust)

have finished in eighth place overall at a higher speed than any Le Mans winner before 1957. The magazine went as far as to say that "the race was saved for Britain" by the car's outstanding performance. In the light of class wins that year for a Lotus Elite, MGB and a Jaguar E-type, this assessment may seem a little harsh, but it did perhaps underline the fact that British cars were no longer winning outright at Le Mans. Autosport's John Bolster pointed out that the Rover-BRM was probably the only car in the whole race that did not require any mechanical adjustment. He believed that it could "certainly be developed to out-perform any of the piston-engined cars of 1963." It also, he said, underlined the reliability of the alternator as opposed to the dynamos which, he pointed out, "wilted during the hours of darkness."

There was a feeling that the gas turbine might have a major future at Le Mans. Writing that year, David Hodges said that the Rover-BRM was "perhaps the forerunner of a new era." Hill and Ginther certainly received the loudest ovation at the end of the race. Two years later, Edward Eves, looking back in Autocar, was perhaps more studied in his appraisal. The fact that the car had finished its first race, particularly one of 24 hours duration, "was proof that the propulsive unit was not as delicate a flower as some would have us believe."

Fellow journalist Michael Cotton's main memory of his first visit to Le Mans was the noise, or lack of it, of the gas turbine car, the 'woosh' as it went past. "You could hear the suspension over the bumps and the tyres squealing." It made a lasting impression on him.

British enthusiasts were able to see the car in action when Graham Hill demonstrated it at Silverstone along with the three road-going Rover gas turbine cars. It was also to be shown to the British Grand Prix crowd at Silverstone two years later.

Such had been the success of the gas turbine car in 1963 that The Rover Company and The Owen Organisation, which then owned BRM, agreed to enter the car the following year in an improved guise. Creating the car had been an expensive exercise for the pair, but they both hoped to see future benefits from it. This time it was intended to enter the Rover-BRM in the race itself in the 2-litre class. In 1963 there had been no way to compare the size of a piston engine with that of a gas turbine, but now a basis for comparison had been agreed. Motor Panel (Coventry) Limited built a new GT-style aluminium body for the car complete with pointed nose and square-cut tail. The ugly duckling had become a purposeful coupe.

The car ran at the April trials, although still without the heat exchanger that was planned for the race so as to reduce paraffin consumption by using waste heat from the exhaust. Corning Glass Works had been experimenting with an inexpensive glass-ceramic material, Pyroceram, capable of withstanding very high temperatures. This made it possible to overcome the problem that hitherto, in order to avoid exorbitant costs, heat exchangers had to be made of an unreliable, thin material. Another change was to the rear suspension, which used the same components as

The fact that the car is wearing number 35 indicates that this photograph was taken during April testing; new boy Jackie Stewart is now at the wheel. Out on the Mulsanne straight, and admittedly affected by crosswinds, the coupe was still 8mph slower than when in roadster guise. (British Motor Industry Heritage Trust)

that year's BRM Formula One car, although arranged differently to give the same characteristics as the car in its 1963 guise. The principle used links and radius arms combined with a cast aluminium hub carrier. Otherwise the proposed 1964 contender was based on the previous year's tubular steel spaceframe.

Unfortunately, in May an announcement appeared from Rover and the Owen Organisation stating: "The car is ready and progress with the Corning ceramic regenerative hear exchanger is satisfactory, but more engine endurance running is required than can be achieved in the time available to ensure that the car reaches the standard of reliability demonstrated in the 1963 race. The general public will share with the Rover Company and the Owen Organisation the acute disappointment caused by this decision." It did not help that the car was damaged on the way back to Solihull after the trials. The drivers, who were to have been the same as the previous year, were left to look for alternative drives for Le Mans. Graham Hill found his way into the Maranello Concessionaires Ferrari 330P, in which he and Swede Jo Bonnier were to be placed second.

Despite the withdrawal of the 1964 entry it was made known that the Rover-BRM would be racing at Le Mans the following year. Once again the car had to be entered in the 2-litre class. This was a bitter disappointment to the team, which had hoped to see it moved into the 1.6-litre category. It was said that the car had a nominal horsepower of 145hp (at 150°C) and was therefore competitive with a 1.5-litre car. Peter Spear, research director of the Owen Organisation, and Noel Penny, chief gas turbine engineer of Rover, had worked on a comparison formula to equate gas turbine and petrol engines. Although the ACO planned to

"It was taken for granted," recalls Sir Jackie Stewart, "that as BRM (team members) we would drive the Rover-BRM." He and Graham Hill discussed piloting it ("I thought it was a beautiful looking little car") at great length, the fact that the Englishman had driven the car during the race two years before (sharing with Californian Richie Ginther) being "very useful." Lap times, though, were to show that the experienced Formula One man and the newcomer ran at about the same speed. The pair understood that they were never going to win the race, but were involved in what appeared to be "an exciting technological breakthrough." Stewart recalls that he was "excited to be part of that, although the drive would not in the fullness of time be regarded as one of the more significant in his career.

Although he did not test the competition car before the race, Stewart did have the opportunity of using the Rover T4 gas turbine on the roads and at the MIRA test track. Even driving that car on the road was "a bit different." Peter Spear advised him not to stop at a pedestrian crossing as the heat from the rear of the car could burn the paintwork of the car behind or perhaps injure a following cyclist.

The biggest difference between the Rover-BRM and conventional racing cars was, says Stewart, "the enormous delay. The smaller the turbine, the longer it takes to get up the revs." He describes the anticipation required as being "a balancing act." However, it is his belief that racing drivers learn to cope with new experiences such as this quicker than most.

Stewart admits that the fact that the car had only two pedals, with the opportunity for left-foot braking, made it "completely foreign." Unlike today's young drivers, there had been no kart racing on which he could learn his craft. At Indianapolis, where he competed in 1966, left-foot braking was common, but he felt that he had enough to learn racing round the famous oval for the first time without that. The fact that he was leading the '500' by two laps before his engine began to seize, with only 20 miles to go, means that he must have learnt fast…but left-foot braking was still out. It was only when he raced the Chaparral 2J Can-Am car with its clutchless torque-converter transmission in 1970 that he learnt this art, something that one of his biographers, Karl Ludvigsen, recalled "he did with astonishing facility."

With no engine retard and no gears to shift, the braking at Le Mans "was terrible" and had to be "in a different zone." Stewart sums up: "One, the sound issue was totally different; two, there was an enormous delay in acceleration response; and three, there was the problem of engine retard. Apart from that it was OK!"

Hill and Stewart tossed a coin to see who would start the race. They joked that whoever did would aim to sail into the sand at the bottom of the Mulsanne straight, too deep into the mire to be able to get the car back on the road. They were not the only team in the history of Le Mans to allege such a pre-race plan, but as with others who have claimed similar thoughts since, it was merely banter. Hill 'lost' the toss and had to start. Embarrassingly, given the so-called plan, he did go off at Mulsanne and it may have been that which caused the turbine blades to be blunted.

Along the straights the car was never very quick. "We were so much slower than we should have been. I remember going down the Mulsanne and being passed by a Triumph Spitfire!" Lesser mortals have given up their racing careers for less. One of the eventual overall winners that year was Jochen Rindt, a particularly close friend of Stewart. Every few laps he would overtake the gas turbine car in his Ferrari 250LM, "waving two fingers at me."

"It was a very long race."

Looking back, Stewart reckons that he is glad that he raced the Rover-BRM. "It was a very historic drive." But he never raced again at Le Mans. In 1964 he had been the reserve driver for Maranello Concessionaires and had qualified the Ferrari 330P of Hill and Jo Bonnier and the GTO of Innes Ireland and Tony Maggs, but did not start.

In a career that ended with many records, surely the strangest must be that Sir Jackie Stewart is the only person to have raced a gas turbine car at Le Mans but never a conventional internal combustion machine.

There was almost a postscript to this story. In 1968 Stewart was asked to drive one of Andy Granatelli's gas turbine cars (nine gas turbines were actually entered for the Indianapolis 500 that year). He believes that one of the reasons he must have been chosen for the drive was his experience with the Rover-BRM. However, the drive was not to be as he was put out of action with a fractured wrist following an accident in a Formula Two race at Jarama. Stewart was to win the Formula One World Championship on three occasions but, as at Le Mans, he was to race at Indianapolis only the once.

The year 1965 was a significant one for Jackie Stewart. Shortly before Le Mans he recorded his first outright Formula One win, taking the International Trophy at Silverstone in his BRM P61. (In the December before, in a one-off drive for Lotus, he had won the second heat of the Rand Grand Prix having retired from the first.) Within less than a year he would have taken his first Grand Prix victory at Monza. *(Author)*

introduce this for 1966, the club flatly refused to bring it forward a year. Nevertheless, Rover and the Owen Organisation went ahead with their entry knowing that it would be up against the much quicker works Porsches. Once again the drivers would be the BRM Grand Prix pairing, although Jackie Stewart had now replaced Richie Ginther in the team. It was to be the Scot's only time at Le Mans although the three-time World Champion had practised a couple of Ferraris there as a reserve driver the previous year. (His elder brother, Jimmy, had raced an Aston Martin DB3S there in 1954.) The team manager was to be Le Mans veteran W.E. 'Wilkie' Wilkinson.

This time the car was thoroughly tested. Trials included five 24-hour runs on a rig especially built for the purpose. Two Corning heat exchangers had now been installed. The two discs, which each accommodated a large number of thin-walled parallel holes and were driven from the gas generator shaft at about 20rpm, were mounted either side of the engine. At the end of the race the discs were described as being in 'mint' condition except for a slight scoring on one of them caused by the passage of a foreign body. It was felt that the state of heat exchanger art had been advanced by at least two years.

Following the April Le Mans trials modifications were made to the bodywork. The most distinctive of these was the addition of twin ram-type air intakes on the tail unit, these having been fitted to improve the engine performance at high speed. The pointed front end was also slightly changed to incorporate long-range driving lights and side flasher units. The headlights rotated into a flush position when not in use.

Modest practice times did not give much hope for a

good result in the race. However, this was Le Mans and the car gradually worked its way up the leader board. It made just one unscheduled pit stop late on the Sunday morning. By the afternoon the temperature was rising and the car began to experience overheating. This was to result in an average speed over 9mph slower than the 1963 effort. After the race it was discovered that some of the engine's compressor vanes had been damaged, possibly as the result of the entry of a foreign body. As a result the turbine inlet temperature had increased.

Today the Rover-BRM sits in the main hall of the British Motor Industry Heritage museum at Gaydon, the racing star of a display that honours the complete Rover gas turbine project. *(Author)*

However, at 4.00pm the Rover-BRM was still in there, 10th out of the 14 cars still running, second in class and the highest all-British entry, the last of these achievements gaining it the *Motor* Trophy. It was pointed out that the car had consumed its fuel at the rate of 13.52mpg, a considerable improvement over 1963 and said to be equal to between 25 and 35mpg had it been running at "family motoring speed." In all the Rover-BRM made 10 pit stops during its 283 laps, used 176.5 gallons of paraffin and three pints of oil. The rear pads were changed once, the tyres never. *The Engineer* magazine stated that "it is quite possible that a developed version of this year's Rover-BRM will be seen at Le Mans in the future, striving for higher rewards than heretofore." Sadly this was not to happen. The experiment was over and the only gas turbine cars to have appeared at La Sarthe since were the American Howmets that ran later that decade. Heavy fuel consumption proved that these could never be competitive. Rover ran down its gas turbine development programme, the Le Mans car being the last of the line.

BRM'S BRIEF RETURN

In 1992 the BRM name did return to Le Mans, although whether the P351 was truly a successor to the line of cars started with the fabulous but troubled V16 Grand Prix car is a moot point. With the exception of the joint project with Rover and a brief foray into Can-Am and Interserie racing, BRM never really dabbled in sportscar racing, preferring Formula One and winning the World Championship with Graham Hill in 1962. John Mangoletsi, with the backing of the Owen Organisation, revived the name in the early 1990s with the Paul Brown-designed, 3.5-litre V12 P351. It was a low-budget affair, but there was little else that the British could wave their Union Jacks at in 1992. Just one of the three drivers, Richard Jones, was British, but he did not get a chance in the car as it ran for 20 laps before transmission problems and then a pit fire intervened. A plan to wheel out the car for a final-hour public relations exercise was eventually abandoned. Five years later the car was back. It was now in open-top form, powered by a Nissan engine and called the P301. It lasted six laps.

The BRM name was not the only famous one to be resurrected in the early 1990s. In 1993 a Cosworth-powered Allard, the advanced J2X, was entered although it failed to run. Robs Lamplough had purchased the car from its in-debt manufacturer and ran it at the Le Mans test day when it was deemed uncompetitive for such a high-speed circuit. It may be that reviving such names is more likely to tarnish their reputation than add to their lustre.

BRM's only other serious sportscar project concerned the Can-Am cars of the early 1970s. They were unsuccessful in North America, but Brian Redman and Howden Ganley took them to two victories apiece in the European Interserie championship. They were then sold to British hill-climb champion David Hepworth, whose finest hour came at the Norisring in 1973. Lack of intermediate tyres meant that his P167 went out on a drying track shod with wet weather rubber. Racing against well-funded Porsche 917-10s he moved up to second place before the track began to dry and, as can be seen here, his passage became fraught. *(Author)*

"Whistling through the esses"

A limited edition print by Michael Turner

The Rover-BRM made history triumphantly at Le Mans. For the 24 hours Graham Hill and Richie Ginther raced against the clock. Although the target was to maintain an average of just over 93mph they did, in fact, exceed this and finished lapping at 109.7mph. They covered 2,553 miles – 300 more than required by the regulations – to make history and win a special award for the first gas turbine car to beat the target.

• Prints are limited to 200 and individually signed by Michael Turner, size 42cm x 54cm •
• Price £80.00 plus post & packing •

SUSPENSION

BRAKES

TOTAL QUALITY TOTAL SERVICE

TRANSMISSION

FILTERS

ELECTRICS

STEERING

COOLING

Today's advanced technology demands replacement components made with surgical precision, and nothing less.

Quality you can always rely on from QH. Over 12,000 part numbers, all made in our own factories to ISO 9002.

So insist on QH, like your life depended on it.

www.qh.com

CHAPTER 15

JACKIE OLIVER

"The nearest run thing you ever saw in your life." (The Duke of Wellington)

The finish of the 1969 race made it one of the most thrilling in the history of motor racing. Much has been written about the tussle between the Belgian and German drivers involved. Down on power thanks to a broken and wired-up exhaust, Jacky Ickx had taken the lead in one of the John Wyer Automotive Ford GT40s, indeed, the very car that had won the previous year in the hands of Rodriguez and Bianchi. However, with around an hour and three-quarters remaining he had been caught by Hans Herrmann in a works Porsche 908. For the rest of the race the two frenetically traded places, rev limits ignored, and with just two laps to go there were only 20 yards between them. Not only

was the Le Mans crowd on its proverbial feet, but back in the UK the drama was being relayed to spectators at a Formula 5000 race meeting taking place at Silverstone.

At this point we should wonder what was going through the mind of Englishman Jackie Oliver, who as Ickx's co-driver was possibly about to win the world's greatest race. Looking back, the former Formula One driver and Can-Am Champion gives the impression of having been a little phlegmatic about the whole thing. Indeed, a post-race photograph that appeared in *Car and Driver* magazine showed him looking somewhat nonplussed. In the closing laps he was also, perhaps,

Thirty-five years on from the event, Jackie Oliver appears laid back about the finish of the 1969 race, but this was the distance between his co-driver, Jacky Ickx and the chasing Hans Herrmann as the flag fell. *(Ford)*

The start of the 1969 race and Jacky Ickx is about to break into what Jackie Oliver describes as a John Cleese-like walk. *(LAT Photographic)*

The rest of the field is on its way and Ickx is safely strapping himself in. Oliver states that he was not upset by the Belgian's protest, even during the tense closing laps 24 hours later. *(Chris Wakley)*

to be anachronistic and dangerous. He was not the only one to be concerned. Vic Elford had suggested that the drivers could be strapped in and their co-drivers could run across the track as of old, either handing over an ignition key or turning on an external ignition master switch. The idea was not taken up, and a rolling start was introduced for the following year. For 1969, though, the dash across the track was still in place. While the other drivers rushed to their cars, Ickx pointedly strolled across the road. The amble, though, was not the nonchalant one now of legend. Oliver recalls that halfway across it turned into a John Cleese-like 'funny walk'.

The protest put the pairing well back. The reliability of the cars and the sprint-style racing are phenomena of recent years and Oliver points out that then being this far back was nothing to worry about. "A number of things had to go wrong for a number of people, but that was the nature of 24-hour racing." Using journalist Denis Jenkinson's measure of how hard a racing driver is trying, Oliver reckons the front-runners at Le Mans in his day were at 6/10ths. Today he believes they are nearer 10/10ths.

One incident was to prove the vagaries of an endurance contest and, given the closeness of the result, show how different it could have been. In those days pit signals were given at the Mulsanne corner, thus enabling the driver to prepare to enter the pits on the same lap. Oliver received instructions to pit, but as he came in so team manager David Yorke wanted to know why. Oliver was irritated that Yorke would not believe his answer, that he had been instructed to by the Mulsanne signallers. He sped out of the pits, paying scant regard to the fact that GT40s did not like standing starts. The same thing happened again the next lap. By now Yorke had decided that the clutch

becoming a little irritated. With Ickx out on the track, Romford-born Oliver was the target for premature well-wishers. One of them he went as far as to actually throw out of the JWA pits; it was a director of Ford France.

As Ickx and Herrmann sparred, Oliver might have been forgiven for being unhappy about the way his co-driver had started the race. However, he says: "No, it was after all a 24-hour race." With cars now equipped with seat belts, the Belgian had felt the famous *en echelon* 'Le Mans start', with drivers having to sprint across the track to climb aboard and start their cars,

should be checked, accusing Oliver of slipping it when he had shot off.

Oliver raced three times at Le Mans, but only two of those drives were of any significance. However, he is indelibly in the record books, not only as one of the winning drivers in the closest finish of the race, but also as the holder of the all-time lap record. In 1971, driving again for John Wyer, but this time at the wheel of a Porsche 917L, he broke the record for what was then an 8.37-mile circuit, leaving it at 151.85mph. Speeds of around 225mph were being seen on the Mulsanne straight that year. An indication that this would happen had been seen at the April test days when Oliver, again at the wheel of a long-tailed 917, had 'destroyed' Vic Elford's existing official record with a time of 3m 21.0s. The increase in speed was simply down to aerodynamics. "The car was still a 917K," says Oliver. He recalls taking the Porsche curves flat. On the Mulsanne, worried about the aerodynamic balance, he kept moving the steering wheel to see if there was any lift at the front.

For 1972 the Ford chicane was redesigned and a new section built to take out the old White House corner. The closest anyone has ever come to Oliver's lap speed since was in one of the Jaguars in 1989 with a speed just under 1.25mph slower.

Come the start of the 1971 race and "Pedro (Rodriguez) and I obliterated the opposition," says Oliver. When he first took over from the little Mexican, their car was already about a lap in the lead. The pair remained at the front until 3 o'clock on the Sunday morning when Oliver brought the car in with suspect handling. A possibly out-of-balance wheel and a shock absorber were changed and he was sent out again. Ten minutes later he was back and the whole corner of the car was dismantled. The long tails of the Porsche 917Ls were putting an unexpected strain on their rear suspension. Eventual retirement, though, occurred when a pipe broke, flooding the cockpit with scalding oil just as Rodriguez was at full speed down the Mulsanne straight.

Oliver recalls Rodriguez as the easiest of his co-drivers to work with, as well as "mighty" in the wet or at Spa-Francorchamps. However, John Wyer liked pairing Oliver with Ickx, "as I did not make a fuss." He also believes that he was quicker than the Belgian during the night. This led to Ickx complaining that Oliver was stressing the car. It was something that Yorke, knowing the Englishman to be particularly smooth in the dark, dismissed. Fittingly, both Rodriguez and Ickx were about the same size as Oliver.

Oliver's initial race at Le Mans had been in 1968, when he had been paired with Brian Muir. During his first stint the Australian put their JWA GT40 into the infamous sand at the Mulsanne corner, becoming a 'digger' in more ways than one. In getting out of the sand he effectively destroyed the clutch. He immediately handed over to Oliver, who completed one lap before bringing the car in to retire and promptly left for home. Even today he seems little amused by the event. A photo was once published of the car being dug out of the sand with a caption that indicated uncertainty whether the man toiling with the spade was Oliver or

Jackie Oliver on his way to Le Mans victory in the same underpowered and outdated Ford GT40 that had won the year before. A French-driven Alpine A220/69 follows. *(Ford)*

Muir. Be in no doubt, it was Muir. Oliver prefers to recall that during that year he had been a Lotus works driver in Formula One and had actually led the British Grand Prix in an early version of one of the team's iconic 49s, having been second-fastest in practice.

Oliver admits that although his most successful time as a professional racing driver was in endurance sportscar racing, he was not enthusiastic about the discipline. Very much an individual, he was not happy that he had to share with another driver, or that success was seen to be that of the manufacturer, rather than the drivers.

His early years in single-seater racing were closely connected to Lotus as he progressed from being the driver for the second-string Lotus Components team, the arm of the company responsible for the manufacture of customer racing cars, to becoming number-two to Graham Hill in the Player's Gold Leaf-sponsored Grand Prix team. Oliver started racing with a Mini, and then drove Marcos, Diva and Lotus Elan sportscars. He moved into Formula Three in 1966, initially with a Brabham and then with a works Charles Lucas-Team Lotus 41. He also competed in one of the early racing versions of the Europa, the Lotus 47. The following year saw him in Formula Two with an uprated 41 entered by Lotus Components. He seemed destined to stay in F2 for 1968, driving an ex-works Lotus 48 backed by the Herts and Essex Aero Club. But fate had other plans.

There are many in British motor racing who remember being at Brands Hatch that April to watch the BOAC 500, an endurance race for Le Mans-style cars. They were stunned when the news came over the Tannoy that Jim Clark, arguably the most perfect racing driver of all time, had been killed during a Formula Two race at Hockenheim. A few weeks later, his logical successor, Mike Spence, lost his life practising for Lotus at Indianapolis. Suddenly Oliver found himself with one of the finest drives in Formula One, although as he records, the Lotuses "were the

At Le Mans in 1969 Oliver may have had to watch as his team-mate raced to the finish. However, he was at the wheel for the final stint of another truly classic event, the 1971 Spa 1000kms. Pressured by fellow countryman Derek Bell he did not put a foot wrong towards the end of what was the fastest road race ever. He stands proudly to the fore ahead of David Yorke, Pedro Rodriguez, Bell and Jo Siffert. *(Alan Hearn)*

best cars and the most dangerous."

An accident on the first lap of his debut race at Monaco almost led to his instant dismissal by Colin Chapman. But the Lotus boss relented and Oliver stayed with the team for the rest of the year. His top result that first season was third place in Mexico. However, the race that could have made all the difference to his future career was the British Grand Prix at Brands Hatch. Here his final-drive unit gave up after he had inherited the lead from his team leader Graham Hill. Historian William Court has described this as his 'High Noon'. Oliver also drove the fastest lap that year at Monza.

The following season he left Lotus to join BRM, his best result of the year again being in Mexico. He remained with BRM for 1971, then returned to Formula One in 1973 with the Shadow team, for whom he was already racing in the US-based Can-Am sportscar series. It was to be his last season at this level with the exception of the Swedish Grand Prix and the non-championship Brands Hatch Race of Champions for the same team in 1977. In all, he was to compete in 49 Grands Prix. Not wanting to retire from the racing world, but not desiring "a path down the slippery slope" like those drivers unable to give up, he became involved in the Shadow operation, bringing the American team to Britain and helping to establish a base in Northampton.

However, as stated, it was in sportscars that Oliver had enjoyed his greatest successes, particularly with the Gulf-sponsored John Wyer team. Included were wins at Sebring with Ickx in 1969 (Ford GT40) and 1971 (Porsche 917), and victories for the Rodriguez/Oliver pairing at Daytona, Monza and, notably, Spa-Francorchamps. That 1000kms event was to enter

A Gulf publicity shot. All three of Oliver's starts at Le Mans were at the wheel of one of the powder blue and orange cars. *(Gulf)*

the history books as the fastest ever road race at 154.765mph. Derek Bell recalls the sense of frustration that he used to experience because David Yorke would not allow overtaking within the team. On this occasion, Bell, who had been quickest overall in practice, was right behind Oliver in the closing laps. Yorke was issuing his usual orders about no overtaking, but Bell's Swiss team-mate Jo Siffert was urging him to ignore this from further down the pit rail. Bell was the first to make his last pit stop and stormed out for "a really good opening lap" of his final stint. Oliver then pitted, coming out of the lane just ahead of Bell. "I thought he's got to make a mistake," recalls Bell. However, there was to be no error and the pair finished the race almost side-by-side.

Oliver also won the Can-Am title in 1974, his Shadow winning all but the last of the five rounds. He had first started racing seriously in North America in 1971 and had angered John Wyer when he asked to be released from his contract for the sportscar race at Zeltweg, Austria, to enable him to compete in the USA. Wyer refused the request and was later to say that Oliver then broke his contract. He was replaced in the JWA team by Richard Attwood, the previous year's Le Mans winner. From now on Oliver's racing career was focused on the USA where, in addition to the Can-Am series, he also competed in Formula 5000 and even NASCAR.

By the mid-1970s, the telephone had stopped ringing with offers of drives and the once busy Oliver realized that "I had stopped being the young star driver years before." Wanting to return to Formula One, he had contacted Ken Tyrrell. The response, he confesses, was "not good." He realized that his career now had to take a different path and thus he joined the ranks of the constructors. In the wake of the problems that occurred at Shadow following the withdrawal of UOP sponsorship, a new team was formed for 1978, called Arrows. Oliver says that he and Shadow's founder Don Nichols "had a divorce. He took the home and I took the kids."

Oliver reckons there was no way that, influenced by Colin Chapman, his former boss at Lotus, he would have wanted the car to be called an 'Oliver'. However, the 'O' of Oliver is there in the name along with those of initial backer Franco Ambrosio, team manager Alan Rees and designers David Wass and Tony Southgate. Oliver's own racing career was over and he was never to drive one of his own cars.

The Arrows story did not start too well. Southgate, who had also jumped ship from Shadow, took designs that he had already made for the latter's DN9 and used them on the first Arrows chassis. Nichols took legal action and a new car had to be built. The team looked a possible winner in its early days, with Riccardo Patrese as lead driver, but a Grand Prix win was never to be. In 1989 the company was sold to the Japanese Footwork Corporation. However, 1994 saw previous owners Oliver and Rees again take over the running of the operation, which they bought back the following year. In 1996 Tom Walkinshaw assumed control of the team, but the man who masterminded Jaguar's 1988 and 1990 Le Mans victories, and whose initials were also on the name of the 1996 and 1997 winner, could not translate his sportscar success into Formula One victories. In early 2003 Arrows went into liquidation having achieved an unenviable record of 382 starts without a win.

Looking back, Oliver admits that the most famous race he won has to be the 1969 Le Mans 24-Hours. "In Joe Public's mind, winning Le Mans is a watershed in a professional driver's career." However, he believes that that year's race was so open and featured so many twists and turns that "anybody could have won." He does not want this to sound as if he regrets it, but Oliver would prefer to be remembered not for this, or even for leading the British Grand Prix, but for "nearly finishing" the 1968 German Grand Prix, a wet and misty affair in which all the contestants were true heroes.

There is a postscript to the story of Oliver (at the time of writing, chairman of SCL, Silverstone's operating company, and a director of the British Racing Drivers Club board) and the JW Ford GT40s at Le Mans. In 2003 he was invited to drive Martin Colvill's former Gulf Ford GT40 in the Legends race that preceded the main event. This particular car had competed at Le Mans in 1965, a works car entered under the name of Rob Walker who, with Ian Connell, had driven a Delahaye to eighth place in the 1939 race. Ford, in fact, had taken over Walker's entry, which was originally intended for his Serenissima. David Piper's wife Liz, then Walker's secretary, recalls how he insisted on Ford agreeing to certain conditions, including the choice of drivers and tyres, and the fact that she could work for Ford at the race. However, this is to digress… The car was then given to John Wyer as one of his team cars for 1967, but was never used again at Le Mans and was sold on to Rodney Clark before Colvill acquired it in 1981.

For the 2003 Legends race it was planned that the owner would drive the pace lap and the first racing lap, then Oliver was to take over. For the occasion the latter had had replica Gulf overalls made *a la* 1969. So clad,

he was waiting in the pits for his turn. Unbeknown to him, Vanina Ickx, Jacky's daughter, was competing on the same day. Walking down the pit lane towards him came her famous father. Seeing his former partner in 1969 guise, Jacky Ickx almost "did a double-take."

"What are you doing here?" he asked. "Sorry, Jacky. I'd like to talk to you but I've just got to race our old car." At that moment the powder blue-and-orange GT40 came towards them for its driver change. For Ickx it must have been a surreal moment.

Still an aggressive contestant, Oliver was determined to overtake David Piper's Porsche 917 in the race. That he chose to do so at, rather than after, the Ford chicane did not amuse the car's owner. However, Oliver had been told, incorrectly, that he was on the last lap. He did manage to squeeze past, but as he did so Piper's

Oliver's first year in Formula 2 was 1967 when he raced a spaceframe Lotus-Cosworth FVA 41. On reflection, his result at Mallory Park is probably best forgotten as the Lotus Components car finished in a ditch. *(Author)*

The 1968 British Grand Prix has gone down in history as the last Formula One World Championship event to be won by a privateer. However, it was also the zenith of Jackie Oliver's career. Here he leads the grid away followed by the two other Lotus 49s of Graham Hill (left) and eventual winner Jo Siffert in Rob Walker's car. *(Ford)*

The Oliver/Rodriguez Porsche neck-and-neck in the Esses with the Martini car of Vic Elford/Gerard Larrousse. The Ferrari 512M of David Hobbs and Mark Donohue is the meat in the Porsche sandwich ahead of the Bell/Siffert 917 and the 1971 winning version of Helmut Marko and Gijs van Lennep. *(LAT Photographic)*

MIKE SALMON

For Mike Salmon Le Mans 1967 was "doomed to failure and disaster." It was one of those rare occasions when everything seems to be against you. For a start, his Dawnay Racing Ford GT40 had to be fitted with a new engine to replace one damaged coming second in the Martini Trophy race at Silverstone. Then the team was contracted to Firestone for tyres. However, because of a strike at the factory no wets were available and so permission was given to break the agreement and change on to Goodyears, a major setting-up operation for a GT40. There was also the matter of Salmon having to replace his Firestone-liveried overalls with less fire-resistant Goodyear ones. Against this, or so it seemed at the time, all the drivers in the race were presented with fireproof gloves to use instead of their usual string-back ones.

It was the first time that Salmon's partner Brian Redman had raced at Le Mans, so he was sent out first in practice to learn the circuit. John Wyer asked him how many revs he was pulling down the Mulsanne straight and, quite frankly, did not believe the answer given. As far as he was concerned, if Redman was telling the truth then this was the fastest GT40 ever. Sure enough, Salmon took the car out and found that he was pulling at least 500rpm below Redman's claimed figure. As it became dark he did, though, shut the car's small quarter-lights to find that, indeed, the young Lancastrian had been telling the truth.

Salmon elected to take the start and not to do up his seat belts in order to get away quickly. Indeed, such was his start that by the time he was under the Dunlop bridge the driver's door had burst open. He had to hold the door to while driving down the straight and then pit at the end of the first lap, "absolutely furious."

"I was still not in a good mood when we refuelled." As he set off from the pits he thought that there seemed to be a lot of petrol around the filler cap. As he went under the Dunlop bridge the door burst open again. Anxious not to do another pedantic lap, he slowed down, jammed his knees up against the steering wheel and pulled down the door.

As he approached the hump towards the end of the Mulsanne straight "all of a sudden the whole windscreen seemed covered with steam. Then I realized it was not steam, it was petrol. From then on it was like the worst nightmare you have ever had. Within a few seconds there was a huge explosion and the car was engulfed in flame." The GT40 had been doing about 210mph at the time so there was no question of getting out. As soon as he put the brakes on, the fuel rushed down the front of the bonnet, and the right-hand front tyre burst. Salmon tried to hold the car in a straight line. Writing in *Autosport*, Gregor Grant stated: ". . . with great presence of mind he continued to the corner where the fire point is situated," although Salmon says: "the good Lord had a lot to do with it." Had he gone down the escape road and into the ditch he would have been trapped. Instead, the car embedded itself into the sandbank on the exit of the Mulsanne corner. It then exploded. Salmon had about five seconds to get out, which he managed on his own. The fire brigade, he recalls, was mesmerized.

He remembers not suffering any immediate pain, "but a huge heat inside oneself." He had been badly burnt on his arms, ankles and back, could not see for five days, and had to spend two months in the famed McIndoe burns unit at East Grinstead. The new 'fireproof' gloves had burnt right through and had to be redesigned.

On the Saturday of the 1967 race Mike Salmon's Ford GT40 burst into flames at the end of the Mulsanne straight. "It was like the worst nightmare you ever had." *(Mike Salmon collection)*

Salmon had precious little time to get out of the car, managing it on his own before help arrived. A Ford France GT40 slows down as it arrives at the scene of Salmon's accident. He was to spend two months in the McIndoe burns unit at East Grinstead, the establishment famed for its pioneering work during the Second World War. *(Mike Salmon collection)*

Porsche caught the Ford's rear wheel, causing the tyre to deflate. The resulting accident left a damaged GT40, although it has to be said that Oliver paid for the damage repair. Perhaps there is a little irony here in that one who had tasted victory in such a car – perhaps *the* victory at Le Mans – after having shared it for 24 hours, had failed 34 years later to finish the 60-minute support race.

Above left: Many of Mike Salmon's drives have been at the wheel of Aston Martin-engined cars, including the Group C Nimrods. A young Ray Mallock (left) listens intently to the words of his experienced team-mate. *(Mike Salmon collection)*

BOB CURL

Bob Curl is one of those who first witnessed *Les Vingt-Quatre Heures* from the spectator enclosures, went on to become involved in the race, and now, although no longer required to be there professionally, still cannot stay away. His first visit was in 1953; he was still there in 2005 and promising to be back. Curl initially went on his own as a 15-year-old, putting his bicycle on the 'Golden Arrow' to Paris, then taking a train to Le Mans, but cycling much of the way back. He did not return until about 1960, but over the next decade he reckons he must have been instrumental in introducing "dozens of people" to Le Mans.

In all, he has attended the event over 30 times. In 1969 he "fulfilled a boyhood dream" by designing a car that actually took part in the race, Mark Konig's Nomad. It was the BRM-engined Mk 2 spyder version that competed at La Sarthe. Significantly for Curl he was located at the old Mulsanne signalling area towards the end of the race. That meant he was one of those privileged few who actually witnessed Jacky Ickx outbrake Hans Herrmann to take the lead on the penultimate lap of the race, only to have to repeat the move on the final round. "You could almost see Herrmann's gritted teeth."

Working with long-time associates Marchant & Cox, he also designed and built the bodywork for the 1978 Cosworth DFV-powered IBEC, as well as the conversion of a Dome into a Group C car for 1982.

Curl continues to make the annual pilgrimage, accompanied by his wife Tracy, "who now understands why I want to stand on the bank at Tertre Rouge as midnight approaches."

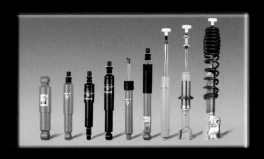

CHAPTER 16

JOHN WYER

"He is an Englishman! For he himself has said it, And it's greatly to his credit, That he is an Englishman!" (W.S. Gilbert, *HMS Pinafore*)

In writing on the preparation of sports-racing cars in the mid-1950s, John Wyer, then manager of the Aston Martin racing team, quoted William Blake: "Mechanical excellence is the only vehicle for genius." Given the success that was to result for his teams' cars – including wins at Le Mans in 1959, 1968, 1969 and 1976 – it is a line that could be applied to himself. It has been said that Wyer brought a level of professionalism to the business of team management not seen since Alfred Neubauer at Mercedes-Benz. Famed private entrant Rob Walker was to describe him as "the most experienced racing manager in the world."

Wyer was a serious person, a disciplinarian, someone who commanded admiration, respect and sometimes fear. Everybody had a high opinion of him and he is certainly looked back upon as one of the greats of sportscar racing. It was a category that he majored in and one that gave him much personal satisfaction. He believed, quite understandably, that it required higher standards of preparation than Grand Prix races.

"Few men make a satisfactory team manager, for the work can be done effectively only by one who has not only a complete grasp of racing but knows every side of the game and, which is more, knows a very great deal about human nature. John Wyer rightly believes that discipline is the foundation of racing success, and woe betide anyone who fails in his duty to a team, for neither friendship nor political protection will avail him anything." So wrote Sammy Davis.

Wyer left school to take up an apprenticeship with Sunbeam, then perceived as the most successful name in British motor racing. As he was to recall, he joined the company just as all that changed. He was to move on to carburettor manufacturer Solex and then, after the Second World War, to Monaco Engineering, a racing car preparation specialist (Roy Salvadori was to become a customer). One of its directors, Dudley Folland, raced a pre-war Aston Martin 2-litre which had been driven in the Tourist Trophy by the 1938 German Grand Prix winner Dick Seaman. The car was entered for the first post-war Spa-Francorchamps 24-Hours, which Wyer was to recall as the first important motor race in which he was involved. His role was team manager, a position in which he was to star. The Aston was also run at Le Mans in 1949, but by that stage it was beginning to feel its age.

That winter Monaco Engineering was sold, becoming a Vauxhall dealership, and Wyer, now aged 40, turned down the opportunity of running the business in its new guise. Although not in a hurry for more employment, advised by the engineer/journalist Laurence Pomeroy, he applied for a post that was to make his name: team manager of Aston Martin. At the interview both Wyer and Aston boss David Brown were insistent that the job should be for one season only.

Wyer inherited an entry for the 1950 Le Mans, reservations at the *Hotel Moderne* and two drivers in Lance Macklin and the ageing Charles Brackenbury. Deciding on the eventual driver line-up proved a little tricky, especially as Brown himself wanted to drive

This chapter is sponsored by:

The British team managers of the 1950s and 1960s, notably John Wyer and Lofty England, were among the finest in the history of endurance racing. Wyer is here flanked by three men who were significant in his career, his lieutenant John Horsman, with David Yorke beyond him, and Grady Davis, executive vice-president of the Gulf Oil Corporation. *(MNF collection)*

Wyer's first success at Le Mans was the long-deserved victory in 1959 for the works Aston Martin. The winning DBR1, seen here in the foyer of Aston Martin's opulent new factory in Gaydon, still competes in historic racing driven by Peter Hardman. *(Author)*

despite limited experience. Brown, however, agreed to engaging Jack Fairman and Eric Thompson, and then George Abecassis and Reg Parnell, the latter the leading British driver of the time, were asked to join the three-car team. Getting the cars – DB2s – built was even more difficult; the racing department did not even have a base. However, by the end of May the first of the cars had been built and was taken down to Le Mans for some very unofficial runs down the Mulsanne straight with Wyer and Brown sitting in the cafe. Thankfully there was little traffic.

Despite Fairman's accident (recorded earlier) on the way to Le Mans, the race proved, according to Wyer, "light-hearted." Two of the three cars ran well to the finish, Macklin and Abecassis coming in fifth and winning the Index of Performance. The race, Wyer was to say, had an important effect on his future life. His race report also included a comment that the *Hotel Moderne* was expensive and noisy (it was also an unofficial press club) and that he had been given the name of another hotel, the *Hotel de France* at La Chartre-sur-le-Loir. Although he was not to use said establishment for another three years, it was to become part of Aston Martin and JWA folklore.

Wyer had learnt the principles of winning Le Mans in the 1950s. His very standard DB2s had not been the fastest in the field, but he had seen that by estimating the highest speed at which they would remain reliable and then sticking to that speed come what may, they would stand a chance of success. In 1959 this philosophy paid off handsomely. Wyer was aware that drivers could be difficult to convince of the wisdom of all this, but as he said, endurance races were usually won from the pits.

That Wyer knew what he was talking about was underlined in 1951 when the DB2s came third, fifth and seventh overall, filling the first three places in the 3-litre class. The year after Wyer tried to play safe with his target lap times in order to gain reliability.

However, as he recalled, this was denied the team and all three cars fell out due to problems with the David Brown five-speed gearbox, which had been designed for the DB3, and with the hypoid gears in the final drive. In 1953 Wyer was enthusiastic about the DB3S that he now had at his disposal, but again all three cars dropped out. However, the team would win every other race that it entered during the rest of the season.

The year 1954 was, Wyer recalled, as bad as 1953 was good. He took on the role of directing racing engineering policy to add to that of racing manager. It might, he said, have worked if he had relieved himself of some of his other tasks as David Brown urged him to do. The DB3S had shown great potential, but Wyer also had to take under his wing the under-developed Lagonda V12, a car by which Brown set great store. Until this time Wyer had undertaken the testing role himself, but now began to realize his limitations in this department. Accordingly he hired Roy Parnell, nephew of Reg, to take over testing.

The team attacked Le Mans that year "in the grand manner." However, the Lagonda crashed after 20 laps and the two DB3S coupes were "terribly disappointing," also crashing within yards of each other. A supercharged DB3S lasted the longest but blew a head gasket after completing 222 laps. Wyer had a nervous collapse and was sent away to recuperate. When many years later he reminded David Brown of this episode in 1954, Brown replied that he thought he had a breakdown after every race.

The following season, the tragic 1955, one of his cars, that of Peter Collins and Paul Frère, finished second. Wyer believed that the ACO over-reacted to that year's crash in producing a set of very safety conscious regulations for 1956. However, again, one of his cars came home second, Stirling Moss and Peter Collins having led the race for seven hours. At the end of the year Brown invited him to become general manager of Aston Martin and Lagonda. Happily for Wyer, Reg Parnell took over as racing manager. Wyer was to say that it was Parnell's control of the race, with the battle being fought on his terms, that was to bring Aston Martin the Le Mans win that it so craved in 1959. Roy Salvadori and Carroll Shelby's victory in the DBR1 was to be the first of four for Wyer at La Sarthe.

The next two were to come with the GT40 wins of 1968 and 1969, but we have to go back to 1963 for Wyer's first involvement with Ford's Le Mans attempt. In an effort to win the 24-hour race, the American company talked about buying Ferrari or perhaps Aston Martin. Neither happened, but Wyer left Aston to become a key member of the Ford assault. He worked closely with Lola in the early days, mediating between Eric Broadley and Ford, eventually setting up Ford Advanced Vehicles in Slough to look after the GT40 in Europe.

Stuart McCrudden was an apprentice at Ford in 1965. He inquired whether *Ford News* would be interested in his covering Le Mans for them and then wrote a letter to John Wyer. The result was an interview with Mortimer 'Mort' Goodall and a trip out of the country for the first time as 'tea boy' for the Ford Advanced Vehicles team. He recalls Wyer as "elegant, stylish, aloof, but much respected. He clearly enjoyed life." It was evident to McCrudden that matters were not as they once were. Those who had been with Wyer at Aston Martin now felt constrained by the Ford yoke, while Wyer seemed to be constantly arguing with designer Roy Lunn.

In 1966 Wyer met Grady Davis, the executive vice-president of the Gulf Oil Corporation, at Sebring. Initially, Davis wanted to buy a road-going GT40 and the pair started to meet regularly. At one point the American asked Wyer for his views on oil company participation in motorsport. Wyer's answer was to form the basis of what was to come. The major companies, he thought, had spread their nets too wide and failed to benefit from being specifically identified with winners. For Wyer, the solution was to become involved with a single, successful team. Somewhat understandably, he suggested an endurance racing one. Davis soon asked him to run such a team and, with Ford Advanced Vehicles likely to be disbanded at the end of the year, Wyer found himself in a position to accept. The result was the creation of JW Automotive Engineering and the famous powder blue-and-orange livery took to the tracks.

The Le Mans careers of the JWA GT40s, Mirages and Porsche 917s are recorded elsewhere in this book. The Fords and the Mirage were to bring Wyer further success at La Sarthe although, perhaps surprisingly, no Porsche won the race in Gulf colours, although some who have watched the Steve McQueen film *Le Mans* probably believe one did.

Wyer's name is often joined with those of his two able lieutenants, John Horsman and David Yorke. Horsman first met Wyer when he went for a job interview at the David Brown showrooms in London's Piccadilly in 1958. "At the time I felt he did not have

long to live, he looked so ill, but I am glad to say that he survived another 34 years."

Horsman was to work directly for Wyer from 1961 until his semi-retirement in 1971, and then continue to work with him until 1975. Wyer also assisted his former number-two during the years that Horsman ran the Mirages for Harley Cluxton. To Horsman, one of Wyer's greatest assets was his ability to enter the pit at Le Mans, having been absent for a few hours, pick up the last hourly position from the ACO showing the number of laps each car had completed at that given hour and, within 10 to 15 minutes, work out the exact time gaps between each car and the race order at that very moment. "I have tried to do that and know it takes great concentration of the mind, with absolutely no interferences, but I never mastered it like John. Nowadays I expect it is a lost art, it all being done by computer." Wyer, says Horsman, "possessed a mind capable of great concentration and mathematical ability."

Derek Bell remembers a time when the JW team was testing a Mirage at Sebring. There was a major problem and Wyer reacted by saying: "Phone up Slough. Look up the records from when we had a problem testing the GT40 here in 1968." Bell was impressed by Wyer's immaculate record keeping, everything being carefully noted down in pencil. Nobody else in those days took the temperature of the track. Roy Salvadori also recalls those records, in particular the notes Wyer made about the comments of drivers new to his team. He would always go out of his way to take an interest in such drivers.

Horsman believes Wyer's greatness "to come from his ability to delegate. I don't believe this came naturally to him, but after his many years at Aston Martin, followed by his three years with Ford, he had learnt he could not do everything himself, as was his nature." At JWA he forced himself to delegate the

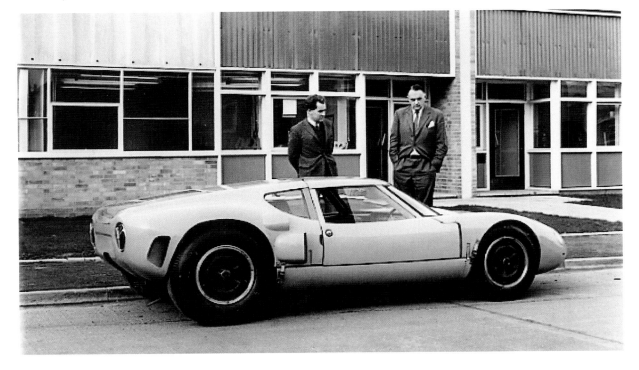

It has been said that the Ford GT40 evolved from the Lola GT. Wyer emphatically denied this although he admitted that the GT40 did incorporate many of Eric Broadley's ideas. Here Wyer (right) and the Lola designer discuss the latter's first endurance car. Wyer pointed out how simple it was compared with the Ford's over-engineering. *(Lola Cars International)*

Belgian Lucien Bianchi gets into the 1968 winning Ford GT40. It was to be victory number two for Wyer at Le Mans. *(Ford)*

engineering, race car development and preparation to Horsman and the race operation to David Yorke. "It worked out very well on the whole," says Horsman.

There is also a tale of how Wyer, on learning that the British Racing and Sports Car Club's Nick Syrett was visiting the Daytona 24-Hours, invited him to join the team in the pits. Twice Syrett turned up at the JWA pit and twice David Yorke threw him out. Eventually Syrett bumped into Wyer elsewhere in the paddock and reported how Yorke had been unwilling for him to be in the pits. "My dear Nicholas," said Wyer, "I would not take too much notice of him. I am afraid he is not very well bred." JWA mechanic Gordon Wingrove remembers that David Yorke must certainly have been brave, though. In an effort to stop his drivers overshooting their pits he stood on the line where they had to halt. "He had bruises on his shins."

Jackie Oliver recalls John Wyer as "a Darth Vader figure with a very hooded complexion." His contact with Wyer was limited, as he would deal with the strategies that Yorke – "an excellent team manager," says Oliver – and Horsman would implement. "He orchestrated through these two individuals. I don't remember him giving me any instructions at all." It was a fixed and impressive command structure. Wyer, anyway, says Oliver, was a man of few words, but with a very dry sense of humour. Mike Salmon recalls reporting a problem on the brakes of his Aston Martin Zagato. Wyer replied, "My dear Michael, I think the situation is more apparent than actual."

Wyer was somebody who did not care for political correctness and would not, reckons Derek Bell, fit in these days, "but he would probably be just what is needed." Bell believes that Wyer set that standard for the rest of his own career. "At Ferrari there had been all the passion of Ferrari and you were not really part of a team. With Wyer you were. There were two cars and you were one of the four drivers."

He certainly made a great impression on the young Bell, although during the year that he drove the JWA Porsche 917 he did not get to know him that well. "The team was gelling and doing a great job and Wyer was like the figurehead behind it all." He certainly nurtured the people around him. "He had such a wise head on his shoulders. His attention to detail reflected on everyone in the team." Wyer, says Bell, was "really one of the old school, self-opinionated, very bright and knowledgeable." He recalls him drinking a Martini in the evening after a race, walking around slowly in a positive way with his head slightly stooped.

"He always had one-liners. He could walk past you without saying 'Good morning' even if you had not seen him for a month. I said 'Good morning, John.' He looked slightly to one side. 'Hello, Bell, a riot of colour again I see.' That was Wyer. He was just like a headmaster to me. It was like a furtherance of further education."

Journalist Michael Cotton spent a lot of time with the John Wyer team and remembers a "very good atmosphere." He does say, though, that Wyer and Yorke "were not people to be argued with." Brian Redman, he remembers, always called him "Mr Wyer."

Gordon Wingrove, a JWA mechanic in 1970 and 1971, recalls a strict hierarchy in that Wyer would tend to speak to a shop foreman rather than the mechanics themselves. It was only at a test day that the likes of Wingrove would get the chance to talk to him. It was probably, he reflects, a legacy of the way they worked at Aston Martin.

"He did have a sense of humour, but most of us were frightened of him." Wyer was also a master of the understatement. Wingrove recalls a cold day at Silverstone with Derek Bell testing a Mirage. Out, somewhere in the distant reaches of the former Northamptonshire airfield, Bell went off. Wyer cut the resulting silence: "Well, I think that tested that enough."

Bell also recalls testing that Mirage, which Horsman states was the Ford GT40-engined M4, a backup car intended in case the Porsche 917 programme fell through. It was, he says, a handful thanks to the heavy lump of an engine in the back. Perhaps not surprisingly, Bell made a habit of going off the road with that particular beast. He remembers that Wyer had said that if lap times were brought below a certain point then the unloved car could be entered in the Can-Am series. To Bell at the time, this North America championship seemed such a glamorous series. Horsman says that the car was never intended for Can-Am. It just did not have enough power for that.

As the day ended and the target time was nowhere in sight Bell suggested locking up the roll bars, tightening up the shock absorbers and making the car "like a go kart." On his first timed lap he was flying and the car, although still nervous, did not feel too dire. Out of Stowe corner he caught a bit of concrete curb and crashed. "Everything fell off the car," so Bell started to pick parts of the bodywork up, putting them back

to make the damage look not quite as bad as it really was. Wyer drove up, looked at the hapless driver, and merely said: "I saw it all, Bell" and then drove off again. "He didn't even pick me up!"

Wyer often had a good quip. If a journalist told him that the opposition was in trouble during a race he would remark: "Nothing trivial, I hope." On one occasion Wyer and Horsman were at the Porsche factory and Ferry Porsche had denied that there was such an engine as the 16-cylinder 917 unit. Immediately after the meeting Ferdinand Piech took the pair to the dynamometer room and showed them the 'non–existent' 16-cylinder. Piech, whose English was good, but not quite as good as he thought, said: "Auntie does not know about this," meaning that his uncle Ferry was unaware of its existence. As they were leaving, Wyer said quietly to Horsman, "If 'Auntie' does not know about that, she must be pretty thick!"

Horsman also calls Wyer "a great orator," despite

The David Hobbs/Mike Hailwood GT40 receives attention during 1969. Wyer's cars unexpectedly came first and third in the race that featured the most exciting finish in Le Mans' long history. The man himself, though, was back in London, unwell. (Alan Hearn collection)

GT40 number 1075 was usually Jacky Ickx's mount, but the Belgian had broken his leg at the Canadian Grand Prix. Gulf's Grady Davis came to the rescue by signing Pedro Rodriguez to partner Bianchi for the 1968 Le Mans. Jackie Oliver was also recruited for the team for the first time. Number 1075 would win Le Mans for a second time in 1969, on this occasion with Ickx and Oliver. (Ford)

the fact that he did not like making speeches and was always nervous when called upon to do so. He did, though, have what Horsman calls "one strange oddity."

"In our days at JWA he would give me a set of specific directions as to how he wanted a project to be done, together with good reasons for this decision. Before I knew him better I would go to the workshop to work out with the chief mechanic or foreman how we should go about the project, personnel, materials, etc, only to find next morning that he had made a 180-degree turnaround with completely logical reasoning. After a while, I would not make any changes until the following day."

"We called John Wyer 'Death Ray' because he was such a serious looking bloke, but he had a very cheeky sense of humour," says Richard Attwood. He first met Wyer through his father, Harry, who sold Astons in about 1960. "My father was trying to get me involved in whatever Aston Martin might be doing, but they had just finished racing…so it was a complete waste of time!"

John Horsman describes that 'Death Ray' look as "notorious and piercing," but being fortunate to get on well with Wyer he says that he was never on the receiving end of it. "He had this certain look," says Alan Hearn, who worked for Wyer from 1967 to 1975 and succeeded Ermanno Cuoghi as his chief mechanic. It made Hearn think: "He's going to fire me!"

Wyer regarded Attwood as an ultra-reliable driver whom he could call upon when he had a crisis. On one occasion he was asked to drive a Mirage with Jacky Ickx at the Nürburgring. Ickx had carried out plenty of practice, and then Attwood was allowed out for a few laps. He was just getting into his stride when he received the 'in' sign. He ignored it. "And this," Attwood reminds us, "is John Wyer." Having been quite a bit slower than Ickx he was now almost as quick on this extra lap. "Now I feel great. I can do it." About half an hour after his return to the pits,

Wyer quietly asked him if he had seen the board. Attwood admitted that he had, wanting to explain why. Wyer merely said "that's fine." There was, recalls Attwood, "no bollocking…but if I had thrown it off the road…"

He did exactly the same thing when he drove with Pedro Rodriguez in 1971. At the beginning of that year Attwood had determined that he was going to retire from racing and was only competing in selected races. He was called in at the last minute by Wyer to replace Oliver at Zeltweg. Rodriguez set the car up. This was right at the end of the development of the Porsche 917 and it was, says Attwood, "absolutely perfect." He admits, though, to have been "rusty" by this stage. He was about five seconds slower than the Mexican in practice and then, on what should have been his final lap, he brought this down to about two and a half seconds. False logic told him that with another lap he could be competitive. However, by this stage in his career Rodriguez and the Porsche 917 were as one, "he had such confidence in the car." Attwood stayed out for a lap more than he should. Again Wyer asked him if he had seen the board, but again the legendary "wrath of Wyer" never happened. "He was so understated," says Attwood. "Wonderful, wonderful, typical British calmness and efficiency; almost efficiency gone mad."

Attwood was never on the wrong end of Wyer's wrath, but there is an incident with Mike Hailwood that shows it was not a good idea to upset him. It had started to pour with rain at Le Mans. The pit lane suddenly became overcrowded and, unable to get in to change onto wets, Hailwood started on another lap. He never made it, flying off the road before he could get round. He walked back. Wyer looked at him on his arrival back at the pits. "Don't worry, Hailwood. Don't call us, we'll call you." With that he turned round and walked away.

Roy Salvadori says that Wyer could be cutting with "the old hands" and would chop down to size anyone he thought had got out of hand. He also states that Wyer had black moods when everyone would be at pains to stay out of his way. For all that, he was the one team manager Salvadori always wanted to do well for. The respect was mutual, with Wyer regarding the 1959 Le Mans winner as "a very valued friend."

It was not likely that a driver would answer Wyer back, but Reg Parnell, who usually wanted to be out in front in an endurance race, came near during the 1956 Le Mans. Aston designer Ted Cutting recounts how Parnell's lap times had started slipping. Wyer wanted to know what on earth was happening. "It's alright. I got to thinking about the pigs," said the part-time farmer. Another press-on driver, whom Roy Salvadori says treated Le Mans like a 10-lapper, was George Abecassis. After one of his many accidents, the former RAF pilot is supposed to have told Wyer that when he crashed a bomber in the War he was given the DFC, but when he shunted an Aston he got a "rollicking."

Perhaps it is best to leave the last word on John Wyer to his colleague and friend of many years, John Horsman. "John Wyer was a very great man, the likes of which do not appear very often. It was my privilege to work for him, and to be his friend and confidant."

Bianchi (left) and Rodriguez test the roof of the 1968-winning car with chief mechanic Ermanno Cuoghi. (Ford)

Alan Hearn first went to Le Mans as a mechanic in 1960 although he had already been working on cars for the race for five years. As a trainee mechanic at Motor Work, Chalfont-St-Peter, he had helped to look after the Cooper-Jaguar of the Whitehead brothers and then their two Aston Martin DB3S racers. There was also the only DBR1 built for private ownership, this being the 1959 car DBR1/5 for Graham Whitehead; Hearn remembers travelling to Feltham to collect parts for the car. Brian Naylor crashed it during the Le Mans race that year, the abandoned car being further damaged when a Stanguellini then ran into it.

The following year, Whitehead raced a Ferrari 250 GT at Le Mans with Henry Taylor. However, Hearn was able to work on the previous year's winning DBR1/2 that had now been sold to Major Ian Baillie of the Grenadier Guards. It was his first opportunity to travel to La Sarthe with a car. On the Friday night the team planned to drive to the Mulsanne straight to set up the lights. The 21-year-old Hearn was told to get an early night and prepare for the long race ahead, but instead he took the team's ex-works Aston Martin transporter off for a trip round the track. As he drove down the Mulsanne straight so the team spied him. "In the morning I got a right old ear-bashing."

In the event Jack Fairman became entrenched in the Mulsanne sand for nearly an hour before extricating the car to finish ninth. For Hearn it was to be an isolated trip to Le Mans because the following year Whitehead moved away from Motor Work. Instead, Hearn settled down to a life of working on road-going Jaguars, getting married and having children.

By 1967 he was itching to return to racing and applied for a job with John Wyer at Slough. He had not realized just how many of Wyer's staff were ex-Aston Martin. "Having worked for the Whiteheads proved useful," he says. Initially he toiled on customer Ford GT40s for people like Mike Salmon. The changes that had taken place in sportscar racing since the start of the decade took him aback. "Everything was so big…and they were rear-engined." In 1968 he joined the works team, remaining with it until 1975.

After a debut at Daytona, Hearn went to Le Mans to work with senior mechanic John Collins on the David Hobbs/Paul Hawkins GT40. During practice the drivers complained of a vibration, which it was felt was caused by an engine mounting fouling the chassis. "We shimmed it up with a washer to give it clearance." The drivers then tested the car on the roads around La Chartre and reported that it felt better. Hearn can only wonder at the speeds they must have been doing to notice this. During the course of the race, Hearn and Collins had to change the clutch only for the engine to blow up.

The following year Collins had left and Hearn was now senior mechanic on the Hobbs/Mike Hailwood GT40, working with Ray Jones. The year 1969, of course, is remembered for the thrilling victory for the other JWA car. However, Hearn points out that his GT40 was ahead of its team-mate for much of the race, but unfortunately

on the Sunday Hobbs found that the brake pedal appeared faulty. David Yorke said that the problem must be the pads, but a lap later Hobbs was back, saying that this had not helped. Hearn removed the left rear wheel to find that the bridge pipe over the caliper had been knocked off by a wheel weight. "That is when we were overtaken," he remarks. His disappointment dissolved at the finish. "The tension in the pit was unbelievable. We really did not know who would come by first; we knew the car was low on fuel."

The next season was the first for Wyer with the Porsche 917. Hearn says that the factory mechanics were looking forward to working with the JWA team at Le Mans. They had heard that Wyer gave his mechanics the Friday before the race off to go fishing in the Loire. Hardly, recalls Hearn…that was more likely to be the drivers. "We would be in the garage rebuilding the cars." The villagers would turn out to watch the work being done and lunch would be brought out from the hotel. Food was not always easy to come by in those days, and Hearn views today's team catering facilities somewhat wistfully.

Indeed, the conditions for mechanics in the 1960s and 1970s were "terrible," small concrete bunkers with a narrow alleyway out the back and nowhere to sit down. "It became my second home, but it was uncomfortable." There was also no protection for the mechanics out on the pit lane. As the senior of the two, Hearn would always take the outside for himself.

In 1970 he was again working with Ray Jones, this time on the Pedro Rodriguez/Leo Kinnunen 917. JWA, which had already won the Daytona 24-Hours that year, was looking for the hat-trick, "but it all went wrong." The highlight of that year for Hearn must surely have been at Brands Hatch, not at Le Mans; how Rodriguez drove that race in the pouring rain is the stuff of legend. Often quoted is the tale of how, after six laps, clerk of the course Nick Syrett ordered the little Mexican in for ignoring the yellow flags. It was Hearn who held the door open as Syrett lectured the driver. "Pedro just sat there, eyes ahead." Lecture over, Rodriguez shot off into the storm and delivered one of the great drives of endurance racing history.

Hearn was Rodriguez's mechanic throughout 1970 and 1971 and although these were great years, success at Le Mans did not come their way. He recalls the frustration

Alan Hearn (centre) acted as mechanic for the ultra-rapid Pedro Rodriguez (left) throughout 1970 and 1971. *(Alan Hearn collection)*

when Porsche ordered the JWA team to slow down the second-placed Richard Attwood/Herbert Müller car in the closing stages.

The Mirage years followed, with 1974 in particular recalled as "a very busy race." The team was using titanium drive-shafts and CV joints. However, the latter's rubber covering was faulty and throwing out grease. The mechanics were thus continually packing the CV joints. "We were as black as the ace of spades."

About this time Wyer arranged for the mechanics' wives and girl friends to be present at the race. Hearn was "somehow elected" to drive the minibus with them in back to La Chartre after the event. It did not seem fair considering he had been up working for about 36 hours; it was even worse when all his passengers fell asleep. The drive still seems to rankle even after all these years…

The same journey, after the same amount of time awake but in a Ford GT40, now that is a very different

matter. It was a tradition that the mechanics drove the cars back to the hotel after the race. In 1969, chief mechanic Ermanno Cuoghi led the way in the winning car with Hearn following. The *gendarmes* refused to let them go down their normal route, and they were forced to make their way through villages that they had never seen before, asking for directions as they passed by. The drive to La Chartre was a carry-over from Aston Martin days, "a special treat for the mechanics." However, Porsche did not like the idea at all and put a stop to it in 1970.

In 1972 Hearn succeeded Cuoghi as chief mechanic, with Jones as his number-two. In his final year with Wyer, 1975, the team again won Le Mans, that season's Gulf GR8 being, he says, "much better" that its predecessor.

Although Hearn now moved away from motor racing for his daily living, he would still return to Le Mans for a week each year at the request of John Horsman, who was now team manager and engineer in charge of Harley Cluxton's Mirages. In 1977 Horsman invited him to Arizona to help convert the cars into Renault-powered M9s. When the cars went back to Cosworth motivation two years later Hearn again spent a while in the USA.

Hearn's time at Le Mans now mirrors that of Horsman, which meant that in 1982 he was privy to the infuriating saga of the Mirage M12 (see Chapter 18), another car that he had worked on in Arizona. It was he who had the task of driving the car off the grid. Round the back of the pits he almost ran over a little old lady who was dressed in black. To this day he has no idea what she was doing there.

Horsman also assisted with Vern Schuppan's team of Porsche 962s from 1988 to 1991 and it was in the first of these years that Hearn made his last of 14 working appearances at Le Mans, again taking a week's holiday to do so.

THE FORGERS

Don Wilkinson knew someone who had acted as a timekeeper for John Wyer. He reckoned that if he and his friend Roger Ellis turned up at Le Mans on the Tuesday before the 1970 race, said Mr Wyer would give them passes and jobs in his pit crew. As a backup they had two passes from the previous year.

Arriving at the circuit they found an area behind the pits used as a car park for the signallers at Mulsanne corner. Unchallenged, they put up their tent. Still unchallenged, they then drove up to the start area and attended a Porsche press conference in the tribune. So far so good. Wilkinson's friend, the real timekeeper, introduced them to Wyer who, as Ellis puts it, "easily sussed two clueless freeloaders and declined our offer of assistance."

Plan B was also looking rocky; the 1969 passes were a different colour to those used in 1970, although the design and layout were the same. Out of desperation they drove into the town to buy a bottle of ink in which they would soak the offending passes. They returned to the campsite to find that the Grand Prix Medical Unit had parked right next to them.

The next step was to see if the 'new' passes worked. In the morning, spectators with valid tickets were being allowed into the paddock to see the cars close-up. The ticket inspector failed to notice the forgery and the pair spent a pleasant day admiring 917s, 512s and the like and standing next to a 'rookie' by the name of Derek Bell.

For days Wilkinson and Ellis used their forgeries without any problem, watching practice and test sessions. But come the race they were concerned because the checking stations were manned not just by marshals but also by *gendarmes*.

However, the two had been making friends with their neighbours down at the Mulsanne corner, who lent them some spare Medical Staff passes. These worked for a while until the last possible check point, when a *gendarme* refused them further passage. Ellis was placed "under arrest in the back of a police jeep, a pistol firmly pushed into my ribs," while Wilkinson went in search of some alternative tickets. Thankfully, the Wicky Racing Team back at the signalling pits helped out with some more passes and Ellis was freed to watch the race. "The only time we used correct and legitimate passes we got arrested," he says.

Gordon Wingrove was out of work. However, the interview that he had just failed was on the Slough Trading Estate, home of, among others, JW Automotive Engineering. On the strength of the fact that he had run a Clubmans car, Wingrove decided to knock on the door. Proving that anything is worth trying, whatever the odds against it succeeding, JWA took Wingrove on for a trial month with the warning "if you're no good you're out on your arse."

It was the spring of 1970, and Wingrove was given the responsibility of looking after the Mirage M5 Formula Ford project. He occasionally worked on the Porsche 917s, but it was not until the following year that he found himself full-time as a mechanic on the World Championship sportscar programme. Three JWA 917s were entered for Le Mans, two long and one short-tailed, with Wingrove working on the latter, which was to be driven by Richard Attwood and Herbert Müller.

Wingrove recalls the "huge speed difference" between his car and that of the two long-tails. However, that probably did not faze him. "Some people say that top speed is what you need at Le Mans, but that's not necessarily true. There are some twisty sections that definitely require downforce as opposed to low drag.

"The first thing that surprised me was how rough and dusty the paddock area was. There was nowhere much to work on the cars except the pit lane and that was heaving with people. The place was so different to other circuits; it was all a bit daunting. The pit box was a small room with a door and a counter. Within that you had everything, "including the folks from Gulf Oil."

Wingrove still recalls the traditional JWA base at La Chartre-sur-le-Loire with some affection, and the excellent meals at the *Hotel de France* that the grubby mechanics enjoyed, having simply removed their overalls and washed their hands.

During the season two mechanics were assigned to each of the two team cars, while Wingrove and chief mechanic Ermanno Cuoghi would tend to what was referred to as the 'trainer', the spare car. Three cars were to be raced at Le Mans and Wingrove found himself in the front line. He admits, though, that it was safer to use the more experienced mechanics from the other two cars to perform some of the trickier tasks such as changing the brake pads. However, perhaps his most abiding memory is of a significant task that he performed on behalf of the Jo Siffert/Derek Bell entry. The car was dropping oil and a crack in the crankcase was diagnosed. End of the story, one supposes. Certainly most of the team did, but not Cuoghi, who Wingrove remembers as "an incredible innovator."

The chief mechanic told Wingrove to "go and get some chairs." Yes, that's right, chairs, not something normally associated with the repair of any kind of car, let alone a Porsche 917. However, standing in the box and in the dark alleyway that used to back the pits complex, Wingrove found four chairs that he describes as being typically '1960s', with thin sponge seats and leatherette covers. He dragged them in to the pit where Cuoghi cut the sponge

Gordon Wingrove, who spent two years working for John Wyer's team at Slough before leaving to pursue a career in microprocessors and electronics. *(Gordon Wingrove collection)*

seating away. "I'm making a nappy," he informed the bemused Wingrove. Using liberal amounts of tank tape they then applied the sponge around the bottom of the engine to absorb the oil and sent the car on its way. It is amazing to what lengths some people will go in order to keep their cars going at Le Mans. But not surprisingly, all was in vain and before long the car really was retired.

Earlier, Wingrove's 'own' short-tailed car had been running near the front, indeed it had taken the lead at one point, both drivers, recalls Wingrove, "going well." Then during the night the car lost fifth gear. The torque on third and fifth in these gearboxes could actually unscrew the syncro. It was a problem that Porsche had known about since it occurred at Daytona earlier in the year. The head of transmissions at Porsche had promised John Horsman that he would carry out his suggestion of making third and fifth gear cones/rings with left-hand threads to avoid a repetition. However, when the cars arrived at Le Mans Horsman found that this had not been done and that the rings had simply been peened and Loctited. That did not stop them from coming unscrewed and, as Horsman observed, ruining the team's last hope of winning that year.

The resulting work took 27 minutes. At the end of the 24 hours the car was in second place just two laps behind the winner. The fastest lap that year – the all-time record – was set by one of the other JWA Porsches at 3 minutes 18.4 seconds. The maths is obvious.

It was to be Gordon Wingrove's only season as a mechanic at Le Mans. The next year he started a long career in electronics and microprocessing, which is what he had been after in the first place that day in spring 1970.

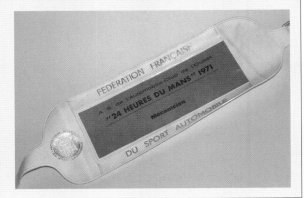

Solitary Mirage

"I never really 'looked over the fence' and paid any attention to Le Mans." Derek Bell may not have set out to be an endurance racer, but he was easily to become Britain's most successful Le Mans driver. The first of his five victories came in the 1970s. Here his Gulf GR8 leads the sister car of Vern Schuppan through the Esses. *(LAT Photographic)*

CHAPTER 17

THE BRITISH AT LE MANS 1970-1981

". . . the march out into the desert displayed under all its circumstances a courage and dash worthy of our best military traditions." (Alex MacDonald, *Daily News* Correspondent)

As far as British manufacturers are concerned, the 1970s saw just the solitary Mirage that appeared briefly out of a desert of German and French cars. Winning British drivers numbered but just three with Richard Attwood, Graham Hill and Derek Bell.

The decade had begun well, as will be underlined in a subsequent chapter, with Attwood overcoming mumps plus a grid seemingly full of bigger-engined and faster Porsche 917s to score the first victory for the Stuttgart marque and for the Porsche Salzburg team. Perhaps the magazine that headed its report "Porsche makes it at last – without Wyer" was a little unkind, but the record books certainly look unfinished given that the team most responsible for making the 917 legend what it was only won Le Mans with a Ford GT40 and the Gulf GR8.

Unlike the Wyer team, Englishman Vic Elford never won Le Mans and there are those who say that his press-on spirit made it unlikely that he should do so, even though his car had been so far ahead the year before. To win Le Mans needs the guile of a Richard Attwood, and in 1970 he had found an arguably slower partner who was more likely to finish. Elford showed, though, why he was so held in awe in practice, preventing Ferrari from taking pole with his Porsche Salzburg long-tailed 917.

There were British drivers in most of the 917s that stormy year including Brian Redman, David Hobbs, Mike Hailwood and David Piper, as well as Elford and Attwood. The opposition in the Ferrari 512 camp included Michael Parkes, Alistair Walker and another newcomer, one Derek Bell. Walker, in his sole Le Mans, was the only one of the above apart from Attwood to be among the select and small band of finishers.

The following year was the last of the charismatic Group 4 leviathans. Attwood and Elford were back in 917s, Parkes in a 512M. Bell and Hobbs had swapped manufacturers, while Jackie Oliver had returned to the race for the JW Automotive Engineering Porsche team. Chris Craft and Alain de Cadenet were driving the big Ferraris for the first and last time at La Sarthe. It looks a mighty assault by the British, but the only

ones around at the finish were Attwood in second place and Craft in fifth.

Every now and again the French become serious about winning Le Mans and succeed, usually in the face of little opposition. Now begins such a period although in the first of Matra's two victories we find the archetypal Englishman complete with moustache, Graham Hill. The rules had changed, limiting the sports-racing cars to the then Formula One size of 3 litres. The Porsche 917s and Ferrari 512s were now obsolete, but not so the French Matras. Perhaps it was indicative of how the British felt about this that the attendance was obviously down in 1972. Still,

The Gulf brand continued to be to the fore during the first half of the 1970s although one of its cars was not to win again until 1975. Mechanic Alan Hearn (right) listens to what his driver, Pedro Rodriguez has to say about their Porsche 917. *(Alan Hearn collection)*

there were British drivers in the Matra-Simca team with Hill in one of the 670s and David Hobbs in an older 660 C. Girling disc brakes had also replaced those of the German manufacturer ATE. British-built opposition came from a couple of Jo Bonnier-entered Lolas and the Duckhams Special of Alain de Cadenet, all three with Cosworth DFV power. Sadly, the vastly experienced Swede Bonnier was to crash fatally in one of his cars, having led for a couple of laps early on. John Wyer chose to stay away with his Mirages.

Two of the Matras swapped places for most of the day and night. During the morning one of them fell behind thanks to a stop because of wet electrics. This put into first place the car that Hill was sharing with Frenchman Henri Pescarolo, a position that it held to the end.

Eleven Lolas had been entered for Le Mans prior to the 1972 race, but not one had finished. That year a Lola T290 not only completed the 24 hours, but also won its class. However, it was not something the winning team wanted to broadcast.

Briton Barrie Smith, winner of the Ford Grand Prix at Denmark's Jyllandsring back in 1968, had entered with the French-based Kodak team. A request for the loan of a spare nose cone from Lola had fallen on deaf ears. Smith remembers "they thought we were crazy doing Le Mans and tried to talk us out of it." Such was the feeling about this that after the event the Kodak team took advertising space in *Autosport* magazine, thanking all those who had helped them on their way to the 2-litre class victory, but deliberately neglecting to state the make of chassis that had been used.

Wyer's Mirages were back the following year, but it was not yet their time. That of Mike Hailwood, John Watson and Australian Vern Schuppan raced as high as third. However, Schuppan ran wide at Tertre Rouge and the car overturned, although the driver was uninjured. Not one British car finished the race, although it has to be recorded that Vic Elford, never an overall winner, nevertheless claimed a first in the GT class at the wheel of a Ferrari 365 GTB. There was some name changing for 1974. The Gulf Mirages had become simply Gulfs, but the plucky Duckhams Special had lost the name of its sponsor and was now a De Cadenet and coloured a patriotic British Racing Green. Derek Bell and Mike Hailwood came fourth in

Jackie Oliver leaps into the JWA Porsche just vacated by Pedro Rodriguez. Both had excellent drives in 1971, the Englishman setting the fastest lap of the race at 151.854mph, a record that still stands. A broken oil pipe brought a dramatic end to their race. *(Alan Hearn collection)*

Oliver sets off from the pits. He and Rodriguez dominated the first 10 hours of the 1971 race. However, just before 3.00am the event took on the proverbial pear shape for them. A broken shock absorber dropped them down to third and the 917 that Richard Attwood was sharing with Herbert Müller temporarily took over at the front. *(Alan Hearn collection)*

In 1972 Graham Hill achieved a unique triple, adding victory in the Le Mans 24-Hours to his Formula One World Championship and Indianapolis 500 wins. However, in driving for Matra, he assisted in the first French win for 22 years. *(MNF collection)*

THE TRIPLE CROWN

There is no definitive description of motor racing's Triple Crown. It could be the three most prestigious races – Le Mans, the Indianapolis 500 and the Monaco Grand Prix – or it could be Le Mans, Indy and the Formula One World Championship. Either way, it does not matter, just one man has been able to lay claim to the title, Englishman Graham Hill.

His victory at Le Mans occurred in 1972 on the last of his 10 appearances at the circuit. The era of the magnificent Group 5 cars was just over and Hill was at the wheel of a 3-litre works Matra, sharing the car with France's Henri Pescarolo. His previous best finish had been back in 1964 when he had come second in a Maranello Concessionaires Ferrari 330P with Jo Bonnier. Other drives ranged from Lotus Fifteen to the gas turbine Rover-BRM, while his son Damon raced at Le Mans just once, in the Richard Lloyd Porsche 962 that retired during the 14th hour of the 1989 event.

That there was even one winner of the Triple Crown hangs by a proverbial thread. Hill's 1966 win at the Indianapolis 500 was one of controversy. "What a glorious mix-up!" headed the short-lived *Auto News*. Even so, it was Great Britain's finest hour at the 'Brickyard'. After the race it was argued that Scot Jim Clark was still ahead at the finish and that Hill had merely been unlapping himself 30 tours before the end. The organizers double-checked the official records and awarded the £75,000 prize money to Hill. Jackie Stewart, who was firmly in the lead himself when he had to retire eight laps from home, believes today that the result was the correct one. However, Clark is said to have received quite a shock when he went into Victory Lane, only to discover that Hill's Lola was already there. Britain had three likely winners at Indianapolis in 1966; one of its sons was not to win there again until 2005

Clark was also on the wrong end of Hill's first World Championship, that of 1962. Had a bolt not dropped out from the crankcase of his Lotus at the final round, the title might have gone to the Scot. There is also a sad irony in that Hill's 1968 title came after he had assumed the mantle of Lotus team leader following Clark's tragic death earlier in the year.

Monaco, though, was firmly Hill's during the 1960s. From 1963 to 1969 he dominated the race, only missing out in 1966 and 1967. In these days of longer drivers' careers, five or more victories at one specific Grand Prix have become commonplace. Back then it was a remarkable achievement.

Quite who won the Indianapolis 500 in 1966 is a contentious issue. Whatever, Graham Hill was given the verdict over fellow Brit Jim Clark. Two sides of the triple crown were now his, but the Le Mans win would have to wait until 1972. It would be considerably longer before another Englishman, Dan Wheldon in 2005, was to win at 'the Brickyard'. *(Lola Cars International)*

one of those Gulfs, but otherwise there is little to say. As far as Britain was concerned, Le Mans was still a desert.

Then came the race of 1975. Le Mans had lost its World Sports Car Championship status. A fuel consumption prerequisite of at least 7.1mpg meant that many described it as an economy run, a term more associated with something likely to be run by the Hants & Berks Motor Club (although said club's event was, at times, anything but pedantic). The turbocharged Porsche and Renault and the V12 Alfa Romeo engines that might have contested Le Mans were just not capable of such figures. A detuned Cosworth DFV engine looked the best bet for 1975. The previous year John Wyer's Gulf had recorded a best consumption figure of 6.1mpg. However, further

The 1975 winning Gulf GR8 in the pits. The ACO ran that year's race to a fuel consumption formula, which meant that it was no longer part of the World Championship. Alfa Romeo, Alpine, Ferrari and Matra all stayed away. (LAT Photogaphic)

ALAIN DE CADENET

Can there have been anyone more British at Le Mans than Alain de Cadenet? Probably not, and yet his father fled from Nazi-occupied Europe to join the Free French Air Force during the Second World War. The story goes that Winston Churchill had asked the British people to befriend the many displaced foreigners who had been washed up on these shores. De Cadenet's grandmother took heed of this and invited back to her home the lonely Frenchman that she had found feeding the pigeons in Trafalgar Square.

De Cadenet is one of those born in the late 1940s and early 1950s who were brought up by a generation that had been dominated by the war. They have only known peace, yet their parents had experienced anything but for almost six years. We have already seen how conflict probably influenced the minds of men like Birkin (one of de Cadenet's heroes) and Hamilton. For de Cadenet it was something different. As his neighbour, Douglas Bader, would sometimes tell him, "what you need is a bloody good war." The legendary Bader lived opposite de Cadenet and would invite him to impromptu dinner parties where the guests might include such as fellow fighter 'ace' Peter Townsend or one-time destroyer captain Lord Mountbatten. De Cadenet, who admits to "a colossal respect" for this generation, imbibed their spirit. They were all, he says, brought up with a sense of duty, loyalty and honour. It means a lot to de Cadenet to be British. When sponsorship has allowed, his cars have been coloured green and one even displayed the legend 'Made in Britain'.

In the early 1970s he was running his own Formula One team but was becoming increasingly aware that his only chance of real success would have to come in some other form of racing. He also admits to having "an urge to go to Le Mans like all proper Brits." That almost came off in 1969, but a planned drive in a Ford GT40 with John Jordan did not materialize. Instead, de Cadenet's debut at La Sarthe was to come two years later in a Ferrari 512M that Derek Bell had raced the season before.

His Brabham BT33 Grand Prix car brought him into contact with the "impressive" young designer Gordon Murray. The resulting partnership, the Duckhams Special, is examined in Chapter 26. During its creation, de Cadenet developed a fascination for building his own cars. He reckons to have been inspired down this path by other drivers who have become sportscar constructors,

detuning and a new, slippery body shape made them the favourites. Even so, the cars that finished first and third had to be nursed towards the chequered flag.

Derek Bell took an initial lead, but he and Jacky Ickx knew the kind of race they had to run and the Englishman soon dropped back. Nevertheless, when the Belgian took over the car he returned it to a lead it was never to lose. Cosworth DFV engines powered the first three cars home in front of a meagre crowd. It was hardly a great 24-Hours, but out of the desert had emerged one tantalizing Mirage and the far from imaginary shape of Derek Bell, who, during the next decade, became the English face of Le Mans. "Britain Wins Euro Enduro," said *Motor*. The magazine was

notably Mark Konig, whose V8 BRM-engined Nomad competed at Le Mans in 1969, driven by the owner and Tony Lanfranchi. In his turn, de Cadenet is proud to have had a similar effect on some other Le Mans notables such as Gordon Spice, Steve O'Rourke and Jean Rondeau.

The latter was to manage what de Cadenet had set out to do, namely to be the first to win Le Mans in his own chassis. Even if the Frenchman achieved what the Brit had failed to do, 1980 was still a special year for de Cadenet. His car was one of the race favourites, having already won at Monza and Silverstone. However, in practice Desire Wilson had a major accident and, with all four wheels "ripped off," de Cadenet thought that was it for another year. But chief mechanic John Anderson told him to just go away and leave it to the team; come the Saturday the car was ready, although Wilson was not permitted to drive. For the second year running, therefore, de Cadenet was teamed with Francois Migault. At one point the car ran as high as second. However, a broken cross-member, probably the result of the earlier accident, broke on the Sunday morning and the resulting pit stop cost 55 minutes. Seventh place at the finish was described as an outstanding achievement and the car was cheered home in the final minutes by the British fans. Rondeau had won, though. For de Cadenet it was as if a protégé had been victorious. "I gave him a huge old hug," he says.

De Cadenet ran his own cars from 1972 to 1981. A Lola T380 that used 'lifed' components from Brabham and McLaren followed the Duckhams Special. Gradually the car metamorphosed into a 'De Cadenet'. In standard shape the Lola had been as much as 20mph down on the Duckhams along the Mulsanne straight. For 1976 the car appeared with new Len Bailey-designed bodywork plus other "Murray/de Cadenet tweaks." At night, during the race, it achieved 208mph, 30mph faster than the previous season.

There is a story that a lorry driver that year reported to the police that a missile had landed on the M4 motorway in the region of Swindon. There is a 14-mile stretch there between junctions where one could, if one was so inclined and was up at about 5.00am, try out new bodywork at 205mph. What can be said is that, with sponsorship from *Motor*, de Cadenet was also able to test in the MIRA wind-tunnel. By 1977 the car was up to about 228mph down the Mulsanne, which de Cadenet believes to be the fastest by a DFV-engined car. The rear of the car came to look rather like that of a 1978 Alpine-Renault. Maybe the fact

Kim Argyle of Argyle Engineering steers de Cadenet's Duckhams Special out onto the grid. Former Cooper and Brabham mechanic Mike Barney undertook construction of the car, being joined in the later stages by Argyle, Bill Harris and finally John Elliott. *(Gordon Murray collection)*

that de Cadenet was lurking around outside the French team's factory with a camera when some bodywork was loaded out of a van had something to do with this.

De Cadenet's best result was the podium finish of 1976. That, he says, was "a wonderful run." The team worked on the principle that the longer you stay out of the pits the better you will do, and accordingly they drove as carefully as possible. De Cadenet was often Britain's major flag carrier and won the *Motor* trophy for the highest placed car from this country on four occasions. For the last five of his 15 Le Mans, he drove for others including Courage. It was at the wheel of one of the Frenchman's cars that he became one of the very few to achieve 250mph down the Mulsanne straight.

However serious his intent, it has always been important to Alain de Cadenet that Le Mans should also mean 'fun'. Post-race parties at *Le Hunaudières* and other unpublishable tales bear witness to that. "The Germans could never understand how we did so well while taking it so lightly."

He has now moved on to television presenting with such as the SPEED channel, a life that enables him to drive the cars most people just dream of. On just one day he tested four Lotus Formula One cars, a 25, a 49, a 72 and a 79 – "and got paid for it" – while a drive in the 1968/69 Le Mans-winning GT40 chassis 1075 was also on his schedule. "I'm a lucky bastard," he says. Few would dispute that.

Alain de Cadenet, who despite his name exemplifies British passion for Le Mans. *(MNF collection)*

at least able to present its own trophy, which used to go to the highest placed British team, to the outright winners. It was also the last Le Mans win for the enduring John Wyer.

For the next few years Ickx, paired with a number of different drivers, continued on his winning ways. Bell during this time drove Mirages in 1976 and 1979, and in between was the only non-French member of the Alpine-Renault team, leading the 1977 race until 9.00am when piston failure intervened. That year Bell is said to have recorded the fastest time in the official qualification session. However, by the time the grid was drawn up, his partner Jean-Pierre Jabouille appeared to have been fastest…well, this is France. In 1981 Bell

was reunited with Ickx and again found himself on the top step of the rostrum.

The noticeable feature of the 1976 race, as far as the British were concerned, was the surely sweet third place of the privately entered, Tate & Lyle and Hammonds Sauce-sponsored Lola-Cosworth DFV T380 of Alain de Cadenet and Chris Craft. Managed by one-time Formula One racer Keith Greene and mainly consisting of part-timers, the de Cadenet team, which only came together for this race, seems to have epitomized the spirit of the British privateer at Le Mans. The body of the car had proved troublesome the previous year. At one point in the night the whole tail had come adrift, hence much work had been

Aston Martin dealer Robin Hamilton entered an AMV8 in 1977. It was the first Aston-powered car to be seen at La Sarthe since 1964 and can be said to have heralded a variety of similarly motivated cars that appeared over the next 12 years, including the Nimrods, EMKA, Cheetah and Group C AMR1s. Initially on the reserve list, the AMV8, which was driven by Hamilton, Dave Preece and Mike Salmon, was slowed by brake problems but finished 17th. *(Mike Salmon collection)*

done before the car had been allowed out again. Its rostrum placing delighted many, including Greene, who was particularly gratified to be congratulated by hierarchy from the winning Porsche team. Writing a diary for *Autocar*, and with half an hour to go before the end, John Wyer said: "Alain de Cadenet is going magnificently…I think they would be very happy to finish third. That will be a great achievement. Alain is an old-style Le Mans privateer who has this one race a year. He is a highly professional amateur if you will forgive the apparent contradiction." De Cadenet and Craft followed up their third place with a fifth the following year.

The year 1977 also saw Aston Martin back at Le Mans for the first time since 1964 and, once again, Mike Salmon was one of the drivers. The car was far removed from the shapely DB 214 that he had shared with Peter Sutcliffe. The bulky 520-530bhp V8 was entered by Aston Martin dealer Robin Hamilton, only getting onto the grid as a reserve following the last-minute withdrawal of another car. Despite brake problems, the car ran an excellent race, finishing 17th and coming third in class. Hamilton returned two years later, again with Salmon and Dave Preece, but the now turbocharged car, "a fearsome beast" said the entrant, retired with an oil leak at 5.15pm, Hamilton having done most of the driving until then.

By 1978 a number of the British specialist race car manufacturers were entering the fray against the major manufacturers Porsche and Renault. De Cadenet and Craft were back to finish 15th with a new Len Bailey tub, their old car also being on the entry list for new owner Simon Phillips with Nick Faure, Martin Raymond and John Beasley. De Cadenet ran the new car for just one year, replacing it with a John

Thompson-built car that ran at Le Mans from 1978 to 1981.

There was also the Harvey Postlethwaite-designed and Lyncar-revised Ibec-Hesketh for Ian Grob, Guy Edwards and Ian Bracey. Lolas and Chevrons abounded in the 2-litre Group 6 class, the winner of that category being a Chrysler Simca-engined Chevron. There were two significant firsts that year. Brian Redman, who had first competed at Le Mans in 1967, sharing the ultimately fiery Ford GT40 with Mike Salmon, was one of the great sportscar drivers of this period. Yet his class-winning fifth place in an otherwise US-crewed Porsche 935 was his first finish at La Sarthe. Stirling Moss also won for the first time at the track that year, albeit in a Saturday morning half-hour race for historic Le Mans cars. His mount was a Formula One Maserati 250F, which hardly constituted a Le Mans car of any era, but who was counting? Fellow Brits Willie Green and Martin Morris came home second and third in Jaguar D-types, which sound a trifle more appropriate. The Jaguar marque was also recalled with a pace lap by 1953 winners Duncan Hamilton and Tony Rolt in a C-type.

Cosworth engines were still popular in 1979; Mirage had returned to the Northampton manufacturer, there were three Lolas including the loyal de Cadenet, and the locally built Rondeaus were all DFV-motivated. So too were a couple of Dome coupes from Japan, managed by Keith Greene and both with British drivers: Chris Craft/Gordon Spice and Bob Evans/Tony Trimmer. There was again plenty of British interest in the 2-litre class with five Chevrons and six Lolas.

However, British hopes of a decent result faded early. Indeed, it was not a good year for the larger Group 6 cars, even the works Porsches. The best at the finish was one of the Rondeaus in fifth. At least it had a British engine. This country, well Scotland to be precise, did better in the 2-litre class with the Mogil Motors of Dumfries Chevron coming first, driven by Robin Smith and Richard Jones. Otherwise it was not a great Le Mans unless you were American. Even Alain de Cadenet failed to finish, thanks to gearbox failure.

The following year the French took over the shout from the Americans. However, Britain could raise a faint cheer in that a Cosworth DFV engine powered the winning Rondeau. Alain de Cadenet's car once again completed the full 24 hours, this time finishing in seventh place, the highest placed British entry.

A number of vignettes from this year: A Janspeed Triumph TR7 V8 turbo was entered with co-sponsorship from the TR Register. Had it got past qualifying it would have been the first Triumph to race at Le Mans since 1965. The now notorious Mark Thatcher, son of the then Prime Minister, started in an Osella-BMW. It was felt that he was somewhat inexperienced. Derek Bell, so used to being in a front-running car, raced a factory Porsche 924 Carrera in the GTP class, finishing 13th with American Al Holbert. The pair had got the car up into the top six before an engine malady temporarily curtailed them. Bell and Holbert were to drive together many times over the subsequent seasons and were to win Le Mans outright together in 1986 and 1987, as well as more than one Daytona 24-Hours.

The final year before the advent of Group C saw Bell and Ickx partnered again, the Englishman now where he would be for a number of years, at the wheel of a potential winning Porsche. For 1981 his mount was a 936 Group 6 car powered by a 2.6-litre turbocharged engine based on Porsche's abortive Indianapolis challenger. A four-speed gearbox had replaced the troublesome five-speed boxes of yore. By the fourth hour the Anglo-Belgian pairing was in the lead, where it stayed for the duration. The margin of victory was 14 laps; it was one of the easiest of Le Mans victories. With Gordon Spice third in a Rondeau and Dudley Wood and John Cooper at the wheel of the fourth-placed Porsche 935 K3 it was not a bad year for British drivers. The same cannot be said, though, for British cars with the Lola T600 of Guy Edwards the first representative in a lowly 16th place.

Like the preceding decade, the 1970s was not a glorious one for British marques. By the end of the period Group C was on the horizon, a new formula that, despite concern over initial fuel regulations, developed into one of the great eras of endurance racing. Eight of the Group C cars that raced at Le Mans during the first year of the category were to be British. Did this herald a new dawn for the Brits? Ultimately it did, but it was going to take a long time.

In 1981, the highest placed car from this country was Guy Edwards' Lola T600 back in a troubled 16th place. Edwards first appeared at Le Mans in 1971 in a Lola T212. He recalls how the track's high speeds took some getting used to. "You could see this long road stretching ahead." Driving the Hesketh-based Ibec in 1978 he had "the most horrifying experience of my life". Finding the car weaving on the straights he pitted to discover that there were only one and a half threads left on the front right upright; the wheel was perilously close to falling off. Edwards later became a sponsorship specialist and was responsible for finding backing for the Group C Jaguars. *(Kaliber)*

A French car driven by Frenchmen won in 1980, but it needed a British engine to do so. Jean Rondeau's eponymous car was powered by a Cosworth DFV engine. Another Rondeau finished third, winning the GTP class with Englishman Gordon Spice one of its drivers. *(Ford)*

149

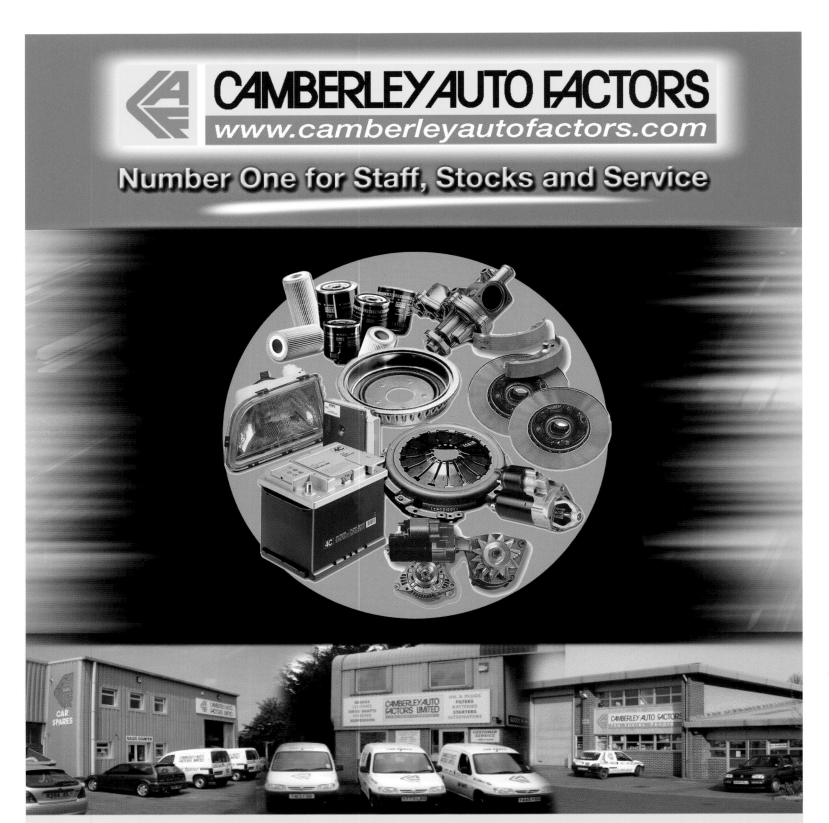

CHAPTER 18

THE GULF GR8 AND THE COSWORTH DFV

What is it…Is it the quick gleam of English steel, or but a desert-dream? Help — or, that last illusion of distress, the mocking mirage of the wilderness." (*Punch*, April 12, 1884)

"The (Gulf) GR8 was a fine little car but it should never have really won Le Mans with a Cosworth engine." So says Derek Bell of his 1975 mount. "It wasn't bad to drive, it just wasn't fast enough." Given that John Wyer had raced Porsche 917s, Ford GT40s and Aston Martins at Le Mans, the car that he used for victory in 1975 was hardly a classic. However, it has to be seen as a car for the times.

That year, as John Horsman points out, was an engineering test because of the fuel consumption regulations. Alfa Romeo's Carlo Chiti told John Wyer that his own cars would be too thirsty to meet the new rules. Wyer obviously thought differently and took on the challenge. As for the GR8's speed, Bell is right in that Gulfs had never been the class of the endurance racing field, indeed they had been dominated throughout the previous season by the Matras, but, says Horsman, at Le Mans in 1975 the Len Bailey-designed GR8 was only one lap short of the previous year's winning Matra.

The end of 1971 was also the end of an era. Lamentable rule changes had confined the Porsche 917 to history. John Wyer's two lead drivers Pedro Rodriguez and Jo Siffert had both tragically been killed towards the end of the season, the Swiss at a non-championship Formula One race at Brands Hatch, the Mexican at an even more pointless event at the Norisring. At JW Automotive Engineering Derek Bell found himself team leader. Another car also had to be found and the team turned to its own Mirages.

The initial Mirages had been a Ford GT40 development, retaining that car's lower steel structure but with a shaped upper body in aluminium. Neither of the two M1s, as they were known, were in a position to challenge at Le Mans in 1967 and, within five hours, both had retired. Wyer was back with GT40s the following year. The M1's successor, the Len Terry-designed M2/300 of 1969, was a bulky, 3-litre closed car that became the neater, open-top M3/300 a year later. Initially, the M2 was BRM V12-powered, but a subsequent version and the M3 had Cosworth DFV V8 motivation. The M3 was also tested with a Ford GT40 engine and was known as the M4 in this configuration. None of these appeared at Le Mans, and once Wyer had been approached to run Porsche 917s they were shelved.

With the termination of the Porsche contract, Wyer revived the Mirage appellation for 1972. The name had come about, said Wyer, after considerable discussion. Any combination of his name with that of fellow director John Willment was instantly rejected, so eventually were names from the big cat family, which sounded too much like Jaguar. Peregrine was considered, but eventually Wyer suggested Mirage and it was accepted.

The year 1975 saw the poorest entry at La Sarthe for many years but the Gulf's victory caused *Autocar* to head its report "Britain's back at Le Mans". It was also the first win for Derek Bell, who was to become the most successful Englishman ever to compete in the 24-Hours. *(LAT Photographic)*

Designed by Len Bailey and with a chassis made by Mo Gomm, the M6 (the M5 was allocated to a Formula Ford car) was a conventional, but overweight, endurance sportscar. Initially the plan had been to use a new Weslake-designed Ford V12 engine, but when this was delayed Gulf Research Racing, as it was now known, reverted to the Cosworth DFV mated to a Hewland DG300 five-speed gearbox.

Bell, on whom much of the test driving of the first car fell, recalls that "the car was never that brilliant, but we did get pole once in front of the Ferraris. There was nothing wrong with it, but it just did not have a good enough chassis."

The Mirage M6's one win was at Spa-Francorchamps in 1973 with Bell coming in first, paired with former motorcycle world champion Mike Hailwood, ahead of the second team car of Vern Schuppan and Howden

Ganley. The team had missed Le Mans in 1972 and had little luck on its return the year after. Schuppan crashed the car that he shared with Hailwood and John Watson, which had been as high as third at one stage, while the Bell/Ganley car retired when the left bank of cylinders partially seized due to lack of water flow. From then on the cars had a second water pump fitted to feed the left hand side only.

For 1974 the car was renamed the Gulf GR7 in deference to the sponsor. Certain titanium components were also used to reduce its weight by about 140lb which, added to various other changes to suspension and drive-shafts and the fitting of an air box, made it at least reasonable on the faster circuits. Bell worked hard to make it competitive, but the French Matras had taken over at the head of the field. The event that sticks in Bell's mind that year was at the Nürburgring. Hailwood had "flown off the road" with their car and Vern Schuppan in the number-two Gulf had come into the pits complaining that the steering column bracket had broken. Team manager John Horsman was anxious for the car to continue and so he had the chief mechanic bind the broken bracket with heavy-duty straps to his satisfaction. When the repair was complete Schuppan's fellow driver James Hunt was reluctant to take over. Bell and Horsman now recall what happened slightly differently, although one wonders if the former is being a little coy. He says Horsman told him to take over the car. "I was a bit concerned!" he says. The way Horsman remembers it is that Bell was simply standing there and said, "I'll drive." He says that "he was in and away in a flash!" The repair held, "probably stronger than the original bracket," quips Horsman, and the car finished fourth. "Such enthusiasm and such confidence in the team," he says of Bell. The driver himself, understandably, has a slightly different take. "We had to get a good result," he remembers.

At Le Mans that year the Mirages used a ZF transmission rather than the Hewland used at other tracks. Bell reported, fairly early in the race, that the gearbox felt "odd" and that it was "never going to last." "Let's wreck it," said the ebullient Hailwood, "and get out to dinner tonight."

"So, that was what we tried to do, but it didn't break and we finished fourth," recalls Bell with a laugh. It was not, though, an easy run to the finish. The CV joints had to be continuously repacked with grease during a series of long pit stops.

The following year the Gulf Research Racing team contested only Le Mans. Two cars, with lengthened wheelbases and new, lower-drag bodywork and now known as GR8s, were entered. The ACO had its own regulations that year with regard to fuel consumption and the race was not included in the World Championship for Makes. The team detuned a pair of Cosworth DFV engines itself with the drivers only able to use 8,000 to 8,400rpm compared to the 10,400rpm of the previous season. It was the first year of that most magical of driver pairings, with Bell teaming up with Jacky Ickx. They easily brought the GR8 home to victory, the first of the three times that they would win Le Mans together. The second GR8 of Vern Schuppan and Jean-Pierre Jaussaud came in third. An aluminium mount, which connected the stressed-member engine to the chassis, broke through one bolt hole on the winning car and both bolt holes on the third-place one. The chassis held up – the engine being still firmly attached at the top with a plate each side between the cam covers and the top of the steel bulkhead – but with a loss of rigidity for the last few hours.

Although British-built, the story of the Mirages, as they must now be called again, takes on an international flavour at this point. An American, Harley Cluxton, ran them, with the now French-driven GR8 coming second in 1976. The same place fell to the car again the following year, although by now it was powered by a Renault engine and called the M9. There was little luck for the Mirages in 1978 and 1979, the cars reverting to Cosworth DFV power with new ZF gearboxes in the second of these years.

The final chapter in the story of the Le Mans Mirages is an unfortunate one. A new Group C coupe, the M12, was entered for 1982. An attractive body had been designed by Horsman. The monocoque was constructed by Tiga Cars and a Cosworth DFL and Hewland VG gearbox fitted. There should have been two cars, but only one could be readied for the race. Unhappily a mistake was made in the design and the gearbox cooler was located just 3 inches behind the gearbox, contravening a regulation that had only been introduced that year. How this was handled, though, does not reflect well on the organizers.

The car was taken to France and, at scrutineering on the Wednesday, examined and passed. Nothing untoward happened until the Saturday. Let John Horsman himself take up the story. "At about 2.30pm on race day a little man came to me as I was standing beside the M12 by the pits. He was holding a page torn from someone's relatively expensive FIA rule book. The page referred to the rule regarding the location of the oil tank and cooler(s). He asked me which were the water coolers and which were the oil coolers – I showed him, then he went away."

Half an hour later Horsman was summoned to the Clerk of the Course's office where several members of the ACO were assembled as well as Jochen Neerpasch who, as Horsman points out, "had an 'interest' in the Ford C100 entry." Make of that what you will. Horsman was told that the coolers were in an illegal position and would have to be moved, otherwise the car would not be allowed to start. "I told them it was not possible to make safe changes to the cooler mounting, ducting and hoses in the time remaining before the race started. They said they would discuss the matter." Horsman asked why the error had not been noted at technical inspection, to be told that it was only items of safety that were inspected at that time. "I asked on what grounds were we to be penalized and was told 'on the grounds of safety'."

Horsman returned to the pit and the team looked to see if there was any way in which the coolers could be moved in the time available, even if the car had to start from the pit lane. There was not.

The next Horsman says he knew was that the car was on the grid with Mario Andretti strapped in.

Then, with about a quarter of an hour to go and without the team being officially advised of the ACO's final decision, Andretti "was pulled unceremoniously out of the car."

Horsman says that the problem had originated when the car was designed with a water-to-oil intercooler that required no ducting. This was thought to have worked well on the 3-litre Formula One cars, which is why, states Horsman, Tiga incorporated it. "I had, of course, read through all the 1982 FIA regulations, noted the oil cooler limitation but dismissed it since we were not using regular coolers." When, during the short development period of the car, the oil overheated the 3.9-litre engine, normal coolers had to be rigged

In 1973 the Mirage M6 of Mike Hailwood, John Watson and Vern Schuppan ran as high as third only to drop back and then retire after the latter had crashed. Hailwood, however, had won earlier in the year at Spa-Francorchamps when paired with Derek Bell. (LAT Photographic)

The GR8 could be said to have bridged the gulf between the Aston Martin victory of 1959 and the Jaguar win in 1988. (Ford)

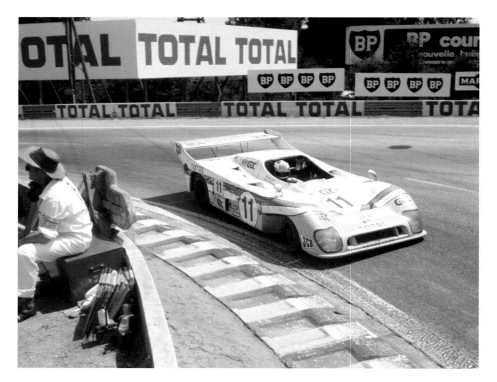

In 1976, the cars were back to being called Mirages. The Derek Bell/Vern Schuppan entry was sixth fastest in qualifying, but suffered from a fuel pump problem and finished fifth. Its French-driven sister car came home second, thanks to a sensible race strategy. *(LAT Photographic)*

and parts were still being made and installed as the car left for France. "In the haste and intense pressure of the time, I missed the new regulation," admits Horsman, "and it was my fault."

On the track the new, previously untested cooler arrangement proved almost too successful with the oil running over-cool during night practice. However, it is Horsman's belief that another team tipped off the ACO having waited to the very last minute to inflict maximum damage. If that is so, it certainly succeeded. "It was a very bad affair, which should never have been allowed to reach the point of no return just before the race," says Horsman. He observes that Mirages were never to appear again at Le Mans.

Motive power for the 1975-winning Gulf GR8 was supplied by a specially detuned version of what was arguably motorsport's most successful engine, the Ford-funded, 3-litre Cosworth DFV V8 (the initials standing for Double Four Valve). However, when John Wyer first told Keith Duckworth that he was thinking of entering Le Mans using a DFV in a Mirage, the Cosworth founder advised him not to do so. But John Wyer being John Wyer, he decided to ignore this. If he was going to Le Mans then, as John Horsman points out, after the failure of the Weslake engine, the DFV was the only choice possible.

Although part of Cosworth's history was spent under Ford ownership, the Northampton-based company must, at least until very recently, be regarded as essentially British. Its DFV was incredibly successful in Formula One, winning the first time out at Zandvoort in 1967 and then adding a further 154 victories in World Championship races. However, it was designed specifically for relatively short Grands Prix, so it is not surprising that the DFV only won twice at Le Mans, the second time in a French chassis. What is impressive is the way that its derivatives went

on to dominate Group C2, the junior category at Le Mans, two decades after Jim Clark's initial win in the Dutch Grand Prix.

The DFV first appeared in a sportscar, the Ford F3L, at the Brands Hatch BOAC International 500 in 1968. There were those who, knowing it to be a Grand Prix engine, said it would not last more than two hours. After about 1 hour 55 minutes Mike Spence parked the car on the exit to Clearways, raised the gullwing door, got out and ran across the track; an inner driveshaft coupling had broken, damaging the exhaust pipe and rear chassis bulkhead. The Alan Mann Racing-built car was to prove unsuccessful and never raced at Le Mans. The DFV and its later 3.3- and 3.9-litre DFL sportscar derivatives would, though, become familiar there, starting in 1971 when a detuned DFV was installed in a French Ligier.

Over the years the engine was to appear at Le Mans in a wide variety of chassis, the first to be classified as a finisher being Alain de Cadenet's 1972 car, called in deference to its sponsor, the Duckhams-Ford. This special was designed by a young Gordon Murray, of whom more later. It ran as high as fifth with less than two hours to go when it hit a post at Tertre Rouge during a freak thunderstorm. From then on it had to be held in the pits with damaged steering before being allowed a final lap to finish 12th. With the spectre of Jo Bonnier's earlier fatal accident still before them, the organizers were concerned about letting de Cadenet out any earlier.

The DFV installed was one of the first built and had been used by Bruce McLaren to win the 1968 Belgian Grand Prix. Engine man John Nicholson, whose career was to become linked with the DFV (and who was later to race for de Cadenet at Le Mans), had recently joined McLaren but had yet to work on a DFV. If de Cadenet was willing, Phil Kerr, then manager of the McLaren race team, would give Nicholson the opportunity to practice on the engine and then it could be used in the race. When de Cadenet asked how much this would cost, Kerr asked him how much he had. Even now de Cadenet is amazed that he once became the owner of a John Nicholson-rebuilt Cosworth DFV for a mere £1500.

A telegram soon arrived from Keith Duckworth pleading with de Cadenet not to use one of his creations for a 24-hour race, as failure would be bad for Cosworth. To give Duckworth his due he did send another after the race offering his congratulations ("on your great result for Cosworth") although, as recounted, he was to react very much the same way when he heard that John Wyer wanted to use a DFV at Le Mans.

Those who were to use the later DFL variants would probably be chagrined to know that not only did the Duckhams' DFV last the full 24 hours, but that it was found to be in such excellent shape that de Cadenet decided to leave it undisturbed for its next outing, a six-hours race at Watkins Glen. DFVs at the time were normally rebuilt after every second Grand Prix – in other words after about four hours. Then it was learnt that he would be using the same engine for the next year's Le Mans, still without a rebuild.

Duckworth queried his sanity, saying that the engine should have blown up long ago. De Cadenet pointed out that he could not afford a rebuild, at which point Duckworth must have decided that he was beating his head against the proverbial brick wall and stated that he would give de Cadenet the new components that he needed. De Cadenet looks back with fondness to that engine. "It never blew up, although we used it five or six times at Le Mans."

Many others were similarly motivated. However, it was not until the Gulf GR8's win that the engine scored its first outright victory at La Sarthe. John Wyer's team had planned to use the Weslake-designed Ford V12 WRP190 engine for the Mirage M6 in 1972. However, when this failed to materialize, it fell back on the DFV. At the Le Mans trials the following year a Weslake-Ford V12-engined coupe appeared but was plagued by fuel feed and electrical problems and not raced. Horsman took the decision to drop the Weslake. During testing at Daytona and Vallelunga the car would not start unless towed or pushed, and during the Le Mans trials it would not start at all. Wyer continued with the DFV, although in 1977, as mentioned, the GR8, revised as the M9 and now run by Harley Cluxton, changed to Renault V6 turbocharged power. In 1979 Cluxton reverted to the DFV.

The year 1975 was to be the most successful for the DFV at Le Mans with the top three places. The fact that it was not just the British that were now using it was highlighted by the second-place Ligier. The following year French drivers piloted a Mirage to second place

ahead of de Cadenet and Chris Craft in their Lola-DFV T380. That might have been it for the DFV at Le Mans had it not been for another Frenchman, Jean Rondeau. The local man used a DFV, prepared in Geneva by Heini Mader, to win in 1980, becoming the only driver/constructor to win the 24-Hours. A second Rondeau came third that year with Englishman Gordon Spice one of the drivers. As will be seen in a future chapter, in the coming years Spice was to use the Cosworth DFL in his C2 cars, giving the engine an Indian Summer in the mid-to-late 1980s.

In 1982, the Cosworth V8, now in DFL guise, appeared once more in a Ford chassis, the C100, as well as other contenders in the new Group C class. The 3.3- and 3.9-litre DFLs were a genuine attempt to produce a long-distance engine, rather than just a modified Grand Prix unit. The Ford C100s ran unsuccessfully with them at Le Mans in 1982, the first year of Group C; the following year there was just one privately entered C100 from current Lola owner Martin Birrane. It retired during the second hour with no fuel pressure. The problem with the DFL in 1982 was severe vibration. Duckworth realized this and, prior to Le Mans, produced a new rubber crankshaft damper, which in turn caused a wealth of problems. Many of the 15 DFL-powered cars went out that year with vibration maladies, including the Rondeau of Spice, which dropped out while in the lead. It was the last chance the Cosworth V8 ever had of winning the 24-hour race.

It became clear that, to compete with the Porsche

And this was as far as it got. The Mirage M12 sits on the grid in 1982 prior to being ordered away by ACO officials. It was the last time that a Mirage was to appear at Le Mans. To its right is the Ultramar-sponsored Lola T610 of Guy Edwards, Rupert Keegan and Nick Faure that would retire after 72 laps. *(Author)*

A true Brit. Alain de Cadenet showed off his country's colours whenever possible. More than once his DFV-powered cars appeared in British Racing Green with a striking Union Jack rear aerofoil to underline the point. *(LAT Photographic)*

The DFV was never as successful in endurance racing as in Formula One. It was first used in the Ford P68 at the BOAC 500 in 1968, during which it perhaps indicated the engine's origins by retiring after what was roughly a Grand Prix distance. Here Mike Spence exits the car prior to running across the track to the pit. *(Author)*

956, tubocharging was necessary. That was part of the thinking behind the 1983 stillborn Ford project with which Spice was to have been involved. As we will see later, the plug was pulled on this and, apart from the occasional foray, such as the use of a 3.3-litre turbocharged DFL in Tim Lee-Davey's Tiga in 1988, the Cosworth name virtually disappeared from the C1 class until a change of regulation for 1989. The 540bhp, 3.9-litre DFL was never able to acquire the reliability for long-distance racing. In 1983, out of the 13 DFV/DFLs entered in Group C at Le Mans, only one was classified and that in penultimate place.

In Group C2 the story was to be different. Spice, as will be seen, made the DFL popular, although not all of his customers used the Cosworth engine. Other one-off constructors like ADA and Bardon likewise installed the DFL. Spice was also involved in the final chapter of the Cosworth DFV V8 Le Mans saga. In 1989, over two decades after the DFV had first appeared in a sportscar, he took advantage of a change in C1 regulations to enter that class with a 3.5-litre Cosworth DFZ-engined car. That variant lacked in top-end power, but that season was regarded as a learning year. The following year a Nicholson-prepared Cosworth DFR was used. Other teams also took advantage of the change in the C1 rules to use Cosworth DFZ and DFR engines in Spice chassis, but the category was now in its twilight years.

John Wyer ran the Mirage M1s at Le Mans in 1967. The David Piper/Dick Thompson car burnt a hole in a piston during practice and both cars had their 5.7-litre engines replaced with 5-litre ones. Both cars were out with engine problems before 60 laps were over. *(Ford)*

The second GR8 driven by Vern Schuppan (seen here) and Jean-Pierre Jaussaud finished third in 1975 having been in a comfortable second place until, late on the Saturday evening, an alternator failed. *(Ford)*

Innovation from Bosch?
Yes

Diesel Direct Injection.
Saving nonstop.

Munich

London

Bosch innovations, such as Diesel Direct Injection, save you twice as much. First of all you save time. Greater fuel efficiency means less stopping to refuel. Second, you save money. Diesel cars consume around 30% less than their petrol engine counterparts. What's more, Bosch Diesel High Tech brings you top performance with low noise emission. That's why more and more drivers – one in every two in Western Europe – are changing to diesel. Bosch technology saves you time and money. **www.bosch.co.uk**

BOSCH
Invented for life

CHAPTER 19

RICHARD ATTWOOD

"I've been very poorly but now I feel prime." (R.P. Weston and Bert Lee)

Mumps is an ailment caused by a virus that usually spreads through saliva and can infect many parts of the body, especially the parotid salivary glands. These are found toward the back of each cheek, in the area between the ear and jaw. In cases of mumps, these glands typically swell and become painful. The disease has been recognized for several centuries, and medical historians argue over whether the name 'mumps' comes from an old word for 'lump' or for 'mumble'.

It was a common disease until the mumps vaccine was licensed in 1967. Now doctors rarely see patients suffering from it. Mumps has usually occurred in children aged between five and 14. However, adults have been known to suffer and for them it is particularly unpleasant. Richard Attwood was suffering from mumps, and Richard Attwood was about to win at Le Mans.

Attwood's wife Veronica remembers the race well. It was her birthday that weekend and he had forgotten to give her a card. They had married the year before and it was also her first time at Le Mans. Indeed, apart from witnessing her husband winning at Kyalami, whilst on honeymoon, she had seen nothing else in the way of motor racing. "There's a lot of razzamatazz at Le Mans. It was a bit frightening for me."

The weather was mixed in 1970 with plenty of rain. When Attwood came into the pits complaining that his neck ached and that he could not swallow, Veronica assumed that this was caused by the damp. He was fed on milk and mashed bananas, hardly the diet for someone leading a 24-hour race, but it was all that he could manage. It was only when the couple returned to England after the race that they discovered Attwood had mumps. "I caught it two weeks later," says Veronica. There are obviously some things that stick in the mind.

At the start of the race there had been little thought of Attwood and his partner, the previous year's runner-up Hans Herrmann, actually winning the thing – they were way back on the grid. Even when it had finished Veronica remembers: "I couldn't believe it and I don't think that Richard could either. They took him away. I

couldn't get to him as the excitement was so great for the Germans. They were over the moon. I felt a little bit out of it." Remember this is 1970; before the race the score was England 12 Germany 1, and that achieved by a Mercedes-Benz. Porsche, having missed out by yards the previous season – and with Herrmann at the wheel – had at last won its first Le Mans. The first victory is always the sweetest and nobody can have dreamt that Le Mans would fall to Porsche another 15 times before the century was out. No wonder Mrs Attwood could not get through to Mr Attwood.

The fact remains that when Porsche finally arrived at the top step of the podium it was represented by a British driver. It was to happen again, of course, with Messrs Bell and McNish, but Richard Attwood was there at the beginning.

Porsche has scored 16 victories at Le Mans. On both the first and most recent occasions one of the drivers was British, Richard Attwood in 1970 and Allan McNish in 1998. In 1970 a race of attrition played into Attwood's safe pair of hands. *(LAT Photographic)*

Attwood shared the Mk 6 Lola GT with fellow Englishman David Hobbs in 1963. The project was an ambitious one for such a small manufacturer. Four cars were eventually built, one of them winning the Nassau Tourist Trophy in the Bahamas driven by American Augie Pabst. *(Andre Loubser)*

Richard Attwood had the ideal temperament for an endurance racer, something that was recognized by John Wyer. In May 1968 he also proved his worth in a Grand Prix, finishing a fighting second to Graham Hill at Monaco and setting fastest lap in the process. *(Alan Hearn collection)*

Attwood's introduction to Le Mans was with Eric Broadley's Lola GT in 1963. "I think it was such a significant car." He recalls it as being "so small and neat." The drivers David Hobbs and Attwood had to visit the modest Lola factory at Bromley to help finish the car off, so far behind schedule was the project. An incredible atmosphere of team spirit was generated, particularly as the British had not done too well at Le Mans for a few years.

Designer Tony Southgate, then working for Broadley, recalls how the Lola founder drove the car out of the building for the first time. The wheels fouled the wheelarches and emergency work had to be carried out before the car could proceed on its way to France. Eventually it set off through Bromley with chief mechanic Don Beresford in the passenger seat, a toolbox on his knees. The next problem was a sticking throttle; Beresford is said to have fixed that on the boat.

It was planned to race two Lolas at Le Mans, but the second was finished so late that, although it was also driven to France, it missed the scrutineering. The first car failed this hurdle "hopelessly." The rule in question said that the drivers had to be able to see behind through a rear-view mirror. However, the air ducts to the carburettors made it impossible to see through the steeply raked rear window. "We had made this fantastic effort to get there and the bloody car was not even going to start!"

The British spirit, though, was not going to be beaten. The team "hacked away" at the car and the induction system was taken through the sides. Such was the huge effort that even the French started to get behind them.

"For some reason we were totally undergeared and we weren't doing the speeds we should have been achieving down the straights," says Attwood. The team also started to experience gear-selection problems as early as practice. Hobbs, heading down towards the Esses in the race, could not select the right gear and went off the circuit, badly damaging the car. "I went absolutely savage. We knew we had gear-selection

problems, so why go into a corner like that? I could not forgive him for it, I probably still can't, even though we are best mates!" says Attwood laughingly.

"It was hugely disappointing." Lola was a very small company at the time and Attwood was worried that it could have been a financial disaster for the concern. As it was, from a business, if not racing point of view, matters worked out differently. Ford took over the project, and although Broadley, unhappy working for the American company, which ignored many of his ideas, soon left, the Lola turned out to be the progenitor of the GT40.

Attwood was to drive one of the works Fords the next year, paired with Frenchman Jo Schlesser. It was "a huge disappointment," the main reason being that the team was using the 4.2-litre Indianapolis engine which would not manage the torque reversals. John Wyer was running the three-car team and, as usual, had deputed one to be a hare and one to be a steady finisher; Attwood and Schlesser had the latter role. At about the four-hour mark Attwood was looking out of the rear of the car when he saw flames licking around the induction system. "I had heard a theory that, if you kept the engine going, you could suck the flames back down into the engine. I tried to do this about halfway down the straight, but noticed that the flames were not going out. I thought I had better get out of here." Mistakenly, he drove round Mulsanne corner and parked on the right just past the signalling pits. "What I should have done was head towards the fire truck area down the escape road. I thought I ought to do something so I popped the catch on one side of the engine cover. I heard something like a 'bouf' inside, probably one of the carburettors. I thought I had better get away from this lot. So, I climbed onto the bank and watched it burn."

The following year Attwood was scheduled to drive a *Daily Express*-sponsored GT40 with Innes Ireland. However, he did not make the race, having been burnt following a high-speed crash on the Masta straight at Spa racing a three-year-old, Reg Parnell-entered Lotus 25.

In 1966 he was down to drive a Maranello Concessionaires Ferrari P2 with David Piper. Effectively they went out of the race on the first lap. At the end of practice the V-belt on the water pump had come adrift. Attwood asked for another pre-stretched belt to be fitted only to be told that the team had plenty of new ones. He pointed out that this was effectively the end of their Le Mans as a new V-belt would simply fly off. Naturally, that happened during the opening laps, so for the next 25 laps Attwood crawled round "being a pain in the arse." The regulations said that water and oil could not be replenished during the first 25 laps, but to Attwood's surprise the car made it through that distance. He then pitted, the engine was allowed to cool down and water poured in. After about 20 minutes Attwood went out again. On the fourth lap, the belt fell off again.

A year later, he was back again with Colonel Ronnie Hoare's Maranello team. This time he was partnered with his friend Piers Courage. It must have been an ideal pairing – "probably Utopia," says Attwood – for

the Cambridge-educated Colonel, Attwood having been to Harrow, Courage to Eton. Indeed, Courage copied Attwood's idea of having his old school colours on his helmet. The pair drove down to the track together in Courage's new Porsche 911. Attwood recalls Courage as "driving absolutely beautifully" in the race, but thanks to a bad batch of pistons the car dropped out after about 14 hours. By now I was beginning to wonder if I would ever finish this race."

In 1968 Attwood was back with David Piper, again in a Ferrari, but this time Piper's own LM. It was a partially wet race, but probably the easiest and most relaxed that he did at Le Mans. At one point Piper reckoned that the gearbox was making a strange noise, but Attwood, enjoying himself and totally in the groove, could hear nothing and was going faster and faster. The team suggested he slowed down. Eventually they even 'waved' a spare gearbox at him, but he still went faster. "We finished and we finished well."

The following year both Porsche and John Wyer were after Attwood to drive in sportscar racing, but by this time the Ford GT40s were becoming dated. Attwood, therefore, had to tell Wyer that he had chosen not to drive for him. Wyer was particularly upset having believed that he was getting a dream team together.

Veronica points out that Attwood was – and indeed still is, racing such as a mid-1960s BRM P261 Grand Prix car – a steady driver. It was an attribute that endeared him to Wyer, who needed drivers who could finish races to partner the truly greats of the era such as Pedro Rodriguez and Jo Siffert. "He has a feel," says Veronica. "I liken it to being a musician."

However, in 1969 Attwood found himself driving a Porsche 917 on the car's debut at Le Mans. Forget, for a minute, what was to come a year later. This is the 1969 917; "absolutely dreadful," says Attwood.

However, at one point he and Vic Elford were leading the race so easily that "it was a joke." It was not until about 2002 that Elford confessed he had nominated Attwood to drive with him in a 917. Like virtually all the other factory drivers, Attwood would have much preferred to have been in an infinitely safer 908. At the Nürburgring, all the regular works team had refused to drive the 917. Attwood assumed when he heard he

Conditions in 1970 were pretty appalling with few entries finishing. At the end Attwood's Porsche was five laps ahead of its nearest competitor. *(Porsche)*

was to drive such a car at Le Mans that it was simply his turn. Years later he discovered that it was because Elford had put his name down for it.

During practice, the three 917s – the two factory cars and the John Woolfe private entry – were "absolute nightmares." The cars were "lifting everywhere." The shape of the long-tailed 908 and the 1969 917 was virtually identical. At 195mph the 908s were almost lifting at the front, but at 230mph the 917s did take off. It was certainly impossible to take the Mulsanne kink flat.

Digby Martland had to do his requisite three practice laps in daylight and three in the night time to qualify in the John Woolfe car. He carried out his three daytime laps and the car was "such a wild animal," says Attwood, that he got out of the car, thanked Woolfe

The name on the overalls would indicate that this is the real McQueen and not 'Michael Delaney'. During the filming of *Le Mans* it was evident that the American film star desired the approval of the professional drivers. Is he seeking Richard Attwood's advice here? *(Richard Attwood collection)*

for allowing him to drive it and announced that he had now retired from racing. The factory stepped in and loaned Woolfe Herbert Linge. It was also recommended that Linge start the race, but Woolfe turned down the suggestion. The Englishman insisted on driving the first stint despite Linge's far greater experience, and he crashed fatally at the White House. New Zealander Chris Amon, who was following the Porsche, observed that "it was an accident waiting to happen." Michael Cotton remembers how the leading cars came through, followed by a gap. In those days there was a straight line of sight from the press box down to the White House and somebody with binoculars reported that they could see the following cars taking to the grass to get past an obviously serious accident.

In the works 917 of the two Englishmen, Elford had started the race, carried out a double stint and then Attwood did the same, after which "I was as deaf as a post and had a blinding headache. From then on I just wasn't interested in driving this car any more." Elford encouraged him to go faster; not a good idea, thought Attwood, if they were to finish the race. He recalls that he had never driven a car with such "huge" power. His neck was aching so much that he was resting it on the bulkhead. "The whole exercise was so uncomfortable."

Eventually, the casing of the gearbox started to crack and with the engine sagging the clutch release became impossible to use. By that time, though "we were six laps in the lead." Attwood was "happy and relieved" to retire. In retrospect, people have pointed out to him that it is easy to say this now, for a year later he won the race. However, he is emphatic that this was how he actually felt at the time. "I hadn't won it then, and I couldn't have cared less. It was such an uncomfortable experience." Elford, whose press-on style was perhaps less suited to Le Mans, was convinced that the race had been theirs for the taking. Given that Attwood had turned Wyer down for this season, this is perhaps not the best place to repeat that it was one of those outdated JWA GT40s that outlasted the Porsches to win.

The following February the factory rang Attwood and asked him what configuration of car would he like to drive at Le Mans. By this time the 917 had been sorted out, so that was a given. Also, because the gearbox had broken the previous year, he asked for a standard 4.5-litre engine and not the then new 5-litre. Finally, he requested that he drive with the dependable Hans Herrmann, who had so very nearly won the year before.

By June the 5-litre had proved itself a great engine and its torque was so much better than the 4.5-litre's. Thus, following practice, Attwood and Herrmann found themselves way down on the grid and the Englishman was worried that he had made a major mistake in requesting the smaller engine. "In my mind I was saying I would have to wait for about 15 cars ahead of me to have problems for us to have a chance of winning. I really did think I had made the biggest mistake of my life. We were going to be completely outclassed and I was not looking forward to the

Attwood's final year at Le Mans was with one of Viscount Downe's Nimrod-Aston Martins. Co-driver John Sheldon was seriously burnt in an accident that caused the race to be halted for over an hour. Here the car they shared with Mike Salmon leads the Group 44 Jaguar XJR-5 that Ulsterman John Watson drove with Claude Ballot-Lena and Tony Adamowicz. *(Roger Stowers)*

race."

That year, he recalls, the start of the race really was like a Grand Prix. The attrition was accordingly huge, playing into Attwood's and Herrmann's hands. After 10 hours they were at the front. "I didn't want to be in the lead at 10 hours." The pair had then to defend their lead in atrociously wet conditions. "That was really quite nerve-racking." However, as the cars behind were also Porsches, team orders came into play and the pressure was taken off. Perhaps the main fear was the way in which the ignition was getting damp. In trying to keep the engine clear Attwood was blipping the throttle in neutral. On one occasion he overdid this and revved to about 8,400-8,500rpm; Herrmann was not too amused when he saw that this had happened. A tremendous slide in the morning also caused Attwood a moment's considerable concern, but otherwise there were no real dramas.

Even now the 1970 Le Mans win does not have same impact for Attwood as his second place in the Monaco Grand Prix in 1968, when he superbly chased the circuit's master Graham Hill for lap after lap, setting a new lap record in the process. Hill reckoned it was Attwood's best race and said that the BRM driver gave him a lot of trouble. One presumes that Attwood was fully fit that day.

In 1970 there was no pressure that this was to be Porsche's first win at Le Mans. "It was just another race, really," says Attwood. Only some years later did it hit him that this was such a major event to win. For Attwood, a win at Le Mans is "a team thing, it all needs to go together or else it is not meant to be." He underlines this by relating the story of the following year. Now, at last, driving for John Wyer, at Le Mans he was paired with Herbert Müller, who had a reputation as "a really wild child." However, Attwood spoke to the Swiss about the way to go about the 24-

race and the pair gelled. Müller drove impeccably. Unfortunately, the gearbox jammed in one of the gears, and the regulations were such then that the gearbox could not be changed, only the internals. The repair took about 45 minutes and the car was fine for the rest of the race. The Martini Racing Team car that won had the same trouble about two hours later, but the mechanics completed the work in 25 minutes. Attwood and Müller lost the race by just two laps, which they could have 'cruised' in less than seven minutes…

Attwood, by now in his mid-forties, went back to Le Mans in 1984 with an Aston Martin-powered Nimrod. "I don't know how it came about. I had expressed a wish to get back into racing." Mike Salmon suggested they should do Le Mans, but his first race in the car was at Silverstone and there he did not like it. "It was

Herbert Müller shared a JWA Porsche 917 with Richard Attwood in 1971. Following the Englishman's victory of the previous year, the pair finished in second place, just two laps behind the winners. *(LAT Photographic)*

Richard Attwood, seen here at the Goodwood chicane in 2005, continues successfully to race in a handsome, 1965-vintage BRM P261. *(Author)*

Attwood perhaps takes a moment for reflection during the 2005 Goodwood Revival meeting. *(Author)*

There are those who said that the Cosworth FVC engine in the back of Ian Skailes' Chevron would not last the full race. While it has to be admitted they were right, it did survive for over 22 hours before losing one cylinder. Mary and John Hine, Skailes' wife Angela, Clive Baker, Digby Martland and, with his back to the camera, Skailes himself talk prior to the race. *(Ian Skailes collection)*

a downforce car, in short-body shape, and I would rather have had the long tail, which was installed by the time of Le Mans."

Salmon started the 24-hour race and carried out two stints, Attwood then did a double stint and found himself going quicker and quicker "without any extra effort at all." Team manager Richard Williams said perhaps he should be slowed down as, of the two cars in the team, this was the one that was meant to be driven circumspectly to finish. "They might have hung something out for me but I ignored it." Attwood was well within his capabilities, braking at perhaps 600 yards where he could have braked at 300. He was really enjoying himself.

Now that the two professional racers had done their first stints, dentist John Sheldon took over the car. Sheldon was about 300 yards ahead of Drake Olsen in the other Bovis Homes-sponsored Nimrod when the car picked up a puncture. Entering the Mulsanne kink at about 190mph it went out of control, hit the Armco barriers and burst into an intense fireball. Jonathan Palmer, who was lapping the two Nimrods in his Canon Porsche, slowed in horror and was able to avoid the carnage. Olsen, though, was hit by flying wreckage and also hit the barrier, although he was unhurt. Sheldon managed to extricate himself from the inferno, lucky to be alive but suffering from 30 per cent burns. Two marshals had also been hit, one of them fatally. "It was just like an aircraft crash," says Attwood. For Veronica it was a worrying time as she did not know for about half an hour which drivers had been out at the time.

After the race Attwood asked Richard Williams what was the condition of the car before the crash. "He said everything was perfect. I asked where we would have finished. He said we would have won. I was staggered."

It was to be about two decades before Attwood returned to Le Mans again. During the 1990s he had been assisting Audi in promoting cars such as the A8. As a result he was invited to attend the 2005 race as a guest of Audi UK's David Ingram. Although he was entertained royally he was not impressed by the changes that had taken place at the track. "To me, Le

IAN SKAILES

The 1790cc Cosworth FVC engine may have been ideal for the 2-litre sportscar racing that was to prove popular in the early 1970s, but it hardly seemed the stuff for Le Mans. "It was," says Ian Skailes, "a terrific engine but reliability was not one of its strengths." Four hours was about the maximum time between rebuilds, which might be why a certain amount of scorn was poured on his FVC-engined Chevron B16 when it turned up to race at La Sarthe in 1970. Just before the start, Patrick McNally, then an *Autosport* journalist, asked if Skailes had booked a decent table for dinner that evening.

He admits not to have been happy about the whole idea. The car was his own, but he had been approached by the Chevron management of Derek Bennett and Paul Owens, who wanted to run it as a works car at Le Mans. The deal was that they would prepare it and provide all the support. Skailes was uneasy about the way this might compromise his chances in the European 2-litre Championship. However, Adrian Hamilton, a friend of Skailes in addition to being the son of the 1953 winner, talked him into going along with the plan. The Derby engine tuner Alan Smith worked on the engine to improve its chances of ever seeing the 4.00pm clock, fitting chrome piston rings to cut down bore wear and camshafts from the smaller Cosworth FVA engine to help overcome valve seat recession.

That meant the 23-year-old Skailes was "a little more confident" about the engine. There was another problem, though. He had been studying for a degree in business studies at the same time, and the examinations were the week of the race. He took an exam on the Wednesday,

flew out for the evening practice, flew back to the UK in the early hours of the morning for another exam and then returned to Le Mans again for final practice. Imagine him sitting on the pit counter studying a book on accounting. It happened.

The cars were still lined up *en echelon* in 1970, but with the drivers already in them. The patter of feet across the track had been consigned to history. As one of Chevron's mechanics went to park the car in first gear so the gear lever came off in his hand. "All we could do was to tape it up and start with a three-inch gear lever." After one lap Skailes pitted for a new one.

For about half the race the Chevron, with Skailes and John Hine at the wheel, performed well, although there was some concern with oil consumption during the early stages when topping up was illegal. Adrian Hamilton, who was managing the car, had to persuade officials that the oil can in his hand in fact contained some kind of petrol additive. Skailes recalls how Hamilton had arrived with much of his father's pit equipment including signalling lights from an aircraft carrier.

In the pouring rain the car moved up to 13th place, the best placed British entry. The weather, Skailes reckons, was probably working in the team's favour. However, after about 16 hours, the engine started to lose compression. During a long pit stop Bennett and Owens re-shimmed the valves to improve the situation.

Eventually the engine went onto three cylinders and then, with about an hour and a half to go and with Hine at the wheel, the metering unit belt flew off round the back of the circuit. The FVC may not have done 24 hours, but it had lasted a lot longer than four.

CHAPTER 20

THE BRITISH ON FILM

"The final test for a novel will be our affection for it." (E.M. Forster, *Aspects of the Novel*)

Another Englishman to win the Le Mans 24-hour race was, of course, 'Larry Wilson' in a Gulf-sponsored Porsche 917. The year was…well, it looks like 1970, but the Englishman in the winning Porsche that year was called Richard Attwood and the car certainly was not in the iconic Gulf colours. However, there it is on film, 'Wilson' winning at Le Mans in a finish that makes the end of the 1969 race look quite tedious.

Perhaps the reason why one tends to overlook 'Wilson' is because he was upstaged that year – whatever year it was – by an American, 'Michael Delaney'. The latter is the name assumed by Steve McQueen in his splendidly self-indulgent film *Le Mans*. 'Larry Wilson' is the character played by British actor Christopher Waite. Not only does 'Delaney' appear to be the hero, assisting 'Wilson' to a famous victory, but while McQueen's career is the stuff of Hollywood legend, *Le Mans* was to be Waite's only film.

'Wilson' is not the only reason why we can claim the *Le Mans* film for the list of British victories. The example of John Wyer gave rise to the use of English actor Ronald Leigh-Hunt to play 'David Townsend', a Wyer-like figure in charge of the Gulf Porsche team, assisted by another Englishman, Alf Bell playing the part of his David Yorke-like assistant, 'Tommy Hopkins'.

Leigh-Hunt has the dubious privilege of uttering the corniest lines in a film not known for its flowing dialogue. "I want Porsche to win at Le Mans," he states emphatically. Over 30 years and 16 real-life Porsche victories later, it seems to lose some of its purpose. However, an Englishman said it, so it must deserve at least a mention. Leigh-Hunt, who died in 2005, was ideal for this terribly British role, having first come to the public's notice in the 1950s playing King Arthur in the television series *The Adventures of Sir Lancelot*. In the late 1960s he was 'Colonel Buchanan' in the children's series *Freewheelers*, again playing the patriotic type. A regular in both *Dr. Who* and *Z cars*, he was also 'Lord Northbrook' in the film *Khartoum*.

McQueen and his Solar Productions company relied heavily on the British in making the film. A couple of the British drivers gave beyond the call of duty; it might even be said that some of the British cars did too. The American actor certainly respected the expertise that the British drivers brought to the film. He was perhaps less sympathetic with the actors from this country. Michael Keyser and Jonathan Williams in their weighty tome on the making of the film recalled how, at an early gathering of the actors, McQueen asked all the British to raise their hands and then to step back 20 yards. That, he said, was as near as he wanted them for the rest of the shoot. The authors believed that although this was said 'tongue in cheek', he was still smarting from being upstaged by that fine English actor Denholm Elliott during the filming of *The Great Escape*.

The British come early into the story of McQueen and his Le Mans obsession. In the UK for the shooting

There were times when Derek Bell (left) was meant to be the German driver 'Erich Stahler'. The overall and proximity of a Ferrari would suggest that this might have been one of those occasions. Brian Redman (centre) is, fittingly, a Gulf pilot, a team-mate of 'Michael Delaney'. *(LAT Photographic)*

of an earlier film, *The War Lover*, McQueen, who had already proved himself to be a more than capable competition driver, wanted to do some racing here. He contacted the BMC competitions department and, in particular, its manager Marcus Chambers, veteran of the 1938 and 1939 Le Mans races. Chambers, not really aware of the actor's standing, passed him on to Sir John Whitmore, who was to race five times at Le Mans, his only finish being in 1959 when he and Jim Clark came 10th in a Lotus Elite. Whitmore secured

McQueen saloon cars drives at Oulton Park and Brands Hatch.

McQueen was after authenticity, and no depiction of Le Mans could be authentic without a certain British ambiance. Nigel Snowdon, a well-known British motor racing photographer, was asked to play himself, for example. Snowdon was to influence a memorable moment towards the end of the film, when 'Delaney' gives a rival the V-sign. Being American, McQueen was simply going to give 'the finger', but Snowdon reckoned it to be more likely that the character would have shown he still had his bow fingers intact. McQueen proved a willing pupil and took delight in giving this very English gesture.

A major British involvement, of course, was in the driving with former Ferrari works driver Jonathan Williams having a foot in both camps as he earned extra pennies for playing 'Jonathan Burton', a non-speaking 512S pilot. He was listed as such among the credits. Williams also drove the Porsche 908/02 entered in the real 1970 Le Mans by Solar Productions. This was kitted out with on-board 35mm Arriflex cameras fore and aft, bulky items far removed from the on-board cameras often seen on modern racing machinery. The idea was to secure some genuine racing shots for use in the film. The cameras had a serious effect on the handling of the car, which did not complete sufficient laps to be classified. Given the number of times it had to pit to change cameras, this was not surprising.

David Piper was one of those who lent their cars, in his case a Porsche 917 and a Lola T70. He was also among the long list of stunt drivers whose names appear at the end of the film, although he was

Richard Attwood gets film star treatment. *(Richard Attwood collection)*

Attwood seems amused; McQueen looks worried. *(Richard Attwood collection)*

to receive a special mention. Other British drivers included Richard Attwood, Derek Bell, Vic Elford, John Miles, Michael Parkes and Brian Redman. Racing commitments meant that Elford and Redman did not spend long on the set. Piers Courage, a close friend of Jonathan Williams, was also contracted to assist, but tragically was killed in the Dutch Grand Prix just prior to work starting. Courage had raced an Alfa Romeo at Le Mans the week before his death. Jackie Oliver could have been on the list of the film's drivers, having got to know Steve McQueen some time earlier through Sir John Whitmore. It was not to be, though, as that year was particularly busy with Oliver competing in some 32 races. Mike Salmon is another who recalls being asked but was unable to give the time.

As stated, Piper received a special mention for what he had given to the film. Both he and Derek Bell were involved in genuine accidents during the shooting. The Ferrari 512 that Bell was driving in the guise of 'Erich Stahler', an open-faced helmet wearer, caught fire. The fire extinguisher failed to work and in the time that Bell took to get out of the car he was burnt on the face. It did not help when the doors of the ambulance were not fastened and he almost shot out of the back as the driver drove off. McQueen insisted that Bell be taken to Paris to ensure that the burns were not serious. However, it was the end of the Englishman's involvement with the film.

Piper's accident had a far greater lasting consequence. Just before White House, he inexplicably hit the barriers in a Porsche 917. The car vaulted over the guardrail and Piper was taken to hospital with a triple compound fracture of the right leg. The bones would not knit and his leg eventually had to be amputated, but this infirmity has not stopped Piper from racing

his collection of Porsche and Ferrari Le Mans cars. In 2001, driving his Ferrari 250LM, he won the Legends race that preceded the 24-Hours.

McQueen was eager to prove himself to the professional drivers, but probably went too far by lying in the middle of the track with a hand-held camera. Derek Bell found the prone actor in his way as he accelerated out of White House at the wheel of a Ferrari 512. He recalls going past at about 160mph a couple of feet from McQueen's nose. Later, starting from the same corner, Bell and Jo Siffert sandwiched in McQueen, now at the wheel of a Porsche 917, and hustled him all the way to the Ford chicane. Bell recalled that, despite obviously scared after the event, he did not back off. McQueen subsequently introduced Bell to dirt bike riding and got revenge luring the Englishman over a hummock, 10 feet into the air, before landing in a rubbish tip. McQueen stood back and laughed at the Englishman's predicament.

At the time Bell was one of the leading Formula Two racers. His Church Farm Racing Brabham was in France for a race at Rouen and the team brought the car to Le Mans for McQueen to try on the Bugatti circuit. The American eventually lapped just three seconds slower than its owner. "He had already done Sebring by then (the actor had finished second in the 12-hour race there with Peter Revson in the March), so we knew he was good," says Richard Attwood.

There was a chance that McQueen could have raced at Le Mans himself. This concerns a story, it has even appeared in print, that his co-driver was to have been Britain's leading racing driver of the time. However, Sir Jackie Stewart will tell you that it was nothing more than a popular myth. Stewart knew and liked the actor. He and Jim Clark, in fact, had signed up to work on

Preparing to film a sequence: this shot from Derek Bell's own collection shows two of the Gulf Porsche 917s including the iconic number 20 of 'Michael Delaney'. *(Derek Bell collection)*

Does Derek Bell (left) really believe Jo Siffert's story? Steve McQueen's assistant, Marko Iscovich, McQueen and Hughes de Fierlant seem to. *(Derek Bell collection)*

an earlier project for a Formula One-based film with McQueen, perhaps because everyone else seemed to have gone with the rival John Frankenheimer scheme, which was to become the movie *Grand Prix*. With the cancellation of the McQueen idea, Stewart followed his fellow Formula One drivers onto the rival film, in which he appeared as 'Scott Stoddart'. He was never asked to partner with McQueen at Le Mans, although he believes that Jo Siffert may have been.

Derek Bell had only raced once at Le Mans before being asked to drive for the film, "but they seemed to like me." His debut had been with Ronnie Peterson in a works Ferrari 512M. "It was not as if I had done well," he recalled, because the car had dropped out fairly early on. The three or four months that Bell spent working with McQueen could be said to be the

start of his close association with the track. "That year I got to know Le Mans very well."

The original director of the film, John Sturges, told him that he had begun to wonder why he did not just use drivers and forget the actors. Bell and his family shared a small chateau with the McQueens for a couple of months and got on "incredibly well" with them. Although the actor was said to be a difficult man to work with, he showed no signs of this to the motor racing fraternity.

Bell was to maintain contact with McQueen, visiting the actor some years later in Hollywood and dining out with him and his then wife Ali McGraw. They drifted out of contact after this, but in 1980 McQueen made a telephone call to the office at Church Farm, Pagham, where Bell was based. He recalls this poignantly as he was out at the time. McQueen had left no number and the Englishman had no way of calling him back. Within four months McQueen had died of cancer. Bell wonders wistfully if he had called to say goodbye.

The real winner of the 1970 race, Richard Attwood, was involved in the film from day one. "I think Derek was a lot closer to (McQueen) than I was," he says. However, because he was retiring from competitive driving he was able to be on call most of the time He mostly drove the camera Porsche 917, and coincidently he was to buy this very car from Brian Redman in the late 1970s. It was in Gulf colours and had a long tail. Wanting it to look like his own winning car, Attwood swapped the tail with David Piper, who had a spare short tail. Only 10 years after he had bought it did he discover that this was the film car, probably the one that he had driven more than any other 917.

Filming was exceedingly boring, and many hours were lost because things were not quite right. Attwood recalls how finicky they were. "You hung around for days, bored out of your head because nothing was happening. It was quite stressful." Bell says that the cars were garaged at Arnage and driven to the circuit at 8.30am. The morning would then be spent setting up the scenes prior to a 2.00pm start of filming. There

The Brabham BT30 is Derek Bell's, but the driver is Steve McQueen. Following a Formula Two race at nearby Rouen, the Church Farm Racing team stopped off at Le Mans. Bell took the car out on the Bugatti circuit and then handed it over to the film star who within half an hour had recorded a lap time just three seconds slower than the car's regular driver. *(Derek Bell collection)*

was no way that the drivers could leave the set, though, as all manner of things could change, particularly the weather.

Attwood remembers a scene early on when he, McQueen, Michael Parkes and a fourth driver, all in 917s, were "rushing in and out" of Mulsanne. McQueen made a mistake, missed a gear and blew the engine. "This was in the middle of a season when Porsche needed all the engines for itself." All the factory had was a brand new engine. The insurance company became involved and asked if it was a professional driver at the wheel. That was the end of McQueen's driving for the film.

Attwood also recalls McQueen saying that he liked kippers. He promised to later bring some for him and still has a letter thanking him for this act. "He was so personable, you couldn't help but like the guy."

Other British personnel found themselves involved in the film including Peter Samuelson, a young student who started off as an interpreter and ended as a 'Mr Fix It'. Most of the 'signed' photographs of McQueen that were given away to visitors to the set were really signed by Samuelson. Another Briton to work on the film was former Formula One team manager Andrew Ferguson, best known for his various times with Lotus, who headed up the production team's 'racing department' and whom Richard Attwood recalls signing up the drivers.

Bob Leggett, whom we have met elsewhere in this book running the Mulsanne signalling crew for John Wyer and others, found himself at his usual location for the film. McQueen had asked Wyer for a 'crew chief' to take charge of the Mulsanne corner location. As a result, Leggett and his wife Liz found themselves back at Le Mans at Solar Productions' expense. Having experienced the delights of Solar Village, the encampment that had been set up in the centre of the track, they were taken down to the Mulsanne corner at about 8.00am the next day to meet the extras who had been brought in from Paris. Leggett remembers them as a group of "budding Bridget Bardots." He had to organize them to look like a group of signallers. Given that everybody wanted to be in the front row, it was not easy.

The next day, recalls Leggett, started with one of those gorgeous September mornings, when the script called for it to be raining. So out came the bowsers. At a radio-controlled command, the cars sped down from about where the second chicane is now located, at racing speeds (Leggett, contemptuous of the Frankenheimer movie with its disguised Formula Ford cars speeded up on film, is at pains to point out the speed). The spray shot up from behind the cars; Liz Leggett "got a soaking…and a free hair-do."

Curious to know what the signalling teams actually did, the second unit director asked Leggett for advice. He was told about the landline back to the pit, something that Liz operated in real life. It was decided that she should perform the same role in the film and had to call back to the pit with a stilted line that Leggett says was far from reality. Because of her new role as an actress, Liz ended up being paid more than her husband, although ironically, her moment of

Richard Attwood and Steve McQueen are obviously amused by something said by the great French journalist Jabby Crombac. *(Richard Attwood collection)*

glory ended up on the cutting room floor. It took four days to film the Mulsanne sequence, says Leggett.

In a race that seems to be all about Porsche 917s and Ferrari 512s, it is difficult to realize just how many British cars were involved. Tony Southgate, who was then at Lola, recalls McQueen visiting the factory wearing a blue metallic suit, "which was fairly unusual for Slough." He wanted a camera car to be built, so Southgate designed a tubular framework to go round the back of a Lola T70 complete with a backwards-facing seat for the cameraman. There was also a camera platform on the side where the door would have been. There were, in fact, more Lola T70 GTs in the film than even the most eagle-eyed anorak might have noticed. Lola T70s being less valuable than the Porsches and Ferraris, some of them were sacrificed for the greater good of the film, earning nicknames like the 'Lolari' and the 'Porschola'. Unlike some of the lesser single-seaters poorly disguised as 3-litre Formula One cars cars in the film *Grand Prix*, the Lolas crashed in the guise of Porsches and Ferraris really did look the part, such was the accuracy of the bodywork. The only flaw came in the colour scheme of a yellow Lola. While the new body was in Gulf powder blue and orange, there were still elements of the original colour on the car that only became apparent once the car was crashed. It seems that nobody thought what would happen when the disguise flew off in the crash. It is the Le Mans equivalent of the *Star Wars* stormtrooper hitting his head on the doorway.

The demise of the first 'Lolari' ended up in a potentially lethal farce. Involved was an Englishman, Malcolm Smith, who was in charge of the special effects crew. Having rigged up the car with servomotors that enabled him to work it by radio control, Smith seated

himself at the top of a 15-foot scaffold. Bob Leggett, a 'marshal' for this scene, remembers that the local radio-controlled model aircraft club was warned about what was to happen. Its members may not have interfered that day, but the car decided that it had a mind of its own and, instead of obeying Smiths' instructions, charged the scaffold. Everybody ran for cover except the trapped Smith. Thankfully, the car fishtailed into a guardrail and the engine died before it could reach Smith's perch. Derek Bell remembered that it gave everyone "a good laugh" when viewed on screen. When the second 'Lolari' was sacrificed instead, Smith was atop a van with the engine running. English

actor Alf Bell was the one who found himself in danger this time. He had decided to take some photographs of the scene and went in too close. With debris falling all around him he was lucky to escape. Ironically he had forgotten to load his camera with film. "The shot turned out better than we had anticipated," says Leggett.

Another British car said to have been a stand-in during the filming reappeared at Le Mans for the 2003 Legends race. The car, which owner Jon Minshaw shared with Martin Stretton that year, still retained its Gulf livery. It is not, though, a Porsche 917 but a Chevron B16 used as a double to minimize the risk of damage to the 'star' cars.

Over three decades since the film was made, it can now be appreciated as an atmospheric reminder of what Le Mans was like in the days of the great Group 4 cars. At the time it was, perhaps quite rightly, criticised for its almost total lack of plot. In his effort to be authentic, McQueen had created something that was neither documentary nor story. Sir John Whitmore warned him that this could happen, but the American did not learn. Stirling Moss described it as "a ghastly film," but it remains a must-see for any Le Mans fanatic. Just prior to the 2005 Le Mans, Allan McNish was observed near the track's museum shop trying to borrow some money from Audi UK's ever-efficient PR man, Martyn Pass. The latter wanted to know what the cash was for. McNish replied that, despite having won the race in 1998, he still had not seen the McQueen film and wanted to buy a copy. The DVD, in fact, had been given free with every programme the year before but, given that he had been concussed in an early-hours accident, McNish probably had not been in a fit state to notice.

THE DECCA RECORD

In the early 1960s, stereo recordings were the latest thing; the record companies were competing to release 12-inch LP sound-tracks of railway trains, aeroplanes or perhaps marching bands to demonstrate how it enabled us to hear things moving around in the living room.

Martin Borland's father Colin was marketing manager for Decca Records, one of his colleagues being recording manager Hugh Mendl, famed as producer of the classic Moody Blues 'Days of Future Passed' album amongst many others, and a racing fan since his childhood. Mendl, who had first visited Le Mans in 1938, convinced Sir Edward Lewis, Decca's chairman, that the company could sell a stereo record of the 24-hour race and its surrounding atmosphere, enabling him to take the ultimate busman's holiday.

Mendl and sound engineer Arthur 'Butch' Bannister arrived during the preceding week to record the sounds of practice. Some of the interviews with drivers, and James Tilling's commentary, were recorded later and mixed in.

The Borlands, father and son, flew over on the Saturday to discover that Mendl had arranged press passes for them. Four o'clock on the Sunday morning found them crouching in the pits as a Porsche screamed in for tyres – Martin with a microphone at left-arm's length, his father with another mike at right-arm stretch, 'Butch'

in the middle checking his tape-recorder levels with a torch, capturing all the noise in stereo. The team also walked through the crowds to the Mulsanne straight and recorded there, before visiting the funfair, having cognac with friends in a caravan somewhere in the early hours, and to the open-air chapel service on Sunday morning.

The race-winning entrant, Ford, was most co-operative, its help including arranging for Graham Hill, who shared one of the 7-litre Ford GTs in the 1966 race, to be available for interview in Decca's Hampstead studios. There were also launch parties for the Le Mans press contingent, and at the Steering Wheel Club in London.

Martin Borland still has the programme, tickets, passes and, of course, the LP record, 40 years on. A woven badge from the event, still sewn on his overalls (he is chief paddock marshal at Oulton Park), has provoked some derisory comments from fellow marshals as for some reason it depicts a single-seater car. "But what the hell," he says, "it's still one of my favourite souvenirs!"

Borland was to return to Le Mans in 1993. He had been considering applying as a marshal, decided he could not afford it, but would try for the following year. Not surprisingly, he could not resist investing £2 to enter a raffle organized by the British Motor Racing Marshals' Club, as the prize was a visit to Le Mans. He drew first prize.

David Piper rightfully receives a special mention among the credits at the end of *Le Mans*. Despite losing his leg during the filming, he has continued to race to this day, winning a Le Mans Legends race in one of his Ferraris. *(Author)*

THE UNIPART CALENDAR

The annual calendar from automotive parts supplier Unipart tended to be photographed by Lord Lichfield. In 1987 Le Mans was chosen as the location but his Lordship was not available. The result, as former Unipart group communications manager Patrick Fitz-Gibbon recalls, was one of the most fraught (and hardly the best) in the calendar's history.

"I was told: 'Lord Lichfield cannot do the calendar this year, but don't worry, David Bailey is available.' So the Unipart Calendar entered a new era, albeit for one year, with photographer Bailey retained for the shoot.

"The venue Le Mans and the *Vingt-Quatre Heures du Mans*. I thought it very appropriate for a parts company and that perhaps the models would add a certain *je ne sais quois*.

"A chateau was retained as a base and the calendar team arrived. It became fairly obvious early on that Bailey had absolutely no interest in motor racing whatsoever, and certainly no intention of using it as part of the calendar. This came as somewhat of a blow to the client as the shoot also included a television crew filming another hour-long documentary on the Unipart Calendar, with all the attendant PR and marketing opportunities. Unipart also had a party of 20 major customers at Le Mans, together with Clive James, who was involved with the TV film.

"Problems are only interesting opportunities, or so they say. Over the next 10 days a calendar was duly produced, which did indeed feature the Le Mans circuit in some of the pictures and produced that so important link for Unipart. There was, however, a certain amount of persuasion and coercion required to ensure that the photographer joined everyone at the circuit.

"Indeed, for some of us the shoot went beyond the call of duty. I actually featured in the month of April with one of the models. Sadly my eyes were blacked out – not to

preserve my anonymity but so that I did not get model fees.

"Other highs or lows of the shoot included a 'slight difficulty' with the circuit when it found out about Bailey's 'creative' photographic plans just before the start of the race. However, it did eventually agree, with 'adjustments' and a suitable 'accommodation'. There was also the problem that madame, who owned the chateau, accused us all of stealing her jewels. The result was a raid by five car loads of police in answer to madame's *neuf, neuf, neuf* call, a full day's questioning of everyone, particularly the models, and the relief when *monsieur l'inspector* informed us that they did not believe madame anyway as she was known to be 'bonkers'. However, having heard about the calendar shoot, how could they not spend the day at the chateau talking to a load of very pretty girls?

"And I only got to see the start and the finish of the race."

Ironically, Lichfield was at Le Mans that year, shooting the Silk Cut calendar. He was to be reunited with Unipart in the coming years. Bailey, who declared racing drivers were the biggest posers ever, was never used again.

Unipart has had an involvement with Le Mans that lasts to this day. In addition to such as its 1995 sponsorship of the Jaguar XJ220s, it also used its Supreme oil brand to back a Spice-converted Tiga-Lamborghini that was intended for the 1986 race. The car, the project of Lamborghini importer Portman Garages, was underfunded and never appeared at La Sarthe. Recently Unipart has been a personal sponsor of Allan McNish. For 2006 the Board of Unipart Automotive planned to be at the race to support the Scot in person, three of them intending to travel there in very British cars, managing director Chris Etherington and fellow director Mike Stringer in Aston Martin V8s and commercial services director Tony Sackett in a TVR 350GT. *(Unipart)*

The Group C Era

"No man is an *Iland*, intire of it selfe." Derek Bell had some notable overseas partners, particularly Jacky Ickx and Hans Stuck, and apart from his first victory, raced for the German factory Porsche, but he is still the flag carrier for the British at Le Mans. His win with Ickx in 1982 ushered in the Group C era. *(Original painting by*

CHAPTER 21

THE BRITISH AT LE MANS 1982-1991

"Now is the winter of our discontent made glorious summer…"
(William Shakespeare, *Richard III*)

Ah, to have been British at Le Mans in 1988. A British car had not won since 1976 and, to be fair to the Gulf GR8s, they hardly set the patriotic pulses racing. You had to go back to 1959 for a win by a true British marque, and the majority of the huge British crowd present in 1988 probably were not around then. Also, by 1959, British victories had become fairly commonplace. Surely, 1988 was something special.

It was also an incredibly exciting and close race, with the result in doubt right until the end. Would the British crowd have taken solace in the fact that Englishman Derek Bell was one of the drivers if the leading Porsche had come home first, something that could well have happened if Klaus Ludwig had not run out of fuel much earlier in the race? One doubts it; the national anthem was played three times to underline the fact that the British really had won at Le Mans again. Jaguar, unsuccessful the previous two years, had promised that it would be back. And it was.

It was never going to be easy for Jaguar, even when the Sauber-Mercedes were withdrawn during qualifying. The Porsche 962 was still a competitive piece of machinery and there were three works cars backed up by eight private entries. However, Jan Lammers, a Dutchman, but surely an honorary Brit that day, showed how it would be. Although the Porsches had been quicker in practice, only one was still ahead of him at the end of the first lap. On the seventh tour he shot past on the Mulsanne straight and the British spectators dominating the grandstands erupted. For Jaguar designer Tony Southgate, watching on a pit monitor, it was a sublime moment. Top speed on this famous stretch of road had been a crucial element in the XJR-9's design. "We had put a massive effort into trying to get it to go quickly down the straight. As (Lammers) went down Mulsanne he overtook (Stuck) beautifully thanks to his superior straight-line speed. I was really chuffed about that." Stuck was to report that Lammers had the cheek to wave at him as he went past.

Southgate recalls that the winning Lammers, Andy Wallace and Johnny Dumfries trio was "the

nutty team." However, it was noticeable how serious they became once it got down to the driving. The experienced Lammers was very much the man in charge, the two Britons being Le Mans 'rookies' that year.

Jaguar team boss Tom Walkinshaw planned his early pit stops skilfully while the Porsches all came in at the same time, then the race settled down, if this is the right expression, to a mighty battle. Jaguar was assisted by Ludwig's mistake, although the British crowd probably cannot have realized just how significant it was when they saw him crawling down the pit lane.

Everybody who was there that year talks about how demonstrative the support was from the British fans in the main grandstands. These days the officials make sure that the crowds do not swarm across the track until the last car is safely tucked away. But it was not so in 1988, and the winning car did not actually take the chequered flag, having been swamped by well-wishers before it could get through the Ford chicane. It was

The year 1988 was the proverbial nail-biter: Jaguar had to win Le Mans. Indeed the No 2 car of Lammers, Dumfries and Wallace did so, but the Porsche of Bell, Stuck and Ludwig kept the crew of the British car honest to the end. *(Simon Maurice)*

Richard Lloyd, a regular at Le Mans both as a driver and as an entrant. In 1983 his Canon-sponsored Porsche 956 finished eighth, Lloyd sharing the wheel with Jonathan Palmer and Jan Lammers. *(David Ingram)*

not, though, as if the second-place Porsche, just three minutes down the road, could have taken advantage of this fact; it too was faced with a sea of humanity. Tony Southgate conjectures what might have happened to it had it even tried to move up.

All this euphoria could not have been predicted when the first Le Mans 24-Hours was held to the new Group C regulations in 1982. It was an intriguing entry and, yes, the new cars carrying the Ford oval had been built in Britain. There were others from this country; none were expected to win, but in this new environment, who knew what might happen? After the two Aston Martin V8s entered by Robin Hamilton in 1977 and 1978, we now had a couple of Aston Martin-powered cars hunting in the top class, the Nimrods. Hamilton had taken a Lola T600 chassis and adapted it to take an Aston 5.3-litre V8. One of the Nimrods was a factory car, the other a private entry owned by Viscount Downe. Established specialist manufacturers March and Lola had also built cars for Group C, Ian Dawson had commissioned Geoff Aldridge to design the distinctive Cosworth DFL-powered GRID-Plaza, the last ever Mirage at least got as far as the grid before being excluded for a technical infringement, and one of Alain de Cadenet's old cars, now owned by Dorset Racing Associates, had its active life prolonged by becoming a Group C car.

Of this motley crew, only the heavy Downe Nimrod finished, in an admirable seventh place. However, in one of the Porsche 956s that were to dominate all but the early part of the race, as they were the initial years of Group C, was one Derek Bell. As all challengers apart from the other works Porsches fell by the wayside, so the car that he shared with Jacky Ickx ran almost faultlessly. In the very early hours of the

morning, the pair regained the lead and held it to the finish; victory number three for Derek Bell. Among the Porsche drivers who seemed to dominate the classified list there were a number of his countrymen, notably John Fitzpatrick and David Hobbs in the former's 935 that finished fourth. John Cooper and Paul Smith were two of the three pilots of Charles Ivey's eighth-placed 935K, and Tony Dron, Richard Cleare and Richard Jones brought their Group 4 934 home to a praiseworthy 13th. Porsche may have won all of the five classes that were running at the end, but there were British drivers in four of them.

It was so nearly victory number four for Bell the following year. As the Englishman recounts in a later chapter, it was probably one of his greatest races at Le Mans, yet the spectating Brits did not realize just how close their hero was to victory. After 1982's dominant performance, Porsche 956s now populated the entry in vast numbers. It was almost as if the other early Group C challengers had faded away, although Downe was back with his now lower and lighter Nimrod. Former Pink Floyd rock group manager Steve O'Rourke and his partner Michael Cane had commissioned the vastly experienced Len Bailey to design another Aston Martin-powered car, the EMKA. The latter came in 17th following two long pit stops, but the Porsche 956 was truly in the ascendant and, in the top 10, only the ninth-placed car was not a 956. Two of those, though, were British-entered, Fitzpatrick's thirsty version finishing fifth, driven by the owner with Guy Edwards and Rupert Keegan. Another owner/driver, Richard Lloyd, came eighth sharing his car with Jonathan Palmer and Jan Lammers. Cooper and Smith, this time with David Ovey, were again class winners in Charles Ivey's Porsche 930. The car had led Group B

The start of Group C in 1982. There were a number of British entries in the new category, but none to rival the all-conquering Porsches. *(Author)*

at the end of the first hour, only to lose it to a BMW. That car eventually disappeared and the team then drove an intelligent race to the finish.

And so the Porsche years continued, although Mr Bell was back on the top step of the rostrum in 1986 and again in 1987, his partners now being Hans Stuck and Al Holbert and their car the 962. In 1984, though, something significant happened, "*le retour de Jaguar.*" The American Group 44 team appeared with the Jaguar XJR-5s that it had been racing in the GTP class in the USA, and Brian Redman and John Watson were among the drivers. The cars ran solidly in the top 10 until the Sunday morning, when one succumbed to transmission failure and the other crashed. At one glorious point one of them was actually in the lead. The two Nimrods also ran well in the early stages before John Sheldon's massive crash on the Mulsanne straight, which resulted in the retirement of both cars. Group C2 did, though, fall to a Lola, an American-entered, Mazda-engined T616, after an intense and varied battle, the winners showing a mixture of reliability and speed. Overall, John Fitzpatrick's team had moved up to third place, albeit now with only one British driver in the car, David Hobbs. Richard Lloyd's two GTi Engineering 965s were both out by the 19th hour, while there was no hat-trick for Charles Ivey as his 930 retired with an oil leak at about the same time as the second of the GTi cars.

The following year was the best for Lloyd. He, Jonathan Palmer and James Weaver were delighted with their second place, particularly the latter, who 10 days previously had not known he would be driving at Le Mans. During the first quarter of the race, the team swapped the lead with the eventual winner, but was then delayed with an electronics fault. Palmer

and Weaver took the lion's share of the driving, with Lloyd carrying out just one stint. In Group C2 the Ecurie Ecosse of Ray Mallock, David Leslie and Mike Wilds was the class of the field, but it broke down after 45 laps to allow Gordon Spice to take his first class victory, partnered by Ray Bellm and Mark Galvin. The Needell, O'Rourke and Nick Faure EMKA finished 11th, and two places further down came the first Jaguar to finish at Le Mans for many a long year. Indeed, this Group 44 XJR-5 won the GTP class. You can almost sense the anticipation.

Pink Floyd drummer Nick Mason, the only member to have remained in the band since its inception in 1965, has raced at Le Mans on five occasions. In 1983 he was teamed with fellow Brit Chris Craft and Elisio Salazar in the Colin Bennett Dome-Cosworth DFL RC82/83. *(Author)*

Another Pink Floyd representative at Le Mans was its manager Steve O'Rourke, who probably caught the 'bug' from Nick Mason. He raced there eight times, twice in his Aston Martin-powered EMKA, letters of the car's name taken from the start of Emma and Katherine, his daughters' names. Here the car leads one of the Nimrods in 1983 when it finished 17th. Two years later it led the race for 15 minutes during the first refuelling stops, eventually coming home 11th. O'Rourke's best result was in 1998 when he shared a McLaren with Tim Sugden and Bill Auberlen to come fourth. *(Roger Stowers)*

Perhaps the most valiant British effort at Le Mans in 1982 was the privately entered Nimrod-Aston Martin of Mallock, Phillips and Salmon that finished in eighth place. Here it rounds Arnage on the Sunday morning. (*Author*)

during the morning, leaving a track that was damp in many places and giving rise to uncertainty about which tyres to use. Martin Brundle, with intermediate tyres on his Jaguar, played the 'hare' with two of the Porsches. As the race progressed so the other two Jaguars came up to put pressure on what by that time were just two surviving factory 962s. Richard Lloyd's Porsche, being shared by Palmer, Weaver and Price Cobb, was also going well in fifth. At one point during routine pit stops the Jaguars held the first three places, creating unconfined joy among the estimated 30,000 British spectators. However, Hans Stuck, in the 962 that he was sharing with Derek Bell and Al Holbert, gained some breathing space at the head following a shower of rain. Then the British-run Porsche caught fire, Weaver escaping unharmed, and a short while later Win Percy in the Jaguar he shared with Watson and Lammers had a massive 220mph accident. It was the kind that the Mulsanne straight always threatened. Just before the kink, the rear offside tyre blew, the result Percy thought of running over some debris. The car set off on a series of frightening somersaults yet Percy, his helmet ground down by contact with the road, emerged unhurt. The fact that the cockpit shell had remained intact was said to be a tribute to Tony Southgate's design. However, it was suggested that had Percy been hurt, the professional drivers might well have boycotted the next year's race.

Two hours before dawn, Boesel, in the XJR-8 also driven by Cheever and Lammers, went off the road at Arnage, although it did not take long to replace the damaged nose section. Then the second-place Jaguar of John Nielsen, Martin Brundle and Armin Hahne first began to suffer from vibration and then retired with a cracked cylinder head. Next, Cheever damaged his gearbox, dropping the car right back. The Jaguar challenge had suddenly fallen apart, and fifth place was the best that the survivor could manage at the finish. However, that man Bell had won again, and the C2 victory, as usual, went to Britain, Gordon Spice's team of Spice, Fermin Velez and Philippe de Henning winning its first ahead of the Ecosse of David Leslie, Ray Mallock and Marc Duez, the two cars finishing sixth and eighth overall, respectively.

And so to 1988 and the glorious story recounted above. Spice strode to victory in the C2 class again to add further lustre to the British glow, his co-drivers this time being Ray Bellm and Pierre de Thoissy. In all, Jaguar had entered five XJR-9s in an attempt to finally make it to the top of the podium. Apart from the winning car, only two others were to finish, the pair from its US IMSA programme, those of Derek Daly, Kevin Cogan and Larry Perkins in fourth place, and Danny Sullivan, Davy Jones and Price Cobb in 16th following two complete transmission rebuilds. Mention must also be made of Englishman David Hobbs, who celebrated his 49th birthday with a fine drive to fifth place in a Joest Porsche.

Despite its excellent performances in the World Sports Car Championship during the late 1980s and early 1990s, Jaguar was only to win Le Mans once more. In 1989 the Lammers, Patrick Tambay and Andrew Gilbert-Scott XJR-9 took the lead on the 153rd

The following year they arrived, three purpose-built Group C, factory-entered Jaguar XJR-6s driven by Derek Warwick, Eddie Cheever and Jean-Louis Schlesser, Brian Redman, Hurley Haywood and Hans Heyer, and Win Percy, Gianfranco Brancatelli and Armin Hahne. All right, so all three retired, but Jaguar's second golden era was upon us. The Warwick/Cheever/Schlesser car was even in second place when a tyre blew on the Mulsanne straight…and let us not forget that Derek Bell won again, even if he was in a Porsche. He had now overtaken Woolf Barnato as the most successful British driver at Le Mans. John Fitzpatrick's Porsche 956-running team also recorded another solid finish with fourth place.

The Gebhardt brothers were German, but their C2 car was built at Silverstone. Even more relevantly, one of their JC843s was sold to the workmanlike British ADA team of Ian Harrower and Chris Crawford. It was another year in which all but one of the top 10 finishers was a Porsche, but this time it was the ADA car that spoilt the symmetry with eighth place and, significantly, first in the C2 class, for Harrower, Evan Clements and Tom Dodd-Noble.

The next season, 1987, meant that it was 30 years since Jaguar's last victory at Le Mans, but the script was wrong again. Once more there were three Jaguars entered for the 24-Hours, only this time they were XJR-8s. Already at Jarama a Jaguar had won, at Jerez a Jaguar had won, at Monza a Jaguar had won, and on home ground at Silverstone, Jaguars had come first and second. It looked good. The early laps at Le Mans were confusing due to the fact that it had rained

lap and led for five hours, but exhaust and gearbox problems plus a shunt at Tertre Rouge dropped it back to fourth. The car of the Ferté brothers and Eliseo Salazar came eighth after numerous mechanical problems and mishaps, while the other two Jaguars dropped out. This was, though, a memorable time for Group C, with a high degree of manufacturer interest including that of Aston Martin. Two of its AMR1 cars were entered, the only time that they would be seen at Le Mans, that of Brian Redman, Costas Los and Michael Roe coming home 11th after suspension damage. The instrument panel on the David Leslie, Ray Mallock and David Sears car short-circuited and was changed in a rapid three minutes, but electrical problems continued, causing the car to drop out in the early hours of the morning.

Derek Bell, now driving for Richard Lloyd, retired and the British did not even win the C2 class, so it was not a good year. Still, on to 1990 and the Jaguar one–two that said farewell and thanks to the company's boss Sir John Egan, on his way to the British Airports Authority. The chicanes were now in place on the Mulsanne straight, but it was still described as a classic race, with Nissan (whose drivers included Derek Daly, Julian Bailey, Kenny Acheson, Mark Blundell and Martin Donnelly) and a private Porsche providing the opposition. Again there were four Jaguars, now XJR-12s, with Martin Brundle managing to drive two of them, but Tom Walkinshaw kept them reined in as the faster, turbocharged cars fought at the front during the early part of the race. The Walter Brun-entered Porsche kept the Jaguars honest towards the end, indeed it was running second with about a quarter of an hour to go, when its engine expired on the Mulsanne straight. The Lammers, Wallace and Franz Konrad XJR-12 moved up into second place behind the winning Nielsen, Cobb and Brundle car. Eventual third place went to an all-British crewed Porsche 962 driven by Tiff Needell, David Sears and Anthony Reid, while Derek Bell was in the fourth-placed Joest 962. The C2 class was also back in British hands, falling to the PC Automotive Spice of Richard Piper, Mike

Youles and Olindo Iacobelli.

The rules had changed for 1991. In theory, because the race was a round of the World Sports Car Championship, all the entrants had to be regulars from that series. The championship was now for 3.5-litre engined cars, designed for sprint racing, and furthermore, the other rounds had only attracted entries of 20 cars or less. However, all this was to be circumvented. Regular entrants were allowed to include 'guests' in their team providing they used the same chassis. Thus the Porsche 962C of Englishman Tim Lee-Davey was entered as part of the five-car Salamin Primagaz team, only two of which were really Salamin's cars. Jaguar, as well as Mercedes-Benz, were forced to enter their new sprint cars, but were also allowed to bring along older Group C models. Therefore, in the original entry list there were two of Jaguar's sleek new Ford-engined XJR-14s as well as four XJR-12s. Both the new cars were scrutineered and Andy Wallace was sent out in one of them to go for pole. Originally Derek Warwick had been slated for this honour, but Tom Walkinshaw had been examining the regulations and found that if he succeeded he would have to start in the 3.5-litre car and not be allowed to score championship points when, as he surely would, he transferred to one of the older V12s. There are times when motor racing regulations can be just a little too complex for their own good. So, Wallace, with limited experience of the XJR-14, was sent out to do the job, eventually losing out to one of the Mercedes after a long tussle. On the Friday, Walkinshaw announced that no XJR-14s would actually race, leaving him with three XJR-12s which, because they did not meet the new regulations, had to start further back on the grid than their practice times would have placed them. There was much about

Ian Harrower and Chris Crawford bought ADA Engineering in 1977 and in 1982 built the ADA/01, a car based largely on the de Cadenet Lola, for Frenchman François Duret. Harrower and John Sheldon shared the car with Duret at Le Mans in 1983. The Group C Junior car was not classified, having completed only 214 laps. *(Author)*

the 1991 race that was unsatisfying, not least that the *Restaurant de Hunaudières* had become 'a Chinese.'

Perhaps the most obvious example of frustration was that the 7.4-litre Jaguars were not able to compete properly without using up their entire allotted petrol allowance of 674 gallons. Davy Jones stated that he was changing gear at 6300rpm to save fuel. The Mercedes-Benz, it has to be admitted, were the fastest in the race, but two dropped out and a troubled third one came home fifth. Ahead of it were the three Jaguars that had eventually started…and a rotary-engined Mazda 787B. This was able to stay out ahead once it had inherited the lead from Mercedes because the complex rules said it need only weigh 830kg, despite having the same amount of fuel at its disposal as the 1000kg Jaguars. Consolation must be found in the fact that one Englishman, three-times Grand Prix winner Johnny Herbert, was in that raucous Mazda. Tom Walkinshaw encouraged the British fans to cheer the Brit in the Japanese car as he drove to the finish, so exhausted that he keeled over on getting out of the car and had to be taken to the medical centre. Thus he was missing from the emotional celebrations on the rostrum. Other British drivers in the top 10 included Jaguar team members Kenny Acheson (third), Derek Warwick and Andy Wallace (fourth) and, yes, Derek Bell, back in seventh in a privately entered Porsche 962.

And then it was all over. The FIA's rule makers had castrated endurance racing. Both Jaguar and Mercedes-Benz had gone from the front of the field; it was the end of a tussle that dated back to the early 1950s. The next time the British really had anything to cheer about it would be courtesy of a German vehicle manufacturer.

It is rare for the 'hare' to win the race, but there was no stopping Jan Lammers at the start of the 1988 event. From the very first lap he was harrying the Porsche 962Cs that had proved fastest in practice. As the cars disappeared off towards the Dunlop curve, the other Jaguars could be seen further down the field, perhaps biding their time. However, Lammers' car proved the most reliable as well as the quickest. *(Author)*

MARTIN BRUNDLE

The 1990 winner and current ITV Formula One commentator Martin Brundle describes Le Mans as "the greatest show on earth," certainly as far as motor racing is concerned. His reasoning is that everyone, from driver to spectator, is involved. "It becomes a personal challenge, whoever you are. We are all in it together." He points out how "you hear it from the fans on the ferry. Everyone has a plan. At the end everyone is tired but fulfilled."

As with many Le Mans drivers he does, though, admit to a love-hate relationship with the 24-Hours. There were times when he relished the idea of going out on the track, there were others – long periods behind a pace car or during conditions of rain or fog – when his enthusiasm logically would flag. As he says, it is an intimidating circuit. The worst part of 24-hour racing is, he reckons, the testing – pounding round somewhere like the Paul Ricard circuit for at least those 24 hours. These simulations could often be as much as 36 hours long for there is no circuit in the world like Le Mans and the cars had to be tested past the limit.

Brundle raced eight times at Le Mans, retiring on no fewer than seven occasions – "very frustrating. I guess I would go to Le Mans not expecting to finish." All of his drives were in coupes and, despite having been an experienced single-seater driver, he says when it came to sportscars, "I always fancied a roof over my head."

His one finish was in the place that matters most, first. In 1990 he was sent out as the traditional 'hare' in one of the Jaguars, his sole purpose being to destroy the opposition. As he says now, if he had kept going that would have been fine, but given that the "absolute plan" was to drive as a quickly as possible, this was hardly likely to happen. Brundle recalls racing side-by-side down the Mulsanne with Jesus Pareja. The Spaniard's Porsche 962 was quicker down the straight but the Jaguar had better brakes…which sounds rather like 1953 all over again. (The Walter Brun-entered Porsche was to retire just 15 minutes from the end for the race, having kept the Jaguar team honest to the end.)

As was usual, Brundle was team leader, and Tom Walkinshaw kept back a seat for him in one of the other cars for as long as possible. In the 16th hour and after 220 laps the XJR-12 Brundle was sharing with David Leslie and Alain Ferté cried enough with water pump failure and the Englishman was transferred into the car already driven by John Nielsen and Price Cobb. It was only just in time; a third driver now had to take over if the pair were not to go over the limited time available to them. Eliseo Salazar was race-suited and ready to go, but Brundle jumped into the car instead and set off apace, despite gearbox worries for the car. The ultimate victory was a fitting result for Jaguar's outgoing boss Sir John Egan, the man who had brought the marque back to Le Mans.

Brundle's memory of the win is the sight of officials trying to drag back John Nielsen's wife as the Dane tried to pull her up onto the podium. It was something of a surreal moment. Then there was the champagne with the Jaguar hierarchy, not the best idea for a dehydrated and tired driver.

The win was the last of four Jaguar drives for Brundle at Le Mans. Seven years later he was back with Nissan and then Toyota. The latter's programme was, he recalls, "very serious", but "the gearbox could never live with the engine's characteristics."

His final appearance at the race was with Bentley in 2001. It was a rather frustrating experience as "this was not the year we were meant to beat the Audis. However, at one stage Brundle was able to take one of the green cars into the lead. It was, he says, "one of my most pleasurable moments at Le Mans."

An experienced Formula One driver – he took part in 158 Grands Prix and was at one point team-mate to Michael Schumacher – Brundle muses on the number of F1 pilots who have raced at Le Mans just the once and not wanted to return. "This confused me, I never quite worked it out." Perhaps surprisingly, he believes that there is nothing more dangerous about being at Le Mans than taking part in a Grand Prix. Maybe, he thinks, it is because Grand Prix drivers, who by the nature of their sport have to be selfish, "could not cope with sharing a car. As a sportscar driver you have to work with your team-mates."

Brundle, though, has enjoyed the camaraderie of endurance racing. In the late 1990s he found himself in the same teams as Riccardo Patrese and Thierry Boutsen. He had never really got to know them before despite having been in the same Formula One pit lane for many years. Yet, thanks to sportscar racing, they became good friends.

Martin Brundle drove two cars on his way to victory in 1990. *(Simon Maurice)*

Now more used to being seen on the grid with a microphone in his hand, Martin Brundle raced for Toyota in 1999. He impressively won the pole and built up a six-second lead before the first pit stops. He was then baulked in the pit lane entry and things went down hill from then on. Eventually Brundle picked up a puncture, the car swapped ends at the first Mulsanne chicane and, damaged, refused to proceed any further than Arnage. *(Tim Wagstaff)*

Painted British Racing Green and showing an artistic interpretation of the Union Flag along the sides. Tim Lee-Davey's unique C1 Tiga was powered by a twin-turbo 3.3-litre Cosworth DFL, a complex engine for a small operation. In 1988 the car came to a halt with electrical failure on its sixth lap. (Author)

The C2 class was a major feature for much of the 1980s. Charles Ivey Racing entered two Tigas for 1988, a Porsche-engined version (above right) being driven by Tim Harvey, Chris Hodgetts and John Sheldon. (Simon Maurice)

The year 1991 may have been unique as the only time that a Japanese car has won at Le Mans. However, for the British its true significance is that Johnny Herbert was one of the drivers. His Mazda 787B sweeps down from the Dunlop bridge into the Esses, a sight that will never be repeated following the restructuring of this part of the track. (LAT Photographic)

CHAPTER 22

TONY SOUTHGATE AND THE SILK CUT JAGUARS

"It has been a long time waiting for this moment." (Tony Blair)

It is often said how the Lola GT was the precursor of the Ford GT40. It is also not stretching a point too far to say that the Group C Jaguars may also have had some of its genes. Working on the design of the Lola back in 1962 was a young man, Tony Southgate, fresh from learning his craft as a member of the 750 Motor Club. It was an honourable school that brought forth such as Colin Chapman and Southgate's new boss Eric Broadley. Southgate spent six months drawing that car, earning £13 a week.

Southgate did not attend the 1963 race at which the Lola GT made its sole Le Mans appearance. Afterwards Ford descended on the programme and, as he says, "suddenly a gang of silver-suited engineers appeared on the scene." He took himself off to Brabham to further learn his craft with Ron Tauranac, only to be invited back by Broadley to work on the Lola T70, including the heavy Aston Martin-engined version that, as he says, "failed spectacularly." John Surtees, who drove the car at Le Mans, "was not too complimentary" about the Aston power unit. One of the problems with the T70 was that it was originally designed for Can-Am and was thus a sprint car. "You always had loads of gearbox trouble." Southgate does not remember any endurance testing, but he does recall that he was now on about £35 a week.

He then moved on, first as chief designer for Dan Gurney's AAR team and then into Formula One with such as BRM, Shadows, Arrows and Lotus. He returned to sportscars when Ford asked him to look at its C100. "It was hideous." Southgate and fabricator John Thompson carried out about three weeks' work on the car, a result of which was that it was now 3½ seconds quicker. Then he was asked to design a completely new car, the Mk 3, that was to be run by Gordon Spice. Quite how well a Southgate-designed, turbocharged Group C Ford would have gone we never found out for, as recorded elsewhere, the plug was pulled on the project. Or did we? He was then approached by Tom Walkinshaw Racing to design the car with which Jaguar wanted to win Le Mans. "I took about a millisecond to say 'Yes'."

To be accurate, Jaguars actually returned to Le Mans in 1984, although they were then very much an American effort. In the USA Bob Tullius had long campaigned British cars under his Group 44 banner and in 1982 his team built an attractive IMSA GTP-class, closed prototype powered by a 5.3-litre V12 Jaguar engine, the XJR-5. The following season, and now with a 6-litre engine, the car proved successful racing in the North American IMSA series. In 1984 two of them were entered for Le Mans with Jaguar boss Sir John Egan's blessing. Neither finished, but a year later one staggered home firing on 11 cylinders in 13th place.

Tom Walkinshaw, though, was the man who really brought about the Jaguar renaissance. Tullius' efforts had highlighted the fact that a European-style Group C, rather than an IMSA GTP, would be needed if Jaguar was ever to win Le Mans again. Jaguar thus handed the mantle over to a man who had proved his worth for the marque. Walkinshaw had already been successful in the European Touring Car

Perhaps not the right line to win at Le Mans, but the race does last for 24 hours. Victory first went to one of the TWR Jaguars in 1988, the third year of their onslaught on Le Mans. It was a memorable achievement for designer Tony Southgate. *(Simon Maurice)*

Jaguar reappeared in 1984 with the Group 44 XJR-5s. To be pedantic, they were not really British, having been built in Winchester, Virginia, USA. The car of Ballot Léna, Watson and Adamowicz was retired with gearbox failure just after mid-day on the Sunday, the latter getting it back to the pits having been stranded for some hours following an 'off' at Tertre Rouge. (Simon Cronin)

Tom Walkinshaw already had a successful history with Jaguar and had won the European Touring Car Championship with an XJ-S prior to running its Group C programme. (Rover)

Championship, campaigning an XJS Coupe, when he invited Southgate to design a Group C car.

Group C had been introduced in 1982 as a category for 'two-seater competition automobiles built specially for racing on closed circuits.' There was freedom of choice as far as the engine was concerned as long as it was recognized by a road car manufacturer and ran on conventional petrol. Fuel consumption, though, was limited, a bone of contention during the life of the class. Group C was intended to replace the Group 6 sports-racers then tending to head the field at Le Mans. A second division, initially known as C Junior but renamed C2, was introduced, similar but with lower weight and fuel figures. It did not follow that the C and C2 cars had to be coupes but, although Jaguar was to examine the possibility of a roadster, all those ever entered in this class had closed cockpits. Although the cars were allowed to run at Le Mans in 1991, their era effectively ended at the start of that year when the FIA, in order to bring sportscars into line with Formula One, introduced a 3.5-litre formula that not one of the teams wanted. Attendances fell after what had been a golden period for endurance racing, and Formula One, to the great regret of the sportscar fraternity, achieved the total pre-eminence that it has retained to this day. The British remember Group C with great fondness for it was the class that brought Jaguar renewed glory.

Although Tom Walkinshaw Racing had tested a Group 44 XJR-5, there was little or no intention of adopting the chassis for the World Sports Car Championship. It lacked sufficient downforce for one thing. Instead Walkinshaw took on Southgate to design the V12-engined XJR-6. Initially he drew the car at his home, assisted by Geoff Kingston, and visiting TWR, where the cars were assembled, about once a week.

"It was a big challenge; you were taking on the might of Porsche. They looked good and were super reliable, but they did not have that much opposition. I thought we could get them on a more sophisticated chassis and better aero. The Jag also had plenty of 'grunt,' but it was a bloody big engine with a high centre of gravity. It was a massive challenge to make the car handle with an engine like that. We placed the engine (the work of TWR engine man Allan Scott) as low and as far forward as possible, with a long bell-housing, so that it was right near the driver's shoulder." The chassis was built from carbon-fibre and Kevlar, further distancing itself from Bob Tullius' cars.

It was a very satisfying period for Southgate, not just because of the success of the Jaguars, but also their safety margin, as illustrated by Win Percy's dramatic crash in 1987. Percy himself does not know how many times the car went over, but when it stopped all went quiet, he undid his seat belts and got out. Southgate, Walkinshaw, Percy and team manager Roger Silman had an immediate meeting to discuss what had happened. "Rarely does something take you by surprise when you have done thousands of miles of testing, so we were really worried." Naturally, tyres were suspected, so all the other Jaguars were brought in and changed over to cross-ply rubber. After about two and a half hours the crashed car was brought back to the garage area; the right rear tyre did not have any tread at all. "Now we knew what had happened and could continue on with the rest of the race." Shortly afterwards Percy wrote Southgate a letter thanking him for making the structure so strong.

Being turbocharged, the Porsches could always 'turn up the wick' and out-qualify the Jaguars, but then the latter would give chase with increasing success in the World Sports Car Championship. For the start of the 1985 season, the first in which the works Jaguars appeared, the name of this contest was changed from the World Endurance Championship of Makes to the World Endurance Championship of Teams. New boys TWR Jaguar managed seventh place with 20 points, having shown great promise. For the next season the XJR-6's engine had grown from 6.2 to 6.5 litres and the now renamed Silk Cut Jaguar team finished equal-third in the championship, having scored its maiden victory at Silverstone. Le Mans may have disappointed in 1987, but the championship did not, Silk Cut Jaguar easily winning with eight outright wins. Significantly, the cars now had the ability to finish races to go with their undoubted speed. The year after, Jaguar's championship was even more emphatic with getting on for twice the number of points as its nearest rival. After two years of Sauber-Mercedes, the championship returned for the last time to Jaguar in 1991. TWR's three series victories were something that the famed C-type and D-type cars had never achieved, although the reader should be reminded that the factory always set more store by a Le Mans win in the 1950s than it ever did in the World Championship. Jaguar drivers also won their respective championships in 1987, 1988 and 1991 with titles for Raul Boesel, Englishman Martin Brundle and Teo Fabi respectively.

The TWR cars progressed from the Design Council

Award-winning XJR-6, 8, 9 and 12 concept through to the XJR-10/11 and then the very different XJR-14. The XJR-8 was essentially the same monocoque as the XJR-6; indeed some XJR-8s started life as the earlier cars. Sixty-four detail changes were made, though, and a 7-litre engine fitted. Even more modifications were made for Le Mans, where the cars were known, perhaps rather obviously, as the XJR-6LM, XJR-8LM and XJR-9LM.

The 1988 Le Mans-winning XJR-9LM was, again, basically the same car with detail changes, at least one original XJR-6 being rebuilt to this specification. A 6-litre IMSA version of the XJR-9 was also built, to be followed by a completely new composite chassis, V6 3-litre twin turbo-engined car for the American series, the XJR-10. A Group C version of this, the 3.5 litre-engined XJR-11, was also built, winning just one race – the 1990 British Empire Trophy at Silverstone. The second Le Mans-winning Jaguar, the XJR-12, was a Le Mans/Daytona endurance version of the earlier cars, which was used in both IMSA and Group C specification. The final Silk Cut Jaguar, the Ford-engined XJR-14, was built to the 3.5-litre regulations introduced for 1991. As already recounted, although one was practiced for Le Mans that year it never ran in the race.

Southgate remembers Egan saying to Walkinshaw: "When you came to me saying that we were going to beat the Porsches I never believed you, but I am pleased to accept the fact that we have." Southgate acknowledges "Tom must have done a good selling job".

He recalls the huge team of 1988, five cars and 15 drivers plus hoards of mechanics. Nothing quite like that has been seen since. By this time, factory Jaguars were also competing in the IMSA series in the USA

and two of the cars had been brought back from the States, their 6-litre IMSA engines replaced by Group C 7.4-litre units. The extra oil coolers that were used on the IMSA cars were also fitted to all the usual Group C cars.

"I was like the chief designer, just sitting on the wall observing it all," says Southgate, there to be occasionally called upon to advise. "I used to float from car to car." The previous year the car had been quick but now reliability had been added. At one point, when Jan Lammers was in the lead, his Jaguar's windscreen was damaged and the Dutchman had to drive down the straight holding it to stop it collapsing in on him. The screen was held by six small clamps and would take about 3½ minutes to change, and the

Jaguar ran no fewer than five cars in 1988, two of them, including the Daly/Cogan/Perkins car seen here, borrowed from its IMSA programme. Of the European cars only the winner was around at the end. However, the two US Jaguars both finished, number 22 in fourth place. *(Simon Maurice)*

Group C in 1989 abounded with factory entries from Britain, Germany and Japan, but it was not a good year for Jaguar with only fourth and eighth places. The No 1 XJR-9 of Lammers, Scott and Tambay did, though, lead for five hours. The No 3 car of Jones and Daly stopped on the Mulsanne straight during the Saturday night with valve failure. *(Simon Maurice)*

Flanked by the triple-height guardrail, the 1988 winning Jaguar sets off again down the newly resurfaced Mulsanne straight. The car achieved around 236mph on this famed stretch of French highway. *(Simon Maurice)*

lead was about a lap. However, the replacement went "very smoothly" and the lead retained, "but only just." Before the race sponsor Silk Cut had said: "You will win, won't you."

The 1988 victory obviously meant a lot more to Southgate than the 1990 win "as it was the first one." The year 1991 still hurts, though. He recalls that at one point the Jaguars were running first, second and third, "but because of the fuel regulation, this Mazda came chugging up and overtook us. It was just a fuel economy run." The cars, though, "went like clockwork and all finished." In that respect Southgate regards that as the Jaguars' best performance.

By now Southgate was 50 years old and was looking to move on. Serving out his notice, he did some work on the Ross Brawn-designed 3.5-litre XJR-14. Aston Martin, though, had offered him a lucrative deal to work on its Group C car. Cosworth was going to supply the engine. During the month in which Southgate's contract was being finalized Ford purchased Aston Martin. This meant that Ford, who did not like sportscar racing that much anyway, now had two Group C contestants. Southgate could see that one would have to go. He was right.

He had not finished with Le Mans, though. He went on to work with Toyota on the slippery TS010. The transmission was the weak link in this car, although it did manage a second at Le Mans in 1992. Southgate suggested using an Xtrac gearbox, but the Japanese could not cope with the fact that this was so much

Three British Le Mans competitors in 1990 who all raced in Formula One. Martin Brundle (centre) won the race that year with Jaguar while Mark Blundell (left) set pole position with his Nissan. Martin Donnelly's Nissan was qualified third by fellow Irishman Kenny Acheson only for it to retire on the warming-up lap. *(Simon Maurice)*

cheaper than their own.

"The 3.5-litre formula was never going to 'click'," says Southgate, who now went to assist Ferrari with its low-budget, Dallara-engineered IMSA sports-racing project. "It was terrific working there." The 333SP was not designed as a Le Mans car, and although reliable was not expected to win there. The Englishman was involved with Andy Evans' two semi-works cars, which went to La Sarthe in 1996 with Southgate-designed low-drag bodies which took them from a straight speed of 187mph to 205mph.

He was then to return to TWR and the Nissan R390 Le Mans project that, he says, was "a British car in all except the engine." He points out that the centre-section was basically a Jaguar. The time frame to build the car was short and the tooling still existed for the one-make, Grand Prix support race series car, the XJR-15. By using the 15's windscreen, taking the tub and modifying the tooling Southgate saved "a chunk of time." He describes the heart of the car as "a 'Jag 15' variant."

As the car was being built to then GT1 regulations, it also had to at least have some visual semblance of a road car. "You did the minimum to get through a road-legal requirement." One was actually made for the street, but it had no ventilation. "If it had been sunny you would have fried or suffocated." By this stage the GT regulations had become a joke. As Southgate says, the R390, unlike the slightly earlier McLaren F1, "was built as a racecar from day one." He believes that prototypes are essential for Le Mans and that the race cannot survive on GT cars alone. "You would not get a quarter of a million people to go to Le Mans to watch a Viper go round. You have got to have some exotica cars there." He also reckons open-top cars are ideal. Such versions of the Jaguar were considered and wind-tunnel tested, "but of course, aerodynamically they were not as good."

A proposed reduction in funding by Nissan brought an end to the R390 project. Dallara knew that Southgate was again free and put him onto Audi, which he joined in September 1998 as a technical consultant. At that stage there was obviously plenty of work to do to make its new, but then heavy, Le Mans contender competitive. Under Southgate's direction, Norfolk-based rtn was given the go-ahead to build a coupe-bodied car that was not simply a closed version of the already designed R8R. Southgate looked after the outer package and the bodywork while Peter Elleray, who was to design the 2003-winning Bentley, did the suspension and chassis work. After the 1999 race this project was dropped as the roadster was obviously good enough to win on its own. The R8C was then used as a development car under the Volkswagen name for a variety of concepts, including a diesel that never materialized. Eventually Southgate carried out a development on the car that became the first Bentley bodywork.

Southgate observes the amount of money that has been spent on the Audi R8. "It was more complicated in places than I would have liked. I like value for money, which is why Tom (Walkinshaw) liked me doing his cars!"

THE COMMUNICATORS

In 1988 the ACO instituted the *Club de la Presse et de la Communication* prize, an award given to those who the assembled media had found to be the most helpful. Its first recipient was British, Jaguar's bearded and popular press manager Ian Norris. However, the award does not necessarily have to go to a PR person, and in 1994 one Derek Bell was presented with it.

The first woman to win the award was also British. "I was extremely honoured," says Fiona Miller, who in 1998 was on her own handling the PR for Panoz and up against the might of other manufacturers' publicity machines. Fiona was no stranger to Le Mans, having worked there previously with Jaguar. However, she had no idea what it was about when she was asked to report to the *Module Sportif* at 12.00pm.

Up to that point it had been "a most dreadful weekend" for the team; the award "came like a bolt out of the blue." She continued to work with Panoz until 2001, but has still been of great assistance to the press at Le Mans, mainly as PR for Care Racing, the team running the Prodrive Ferrari 550s. Other clients have included Creation Autosportif and the rival GT drivers Darren Turner and Oliver Gavin.

Janice Minton first became well known as the voice of the pit lane on Radio Le Mans. She had already worked with ADA, Ecurie Ecosse and OSCAR, and had founded her own corporate hospitality business, but prior to Sebring in 2003 had never written a press release. However, she was approached by John Mc Neil to run the publicity for the Nasamax bioethanol project that year. This was a story with a difference that attracted the

Michel Cosson, President of the ACO, presents Nasamax PR Janice Minton with the *Club de la Presse et de la Communication* award in 2003. *(Janice Minton collection)*

attention of the media outside the narrow world of the motor racing press. The way in which Janice handled this earned journalists' admiration and it was no surprise that she was the winner of the prize that year. Well, it was a surprise to one person: Janice Minton. "I didn't know there was an award." At about midday, four hours after the Nasamax Reynard had retired, ACO communication manager Fabrice Bourrigaud found her to tell her the news. "I couldn't possibly have won it. I was new. It was as if the whole world around me went into freeze-frame. It was an amazing moment. I didn't stop grinning for hours."

In 2005 the prize was back in French hands, those of the Paul Belmondo team. It must be pointed out, though, that the publicity for its Gulf sponsor was handled at the race by an Englishman, Simon Maurice.

The performance of the Jaguars in 1988 and 1990 gave Tony Southgate something to smile about. *(Tony Southgate collection)*

First and second, the Nielsen/ Cobb/Brundle and Lammers/ Wallace/Konrad XJR12s are cheered home by the British hoards in 1990. With only two wins in eight years, the Group 44 and then TWR Jaguars did not quite match the record of their illustrious 1950s predecessors. Nevertheless they were memorable years. *(Jaguar)*

JAGUAR • DAIMLER
Heritage Trust

We specialise in Heritage Certificates, Classic Parts, Photographic Library & Exhibition Services

Genuine Jaguar Classic Parts

Genuine Jaguar Engineering approved parts for classic Jaguars and Daimlers available through a selected dealer network.

Heritage Certificates

Production record traces and Heritage Certificate for your classic Jaguar.

Photographic Library Services

Photographic services to the media, agencies and public. Historic motorsport, lifestyle and promotional imagery available.

Exhibitions Services

Other Services

- Historical research facilities and information service

- Classic car hire for film and TV productions, showroom displays, and selected wedding car hire

- Facility Hire

- Museum open weekday during office hours or on the last Sunday of the month

JAGUAR DAIMLER HERITAGE TRUST
Browns Lane, Coventry CV5 9DR
General enquiries: +44 (0)24 7620 3322
Archive enquiries: +44 (0)24 7620 2141
Vehicle hire: +44 (0)24 7620 2870
Fax: +44 (0)24 7620 2835
Parts: +44 (0)1865 383 358
Email: jagtrust@jaguar.com
Website: www.jdht.com

Look out for our range of XJS merchandise

186

CHAPTER 23

DEREK BELL

"Per noctum volamus." (No 9 Squadron, RAF motto)

John Wyer recounted the tale of how he wanted Derek Bell to drive one of the Gulf Ford GT40s at Le Mans in 1968. The young Englishman had made "a very good impression" during a trial at the Thruxton track in Hampshire. Bell recalls how the unfinished car was without windows and that "dust was flying about." That season he was driving for Ferrari in Formula Two and had been asked to be present at the Mexican Grand Prix as a stand-by. The offer regarding the World Championship race was conditional on his not taking the risk of racing at Le Mans; Enzo Ferrari would not change his mind about this. In the event, Bell was not required to race in Mexico. Ironically, John Wyer recalled in his biography, "had he driven for us at Le Mans he would almost certainly have been in the winning car." Instead it would be almost a decade before Bell scored the first of his five victories at the track that would make him the most successful Englishman ever to race at La Sarthe.

"Derek is a very good ambassador for motor sport," observes Richard Attwood's wife Veronica. He is arguably the figurehead for all those British who make the annual trek to Le Mans. Typically of the man, he sees this differently. It has been his belief that the British first of all supported the British cars, and it is only when they dropped out that they turned to the Englishman who was invariably in a German car. Bell manages to combine a tremendous enthusiasm – even now – with a certain self-deprecation. It should also be remembered that, much as he is now associated with Porsches, Bell's first win was in a British-built Gulf, while what he regards as one of his best drives – that of 1995, when he shared a car with his son Justin as well as Andy Wallace – was at the wheel of a McLaren. It would have been fitting if his Le Mans career had ended racing the Bentley EXP Speed 8.

He was taken on as team consultant for the project, becoming arguably its most prominent figurehead. At

Derek Bell regarded the Porsche 917 as the outstanding car of his long Le Mans career. However, he only once raced such a machine at Le Mans, the long-tailed version that he shared with Jo Siffert retiring during the 18th hour after a variety of problems. *(Alan Hearn collection)*

the end of the 1990s he had been approached and told that Bentley intended returning to Le Mans. Would he be interested? "Lead me on." After years of indecision, enthusiasm had returned to the marque, thanks to the investment of the Volkswagen Group.

Now Bentley was coming back and Bell realized that he could become "a small part of that Bentley history." It is obvious that what the 'Bentley Boys' achieved some 70 years before means something to him. "It is the greatest name in British motorsport history."

Now, at last he had the chance to work with a British manufacturer at Le Mans.

"On reflection," he now wonders whether in the first season, after all a test year in which the car was not expected to win, he should have put himself forward as a possible driver. It is again perhaps typical that it is only now that he wonders if he should have been more forward and to have done this. Derek Bell, too shy? Perhaps, in this case.

"To have had my last year at Le Mans in a Bentley would have been fantastic."

Bell did get to drive the Bentley in 2003, but the car that Guy Smith and his colleagues raced throughout 24 hours was to break down before he could even get the length of the Champs Elysees. The day after the race, the famous thoroughfare was closed to normal traffic, and the winning car, with Bell at the wheel, was driven down it followed by the team drivers sitting in the back of a pair of 1920s 4½-litre Bentleys. Bell remembers it as a "great honour."

"We pulled out from the Arc de Triomphe," recalls Guy Smith. "It was surreal."

The conditions proved to be chaotic, the cavalcade was almost forced to halt and all three cars began to overheat. By the time they had arrived at the end of the Champs Elysees, Bell had to turn the engine off, but it was too late. The Speed 8's engine had boiled.

"I was told to be very careful about overheating, but I assumed that the Champs Elysees would be empty and I would just cruise down at about 70 to 80mph, get to the end and that would be it. I didn't realize that the whole of Paris was going to run down the Champs Elysees with us."

Bell had been told that if the temperature rose to $120°$, he was to switch off. As he drove down the road he gave a run-down over the radio of the water temperature.

"Water temperature 80."

"OK, fine."

"Water temperature 90."

"OK, fine."

"Water temperature 100."

"OK, fine."

"Water temperature 115."

"Carry on."

"Water temperature 120."

"OK, carry on."

Eventually he pointed out that the temperature had now reached 125°, and the other end of the radio went quiet. Bell repeated "it's 125." He stopped and everybody leapt upon the car to remove the panels, but although the engine still worked, it was too late. "The only time I blew up a Le Mans engine it wasn't in the race."

As one of its drivers Guy Smith was to observe, 'Number 7' still wears the flies from the race, just not its original engine.

Bell is such an integral part of the Le Mans story that in 2002 he was given the freedom of the city by its mayor, Jean-Claude Boulard, as well as the Spirit of Le Mans award by the ACO. "It was fantastic," he recalls. "I'd never even been given the freedom of Bognor Regis." He points out that "Le Mans is one of the most famous names in motor racing, along with Monaco and Indianapolis. Just to win there is enough." However, Bell regards the accolades and all that went with them, including a huge commemorative "paving stone" (actually a bronze plate), as something really special. He is also quaintly amused by the fact that he beat his old partner Jacky Ickx to the ACO award.

The ceremony in which Bell was made an honorary citizen of Le Mans was a notable event, taking place just before the May practice on the Place du Jet d'Eau, close to the Place des Jacobins and in the shadow of the cathedral. It is a rare tribute, and up to that point had been reserved for General Patton, who liberated the city in 1944, historian Albert Boroch, and former race winners Sammy Davis, Luigi Chinetti and Jacky Ickx. The location reminded Bell of the opening sequence to the Steve McQueen *Le Mans* film, a project in which, as we have seen, he was closely involved.

There are certain years at Le Mans that stick out in Bell's memory and they are not necessarily the victory years (he regards 1987 as his most satisfying win). The year 1992 is an example. Bell achieved an ambition then to share a car at Le Mans with son Justin, who had been entered there the previous year in an awful Spice-Ferrari. The pair was teamed up with Tiff Needell in ADA Engineering's now 'long in the tooth' Porsche 962. The team that had won the C2 category at Le Mans back in 1986 had purchased the car from the now defunct Richard Lloyd squad.

The team had given the car low downforce and then sent it out in conditions that proved appalling. Bell recalls it "slithering all over the road." He also became frightened, not for himself but for the fact that he was going to have to hand over to his son who was still only in his early-twenties. "What was I going to tell him?" In the end Bell advised his son "just to be very careful." He also asked him how it had gone once his shift was over. "'How was it?', I asked, 'Marvellous, dad!' I realized then that I must be getting old."

He also recalls 1994 as the year he was at the wheel of "one of the nicest cars I ever drove at Le Mans," the Kremer-Porsche K8. Bell describes the invitation to race the car as having been "a wonderful opportunity, literally out of the blue." And blue it was, perhaps not the evocative powder blue of old, but the car was fittingly Gulf-sponsored.

"Gulf," recalls Bell, "made a real fuss about it." The slogan was coined 'Gulf – the Return of the Legend.' "Some people thought the 'legend' was me," quips Bell, who by now was in his fifties. The result was that, in the USA, he is still sometimes teased as 'the legend.'

Bell remembers the severe vibration that the car suffered down the Mulsanne straight during testing – shades of the 1974 Gulf – although the problem was overcome in time for the race. Towards the end of official practice, as it was about to get dark ("the best time") Bell went all-out for fastest time. As he came round for his flying lap, he found that another competitor had "dumped oil" all over the track. The marshals were out brushing cement onto the offending lubricant. Nevertheless, Bell "went for it," the car sliding around for the first few bends. "It was one of my most exciting laps. You don't often get the opportunity at Le Mans to go hell for leather." The result was just half a second off pole.

The year after the Kremer drive, son Justin and Andy Wallace asked Bell if he would share their David Price-run, Harrods-sponsored McLaren F1 GTR. "I thought I had finished with Le Mans." However, the first McLaren year was another that has fond memories,

The first of five; the 33-year-old Bell on his way to victory in 1975. *(Ford)*

The victorious Bell/Ickx Porsche 956 of 1982 lines up for Arnage. *(Author)*

The crowds clamour to see the winners, Bell and Ickx, in 1982. (Author)

indeed was one which brought him tantalizingly close to an Ickx-equalling sixth win.

"Le Mans is the sort of race that you have to prepare for months ahead. If anyone wanted me to be serious about Le Mans I needed to know by Christmas. I always started training from January 1." In 1995 Bell was only asked a few weeks before and he was neither physically nor mentally prepared. "I didn't think I was good enough." There was also the fact that the McLarens were in their first Le Mans and Bell did not expect them to be competitive. By the evening of the race Bell and company were in the lead. "It was such a big surprise to us."

In the middle of the night Justin went out to do a double stint, leaving his father to think that he now had four hours off. After about an hour in the pouring rain Justin returned, his eyes "like the size of soup bowls." Bell and Wallace took over until about 6.00am. It was not until the late morning when the clutch release bearing started to pack up that the team lost the lead. Bell believes that if it had remained wet they could have continued up front. He had been extending their lead over the much younger J J Lehto, "something that I was amazed about."

In the end the Harrods-sponsored car finished third, some achievement considering one of its drivers was now in his early fifties. Given what had happened, it was, says Bell, disappointing "but I still call it the most memorable result of my career." At first sight that may appear strange considering that he won the race five times. However, consider standing on the rostrum with your son on Father's Day, and then you appreciate the sentiment. Some years later Bell had the opportunity to drive the actual third-place McLaren, still yellow and green, across France for a few hours. "It was quite magnificent. How many people lead at Le Mans and then get the chance to drive that car on the road later?"

Bell, quite rightly, regards the Porsche 917 as the most outstanding car of his career. "We were doing 246mph at Le Mans," he recalls with relish. However, it was probably the 956 that gave him his most memorable Porsche drive.

He was outspoken about the rules when they introduced Group C in 1982. "That year (Porsche's) Peter Falk told me that we weren't going to win at Silverstone (because of the fuel economy regulations). I did virtually all the lap in fifth gear to get round with the amount of fuel allowed. I thought it was a detestable way of going racing." However, this formula was not only to give him three of his victories, but also perhaps his most impressive Le Mans.

"If somebody said: 'What was your best race at Le Mans?', 1983 was it," he says. That year Bell and Ickx were on pole but lost a lap on the first round when Ickx was pushed off by Jan Lammers, damaging the undertray. At 6.00am Bell regained the lead. It was the last year in which two drivers were allowed, but most teams had by now plumped for three. Who, though, was up to sharing a car with this pairing?

"During the night we made a lap up and didn't lose any fuel – eight miles gained in 12 hours! I think that was our greatest drive together." Bell took the lead down the Mulsanne straight, but during the next lap the engine stopped and he had to carry out repair work on the electrics. He then drove the car back to the pits and Ickx took over. By 11.00am they were back in the lead again. Then a neck on one of the oil coolers split so the oil cooler had to be changed. The car dropped back four laps behind the leading Porsche of Vern Schuppan, Hurley Haywood and Al Holbert.

As the race neared its end an exhausted Bell thought that this was one race he would be happy for Ickx to finish. However, there was a knock on his door and he was informed that the Belgian would be in within 15 minutes. Porsche team boss Norbert Singer had stated that Ickx was having a major problem with the brakes and that the discs would have to be changed. Bell asked how far behind the car now was, the answer being a mere lap, the leading car having been delayed with a collapsing rear subframe and an errant left-side door.

How long would it take to change the discs? Another answer: four and a half minutes, the equivalent of another lap. What were the other options? To go slowly. Bell said he would go slowly then. However, Ickx was already telling the mechanics to change the discs. The Englishman told him to get out of the way.

Their car was now just over a lap behind with an hour to go. Bell no longer needed to use the brakes to save the gearbox and broke the lap record twice in the last hour. Careful use of fuel during the early stages of the race also meant that he could press on. At one stage he heard Holbert call in and say that the water temperature was rising. Then a few laps later he heard that the water temperature had dropped off the clock. There was no longer any water in its engine. "I pressed the button and said: 'Call him in, call him in!'" Meanwhile he was knocking 20 to 30 seconds off the lead car.

Very few people around the track realized the drama

Scot David Leslie is one of a select band of British drivers to have competed at Le Mans 10 or more times. *(Aston Martin)*

that was taking place. About to start the final lap, Holbert's car appeared along the pit straight trailing smoke. Over the loudspeakers, the commentator talked about a tyre rubbing on the bodywork, but the smoke was actually coming from the left-hand exhaust pipe. The official gap was to be measured from the previous lap at 64 seconds, but Bell's stepfather, 'the Colonel', Bernard Hender, stopwatch in hand at the final bend, reckoned that there was only 26 seconds in it at the end. The winning car would not have made it had the race been one lap longer.

John Horsman believes that Bell was lucky when he drove for him in the Gulf Research Racing team. Luck is surely an important ingredient for the success of any endurance racer, and Horsman does not intend this as a criticism. However, he gives an example from Le Mans 1974, when the Gulf GR7s were breaking the CV joints in their rear drive-shafts. The rubber boots were splitting at the high rotational speeds on the Mulsanne straight, letting out all the grease. The Schuppan/Wisell car stopped out on the circuit and had to retire, but Bell's broke on the approach to the Ford chicane, damaging the rear suspension but allowing him to coast in to the pits. The next year the Schuppan/Jaussaud GR8 developed electrical troubles, which dropped the car from a possible win to third place. Bell's car "with identical parts, had no such problem, allowing him and Ickx to win."

Having said that, Horsman rates Bell very highly, even "in the class of Ickx and Rodriguez." When you understand the high regard the British who drove with them have for these two, then you realize that there could be no better praise for an endurance racer.

How does Le Mans sit in Bell's mind as an important race? On his way up through Formulae Three and Two it had no place in his life at all. "To me Le Mans was a sportscar race and I wanted to be a Formula One driver. I had no great ambition to do Le Mans." However, in 1970, when Jacques Swaters offered him a drive in the race in his Ferrari 512M, he leapt at it. At the time he was leading the European Formula Two Championship in his Brabham and probably at the height of his single-seater career. In the end he never drove for Swaters at Le Mans; Ferrari stepped in and said that they wanted him for a works car. Bell felt that he should be loyal to the Belgian, but the latter generously insisted that he take the

factory offer. He was paired with Ronnie Peterson. Bell recalls that neither of them was given any advice by the Ferrari team, simply told to go out and race. In the third hour he just missed a major accident only for his engine to blow a piston on the same lap. He recalls his first impressions of the race as "stark" and "drab and foreboding." His attitude was to change in time. However, in his autobiography he points out that "although Le Mans has been romanticized beyond belief by many people…the truth is that it's not romantic at all. It's hellishly demanding, gruelling and exhausting."

In all, Bell competed at Le Mans 26 times, half of those at the wheel of a Porsche, more if you include the Porsche-engined Kremer. On his third year, and after two with a front-running car, he drove a Ferrari 365 GTB 4. "That was when I had my work cut out." It gave him an understanding of what life was like for those in the slower cars, something that he reckons not all of today's leading drivers share. "Just remember other people out there are having a race as well."

In 1983 the Bell and Ickx pairing came a close second. The Englishman, seen here listening to Bob Garretson before the start, reckons it to have been one of his finest races at Le Mans. *(Author)*

Another fighting second place that could so easily have been a win: the 1988 event in which Bell shared a works Porsche 962 with Hans Stuck and Klaus Ludwig. *(Simon Maurice)*

The Bell/Ickx Porsche sweeps through the Esses in 1983. The pair won three times at Le Mans together. In theory, there should be no 'buts' in motor racing, *but* if the race had lasted one more lap they might have shared a fourth victory. *(Author)*

Bell has proved an ideal team man, a driver who understands the nuances of endurance racing as much as anyone. However, to the British fans at Le Mans this is the man who stood on the top step of the podium in 1975, 1981, 1982, 1986 and 1987. Only Tom Kristensen and Jacky Ickx have been there more often.

In 2002 Derek Bell joined Sammy Davis as the only Englishmen to be given the freedom of Le Mans. *(Bentley Motors)*

CHAPTER 24

GORDON SPICE AND THE C2s

"…and to England then, Where ne'er from France arriv'd more happy men."
(William Shakespeare, *Henry V*)

"At one o'clock in the morning, I saw the 'P1' sign come up. That was something special." Gordon Spice drove 14 times at Le Mans and in his latter years at the track became something of a specialist class winner, he and his eponymous cars dominating the C2 category in the late 1980s. However, it was in 1982, the first year of Group C, that Spice found himself in overall lead of the race.

For the previous two years he had finished third overall at the wheel of a Rondeau. Now, firmly established as part of the works team, late in the evening he had been asked by constructor Jean Rondeau, *"voulez vous faire une double?"* "I thought he had asked me if I wanted a double rum and coke."

Put right about the fact that Rondeau had requested him to do a double stint behind the wheel, he was now driving through the night convinced that he and his two French co-drivers were on their way to victory. Unfortunately, that was the year that the Cosworth engines had pick-up problems. Having returned from his stint he was having "a kip in the caravan" when he was woken by his wife, Mandy, to inform him that the car was out of the race. "It was the biggest downer that I ever had at Le Mans."

Two years later Spice would be back at Le Mans to start a new and highly successful chapter in his relationship with the race. However, it is necessary to return to 1964 to start the story. At the time he was working for Chris Lawrence, who had built and entered a 998cc BMC-engined Deep Sanderson the year before. For 1964 Lawrence had fitted a Downton-tuned engine from the same manufacturer and it was decided to put some mileage on it by driving to the track. Reserve driver Spice was at the wheel. The remainder of the team followed in a Jaguar Mk VII with trailer. Spice claims that the two spins were caused by suspension failures. Whatever, the car was put on the trailer for the remainder of the journey.

Lawrence had hired a professional driver, Hugh Braithwaite, who did less that two laps in practice, declared the car unsafe and departed the track. So, at what in those days was seen as the tender age of

24, reserve driver Gordon Spice was handed his first chance of international competition. His experience to date had been about 20 club races, six in a Derrington-tuned MG TF and the rest in a Lawrencetune Morgan Plus 4... It was to be a brief initial encounter with Le Mans. Within an hour and a half a water leak had caused the Deep Sanderson's engine to overheat. Lawrence was to rebuild the car and to race it again in the Le Mans Classic four decades later. In 2005 it went under the hammer at a Bonhams Goodwood Revival sale.

Spice himself was not to return to Le Mans for another six years. In the interim, he started to make a name for himself in the British Saloon Car Championship as one of the leading Mini drivers during an era of notable Mini drivers. It was a series he was to become known for, moving on in the 1970s to

The Union flag flies high in 1985, even if it was a German overall victory that year. The British still throng the winners' balcony with C2 winner Gordon Spice in Jaeger-liveried overalls. Richard Lloyd (in cap) shared the second-place Porsche that year with Jonathan Palmer and James Weaver, while Derek Bell (far left) was third with partner Hans Stuck *(Gordon Spice collection)*

The nearest Gordon Spice came to outright glory at Le Mans was in 1982. He was fast asleep when team-mate Xavier Lapeyere finally parked their Rondeau (seen here in the Esses on the Saturday) at Arnage. (Author)

Gordon Spice, seen in 2005 at his Old Windsor home, had arguably the most successful long-term career at Le Mans of any driver/constructor. (Author)

become a six-times class champion, scoring 27 outright victories at the wheel of works-supported Ford Capris. The late 1960s also saw him driving a Ford GT40 for Jose Juncadella's Escuderia Montjuich Spanish team, and it was with this team that he returned to Le Mans, in theory to share the driving of its Ferrari 512S. However, team boss Juncadella decided to carry out more than his usual short stint at the wheel, crashed at White House and so Spice did not get to race. In 1977 he qualified at the wheel of Alain de Cadenet's Lola, but again did not drive in the race and de Cadenet and Chris Craft finished fifth overall.

At this point it is perhaps surprising to hear Spice say that he "rather liked Le Mans." Thus he arranged with Charles Ivey to drive his Porsche 911 Carrera RSR the following year. Perhaps this is where the Spice Le Mans story really starts. The car was easily the oldest in the entry list, probably about 10 years old. "We knew that we would have problems qualifying." Over a quarter of a century on, it can now be confessed that the engine initially used in practice was a 'qualifying special.' Spice and his co-driver, Australian Larry Perkins, indulged in what he recalls as a "get stuffed match" until the engine expired with a "big explosion, thankfully when Larry Perkins was at the wheel." The engine was changed for a legal unit, which was accordingly sealed at the end of practice.

Unknowingly, the team had knocked a French entry from the back of the grid. The next morning two scrutineers were sent to team headquarters to examine the engine that had been replaced. It was explained that, much as the team would like to show them the unit, it was now on its way back to England and they didn't even know which Channel port it was being shipped back from. This was met with Gallic shrugs and the scrutineers were invited to partake of some coffee with the team. Eventually, Spice offered them a lift back to the track in his Rolls-Royce. The Frenchmen were so impressed by the car that they arranged for the team to enjoy an excess of that most capricious of items

at Le Mans, passes. And the qualifying engine? That was still sitting under a blanket in the back of a Range Rover in the paddock.

For Spice, one of the most memorable incidents in the race itself was the way in which Charles Ivey single-handedly changed the gearbox in the pouring rain in 47 minutes. That was just five minutes longer than the works mechanics would take in favourable conditions. The team still managed a creditable 14th overall, with second place in the IMSA class. Spice muses on just how far up the field they could have finished that year had it not been for the need to change the 'box. His Le Mans philosophy is based on the premise that "most races are won in the pits." For that reason, he believes the endurance driver's prime duty to the team is to maintain the integrity of the car, which means putting the drivers' egos on hold. It may not be true of today, but then he believed that should a driver, for example, run over something, he must pit immediately.

Spice's mount for 1979 was "the most dangerous car I have ever driven," a Cosworth DFV-powered Dome Zero RL. It had been a perfectly acceptable car at Silverstone when he and Chris Craft raced it on British-made Dunlop tyres. However, the Japanese Dunlops used at Le Mans (for political reasons) were "like concrete" and it was impossible to get enough heat into them. The Dome was "blindingly quick" down the straights, but had no grip in the corners at all. Spice and Craft tossed to see who would start. Spice won and it says it all that he nominated Craft to start.

"We had jokingly discussed parking it gently against the Armco early on – it was that difficult to drive," says Spice. However, a fuel pick-up problem meant early retirement. "I felt sorry for the team, but the feeling of relief was enormous," he recalls.

Then came the three Rondeau years, initially with sponsorship from cigarette company Belga that had already backed his Capri to victory in the 1978 Spa 24-Hours saloon race. Having won in Belgium with both Spice and then with the Martin brothers, the cigarette company "wanted to have a crack at Le Mans." That first year was very much a rental effort with Spice teaming up with the Martins. The team finished third overall, winning the GTP class, but it was a "banzai" lap in qualifying that Spice reckons most impressed Rondeau himself. "He realized we were serious players."

For the next two years Spice found himself the sole English driver in a predominantly French team. However, Keith Greene, son of Gilby Engineering founder Sid and himself a former, mainly non-championship Formula One racer, had set up the car for Spice's impressive practice effort and, at the request of his compatriot, was asked to manage the operation. Suddenly Spice found that he was not only being paid to race at Le Mans, but that his chosen team seemed to have half the paddock to itself with all the gastronomic delights that a French *equipe* could bring to the circuit. His own influence at the delightful farmhouse where the team stayed was to persuade the French drivers that they would relax more, sleep better and drive faster if they drank dark rum and cokes. "I had to send my chauffeur back for more supplies."

Spice recalls the Rondeaus as being easy to drive. In 1981 he and his French co-driver came third. It could so easily have been second but for gearbox trouble. The following year, as recorded, his car was to retire when in the lead.

That was to be Spice's last real chance of overall victory, although matters could have been so different but for a change of heart at Ford. Spice's own

There was nothing really embarrassing about the works Spice's sponsorship in 1986. Well, not compared to the Dianetics backing which came two years later... *(Simon Maurice)*

The second-division category named C Junior and then C2 was akin to the Formula Junior of the late 1950s and early 1960s in that, at the beginning, it was the Italians who were winning, with the British taking over very quickly to dominate the formula. Alba had won the inaugural championships but was defeated on home ground by the up and coming Spice team in 1985. The Alba had a handsome class lead in that year's Monza 1000kms but retired, leaving the Spice-Tiga to win. Ray Bellm takes over here from Spice during the race. Spice Engineering went on to take its first championship. The Monza race also saw the first appearance of 'Henry', the first Ecosse built from scratch. *(Author)*

195

The 1988 race did not start too well for Spice. Twice the car had to stop during the first hour when two fuses blew and the driver's door was left open. However, it then overhauled the early leader, one of Charles Ivey's Tigas, to finish 33 laps ahead of the next C2. *(Author)*

Silverstone-based outfit was contracted to run a new Cosworth DFL turbo-powered Ford C100, which Tony Southgate had developed from the C1 car that had run at Le Mans the previous year. Spice was also down to be one of the two drivers for five races for the 1983 season, and Greene the team manager. John Thompson's TC Prototypes was to build the chassis and the budget was all in place. The car, now known as the C001, but still with an atmospheric DFL, was taken to the Paul Ricard circuit in France for testing, with Spice and Marc Surer driving, and was, recalls the former, "highly competitive."

Then it all fell apart. Spice was in Barbados when he received a telex saying that the programme had been cancelled. Ford had a new Director of European Motor Sports in Stuart Turner, who within seven days had dropped it. The official reason given was that Ford wanted to go back to grass-roots motorsport. Whatever, Spice was left with a factory crammed with the latest equipment. He wanted to buy the car but was told that it was company policy not to sell. Despite this, Zakspeed, which had a parallel development programme in Germany, did manage to salvage a C100. Of the three chassis that Spice would have run, one was converted into a mind-blowing Transit show car and the other two were "put in the crusher." Spice, however, is at pains to point out that Ford was "extremely generous" when it pulled out and paid him his £30,000 driver's fee in addition to commercial compensation. The demise of the Ford C100 programme was also to lead Spice into the C2 class and a series of cars that will forever be associated with this category.

A second division for Group C was introduced for 1983, initially called Group C Junior. The following year it began to be known as C2, a name that became official in 1985. Aimed at teams running on considerably smaller budgets than the front-runners, this became the preserve of a new breed of specialist chassis manufacturers mainly using Cosworth DFV and DFL engines. Spice not only became one of them, but personally would win the C2 Driver's Championship every year between 1985 and 1988, usually in partnership with Ray Bellm. The latter was to join as an enthusiastic, if inexperienced driver with sponsorship money. However, Spice describes him as having been a very fast learner. "He did exactly what you told him to do, a rare quality in a racing driver." He was also to eventually become a shareholder in Spice Engineering. Bellm went on to win (jointly with James Weaver) the 1996 BPR Global Endurance Series.

This company came about initially as the result of an approach by Australian Neil Crang to help run his Tiga-Chevrolet GC83. It was decided to convert the car to C2 for 1984. A Cosworth engine was installed and a new front end fitted that was based on that of the Porsche 956. Jeff Hazell was taken on as manager and Spice Engineering was formed.

Spice shared the car that year at Le Mans with its owner and Bellm. The official excuse for retirement was ignition problems, the real reason that Crang "pranged it." Graham Humphreys now joined as designer and a new car was built, similar to the Tiga but now, in effect, a Spice. Driven by Spice, Bellm and Mark Galvin, it took the first of the marque's three C2 victories at Le Mans. Gordon Spice was at the wheel for all of those wins, Bellm sharing with him again in 1988.

Overall, the British did not do at all badly in the C Junior and C2 class at La Sarthe. A Lola T616, albeit American-entered and Mazda-motivated, won in 1984. The car that split the Spice winning sequence in 1986 may have been from the German Gebhardt concern, but it was built at Silverstone and was entered and driven by the very British ADA Engineering team of Ian Harrower, Evan Clements and Tom Dodd-Noble. Often the Spices' main challengers were the Ecosses that we have come across earlier. The final chapter in the C2 Le Mans story came in 1990 with a win for the Spice SE88C of Richard Piper's PC Automotive team.

Clements competed four times at Le Mans, each time in the C2 class. The 1986 race marked his debut at the track, although he did most of the night driving. He recalls that the Gebhardt "wasn't exactly the most incredible car out there." He puts much of the class win, and the eighth place overall, down to the "great team management" of Chris Crawford and "his way of timing things. He kept the car at a sensible pace and didn't risk anything." The car had been in a major accident at Brands Hatch prior to the 24-Hours and had been virtually rebuilt. For Clements, as for many others at the track that weekend, there was a melancholic downside to the win. He was one of the first to come across the blazing Porsche 962 of Austrian Jo Gartner, who had crashed fatally on the Mulsanne straight. Indeed, Clements ran into some of the wreckage. He recalls that he could see through

the flames "as if it were an X-Ray…" After such an experience, his team understandably called him in and it was Dodd-Noble who took over behind the pace car.

Spice Engineering was commissioned by Pontiac to build a car for racing in the USA in 1986. This was easily adapted to a Cosworth-engined C2 car with customer versions becoming available. Humphreys – "one of the most underrated talents in the business," says Spice – designed new bodywork for the 1988 season. The cars were known to be affordable and user-friendly for the private teams, and in all about 50 Spices were built for endurance racing both in Europe and in the USA. About 14 different engine combinations were also possible.

The first Le Mans C2 victory for the Pontiac-based design came about in 1987, Spice sharing with Fermin Velez and Philippe de Henning. The latter had brought sponsorship with him, but initially did not say from whom. Two weeks before the race he declared it to be the controversial Dianetics sect, which had just been the subject of some decidedly adverse publicity on television. We now have one embarrassed Gordon Spice with no choice except to run his car in the Dianetics yellow livery. The sponsor's people all wore a splendidly funereal black and the movement's founder Ron L. Hubbard was to declare the team's victory was down to the following of his teaching. He also wanted to continue sponsorship for the following year. "I passed him on to a customer," says Spice, still a little unsure of what this episode was all about. What was special about that year was that the team scored a splendid sixth overall, the highest ever for a C2 car. Spice was also voted the Driver of the Year by the UK's Guild of Motoring Writers, an award that fellow Le

Mans racer Derek Bell had won in 1982 and 1985. It remains an accolade of which Spice is particularly proud.

The following year, when Jaguar took overall victory, he won his class again. "Jaguar has such a following and the fans were euphoric. It was good to be part of the British success that year."

By 1989 Spice admits that his mind was elsewhere, particularly with his troubled car accessory wholesale business. Spice Engineering took advantage of a change in the C1 rules that favoured 750kg, atmospheric 3.5-litre cars by fitting larger wheels and an enlarged Cosworth DFZ engine and joining the front-running class. Spice himself drove the works car at Le Mans with Bellm and the American lady Lyn St James. He recalls that the car retired early on the Sunday morning. So did he, "for good."

"At about 6am I felt that car tightening up. I handed over to Ray telling him that I thought the engine was on the way out." Bellm confirmed this diagnosis after a few more laps and the car was retired rather than face a £30,000 rebuild for the engine.

Spice Engineering, so buoyant in the 1980s, struggled into the new decade. There were a few customers for the C1 and private entries continued to dominate C2, but the company was in financial problems, mainly due to agreed sponsorship of over a million pounds for the 1990 season having failed to materialize. It cost twice as much to run a C1 car as a C2, and the global economic downturn meant that customers were thin on the ground. There was hope of a Lamborghini-supported project that came to nothing and, in 1991, Spice, who had retired from his main business, decided to put the company into voluntary liquidation whilst still a going concern.

Mike Cotton, arguably the most loyal endurance racing specialist in the British press corps. (Author)

MICHAEL COTTON

The doyen of British Le Mans journalists has to be Michael Cotton, who joined *Sporting Motorist* in 1962. Lola's Bromley factory ("not much more than a lock-up") was about half a mile away from the office and the fledgling race reporter would spend his lunch times watching the Lola GT being built.

Cotton's first visit to Le Mans was as a spectator in 1963, driving down to La Sarthe in his Mini, sleeping in the car and being impressed by the Rover-BRM. Like the gas turbine car, he was back in 1965, this time with a press ticket.

The ACO's headquarters were then in the centre of the town and passes had to be collected there from an elderly lady known as Mademoiselle Petite. "She'd tell you that you had a very nice ticket, but you would find when you got to the track that it wasn't much good at all."

He did, though, now have access to the tribune press box opposite the pits. This was roofed but opened at the front and the noise would swirl around inside for 24 hours. "I was completely deaf when I came out.

"You had dust in your hair and eyes. To be honest, it was fairly horrible." To find out what was happening Cotton and his fellow journalists would have to go to the paddock via a tunnel that by 2.00pm could be likened to a Black Hole of Calcutta. "I had a pretty strong dislike of Le Mans in those days. It was very hard work." Even in years to come, he would say – like so many others – that you would continue to hate it up to about Christmas time and then start looking forward to it. Le Mans gets you like that. "The drivers endure. The spectators endure. In 24 hours I don't suppose I smoked more than 95 cigarettes," wrote journalist Peter Chambers in 1958. That was a year in which, according to Chambers, "we…accepted defeat with British phlegm."

Cotton missed the next two years. In 1968 he had become editor of *Motoring News* and that year he covered Formula One, Formula Two and endurance racing. Life was less compartmentalized in those days and the drivers would often be the same regardless of the type of racing. He tried staying up all night at Le Mans, a mistake that he has not repeated since. Proceeding home on the Sunday evening in his Lotus Elan he found himself driving on the grass…and on the wrong side of the road. From that day onwards he was to make sure that he had at least two to three hours sleep per race.

At the end of the 1968 season Cotton made a decision that would lead to his becoming the country's leading endurance race journalist. The management of *Motoring News*, often eccentric but in this case probably wise, pointed out that if he was to perform his role as editor efficiently he would have to cover fewer races. His heart was with sportscars. "The longer the better."

Cotton confesses to having been partisan in those days, "more than a journalist ought to be." In particular he was something of a fan of Jacky Ickx. In the closing laps of the 1969 race Cotton found himself "shouting like a football supporter" although thinking, "I shouldn't be doing this."

Having said that, why shouldn't he? Back in 1953 the *News of the World*'s Keith Challen had sent a telegram to Duncan Hamilton saying "Congratulations Magnificent Performance No More Popular Winner."

The tribune did at least afford journalists an excellent view of the action. In those days Cotton would lap-chart for about three hours before then hiking to the pits. There

Roy Baker's C2 Tiga-Cosworth was a ghastly pink in 1988, leading to an association with certain Peter Sellers films. Baker was one of the most faithful users of the High Wycombe-made cars, racing Tigas regularly in the World Championship. Stephen Hines, Mike Allison and David Andrews were the drivers in 1988. An 'Inspector Clousseau' also had his name above the car's door, but is believed not to have driven. (Simon Maurice)

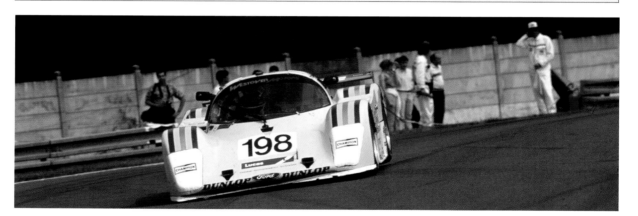

Once Alba had retired from the scene, Spice's closest antagonist in C2 was the Ecurie Ecosse team. 'Pat', the last Ecosse to be built, finished second to a Spice in 1987, driven by Ray Mallock, David Leslie and Marc Duez. (Simon Maurice)

was no protection then for those working in the pit road; a thick white line was all that divided it from the racetrack. "I had a feeling of unease. I never felt safe there." Cotton might then take a walk around the 'Village', the fairground then on the outside of the Dunlop curve that was so much a part of the Le Mans folklore, followed by a visit to the Esses and perhaps as far as Tertre Rouge. At about 11.00am he would settle down to write up the first part of the race, a task he would probably finish by about 2.00pm. Then he would put his head down on the desk for a while. During the morning, less dedicated 'hacks' would return from their hotels and a certain amount of badinage would occur between those who had remained at their posts and those who had left the track.

Occasionally Cotton would get out as far as the Mulsanne straight and it is obvious that, like all those who have been privileged to get anywhere near that stretch of the track, he holds it in awe. "You would see the lights coming towards you at terrific speed and then the Armco barrier would rattle as the car went past going faster than a small aeroplane. I made sure that there was a tree between me and the Armco." The straight's maximum speed in the pre-chicane days, he says, was part of the allure of Le Mans. Cotton experienced just what it was like when, courtesy of sponsor Rothmans, he was taken by Derek Bell round the circuit during a break in practice. By focusing ahead he was able to cope with the extreme speeds of the N138.

In the early 1990s, a new complex was built over the pits, which included a media centre. "In terms of a working environment it is wonderful," says Cotton. There are desks virtually for all, television screens on which one can either watch the action or scrutinize the placings, and power points for computers. It is also much easier to pop down to the pits and paddock to find out exactly what is happening. Having said all this, one notices a certain wistfulness in Cotton's voice…a memory of what it was like, dust, noise and all. "You have now lost contact with the cars. The sound is remote. You can't smell them any more." Now, he feels, there is a partition between the press and the race.

From 1976 to 1983 Cotton was press manger of Porsche Cars Great Britain; it was a period when Le Mans was usually won by the German marque. Today the press is inundated with hordes of bulletins issued on a regular basis during the race by the teams. Cotton believes he was the first to offer such a service. A connecting rod had broken on the 936 of Pescarolo and Ickx. Cotton got out his Olivetti portable typewriter, wrote out a statement and then Sellotaped it to the glass window at the rear of the press box. The journalists lined up to read it. "It went down well, so I produced another bulletin at 12.00pm, and then one at 8.00am and so on." Each was stuck up on the glass window.

In 1983 Cotton returned to journalism and now covers sportscar racing for such as the *Daily Telegraph* and his old paper, now renamed *Motosport News,* in association with his son Andrew. He has been a permanent feature at Le Mans since the late 1960s.

However, in 2004 he gave the race a miss. With Audi looking likely to record another, probably unexciting victory, he left Andrew to cover the French race while he "turned left at Calais" and fulfilled a long-held ambition to see the Nürburgring 24-hour race which clashed with Le Mans. He recalls that many were shocked that he was not at Le Mans, "but I had a ball."

A Spice did not win the C2 class every time at Le Mans even if it may seem like it. In 1986 Evan Clements was one of the three British drivers in the victorious Gebhardt. *(Simon Maurice)*

In 1989 Spice Engineering turned its attention to the C1 class, thanks to a change in the regulations. Bellm and Spice shared one works car – seen here in testing – at Le Mans with American lady Lyn St James. Both the factory entries broke their Cosworth DFZ engines within an hour of each other. *(Spice Engineering)*

PART SEVEN
1992-1998

Lean Years

"From now on the McLaren drivers are in the dark. Their GTRs have never gone this far." *Autocar* summed up the position at 8.00pm during the 1995 race. The designer was South African, the winning entrant was to be Japanese, the drivers an international collection and the engine German – one could even add that the company founder was a New Zealander – but the car was British. *(Original painting by James Dugdale – reproduced by kind permission of Spies Hecker and Bodyshop Magazine)*

CHAPTER 25

THE BRITISH AT LE MANS
1992-1998

"Men have looked upon the desert as barren land…but in fact each hill and valley in it had a man who was its acknowledged owner." (T.E. Lawrence, *Seven Pillars of Wisdom*)

Finding the Britishness in the 1990s becomes a little more complex. Motor racing by this time had become more cosmopolitan. The 1995 victory can be claimed for this country; even if McLaren was founded by a New Zealander, the car's designer Gordon Murray was a South African and its BMW engine was made in Germany. Take the victor of the following two years, though. A car called a Joest Porsche sounds totally Teutonic. However, let us not forget that its chassis was originally designed by TWR for Jaguar. Such is motor racing these days that cars can change their identity, even their nationality, at the touch of a decal.

In one respect this period started well for the British. The 1992 winning Peugeot 905 may have been French, but two of its three pilots, Derek Warwick and Mark Blundell, were English. It was the sixth year out of seven that at least one of the drivers of the winning car had come from this country. However, the next five years were to see a drought until Allan McNish was one of the winning team in 1998.

La Sarthe had lost something of great importance to the British fan in 1992, namely the Jaguars. Tom Walkinshaw had gone off to play in Formula One with Benetton, which did not impress the Le Mans diehards. There was a chance that a privately entered Jaguar might run. A representative of Agip even turned up with a consignment of fuel for the car, only to find it not there. The big cats no longer roamed La Sarthe, and the formerly full camp sites were virtually deserted. Such had been the magic of the British marque. Who in Britain really cared if French Peugeot beat Japanese Toyota or vice versa? Obviously, given the driver line-up, there were a few. Like Peugeot, Toyota had a number of British drivers – Kenny Acheson, Andy Wallace and Geoff Lees – in its team, while its TS 010 had been designed by Englishman Tony Southgate.

There were also some Brits who transferred their allegiance to the lone BRM. This was probably not a good idea given the fact that it was even refused entry to the paddock for not having the right pass following the night-time qualifying session, when it had been stranded out on the circuit. Only one of its drivers

actually qualified for the race, and by lap 20 the car was out. There were also Lolas, Spices and a single Tiga in the main class, but nobody was expecting victory from any of them. In the event the best of these, a Euro Racing Lola T92, finished 13th, with a Chamberlain Engineering Spice next. Only 14 cars were classified, but then it was a pathetically small entry of 28 that year. In changing sportscar regulations, some say to ensure all emphasis was placed on Formula One, the FIA had effectively emasculated endurance racing. Still, it was a two-thirds British driver line-up that led from the second hour, and that was something that has not been seen since.

The following year Tom Walkinshaw and Jaguar were back, although not contemplating another outright win. GT cars had returned to Le Mans and their ranks included three Jaguar XJ220Cs, sponsored

Peugeot may have won at Le Mans in 1992, but it was a mainly British driver line-up that secured the victory. Mark Blundell (second from left) and Derek Warwick (fourth from left) were in the winning 905. The latter "almost had a heart attack" when the car's engine cut out three or four times during one lap on the Sunday morning. *(Peugeot)*

One of the Jaguars, that of Scot David Coulthard, David Brabham and John Nielsen, lost an hour and a half in the night when a fuel bag split. However, it clawed its way back into the lead of the GT class and was still there at 4.00pm. The champagne was sprayed, the success advertising placed…and then the ACO took the victory away from the team. Perhaps this should not have been surprising; the XJ220Cs were built to IMSA specification, to take advantage of the wider wheels allowed, and would therefore have been perfectly legal had they been racing in the USA, where IMSA held sway. ACO steward Alain Bertaut, who has crossed swords with Tom Walkinshaw before, claimed in practice that according to the IMSA rules the cars should have been fitted with catalytic converters. This was despite the fact that no other car in the race had 'cats' and that the ACO's own GT regulations did not refer to them. At one point the Jaguars had been removed from the qualifying timesheets, but had been reinstated pending an appeal to be held in Paris after the race. In the week following the race M. Bertaut had his way and the Jaguar was stricken from the record. So far, no British-built car has won the GT class since, although Aston Martin came close in 2005. "The future of sportscar racing lies in the new GT class," said *Autocar*. Not if it was policed like this, did it.

As has been seen, Derek Bell narrowly missed pole in 1994, and Eddie Irvine finished second in a Toyota, but this was not really a great time for British cars and drivers. The next year was to be different. The ACO's attempt to run a race for road-going cars had fallen foul in 1994 of a cynical entry by a road-legal Porsche 962. Now the British-built, £750,000 McLarens were to show that such a car could really win at Le Mans. It was the stuff of which the race's founding fathers would have been proud. Seven McLaren F1s started the race and at the end four of them were running first, third, fourth and fifth, with the Kokusai Kaihtso

A mere 28 entries started the 1992 race. Euro Racing was one of the few teams to have made any commitment to a lacklustre Sportscar World Championship. It entered two of the disappointing Lola T92/10s, one of which finished 13th, the leading British-built car. The car of Charles Zwolsman, Cor Euser and Jesus Pareja (seen here) retired with gearbox failure. *(Martin Lee)*

by automotive parts supplier Unipart. Lotus was also back, with an Esprit run by one of the prime movers of the new GT class, Hugh Chamberlain. Many of the British spectators absent the previous year accordingly had returned. Front-running British drivers could also be found again in the Toyotas, including Eddie Irvine, who came fourth overall, and again Lees, Wallace and Acheson. Peugeot, though, had forgotten the nation that helped it to victory the year before.

As with the Audis a decade later, Peugeot won Le Mans with British transmission 'know-how'. The first 24-hour win for an Xtrac gearbox was in 1992, followed by the one-two-three victory the following year (seen here). *(Peugeot)*

car of JJ Lehto, Yannick Dalmas and Masanori Sekiya the winner. No other marque had ever achieved so much on its debut. Derek Bell MBE was also able to write another chapter in his personal adventure story of Le Mans. One more point to note: Lister was back, although it was a vastly different outfit from that which had last raced at Le Mans in 1963.

It was said that 1995 was the wettest Le Mans race in living memory. Keith Greene, who had first raced a Lotus at La Sarthe in 1963 and had attended most since, said that he had never experienced one quite like it. There had been years when the rain had fallen harder, but not one where it had been more prolonged. Greene even called it "the wrong kind of rain," not the kind to clean up the circuit. With no downforce the McLaren drivers felt as if they were driving on ice.

By the end, though, the Woking-built McLarens were running first, third, fourth, fifth and 13th, having led for all but 12 laps. There was some, arguably unfair, concern from the massed ranks of the McLaren runners that the eventual winner was a thinly disguised works car, but as will be seen in the next chapter, it was the least likely of them to win. It was run by historic racing

specialist Paul Lanzante Motorsport, but there were four factory mechanics in the team. Ray Bellm, owner of GTC Motorsport and the person who persuaded McLaren's Ron Dennis to build a racing version of the F1, pointed out that McLaren had agreed not to run any works cars in 1995. Fellow privateer team manager David Price was not happy either. However, designer Gordon Murray says that the 'works' taunt was not deserved.

Whatever the arguments, there was no escaping that a McLaren had won on its debut at Le Mans, only the third marque to do so in the history of the race. Given that the others were Chenard et Walcker – and somebody had to win the inaugural event, or did they, given the rules then – and Ferrari, whose victory came after the long war induced hiatus, this achievement is particularly memorable. It also gave McLaren the Formula One World Championship, Indianapolis 500 and Le Mans treble, something that only Mercedes-Benz had ever achieved.

The Bells, father and son, plus Andy Wallace, as already recorded, led for 10 hours in the Harrods-sponsored Mach One Racing entry before clutch

The Le Mans start-line complex was rebuilt in the early 1990s. A British company Showtrax International was chosen by the ACO to be responsible for kitting out much of the permanent garage facility with such as walling and flooring, lighting, gantries and pit lane equipment. In 2005 Showtrax also supplied product to all but two of the teams in the race. *(David Ingram)*

While one of the David Price Racing McLarens finished a fighting third in 1995, the West-sponsored car of John Nielsen, Thomas Bscher and Jochen Mass retired on the 131st lap. The car had been in the lead before the rain first fell, losing and then regaining it before a clutch problem forced a 70-minute pit stop. It regained the track only to get as far as the second chicane. *(LAT Photographic)*

previous year's winning team. There were six of them in the top 11…but none on the podium; the car was no longer fast enough even to win the GT class. The best chance of a podium finish ended when the gearbox of the Bellm, Lehto and James Weaver car had to stop to have its gearbox changed with just four hours to go before the finish, dropping it back to ninth. In the end the leading McLaren was that of Thomas Bscher, John Nielsen and Peter Kox, which came home fourth. Wallace and Bell were unhappy with the performance of the sixth-placed F1.

Back in 19th place was found a famous British name, the Laurence Pearce-entered, Newcastle United-supported Lister of British drivers Geoff Lees, Tiff Needell and Anthony Reid. It was the first finish by a Lister since Bruce Halford and Brian Naylor had come home 15th in 1958. In all there were to be 11 Lister entries between 1958 and 2004, the only other to complete the course being the Storm LMP of the last year, which was driven by Danes John Nielsen, Casper Elgaard and Jens Moller to a troubled 24th overall.

Another British marque to make occasional appearances at Le Mans was Marcos, although like the two LM600s entered the previous year, the 1996 entry of Cor Euser, Pascal Dro and Tommy Erdos retired. Indeed, the only Marcos ever to finish the race was a French-crewed Mini-Marcos back in 1966.

The McLarens were fewer in number but still out in force for 1997. Just two finished this time, but only the Joest-run TWR Porsche was ahead of them at 4.00pm Sunday. There were those who said that if the semi-works GTC team had allowed its drivers, Pierre-Henri Raphanel, Jean-Marc Gounon and Anders Olofsson,

trouble intervened, and what a result that would have been for the British crowd. Other British drivers in this success story included Bellm and Mark Blundell in the fourth-place, Gulf-sponsored GTC car, which had been crashed by the former on the Saturday evening, but which the latter had hauled back up the field. "The future of Le Mans, it seems, lies with McLaren," said *Motor Sport* magazine.

True, there were a lot of them on the grid the next year, and the only one not to finish came from the

Testing the Jaguar XJ220Cs at Silverstone prior to the 1993 Le Mans. Scot David Coulthard, standing behind the car, was one of the drivers who, understandably, thought he had won the GT class before the ACO decided otherwise. *(Author)*

DEREK WARWICK

"My opinion of Le Mans is quite simple," says 1992 winner Derek Warwick. "It's one of the greatest races in the world. Any driver who doesn't agree is a driver who hasn't experienced it."

Warwick had always wanted to race at Le Mans, his first chance coming in 1983 with a call from the Kremer brothers to see if he would drive their Porsche 936-based CK5. The money was good and, as he was earning nothing from Formula One at the time, he took the opportunity. However, "the car was unbelievably dangerous and I was happy when it broke." His first impression of the track, though, was "Wow, fantastic. It had everything from slow first-gear corners to flat sixth-gear and, of course, the famous Porsche curves. The race is amazing because you are always overtaking cars. You can make some 30 pit stops, so you are sometimes leading, then back to third and then leading again. Le Mans was always very demanding because of the nature of the track, the fuel economy and all the slower cars. The track is physical, technical and demanding and, above all, it's dangerous."

It was only when Warwick returned in 1986 with Jaguar that he realized just how "big" Le Mans is "and what a huge following it has from the Brits." The atmosphere when the drivers were parading in front of the grandstand just before the start was such that he admits he had tears running down his face. "It was unbelievable." A punctured tyre when Jean-Louis Schlesser was driving put out Warwick's XJR-6 that year.

At one point in the week Warwick had run out of petrol at the end of the Mulsanne straight. "I parked on the right-hand side of the track just after the kink and radioed the pits to bring some fuel. I then sat on the left front of the car waiting and watching. I heard an engine in the distance, it seemed to take forever to get to me, but when it came through the kink doing some 240mph, it almost blew me off the front of the car. The noise, speed, explosion of air as it went by was the most frightening thing I've ever experienced. I ran to the other side of the barrier."

He also drove for Jaguar in 1991, a year he regards as disappointing "because I thought we could win it." It was the year that turned into an economy run for the Jaguars. For Warwick it was "very frustrating. I think the organizers made a mistake because for Jaguar to have won it that year would have been great for Le Mans and motorsport."

His winning year with Peugeot, 1992, was "a different matter because we were favourites and I was very focussed all weekend." Of course, there was pressure from the French media that year, but the British fans added to that, particularly as two of the three drivers in Warwick's car were English.

As the lead driver, Warwick had the main influence on who should be the third pilot. "I called Mark (Blundell) and he was most definitely up for it." He reckons the team drove "flat-out" for 23 hours that year. It was a very different matter to pedalling the heavy, low-revving V12 Jaguar. The Peugeot was "more nimble, like a thoroughbred." The team may have been the favourite, but with the other Peugeot and Toyota pushing hard for most of the race, it was never that easy.

Drivers have been known to build up a rapport with spectators as they race past. Warwick recalls during his winning year a bar in which during the early evening he could see "a group of guys drinking pints. Every time I came through they lifted their drinks as if to say 'cheers', so I flashed my lights. This went on for two stints. I could see the drink going down and then, on the next laps the glasses were full again."

Four years later, Warwick received a call from Courage to run in the same car as Mario Andretti. "I couldn't resist it." Unfortunately the US legend went off, Andretti admitting that he had been "right on the limit." The car was repaired but could only finish 13th.

Warwick, a veteran of 162 Grands Prix, obviously has a soft spot for *Les Vingt-Quatre Heures du Mans.* "You remember how hard the mechanics worked and how tired they were, but when their car came in they were fresh and ready. Your family and friends were always there when you got out of the car. Le Mans is a unique race, possibly the greatest race in the world."

Derek Warwick, whose victory at Le Mans augmented his heroic career in Formula One. *(MNF collection)*

Allan McNish has become a firm Le Mans favourite and is now one of the regular Audi pilots. However, his only win to date at Le Mans has been in a works Porsche GT1-98. He had been reconciled to second place in 1998 following a 20-minute delay with water temperature problems. However, the leading Toyota broke and the Scot took what he understandably described as the biggest win of his career. Prior to 1998 his only experience of Le Mans had been 37 minutes in a Roock Racing Porsche 911 GT1 before a damper failure caused him to crash. *(Porsche)*

to push harder through the night they might have won. TWR itself was back, having built in Britain, and now running, the Tony Southgate-designed Nissan R390 GT1s with Martin Brundle as a lead driver. The flags on those cars' flanks, though, featured the rising sun of Japan.

By 1998 the McLaren F1 GTR was truly outdated; it was based on a car that had initially been designed for the road, which was more than could be said for the latest GT class contenders. Only two started, both from Gulf Team Davidoff, and one of them, that of Britain's Steve O'Rourke and Tim Sugden, teamed with American Bill Auberlen, came home fourth having spent less time in the pits than any other finisher. O'Rourke described the result as "real *Boy's Own* stuff."

RADIO LE MANS

"Radio Le Mans transformed the British involvement in the race," says Audi UK team boss David Ingram. "It is great entertainment, it is informative and they play my sort of music in the week leading up to the race. Le Mans without Radio Le Mans is like champagne without the bubbles."

In the BRLM era (before Radio Le Mans) commentators such as James Tilling and his nephew Bob Constanduros were permitted to give British-language updates over the Tannoy. The BBC Light Service, with such as Raymond Baxter, Robin Richards, Eric Tobitt and John Bolster, had kept the fans at home informed until it lost interest in the early 1970s. Then came the mid-1980s, and with a caravan in the paddock with a radio transmitter and a phone link to the tribune, Radio Le Mans, the brainchild of marketing man Harry Turner, took its first faltering steps. "I don't think I've ever had so much fun," says Turner. The fledgling team – he recalls such as Alan Brown, Tim Foulsham and the Wireless Workshop crowd – were true pioneers. Turner remembers, for example, an aerial mike having to be attached to a garden cane.

Neville and Richard Hay, along with Constanduros, were among the first voices to be heard, with Ian Titchmarsh and the enduring Paul Truswell joining in 1988. A year later the distinctive Geordie tone of John Hindhaugh was heard for the first time. "I believe that the pictures are always better on radio," he says.

"In 1989 we had our first interaction with the fans," says Hindhaugh, a spoof Miss Radio Le Mans competition. It was won by the station's Anthony Landon in drag, the prize being a '24-carat' necklace of…24 carrots. "We realized that we needed to interact more with the audience. We had not really understood just how many people were listening. People switched on on a Tuesday or Wednesday, when they turned up, and left it on until Sunday night. They relied on us for everything."

The years of dwindling fields in the 1990s were difficult ones, but *Autosport* raised the profile by backing the project. In one year the team had set off from the UK with no funding but were saved by the fans with what

Hindhaugh calls "the great resurrection raffle." Teams and drivers donated prizes, such as Derek Warwick's balaclava. "Every single British team and quite a few of the foreign ones gave us something. It was at that time that I realized how much a part of the race RLM had become."

In 1997 RLM discovered the Internet. "I 'blagged' some service space from a city organization with spare capacity and we streamed live to the world. All of a sudden RLM went from being this odd little thing for a few enthusiasts to a worldwide entity." It had become a global brand. The American Le Mans Series followed. Now the team even assists at Crufts. In 2005 RLM was also broadcast on a satellite radio station. "We have now got a 24-hour, 365-day-a-year radio channel that is blokes talking about cars and sport, and playing a bit of music."

In listing those now involved with the station one has to mention in particular Paul Truswell, who stays up for 30 hours, never moving from the tribune. "A remarkable display of self control," says Hindhaugh, "in that he literally does not move!"

"Amazing," observes Simon Maurice, who once worked as RLM's station manager, adding that the station must be "one of the most brilliant services of any race meeting."

In the pit lane you now find Joe Bradley, who once remarked "we are merely spectators with microphones," and Graham Tyler, while mention must be made of Janice Minton, who used to tread this path. Henry Hope-Frost has come on board in recent years; he takes requests for car noises, a John Culshaw of the automotive world. Gary Champion is another, as are Alan Hyde and Stuart Codling, while Neville Hay returned to the fold in 2002 after 10 years away. From America we have Jim Roller and the encyclopaedic Charles 'Chuck' Dressing.

Such people deservedly develop their own following. Janice Minton was assisting the ADA squad when she first became involved. Neville Hay interviewed her on air about a problem the team had and it was not long before she became a permanent RLM feature in the pit lane. One Le Mans Saturday she was in the medical centre with Joe Bradley, who had damaged his knee, when a group

However, we end this era as we came in, with a least one British driver at the wheel of the winning car. Scot Allan McNish, in his second Le Mans, led home a one–two finish for the works Porsche 911 GT1-98s. For much of the race, the Porsches' main contenders had come from the factory Toyota team, whose drivers included early race leader Martin Brundle and Geoff Lees. As he stepped into his car for the last

hour McNish was expecting a run to second place. His Porsche had already been delayed by 20 minutes with a water temperature problem, and one of the Toyotas, the car which Lees was sharing with Thierry Boutsen and Ralf Kelleners, was still about a minute ahead. This car had taken over the lead from the one that Brundle was driving when it had run into wheel bearing problems during the fourth hour. Now it, in turn, succumbed to transmission failure, enabling McNish to sweep by to a career-reviving win.

The TWR-run, Tony Southgate-designed Nissan R390 GT1s had steady runs to finish third, fifth and sixth, while the name of Bell was back on the podium again, albeit for winning the GT2 class. Two years after his father's last race at Le Mans, Derek's son Justin was one of the three drivers in the class-winning ORECA-run Chrysler Viper GTS-R.

By the following year the McLarens would have disappeared and the Audis would be present for the first time. Times were changing again.

of fans, all clad in T-shirts with Janice's photo on them, visited the RLM base hoping to make contact with her. Sadly, they never returned, so she was never able to meet them

The 'technical bods', including Andy Toms, Carl Landsbert and Bob Dawson, must also surely deserve a mention. The kind of problems experienced at Le Mans tend to be unique. It is not a radio-friendly environment.

"We get access that no-one else gets," says Hindhaugh. However, he does remember when one major team, new to the race, refused to let Gary Champion into its pit to discover what was happening. Hindhaugh decided that they should go live and, on air, asked Champion what the problem was with the car. Champion then told the whole of Le Mans that he did not know as the team would not let him in. "How very F1 of them," said

Hindhaugh. Within seconds the team's PR was ushering Champion in.

At the beginning of 2006, having lost the backing of *Autosport*, Radio Le Mans' future looked uncertain. However, every effort was made to ensure its continuation. At the end of January John Hindhaugh was able to announce that Radio Show Limited, a new company of which he was one of the directors, had been given the English-language broadcasting rights up to 2010. Fabrice Bourrigaud, the ACO's head of marketing, had described RLM as "indispensable."

Aston Martin and Audi had already pledged support for the new operation and there was the promise of a two-hour long broadcast from the Aston team base on the morning of the race. Hindhaugh was also pleased to report that RLM would be reviving its popular camp site tour. "We have come full circle," he said. "We are again a bunch of enthusiasts trying to run a radio show."

There is more to RLM that just the broadcast, it is a community service; one year it even reunited some false teeth with its owner. It has its own shop in the 'Village', a major meeting place, but above all, it is the one aspect of the race that truly unites the British at Le Mans.

JUSTIN BELL

Derek Bell missed 1998, the year that son Justin won the GT2 class at Le Mans; television duty had called him to the Canadian Grand Prix. All the way through the race Bell Senior kept ringing Radio Le Mans to see how his son was doing. RLM even put him on air.

With half an hour to go an excited Derek rang again, recalls presenter John Hindhaugh, "so we put him on the radio again." Twenty minutes later he was back on the phone. Justin was out of the car at this stage. Hindhaugh sent colleague Joe Bradley to find him and to give him a microphone and headset. As his Viper crossed the line so Hindhaugh put him on air to be congratulated. He then said that he had somebody who wanted to talk to him. "Who's that?" asked the younger Bell. "Your Dad," replied Hindhaugh.

"The result," recalls Hindhaugh, "was a powerful piece of radio."

In 1988 the GT victory of Justin Bell (right) was followed closely by his famous father despite a small matter of the Atlantic Ocean being between them at the time. *(Chrysler)*

Unipart then...and now

Sponsoring the second generation of Mansell talent in the 2006 Formula BMW UK championships confirms the developing reinvolvement of Unipart Automotive with motorsport.

Unipart Automotive has a long standing association with motorsport, both commercially and through sponsorship including; Formula One, the Le Mans series, Sydney to London Rally, the British Touring Car Championships and Formula 3.

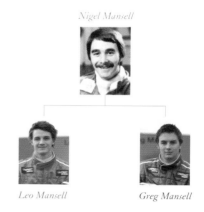

Nigel Mansell

Leo Mansell   *Greg Mansell*

UNIPART *AUTOMOTIVE*
more than just moving parts

CHAPTER 26

GORDON MURRAY AND THE McLAREN F1 GTR

"The British cavalry and charioteers had a fierce encounter…"
(Caesar, *The Conquest of Gaul*)

Today McLaren is perceived as a constructor of Grand Prix cars, as if the only vehicles to come out of the magnificent new McLaren Technology Centre are solely designed for the relatively short races that comprise the FIA Formula One World Championship. However, it should not be forgotten that its roots are firmly grounded in sportscar racing and that recently it has been responsible for the Mercedes-Benz SLR McLaren road car.

The team's origins go back to Roger Penske's Cooper Zerex Special that the young New Zealand Formula One driver Bruce McLaren purchased in the mid-1960s. There followed the first of his own Group 7 sports-racers, the M1A, in 1965 and then the powerful V8 machines that competed in the Can-Am series. On tracks such as Elkhart Lake and Laguna Seca, Riverside and Watkins Glen, the 'Bruce and Denny Show' as it was known was virtually unbeatable. The bright orange cars, with their eight fuel-injection trumpets that seemed to stretch to the sky, set new standards in domination. At this stage, despite its UK base, the team, with McLaren himself and Denny Hulme driving, probably ought to be seen as a New Zealand outfit and therefore outside the remit of this book. However, in June 1970 McLaren – who won at Le Mans in 1966 with Ford – tragically was killed while testing at Goodwood. Today the now Ron Dennis-led operation is almost an integral part of that very British of counties, Surrey. Indeed, in 2004 Her Majesty the Queen opened the McLaren Technology Centre.

It was one of Bruce McLaren's dreams that his company should produce a road car. Twice this occurred, first with the M6 GT of 1969 that never went into production, and then with the iconic 630bhp BMW-powered McLaren F1 introduced in 1992 as the world's fastest and most expensive production vehicle, as well as being the first all-carbon road car. Originally there was never any intention that this car, with its central driving position, should go racing. However, pressure on McLaren from potential customers meant that F1 racecars were built to take advantage of the GT-friendly regulations of the mid-1990s. By the time

of Porsche's 1998 overall victory at Le Mans with its 911 GT1, the GT class had gone far beyond the thought that it had anything to do with road cars. Thus it can be said that when a McLaren F1 GTR won in 1995 it was the last by a true road-going vehicle.

There is also something very cosmopolitan about the 1995 victor. There are those New Zealand origins, the German engine (although, of course, the Bentley EXP Speed 8 also had one of those) and the fact that it was entered by a Japanese team, crewed by Japanese, Finnish and French drivers…and designed by someone born in South Africa. Still, it was the only British-built car to win Le Mans between the disappearance of Jaguar and the arrival of Bentley and should be celebrated as such. As already mentioned, national strands in motor racing have become confused.

It might be said that the success of the McLaren F1

Until recently technical director, McLaren Cars, and a director of the TAG McLaren Group, Gordon Murray is now planning a future that could include a return to Le Mans. *(Author)*

The de Cadenet team had its base in 1972 at a small hotel in Sceaux-sur-Huisne, over 20 miles from the circuit. *(Gordon Murray collection)*

Le Mans story goes right back to 1972 and the Alain de Cadenet-entered Duckhams Special. At first sight this might be said to be pushing a point. However, Gordon Murray, one of the most iconic of Formula One designers, put pen to just two Le Mans cars, the Duckhams and the F1. He would say that they have even more than this in common. Both were run on shoestring budgets and both, he says, were "fairy tales."

It is notable that the man who was responsible for the World Championship-winning Brabham BT49 and 52 and who presided over the ultra-successful McLaren MP4/4, has a soft spot for his two sports-racing cars. More than that, while Murray, given today's straight-jacketed regulations, has no interest in designing a Grand Prix car again, in the future he could well express himself in another GT car capable

of racing at La Sarthe.

Back in the early 1970s, Murray – then in his mid-twenties – was one of just five designers at Motor Racing Developments, as Brabham was known. The future of the company was uncertain and the South African was thinking of moving on. Then "Alain de Cadenet turned up out of the blue," wanting a competitive car for Le Mans. The pair met at a pub. Murray remembers it well – he had to pick up the bill. (De Cadenet responds: "He was earning, I wasn't.") De Cadenet owned an old Brabham BT33 Formula One car and wanted it converting into a prototype. Murray had the opportunity to "do the whole car," his first as far as racing was concerned. Faced with this, he decided to leave Brabham, but Bernie Ecclestone, then the owner of the Formula One team, had different ideas. He wanted to make the other four

Pit stop jottings from Gordon Murray's notebook. It was as well that the Duckhams Special did not use much oil: Duckhams competitions manager Ron Carnell arrived at Le Mans with a limited stock of 'Q' and even had to borrow some from other British enthusiasts as an emergency reserve. *(Gordon Murray collection)*

designers redundant and for Murray to come up with a completely new Grand Prix car. Murray said this was not possible; he had shaken hands on the Le Mans project. Ecclestone, as ever, had a way round the problem. Murray would design the Formula One car by day and moonlight on the de Cadenet project.

It was already late in the year. Murray and his wife Stella were renting a two-room bed-sit with no heating. Water ran down the walls and froze when the temperature dropped. In this Dickensian ambience Murray set up a drawing board between the two rooms. For three or four months he would come home at about 8.00pm and then work, drawing from scratch what was to become the Duckhams Special until about 3.00am. It is little wonder that, one morning at the end of the project, he collapsed; he simply got up and fell over.

The end result carried very little over from the Brabham, except the four corners. It was also very English, de Cadenet having insisted on that. Suppliers – names like Lucas, Lockheed, AP and Dunlop – came from the British component industry. De Cadenet was disgusted when Murray told him that the Aeroquip hosing had come from the USA.

"I was terrified," recalls Murray. "I hadn't done a complete car before." He already knew "what fell off a Grand Prix car in two hours" and so wondered how the Duckhams Special could possibly last 24. "I doubled everything when doing the stress calculations." The monocoque was 16-gauge throughout while there were two complete electrical systems and batteries. Teams could not top up oil in those days so, concerned that the car's Cosworth DFV engine would use too much, he fitted a huge, seven-gallon oil tank. "I was so inexperienced," he says.

His self confidence received a further knock when the team got to Le Mans for scrutineering. He was convinced the 687-kilos car was overweight. Then he saw the figures for other cars. The Porsche 908s weighed 713 kilos, the Matras 718 kilos and the Lolas and the Alfa Romeos even more. "Then I *did* panic."

It must also be noted that the Duckhams had

Gordon Murray's own drawing of the Duckhams Special. The car was originally penned in the Murray's two-room bed-sit. Murray, still working for Brabham at the time, stayed up into the small hours for nearly four months designing the Duckhams. During the race his wife Stella also proved her ability to stay awake, running a non-stop, 24-hour catering service for the team from the Duckhams caravan. *(Gordon Murray collection)*

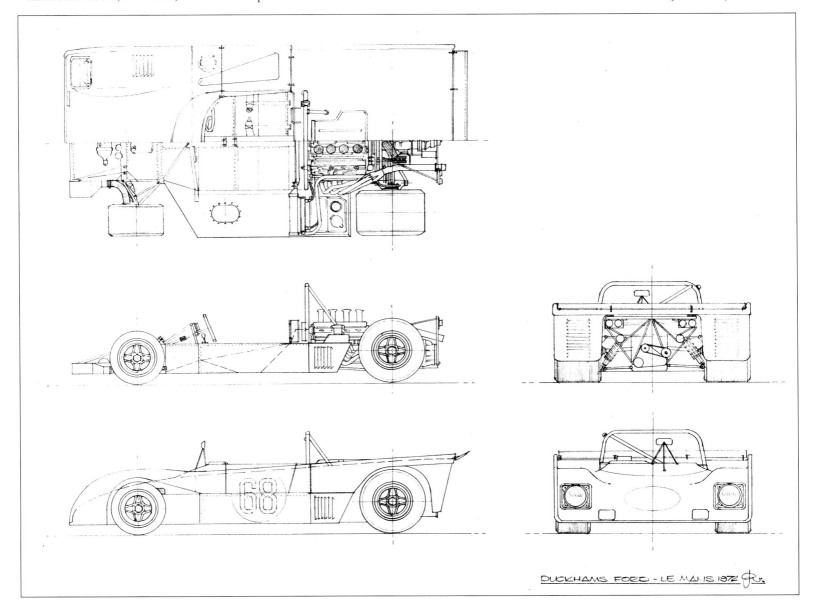

DUCKHAMS FORD - LE MANS 1972

Gordon Murray was one of the finest of all Formula One designers. Over 50 Grands Prix were won by his cars. (Brabham)

Bearded Kim Argyle ponders by the Duckhams Special. In those days Argyle was running his own engineering business just outside Oxford, although he had also assisted at March when it was first established. (Gordon Murray collection)

been finished so late and was on so limited a budget – Murray reckons the total to have been about £5000 – that testing had been limited to 25 laps of Silverstone in the rain. There is also said to have been a matter of 200mph down the M4 (this rumour returns with the later Lola-based De Cadenet) and a run at some equally ridiculous speed along the road to Paris the night before practice, but perhaps, to avoid any questions, this narrative had better stick to those few laps of the Northamptonshire circuit.

De Cadenet remembers the time as "very good days indeed." Downstairs in the garage at Petersham Mews, the car was being assembled under chief mechanic Kim Argyle, while upstairs in the flat, de Cadenet's wife was pregnant. (Murray recalls that Argyle and fellow mechanic Mike Barney were the only professionals, the rest were "mates".) Daughter Amanda was born a couple of weeks before the race, which meant that team duties could include feeding the baby.

Despite all this, the car ran well. Nothing fell off, nothing broke and as the race progressed so it gradually picked off most of its competitors including all but one of the Porsches. Only the three Matras steamrollered ahead. Murray reckons the car was about to take fourth place when it rained. Craft spun off and about 40 minutes disappeared taping up the bodywork. The car dropped back to 12th overall, still good enough for a prize as the best British team. Murray was paid £200 and given a Hewlett Packard pocket calculator – which is still in his office – for his efforts. It was – he repeats the description – "a fairy tale. The car was so competitive. It launched my career." He did not go back to Le Mans, though, until 1995 "and that was an even bigger fairy tale."

The Duckhams was a low-drag car that proved much quicker down the straight than cars with much greater horsepower. It was a simple shape, loosely based on the Ferrari 312, with a very small frontal area and not too much wing, similar in concept to the McLaren F1.

Murray designed the 6.1-litre V12 BMW-engined McLaren F1 as the ultimate driver's car. He pointed out to the McLaren directors that if they wanted it to be a racing car as well the road version would be compromised. They assured him that they wanted something that could be driven to the south of France in absolute comfort, not hauled round a race track. Therefore it had to have air conditioning, a decent sound system, luggage space and good visibility. It was decided, no racing.

Then pressure was applied, first by German banker Thomas Bscher and by Ray Bellm, who wanted to go racing. McLaren kept saying "No," but it is said there was a thinly veiled threat that, if there was no factory support, these private owners would go ahead by themselves. Ron Dennis agreed to change his mind, but only if the whole programme could be funded out of the profit made from selling five racecars. All the design, prototyping time, testing and development had to be carried out within this parameter. A small development team under James Robinson went to work. Just one day in the wind-tunnel could be afforded…and the car was immediately successful.

One of the reasons why the GTR racing version did so well was that, despite saying racing must not come into it if he was to design the ultimate road car, Murray came from a racing background. It was difficult for him to think any differently. All that was needed was for straight-cut gears to be put into the gearbox, a roll-cage and a fire extinguisher included, a couple of the wishbones stiffened up, a body kit – with short-cord rear wing, flat bottom, new side inlets and re-profiled nose – fitted, "and we went racing." The engine was simply remapped. Removal of the active aerodynamics – illegal under BPR GT championship rules – air conditioning, sound system and most of the trim reduced the weight of the car, but the roll-cage and extinguisher put it up again. It is interesting to record that the race F1 was actually about 15mph slower in a straight line than the road car.

The F1 GTR proved successful in the BPR GT series, which led owners to decide they wanted to compete at Le Mans. "Then I really put my foot down and said 'No'," says Murray. The same thing happened all over again and McLaren was forced into carrying out the work itself rather than let a third party loose on its creation. Murray was on very limited time to develop a Le Mans kit, which included slightly beefed-up wishbones, a smaller wing, carbon ceramic brakes, new brake ducts and improved cooling. The electrics were also made more accessible. (One of the privateers that raced in 1995 did not even buy the Le Mans kit but simply ran its car in BPR trim.)

So much development work had been done on the road car that it was, claims Murray, "bullet-proof." This was to rub off on the racecar. "We went to Le Mans feeling that we might be quite competitive and finish, even pick up some positions. We found the thing was dynamite for all the reason the Duckhams was – small car, aerodynamically efficient, well-balanced handling." However, he does add that "what really won us the race was the fact that it rained. The car was so well balanced, 'JJ' (Lehto) at one point at night in the wet was 16 seconds quicker than the next fastest car." (Lehto had given team manager Paul Lanzante, as well as his fellow drivers, cause for concern before the race that he might be a little too quick for an endurance event.)

Murray reckons "it must have been the cheapest Le Mans victory in the history of the race." However, for him the real 'fairy story' (for Murray, Le Mans seems to continually enter the realms of fiction) was the fact that the winner was what he describes as "the old slow car." A sponsor, Ueno Clinic, turned up. "The guy (Kokusai Kaihtso) just wanted to be at Le Mans and have some stickers on a car, bring his mates and his family and have a car at the race." McLaren thought to share out the sponsorship money among the various teams, but fearful that they might upset existing sponsors, they turned Ueno down. "The guy came back to us. This was really last-minute stuff." Kaihtso really wanted to race at Le Mans and asked about buying a car, but they had all been sold. "What about (leasing) your prototype?" he asked. Murray was concerned that the car, chassis 001, had done so much testing that "it was thrashed to death," but "he was so persistent that we took his money, rebuilt the car and got Paul Lanzante, who had never raced at Le Mans, to run a team." Jeff Hazell, the manager of McLaren's racing programme, was also involved. Lanzante had access to works mechanics, "like everybody else," which is where the accusation came about that this was a factory car. "Suddenly this other entry had appeared and the existing teams said 'that's your prototype car.' We told them the truth but they wouldn't believe it. What made it seem worse was that as soon as it looked like winning, we had a lot of our guys in Paul Lanzante's pit, which may have been the wrong thing to do in retrospect. But it was absolutely not a works team."

Murray recalls that Lanzante played it so safe that he kept bringing the car in one lap early as he was terrified it might run out of fuel. Initially the other McLarens rushed ahead, and the two David Price-run cars led for much of the race, first the West-sponsored car and then the Harrods entry. However, both cars had modified clutch mechanisms, which gave trouble.

JJ Lehto's night-time drive in 1995 was the proverbial stuff of legend. John Hindhaugh also remembers it as one of Radio Le Mans' finest hours as the station brought alive the Finn's performance for those still awake. *(LAT Photographic)*

John Nielsen took the now cold West car out after a lengthy pit stop only to crash out of the race.

Ray Bellm also crashed his entry, losing much time while, as Murray puts it, "the tortoise cruised around stopping for fuel one lap early, but when they realized it had a chance of winning they stepped up the pace a bit and won the race."

During the night Lehto's tenacious speed turned the Ueno car into a potential winner, something that became a distinct possibility once the Harrods car had also run into trouble. In the end, only the second-place Courage prevented a clean sweep of the first four positions for McLaren.

Slower on the corners but quicker on the straights, the GT McLarens had, for the time being, proved more suitable to Le Mans' changing conditions than purpose-built World Sports Cars such as the Courage.

Murray now rues the fact that he did not drive the winning car to the track. One would have to go back a long way to find the previous Le Mans victor that could be so easily driven on the road. The McLaren, in this respect, harkens back to such as the 1953

winner, which one can still happily drive around the Hampshire country lanes. It would not happen now; imagine a Bentley EXP Speed 8 on the Basingstoke by-pass. Small wonder that many still regard the McLaren F1 as the ultimate production road car.

In 2005 Gordon and Stella Murray participated in a rally to northern France and took an F1, thinking it would be "original," only to find another two there. One of them was the Harrods-sponsored car that had finished third in 1995. "We started from Jermyn Street at 7.00am and were headed out through east London, which I did not know very well. Dave Clark was in the Harrods car and said 'follow me.' Driving through the streets of London at that time in the morning behind this open-piped car was absolutely surreal. This was not a replica but the actual car that came third at Le Mans 10 years ago."

For all his Formula One experience, Murray believes sportscar racing to be the most fulfilling, indeed he still regards it as unfinished business. "Of all the periods I have done in racing, 1995 to 1997 were the best three years. We saw all the flags. A lot of people were shouting for us."

Britain's Steve Soper was the fastest McLaren driver in qualifying for the 1996 race. However, his Team Bigazzi car only finished 11th following a gearbox change. *(BMW)*

The slower Bigazzi McLaren of Cecotto/Sullivan/Piquet eventually finished higher than its sister car, although it too had transmission problems. *(David Ingram)*

www.ben.org.uk.

1905 – 2005

100

years of help
and support

After Paul's accident,
over 18,000 family members
helped him get back on his feet.

When things come out of the blue – you need all the help you can get.

That's where your family can prove invaluable. The BEN family includes everyone from cycle manufacturers to motor insurance clerks, even their immediate family. What's more, that includes those past and present.

As the automotive and related industries' own charity, we're here to offer vital help and support to all members of our family when they need it most. BEN is your charity, so whether your need is financial, physical or emotional we'll be on hand to help – for however long you need us.

For more information or to request BEN's help simply call 01344 620191 or log on to: www.ben.org.uk

To make a donation to BEN simply call
01344 620191

BEN MOTOR AND ALLIED TRADES
BENEVOLENT FUND
The heart of the industry

216

CHAPTER 27

ANDY WALLACE

"We looked at one another with cheerful foolish grins of joy. The feelings uppermost were 'We've done it'." (Frank Worlsey, member of Shackleton's Endeavour crew)

Andy Wallace had to be asked twice. The first phone call from Tom Walkinshaw Racing came at the start of 1987. Would Wallace, the previous year's British Formula Three Champion and Macau Grand Prix winner, like to test a Group C Jaguar? His eyes firmly set on Formula 3000 and then Formula One, he politely declined. Such opportunities do not usually come around twice. This one did. Twelve months later came the same phone call. By now the young Oxford-born driver had experienced racing F3000 on a Formula Three budget. This time he answered in the affirmative and was soon testing a Jaguar XJR-9 on the long circuit at Paul Ricard. "It was the first time I'd been that fast in anything."

Down the long straight at the French track, Wallace was surprised to find just how much the car moved about. "The only thing," he decided, "was to let it do its own thing." However, revelling in its massive amount of grip, Wallace soon decided that the XJR-9 was "a great car, absolutely solid." In recent years he has had the chance to drive an XJR-9 at the Goodwood Festival of Speed, finding himself still feeling the same about the car. "It still smells the same."

The early months saw him racing for TWR at Jerez (where he came second with John Watson and John Nielsen) and Road Atlanta (fourth with Davy Jones) before being pitched into Le Mans. It was not as if he had not been there before. Like so many, he had travelled there with Page & Moy, his father having taken him three times in the late 1970s. As far as racing goes, though, this was his baptism, and what a position to be in. True, Jaguar had five cars on the grid, but it just had to win that year. Wallace admits that he was very much the junior driver of the number-two car. "I did not know anything about 24-hour races. I was the one who could mess everything up."

However, Wallace was blessed with "two very good team-mates" in Jan Lammers and Scot Johnny Dumfries. The Dutchman, in particular "spent a lot of time explaining what I should do in the race." Even now, a veteran of 17 Le Mans races and a three-times winner of the Daytona 24-Hours, Wallace puts into use what Lammers taught him back in 1988. "In single-seaters you have to develop a sense of selfishness. In sportscars you have to work, three together. You never win races on your own. I trusted Jan and I was right to do so."

Over the last decade Le Mans has become a 24-hour sprint race in which a handful of drivers can go flat-out and still expect to finish. In the late 1980s it was not so, and transmissions were still a weak point; Lammers pointed out that the gearbox was the most likely thing to stop the car. Wallace explains: "The Esses in those days were a third-gear corner. However, if you took them in fourth you would lose only about a tenth of a second while saving on one down and one up shift per lap. The same applied to the Porsche curves, and there were other, similar instances around the lap.

Following his drive in the 1988 winning car, Andy Wallace stayed with Jaguar until the factory withdrew from Le Mans. *(Simon Maurice)*

Before making his Le Mans debut with TVR Jaguar in 1988, Wallace had been sampling F3000 racing on a limited budget with Madgwick Motorsport. (Author)

Wallace prior to the start in 2000. His troubled Cadillac was to cross the line in 21st place, by far his worst Le Mans finish. (Author)

Being gentle on and off the throttle round the Porsche curves was also a kindness to the drive-shafts.

"I did everything that Jan told me," says Wallace of that 1988 race. Even so, about 45 minutes before the finish a shaft snapped putting third gear out of commission. The Jaguar had an H-pattern box, unlike the modern sequential boxes, which meant that Lammers, who was in the car for that final stretch, was able to avoid third. Had he not been able to do so, 1988 might not have become the stuff of legend. Wallace, though, points out that this is what endurance racing is all about. You could make a perfectly valid case as to why he should have won again in 1990, but it will not impress him.

Wallace spent another three years with Jaguar at Le Mans, finishing a weary second in 1990 with Lammers and Franz Konrad. Contemporary reports described him as philosophical about the result. At one point the team had around a two-lap lead. Lammers and Wallace by now were very familiar with the Group C Jaguar and Konrad, the 'guest' driver, was "doing an excellent job." However, during the night, team boss Tom Walkinshaw told the Austrian to pick up his speed. Perhaps as a result, he crashed at the first chicane and the team lost six laps. They finished second, two laps down but, as far as Wallace is concerned, that means second. Conjecture on what might have been is pointless.

In the economy run of 1991 he came fourth, with Derek Warwick and Nielsen, in one of the three XJR-12s, having to watch as the Mazda stayed in front, being unable to do anything about it for fear of running out of fuel. Warwick visited the gravel trap at Indianapolis. That year the car, with added weight and a larger engine to compensate, was, says Wallace, "a bit of a nightmare to drive" and "almost impossible to stop." All of the drivers had problems with the soles of their feet as a result. His other year in a Jaguar, 1989 – in which he shared with Nielsen and Price Cobb – resulted in one of his few retirements; from 17 starts at La Sarthe, Wallace has dropped out on only five occasions. Early in the 1989 race Julian Bailey's Nissan had run into the back of Nielsen's car as the

pair braked for the Mulsanne corner. The exhaust was bent down and Nielsen headed for the pits for repairs. Bailey arrived there as well, but some seven minutes after the shunt. With the Nissan's front suspension pushed into the monocoque there could only be one result and the first retirement of the race was posted. Wallace's car was also now at the back of the field, but the drivers fought their way back to third before the engine gave out.

Wallace now began a peripatetic career that took him from Toyota to McLaren, Panoz, Audi, Cadillac, Bentley, Dome and, latterly, Zytek and DBA. He is at pains to point out the amount of graft that those working on all these cars have put in. "I feel really privileged to have driven for such good teams."

Wallace joined Toyota in 1991, but with no car ready for Le Mans the Japanese factory released him to drive for Jaguar that year. Early in 1992 he went testing with Toyota 'down under' at Eastern Creek. The team ran for a solid nine days continuously blasting over the two large bumps in the road that were part of the fast first corner. "It was really giving the ribs a good old smack," recalls Wallace. Eventually they cried enough and two of them broke. The same happened to the Japanese driver Hitoshi Ogawa. Wallace now had a small problem, a matter of the Sebring 12-Hours being just three weeks away. The doctor said he would be fine in five weeks. At Sebring he was due to drive for Dan Gurney's team for the first time, partnering the namesake and nephew of one Juan Manuel Fangio. "There was no way I was going to ring Gurney (a 1967 Le Mans winner) and tell him that I could not drive." The American Toyota was a "big, heavy car" and the Sebring airfield track is notoriously bumpy. However, as Wallace says with an understandable smile, "we won." The adrenalin must have been flowing as he says he most felt the pain when following the pace car.

Wallace again broke two ribs in 2005, this time by falling off the pit wall at Mont Tremblant. It was the month before Le Mans; on this occasion he came clean and told his entrant, the Creation team, what had happened. The end of the story this time was not so fairytale; the DBA 03S that he shared with Jamie Campbell Walter and Frenchman Nicolas Minassian finished 14th.

Wallace's two years with Toyota resulted in an eighth place and a retirement. During the second season the TS 010 he was sharing with Kenny Acheson and Pierre-Henri Raphanel kept suffering from gearbox problems. But every time the gremlins struck it was in a place where the car could be nursed back to the pits. Eventually in the morning, with Wallace at the wheel, the 'box broke just as he swept past the pits; there was no way this car was going another eight miles. It is said that there was rejoicing in the pits that they would not have to work on the transmission yet again.

Wallace's contract with Toyota was dependent on there being a World Sports Car Championship, and with the cancellation of this he found himself without a Le Mans drive in 1994. It was to be his only absence in a record that so far has stretched from 1988 to the present day.

The mid-1990s saw Wallace with the David Price

Racing McLaren team and a drive to third place with Bell and his son that Derek reckons to have been one of his most memorable at Le Mans. Plenty is said elsewhere in this book about that event, but we should spend a moment looking it at it from Wallace's point of view. He had driven with Bell *pere* in the USA and points out that, though he was by then in his mid-fifties, the five-times winner "was still really good."

Wallace remembers the McLaren reaching 210mph down the straights. It should also be noted that it was he who once recorded 241mph with a production McLaren F1 to make it the fastest ever road car. He recalls those tops speeds, even to the 200mph at 6000rpm that he did the first time he ventured down the Mulsanne straight in a Jaguar. "That'll do for the first lap," he thought and then held the throttle down. It was in the pre-chicane days and Wallace can also quote the 248mph that the Jaguars were then reaching. "Tony Southgate was an absolute master of building cars with low drag." He muses on the fact that this is a public road with cambers either side and truck ruts.

During that first year with the McLaren the heavens opened up and a small river ran across the track just after Tertre Rouge. In sixth gear and at about 200mph Wallace was experiencing "a huge tank slapper" every lap. "It was something to look forward to every four minutes!" He teamed up with DPR and Derek Bell again the following year, this time with Olivier Grouillard. But unfortunately, their particular McLaren was a handful and the trio struggled with insufficient downforce to come sixth.

The front-engined Panoz Esperante GTR1 coupe that he shared with James Weaver and American Butch Leitzinger in 1997 was also an experience, in a different way. Weaver summed it up after a double stint: "Well,

old boy, driving that car for two stints saps your will to live." Wallace describes the experience as being put in a dustbin and having people bang on it with a baseball bat. The noise, with the exhaust's exit about a metre from the driver's left ear, and the vibration were excessive. Wallace drove a Panoz for a second time at Le Mans in 1998, sharing the car with Jamie

Johnny Dumfries (right) only finished Le Mans once in his five appearances, however that was in the place that mattered, partnering Wallace and Lammers in 1988. Now the Marquis of Bute, he admits that his driving was perhaps a little too wild for Tom Walkinshaw and he moved on to two frustrating years with Toyota. His other appearances at La Sarthe were in 1987 and 1991 with a Sauber and Cougar respectively. He is seen here prior to the start of the 1988 race with American Kevin Cogan, who drove the fourth-place Jaguar. *(Simon Maurice)*

Wallace, whose car is seen here during qualifying, spent two years with the Bentley squad. *(Bentley Motors)*

Davies and David Brabham. Apart from a 35-minute night-time stop to replace the dashboard the car ran well and the resulting seventh place was the first time that a Panoz had finished a 24-hour race.

It is easy to forget the Audi R8C, the coupe that was entered alongside the Audi R8R in 1999. While the open-cockpit car was to be developed to great glory, the closed one was quietly shelved. The project had started late. The Ricardo gearbox was weak that year (something that was more than overcome by 2000); there was time to install a paddle-shift change in the R8R, but not in the British-ran coupes. The cars were fast down the straight, but broke so many gearboxes. However, says Wallace, it was nice to drive for Audi. His next move was to Cadillac, whose new prototype had been built by Riley & Scott, a specialist

Very few men have won both Grands Prix and at Le Mans, and only three Englishmen have achieved this feat: Mike Hawthorn, Graham Hill and 1991 victor Johnny Herbert. The latter first came to attention with a legendary performance in the 1985 Formula Ford Festival, overcoming a practice crash that resulted in his starting the first heat from the back, to win the final. In 1988, several seasoned observers who witnessed his performances in Formula 3000 judged him to be the best talent to emerge from these shores for many a long year, and he was promptly selected to drive for Benetton in Formula One. But then a horrendous accident in an F3000 race at Brands Hatch left him with severe foot and leg injuries, which were to prove a massive setback to his career, although remarkably, he eventually still made the Grand Prix grid for his new team in 1989. Subsequently he was to drive for a number of Formula One squads, scoring two popular victories in Britain and Italy for Benetton and then a third at the Nürburgring with the Stewart team.

His Le Mans career is neatly split into two sectors, the first embracing three years with Mazda in the early 1990s, followed by four with the Volkswagen Group from 2001 to 2004. During this time he achieved a 'hat-trick' of successes, winning with Mazda in 2001, then recording the fastest lap in 2003 at the wheel of a Bentley, followed

Johnny Herbert being interviewed before the 2004 race. *(Author)*

by pole position the next year with one of the Veloqx Audis.

For a popular tailpiece to these achievements can be added an entertaining win in the 2005 Legends race with Nigel Webb's Jaguar D-type.

US racecar constructor for whom Wallace had already won the Daytona 24-Hours. The Le Mans yearbook described him as having "the ideal profile for Cadillac in their (*sic*) learning year." Twenty-first place overall – easily Wallace's worst finish – indicates the various difficulties the Cadillacs had that year. Even so, he again says that he enjoyed driving the car.

It rained the next year. Wallace reckons it does so every three years; this may be an exaggeration, but he certainly remembers 1995 and 2001. Wallace was now at the wheel of one of the Bentleys, the first of the new breed of Bentley Boys. Just ahead of him was Stefan Johansson in the Gulf Audi, and just behind was Ralf Kelleners in another of the German cars. As they were approaching Indianapolis a deluge hit them. Struggling to see where he was going in the closed car and travelling way too fast to be on slicks, Wallace was presented with a dilemma. Lift off and the car behind would hit him. He tried to slow down gently and then Johansson started to spin. The Bentley was still doing about 170mph. The Swede hit the guardrail and something powder blue and orange flew through the air, Wallace knew not what. As he went through the right-hand kink just before the bend, he heard the object – it was the Audi's nose – hit the roof of the Bentley, knocking off a door mirror and the airbox.

He kept going and noticed an Audi in the gravel trap at the Porsche curves. It was possible, he thought, that he was now in second place. As he headed for a stop so he heard fellow Bentley driver Martin Brundle radioing in and asking to swap pits. The result was that Wallace could not get into his pit. Brundle got out first, Wallace was held up and by the time he was back on the track a pace car had intervened between

himself and the leader. He was not amused.

Shortly after, entering Mulsanne corner, he found that he could not down-shift, the compressor had filled with water and the gearbox was stuck in sixth. He pulled well over to the left and managed to get through the curve. Seventy-five miles an hour through the Mulsanne corner is pretty impressive. He also managed to scramble through Arnage in sixth and, with only the Porsche curves ahead before the pits, he thought "I've done it." He had, of course, forgotten the chicane-like nature of the pit entrance. There was only one thing for it, straight across the gravel. He made it. The less experienced Guy Smith, suffering the same problem, did not, as we will see. Wallace and his fellow drivers Leitzinger and Eric van de Poele then "got our head down and drove the wheels off the car." As others made mistakes so they now kept it together and finished third. It was the year of 'Wing Commander Wallace'. Richard Lloyd handed him and his team-mates old leather flying helmets and goggles and in homage to the original Bentley Boys they appeared so clad on the rostrum. The following year Wallace was again in the first non-Audi, albeit back in fourth place.

The third year was the one in which Bentley had to win. There were also no works Audis and two of the German make's contracted drivers were transferred to Bentley. It was also the year in which Guy Smith was to be rewarded for his year in the testing wilderness. There was no place for Wallace, so instead he teamed up with his fellow 1988 winner Jan Lammers in one of the Dutchman's Domes. "It was nice to be back with Jan, but the car was getting a bit long in the tooth." Sixth was probably a reasonable result given

ALLAN McNISH

In 1998 a spectator was standing on a box by the exit of the Porsche curves. Allan McNish could tell from his antics whether he was lying first or second in the race. "He was getting more and more animated the closer I got to the Toyota. If I was leading he was going absolutely berserk. That chap does not realize how much he spurred me on. I don't know who it was, but he helped me win Le Mans."

"Le Mans is a roller coaster," says the Scot, "and 1998 was certainly a very good example. We were fastest in pre-qualifying. We had a lot of pressure on our shoulders because on the Monday afterwards it was the 50th anniversary of Porsche. It was also the 100th anniversary of Michelin." Victory was expected, "nothing else was acceptable." In qualifying the team was basically able to repeat what it had done in pre-qualifying. However, the opposition was going quicker and the car was only fifth on the grid.

"We had to play a bit of a waiting game," McNish recalls, "but by about 10.00 at night we were leading. At six in the morning I was doing a long stint when I saw Jörg Müller coming out of the gravel trap. That put us a lap in the lead. 'That's perfect', I thought, 'Thank you very much. I'll take that.'" Within half a lap the water temperature started rising. McNish thought it was a sensor failure but was instructed to pit despite being only halfway through his stint. Now both Porsches were in the pits, McNish with a split water pipe being replaced. "At that point I could have cried. I was seeing a lap lead just slipping through my fingers."

When he did return to the race he was second behind one of the Toyotas. From about 6.30am to nearly 1.00pm "we fought like hell with that Toyota. (That year the race finished at 2.00pm because of the soccer World Cup.) Then, at ten to one, I came out of Arnage and there was a red Toyota sitting by the side of the road. I radioed in 'number 29 stopped, confirm I am in the lead'." For a

while there was no reply. Then going down in the Esses he received confirmation. He was in the lead.

"The last hour was more nerve wracking than anything else. When I crossed the line it was relief. Not ecstasy, not enjoyment, just sheer relief."

When Porsche's Norbert Singer looked over his horn-rimmed glasses at McNish, the Scot realized that he had been "involved in something very, very special and that I had also learned from the master. Norbert will always have a special place in my heart just for that look on a very hot day in June."

McNish has raced at Le Mans six times and there is no doubt about the affection he holds for the event. "It's so much more difficult than a Grand Prix because it's 12 of them back to back." Before his first event in 1997, "I had heard about it but I did not really understand the place. When I watched the cars going out for pre-qualifying I had a shiver down my spine."

Having driven for Porsche for two years and then Toyota in 1999, McNish became part of the Audi R8 legend, finishing second in 2000 and setting fastest lap of the race, after long pit stops had relegated his previously front-running car back to third and then fourth. He returned to Le Mans after a time in Formula One and to literally his least memorable race there…he can hardly remember anything about it. The start was hectic, as he and team-mate Jamie Davies rubbed flanks with the start line still some yards away. Further drama occurred just before 6.00pm when both McNish and another R8, that of JJ Lehto, went off on oil at the Porsche curves. Such was the ferocity with which McNish's Audi hit the tyre barriers that the Finn afterwards said to him, "I looked at you, Alan. Your eyes were like clocks, they were going round and round."

As soon as the car turned in to the corner, McNish realized that he was on oil and about to crash. His mind is a blank as to what happened then until he remembers a fire extinguisher going off in the pits and then waking up in hospital. He is sure that he was on automatic pilot in bringing the car back to the pits. "I don't have any memory of jumping out of the car like a champagne cork coming out of the bottle." However, that is what happened; once he had 'done the job' and brought the car back, he jumped out of it and collapsed. Much of the weekend is now a blank, "although I was, apparently, perfectly compos mentis."

In 2005 McNish was entered in one of the two Champion team's Audis. An off into the gravel trap at Indianapolis and a subsequent 20-minute pit stop to repair the suspension put the car back from second to third place, where it remained.

McNish will return. "I know in my heart of hearts that I will go back to Le Mans as a driver and then as a spectator, and as soon as my little boy can turn up there he will – and it will probably be before his sixth birthday. It is something that gets in your blood. You can't get it out and you shouldn't want to get it out. It's such a special sporting event. Big, sexy, fast cars going past at about 220mph in the dark at three in the morning is one of the finest sights in the world."

Allan McNish gets ready for a spell in the cockpit. (Author)

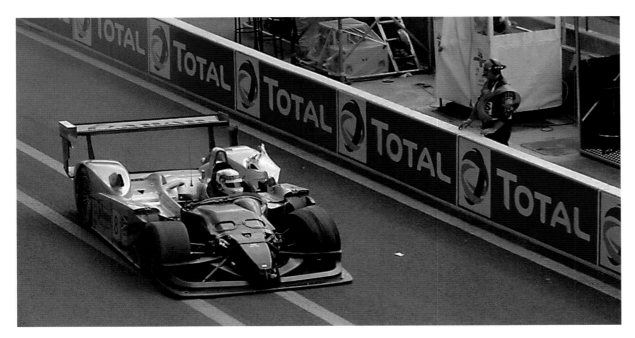

the circumstances, not that any British fan was likely to notice that year. Battery and electrical gremlins had dropped it back one place, denying it the honour of being the first non-Volkswagen Group car home.

The years 2004 and 2005 saw Wallace in the basically similar Zytek 04S and DBA 03S. In 2004, Zytek team-mate David Brabham frightened the Audis in practice. At 10.23pm during the last session he topped the timesheets, only to be beaten at the last moment by the two Audi UK cars. Third place on the grid was still good enough to be ahead of the other two Audis, though. Wallace started the race, but records show that other cars just kept going by him in the early laps. The works Zytek 04S was an ideal car for the shorter 1000kms races, indeed it was to win in both the USA and Europe the following year, but Wallace believes that it was too highly stressed for the 24-Hours. If so, this shows what an excellent job the little Jota team did to bring its less developed, privately entered car so near to finishing the following year.

Unfortunately the engine cried enough in spectacular fashion at about half-distance. Wallace was also troubled by vibration although team manager Trevor Foster reckons he was the only one of the three drivers to be so. It had been the intention, says Wallace, for the drivers to carry out triple-stints. However, by the end of the second the muscles in his legs had given way and he was suffering from pins and needles in his finger and toes.

It was a similar picture the next year. The DBA was the forerunner of the Zytek and had started life with a Zytek engine. However, the Creation team, which Wallace joined for Le Mans in 2005, had replaced it with a Judd V8. Again, Wallace feels that the concept – the DBA had started life in the LMP 675 class – was fragile. Nevertheless, the car came home in 14th place. It was the smallest team that Wallace had driven for in his 17 years at Le Mans. He was impressed by the operation. "It shows how you can go to Le Mans and still do a good job (whatever the size of the team)."

Andy Wallace is now in his mid-forties, but still obviously enjoying his motor racing as much as ever. He insists on pointing out how lucky he is to have had such a career. He appreciates that the sportscar spectators are real fans. "So are we," he says, "I'm a bit of an anorak myself." He also enjoys the technical aspects of the sport.

There have been sportscar drivers who have also had successful Formula One careers, and others who rue the fact that they never really made it to, or in, Grand Prix racing. Does this worry Wallace? He looks at it this way: he might have made Formula One and then been out of work by his early-thirties. Instead, he is still an active and successful, professional racing driver. During 2005 he participated in 25 races. In 2004 he counted up that he had spent 119 days of the year sat in a racing car, much of it with the Dyson ALMS and Crawford Gran-Am teams in the USA. That is a lot of time to spend in a racing car, but Andy Wallace is not complaining.

In 2006 he signed to drive the RML MG Lola EX264, partnering Mike Newton and Thomas Erdos, at Le Mans.

What sparks them into action?

When the race is on and you're aiming for the top, only the best is good enough. That's why time after time, the first choice for reliability and performance is NGK.

THE WORLD'S NO.1 OE FITMENT SPARK PLUG

NGK

www.ngkntk.co.uk

NGK Spark Plugs (UK) Ltd. Maylands Avenue, Hemel Hempstead, Hertfordshire, HP2 4SD. Tel: 01442 281000 Fax: 01442 281001

224

CHAPTER 28

THE CLASS CONTENDERS

"We will drink to the British flag with all honours."
(Private Edward Woodham, survivor of the Charge of the Light Brigade)

The British at Le Mans are known for their active support of the smaller cars, the class contenders, or even those whose sole aim is to just finish the race, even if it is in last place. Ever since the 1925 Austin Seven of Gordon England and Francis Samuelson, they have had plenty to cheer. Over the years such as TVRs, Rileys and Morgans have found their way into the spectators' affections.

It does not matter which British manufacturer goes, the smallest will receive plenty of backing. "The little TVRs get as much support as the big boys and that is something quite special about it," observes 1998 winner Allan McNish.

As recently as 2005, the only British success came in the LMP2 class when the Lola of Ray Mallock Ltd overcame a spectacular attack on the gravel trap at the Ford chicane to overtake two ailing French cars in the final hours. The whole gamut of emotions can be felt for those contesting the lesser prizes. "Everybody was sorry when the gallant MG Midgets were put out of the race, after one had run for about five hours and the other for 12 hours," said *The Motor* in 1930. The RML Lola also carried an MG badge 75 years later, although the link was tenuous.

An early success, which the press at the time said called for the highest praise, was that of a lone Lea-Francis in 1929. It had no works support and was driven by a couple of amateurs – surely a forerunner of many British entries to come. Keith Peacock and Sammy Newsome drove the car steadily for 24 hours, qualifying for the next year's Rudge-Whitworth final with points to spare. The Morgan Aero 8 that ran well behind the rest of the field in 2004, and after a troubled run to the chequered flag failed to be classified for not having travelled the required minimum distance, surely came from the same breed. Looking at the team straight after the race you would have thought they had won. Just finishing Le Mans for such entrants is a great achievement.

Over the last four decades, a hard dividing line has also occurred between outright racing cars, still euphemistically called 'prototypes', and GT cars,

contenders based on production vehicles. Such a division was unnecessary in the early years when entrants could be, and often were, driven to the track. However, at the start of the 1960s, the race was divided into categories for sports prototype and *grand tourisme* cars. The GT cars disappeared briefly during the C1 and C2 era of the 1980s, but are now back as an essential part of the entry list. It is in the GT classes as well as the 'second division' LMP2 prototype class that opportunities now dwell for glory other than an outright win. However, over the years there have been plenty of other possibilities to come away with some silverware.

Perhaps in no year was the British obsession with class wins or just simple participation – rather than outright victory – more noticeable than in 1934. Over half of the biggest field since 1925 were British, yet none of them looked likely candidates for outright

Small British cars populated the Le Mans entries of the mid-1960s. Here the Deep Sanderson 301 of Chris Lawrence and Gordon Spice leads the Lotus Elite of Clive Hunt and John Wagstaff. The two most common little sportscars on British roads at the time, the 'Spridget' and the Spitfire, were also represented. Austin-Healey Sprites first appeared in 1961 and were last seen in 1967, while a team of works Triumph Spitfires raced in 1964 and 1965, the Thuner/Lampinen car winning the 1150cc class the second year. *(LAT Photographic)*

Lotus Engineering was a regular entrant until the ACO upset Colin Chapman over the 'Lotus 23 incident'. In 1958 the 750cc Lotus Eleven of Alan Stacey and Tom Dickson was delayed for two hours as the latter tried to extricate the little car from the Mulsanne sand bank. Although it eventually came home in 20th place it was unclassified. (LAT Photographic)

Throughout their long history at Le Mans, MGs have always fought for class honours rather than outright victory. In 2001 the marque returned and fittingly chose the LMP 675 class to compete in. The MG-badged Lolas were factory-entered for two years, the Julian Bailey/Kevin McGarrity/Mark Blundell car seen here in 2001. Number 21 is another British entry, the Judd-powered Ascari KZR1 of Klaas Zwart, Xavier Pompidou and Scott Maxwell. Both cars retired. (LAT Photographic)

victory. Significantly, three-quarters of the entry had an engine size of 1500cc or less, and most of these came from the UK. Indeed, there were only two works teams in the whole race and they were Aston Martin and Riley. The little cars nearly overturned predictions. The Aston Martin of Mortimer Morris-Goodall and John Elwes ran as high as second before retiring just before noon, leaving one of the Rileys to take over the position. In all, the British cars filled seven of the top places that year. It was a shame about the one Alfa Romeo that headed them; however, the fifth-placed Riley won both the Biennial Cup and the

Index of Performance. Such additional awards, as well as the Index of Thermal Efficiency which is examined in Chapter 32, have given the British plenty of success over the years.

It was in 1934 that the press started recording class winners, with three of the five categories going to British cars. A year later there were six classes, again with British victories in three. In 1937 Morris-Goodall and Robert Hichens may have won the Biennial Cup, but there was only one class win, with J.M. Skeffingham and R.C. Murton-Neale, also Aston Martin-mounted, taking the 1500cc award. The story was similar the next year, with just a Singer victory in the 1100cc class, but the final year before the war saw wins in both the 5-litre and 1500cc classes for British cars.

After the war the classes were again set according to cubic capacity, and the story of British successes continued, HRG resuming where it left off before the world conflict with a 1500cc win in 1949. The next year an 8-litre class was added, which went to Allard. Three other categories also fell to British cars. So it continued throughout the 1950s, when British cars were winning at a variety of levels as well as up front.

In 1958 the CSI decided to limit the World Sports Car Championship to 3 litres, and a year later, with this capacity limit still in force, the entry, as mentioned earlier, was divided into Prototypes and GTs, even though class winners were still also decided on engine size. More new regulations were introduced for 1960, with a mandatory 10-inch depth of screen and 'luggage space' intended to make the cars appear more like road cars, not that they succeeded in this. Fifteen new capacity classes were also introduced. Eighteen cars in that year's field were considered to be GTs, with Lotus Elites dominating the 1300cc category, something that was to be repeated the following year, when an AC Ace also took the 2-litre GT award.

In 1966 the long-standing division between just Prototypes and GTs was abandoned. Only two of the latter, neither of them British, were entered, but a new Sports Car class, for cars of which at least 50 examples had been built, was introduced. Prototypes again dominated and there were only 11 Sports Cars, none of them from these shores. Two years later the Prototypes, which had been of unlimited capacity for some years, were again reduced to a maximum of 3 litres, but the Sports Cars were still allowed to use larger engines. It was a ruling that ultimately was to be abused in such a way that it produced some of the most exciting cars ever to have run at Le Mans. Lola took advantage of it by producing enough T70s to be able to run two 5-litre cars, although both retired. The Slough-built 4.9-litre Ford GT40s were also eligible, although their larger brethren had now been banned. It all meant that there was still a myriad of classes, although none fell to a British manufacturer in 1968.

The year 1969 saw the sports category regulations reduced to a minimum production of 25 cars and Porsche rode the proverbial 'coach and horses' through the rules by building the required number of pure racing 917s. Ferrari was to follow suit with the 512, while Lola continued to also take advantage of the rules. But it could not continue, and for 1972

LMP2 replaced LMP 675 in 2004, the winner the first year being the Lola-Judd entered by Intersport and Anglo-American Bill Binnie. Their B2K/40 was actually a leftover from the old class. However, a purpose-built Lola LMP2, the Ray Mallock car of Warren Hughes, Mike Newton and Tommy Erdos (seen here at Tertre Rouge) won the second year. Effectively this was one of the new B05/40 models but was entered as a Lola/MG Type EX264. *(Author)*

all the Group 5 sportscars, as they were now known, were also reduced to 3 litres in size. The GT category was redefined as Group 4 *Grand Tourisme Special* and a Group 2 Special Touring class introduced. The 2-litre sportscars were also becoming popular at about this time, which meant opportunities for British manufacturers Lola and Chevron leading to four consecutive victories, from 1977 to 1980, in the 2-litre Group 6 class by Chevron B36s. By the mid-1970s we were also talking about three Groups, the prototypes of Group 5 and the GT-like cars of Groups 4 and 3. In 1976 this was changed to Groups 6, 5 and 4, with various other categories added to allow cars in from North America. It was all very complicated, although for the spectator it did not really look much different.

The year 1982 saw the start of the highly successful Group C category as well as a GT-like Group B, which raced alongside the former for a while. Twelve months later saw the introduction of Group C Junior, which became the British-dominated C2, as will be recorded. By the late 1980s the Group B cars were off the scene and there was nothing left but pure-bred racers.

The 1990s brought a further period of confusion with the front-runners reduced to 3.5 litres and the return of GT cars, one of which, a British-built McLaren, scoring an outright victory in 1995. During recent years there have been attempts to straighten out the classes. Two divisions of prototype have arisen, initially the LMP 900 (along with its closed-cockpit LM GTP counterpart) and LMP 675 categories, these having been divided by weight and power. They have since undergone a transitional period into the LMP1 and LMP2 divisions, which should settle down in 2007. Some LMP 900 and LMP 675 cars have been converted into what have been called 'hybrids' to enable them to continue just for 2006. The GT class has undergone a variety of changes, having got completely out of hand with thinly disguised prototypes masquerading as GTs

during the late 1990s. Sanity returned in 1999 with what were known as the LM GTS and LM GT classes. These have evolved into the LM GT1 and LM GT2 classes, with a return to La Sarthe by Aston Martin to contend the first of these. To quote the *Goon Show*: "it's all very confusing really," but it does give Le Mans the depth it requires. As a prototype or GT-only race, it would just not be the same.

Heavy rain was a feature of the Wednesday practice in 2005. Mike Pilbeam was only able to deliver his new MP93 LMP2 to its French customer the week before the preliminary trials. Pierre Bruneau had done enough in the previous year's Le Mans Endurance Series with an older car from the British constructor to earn an entry for the 24-Hours. *(Gavin Ireland)*

British, indeed Scottish, entries can be found in the LM GT2 class. Stuart Roden's Scuderia Ecosse – on no account to be confused with Ecurie Ecosse – entered this Ferrari F360 GTC in 2005 for Nathan Kirch, Andrew Kirkaldy and Anthony Reid. *(Gavin Ireland)*

cars. Five times an outright winner, Derek Bell reflects on the fact that the drivers of such entries "have their work cut out" and can sometimes be involved in their own private contests for class victory. "You just have to remember that there are other people out there and they are having a race as well." He wonders, though, if attitudes have changed. "In my era I couldn't afford to bash a Ferrari 512 or a Porsche 917 into a slower car, but now the Audis are so robust!"

The differing categories have often given possibilities for innovation. After the two Alvis entries in the 1928 race, *The Motor* reckoned that "front-wheel drive has come to stay." In those days it was not a matter of winning one's class, but of covering the minimum distance required to qualify for the Biennial Cup. Thus a 750cc car had to keep going for a mere 900 miles at 37.5mph while a car in the 5-litre group had to race for 1450 miles at 60.5mph. The 1500cc Alvises would have been required to do 1188 miles at 49.6mph, a challenge they easily met, Maurice Harvey and Harold Purdy averaging 59.19mph and covering 1410.61 miles and 'Sammy' Davis and William Urquart Dykes achieving 1396.91 miles and 58.20mph.

The tremendous speed differential at Le Mans, caused by having smaller or production-based cars on the same track as out-and-out powerful racing cars, does of course create problems. Gordon Spice, who was entered in everything from a little Deep Sanderson to a Rondeau with outright winning potential, reckons that it is far more difficult to drive one of the slower

By examining the stories of the lesser lights – many of which are told elsewhere in this book – the drama, and even the humour, of Le Mans can truly be unfolded. For example, in 1949 George Phillips and 'Curly' Dryden were disqualified for giving a lift back to the pits of a mechanic who had gone out to the circuit to help repair their stranded MG TC. Mike Salmon, who raced at Le Mans 13 times, tells

For some years the top GT class has been a battle between the American Corvettes and cars developed by Banbury-based Prodrive, the Ferrari F550 and the Aston Martin DBR9. Usually the former has prevailed, but in 2003 the Ferrari of Peter Cox, Thomas Enge and Brit Jamie Davies won the class. A sub-plot to this tale concerns a battle between two British drivers: Oliver Gavin has been a regular for the Chevrolet team, winning in 2002, while Darren Turner made his Le Mans debut with the Veloqx Prodrive squad a year later. Gavin's Corvette was second in class that year, but won again in 2004 and 2005. Turner was third in class in a Ferrari in 2004, finishing in the same place in an Aston 12 months later. *(Author)*

the story of limping back to the pits with a punctured Aston Martin DP214 in 1964. Such was the faith in the mechanics that the car would not last the 24 hours that by the time he arrived they had packed up in the pits. The car, co-driven by Peter Sutcliffe and run by the Hon John Dawnay, later Viscount Downe, eventually retired in the early hours of the morning with head gasket problems.

If anyone epitomizes the independent entrant hungry for class honours it is Hugh Chamberlain. Between 1987 and 2005 he entered the race 17 times, initially in the C2 class, then in GTs, LMP 675s and in 2005 the LMP2 category. His cars have officially finished the race on eight occasions, the highest placing being 14th in 1992 and 1999.

Initially a driver himself, mainly in the Clubmans category, Chamberlain teamed up with Will Hoy, a rugby club 'mate', who was soon to demonstrate his versatility. Driving a Chamberlain-entered Mallock, farmer's son Hoy dominated the Clubmans title and went on to compete at Le Mans five times between 1985 and 1991, as well as winning the British Touring Car Championship. With the advent of the Thundersports series in the UK Chamberlain turned his attention to a very quick 1800cc turbocharged Hart-powered Tiga sports-racer. But Thundersports was limited in its appeal, so the team "put a top" on the Tiga and entered some races in the World Sports Car Championship. From there the team bought the first European customer Spice Pontiac Fiero and fitted it with the powerful Hart engine from the Tiga. The first Le Mans race for the team was in 1987, the drivers being Nick Adams, Graham Duxbury and Richard Jones. "We had all sorts of hassle," says Chamberlain. The records also say that the Spice did not complete the required number of laps. Chamberlain still contends this. The regulations stated that a car had to do 75 per cent of the class winner's distance, not, as most people believed, a similar percentage of the outright winner's distance. He points out that his car did complete the

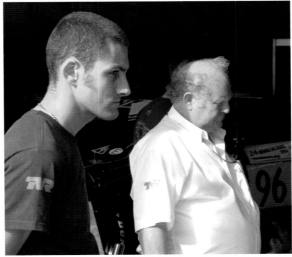

first distance, if not the second. That year someone ran off with the whole of the rear bodywork of the car. It was eventually found on one of the campsites, having been taken by some Welshmen – perhaps they knew of Chamberlain's rugby background.

A year later Chamberlain was back running two Spices, the old Hart-engined SE86 for the reliable trio of Adams, Jones and Martin Birrane and a new Nicholson DFL-powered SE88 owned by playboy Jean-Louis Ricci. He was to run a total of nine Spice entries at Le Mans up to 1993, the "worst downer" occurring in 1989. Having come second the previous year in the C2 World Sports Car Championship, the team was on a high and one of the favourites to do well at Le Mans. Having decided to just go "round and round and round," the Spice was about 45 minutes ahead of the rest of the class. One of the drivers, Spaniard Fermin Velez, was personally backed by Silk Cut Spain and Chamberlain had been told by the cigarette manufacturer that, if he were to win the C2 World Championship, it would put money into his

In 2003 Warnock finished 23rd overall and sixth in the LM GT category sharing this Porsche 911 GT3-RS with Scot Robin Liddell and Englishman Piers Masarati. (*Author*)

DAVE WARNOCK

Le Mans gave Alderley Edge's Dave Warnock a warm welcome. He was really enjoying his 1997 debut at the race. "I was so busy thinking 'this is great' that I went straight on into a gravel trap (at the first Mulsanne chicane)." The exhaust of the GT2 Saleen Mustang he was sharing with fellow Brit Rob Schirle was cracked and the underside of the car damaged. The result was that flames started shooting through into the seat. "I radioed in for a medic as my arse was on fire!" Crew chief Bevis Mush had a water bucket at the ready for Warnock to sit in as soon as he pitted.

Despite this baptism, Warnock, a past winner of the GT class at the Daytona 24-Hours, retains his love of Le Mans. "The whole week – even from the first night in the chateau, and going down to the *Place des Jacobins* – it's just an amazing feeling." He first tried to pre-qualify his Marcos LM600 in 1996, but as the team had never driven round the track, Win Percy was brought in to qualify it. He did just one lap and declared the Marcos to be unsafe.

Warnock's first finish at Le Mans was in a Roock Porsche GT2 in 1998. "We started with a full spare car in the truck, which was used to purloin parts from. At the end it was a shell with an engine. I really felt for the crew of our car. It can be easy to forget the efforts that these guys put in to keep it going."

The team used caravans for the drivers to rest in. The door handle broke locking Warnock inside his and forcing fellow driver Andre Ahrle to drive round for a few more laps while he broke out.

Between 1997 and 2004 Warnock competed at Le Mans six times, his best result being to finish 16th in 2001 at the wheel of a PK Sport Porsche 911 GT3-RS. At one point the team was leading its class but was struggling to keep everything dry in the torrential conditions. Perhaps not surprisingly, he regards the 24-Hours as unfinished business. "It is amazing to me that you can compete with some of the top drivers in the world and, due to the nuances of endurance races and this race in particular, have a chance to win."

The TVRs changed hands for 2004 and various modifications were made to improve on the previous year's poor result. This time they both finished, in 21st and 22nd overall. (*Author*)

effort for the following year. At about 10.00am Nick Adams, who was then at the wheel of the car, reported in that something was up, compression had been lost on one of the cylinders. The team was unable to assess the amount of damage and Chamberlain could not risk a valve dropping. "If I had known it was just a little bit of burning on the edge of one valve I would have continued to run it, but I could not afford that." Reluctantly he signed the relevant form to say that the car had retired.

Thoroughly depressed, Chamberlain was walking back to the team's hospitality tent when he bumped into Silk Cut's Peter Gilpin. The latter enthused about how well the car had been going and could not understand why Chamberlain had retired it, given that it was so far ahead. Hugh explained how he just could not afford to rebuild the engine. Gilpin told him that if he continued to run it on the remaining seven cylinders he would give him a £30,000 cheque for the engine. However, the paperwork had been signed, the car had officially retired and it was too late. Gilpin

Richard Shepherd-Barron drove the 2-litre GT class-winning Morgan Plus 4 in 1962 with Chris Lawrence. Particularly noticeable was a group of people waving their Union Jacks for the entire race. "We waved back every time we went past," he recalls. Thirty years later he met one of them. "Did you see us?" he was asked.

The Morgan had, in fact, been entered the year before but was refused, the ACO describing it as "a museum car from the 1930s with disc brakes." It was felt that a rival team might have had a hand in this, not wanting to see its modern technology beaten by the old. It was true that the previous Morgan entry had been 10 years earlier, a Plus 4 with a Standard Vanguard engine. Before that, Prudence Fawcett's 4/4 had paved the way in 1938 and 1939.

It was a different story in 1962. The car, Shepherd-Barron recalls, was much better prepared than the year before and the entry was accepted without question, perhaps due to pressure on the ACO from the Morgan dealer in France. British component suppliers Lucas ("amazing headlights"), Automotive Products and Lockheed all provided support. "It exuded charm and the crowds loved it," says Shepherd-Barron. The team ran at a steady pace in the incredibly hot conditions and he remembers not actually seeing any other cars "for quite a long time" during one of his three-hour stints. Top speed down the Mulsanne was about 135mph.

The Malvern constructor did not return to La Sarthe until 2002, the Aero 8 GT run by DeWalt Racesports Salisbury making little attempt to hide its relationship to the car of 42 years before despite is aluminium rather than wood construction. Chris Lawrence was still involved, running the technical side of the project. The all-British team of Richard Hay, Richard Stanton and Steve Hyde retired during the morning with engine failure. Two years later an entry was made under the Morgan Works Race Team banner, Hyde now sharing with Neil Cunningham and teenager Adam Sharpe, at that stage the youngest Brit

The Lawrence/Shepherd-Barron Morgan at Indianapolis. "We were very fast here and outran the most surprising cars in this section," says the latter. *(Richard Shepherd-Barron collection)*

to have driven at Le Mans. During the opening laps it was obviously the slowest car in the field, falling back behind the rest…but as in 1962, the crowd loved it.

As the evening light faded, the car, with Cunningham driving, ground to a halt at Indianapolis with fuel starvation and was pushed behind the guardrail by the marshals. It seemed to be all over. However, some hours later the Australian was seen to be driving slowly towards the pits and, just after midnight, the fuel pump was changed. The car continued to the finish, but with only 222 laps under its belt it had not completed the minimum distance requirement to be classified.

The same corner 44 years later and the marshals are seemingly pushing the Morgan Aero 8 to retirement, but just under three hours later it was back on the track. *(Author)*

The Xtrac crew at Le Mans in 2003 celebrating the fact that eight out of the top 10 cars, including the winning Bentley, have been using the company's gearboxes. *(Xtrac)*

THE COMPONENT SUPPLIER

Over the years British component manufacturers have flocked to Le Mans to support their products. In recent times their physical presence has perhaps been less obvious, but one of those whose motorhome is still a meeting point in the paddock is Xtrac, the Thatcham-based transmission specialist.

The company's initial successes came in 1989 and 1990, when it supplied components for the winning Sauber-Mercedes and then the Jaguar. The winning Peugeots of 1992 and 1993 both used its gearboxes, as did the victorious McLaren in 1995 and the BMW in 1999.

The year 2003 was the company's highlight to date, the season that eight out of Le Mans' top 10 finishers preferred Xtrac. Included were the winning Bentleys that used its magnesium-cased inboard, transverse, six-speed gearbox.

Following the Bentley victory, Xtrac has had to content itself with GTS and GT1 wins as the supplier for both the Prodrive Ferraris and the Chevrolet Corvettes. (It should be pointed out that all the GT1 cars also use British-made composite propshafts from Banbury-based CTG.) The Audi R8 used transmission from Xtrac's British rival Ricardo. However, at the start of 2006 it was announced that Xtrac had won Audi over and would be supplying the gearboxes for its new R10 diesel. Despite the enormous torque produced by the V12 TDI engine, the 'box is lighter than that used for the R8. Because of the turbodiesel engine's characteristics, the number of gear-changes to be made in the race will fall significantly, an important factor concerning durability, particularly as the transmission system is subject to extremely high loads. German cars may be more likely to win Le Mans these days, but when it comes to transmission it is the British who dominate the event.

Le Mans is important to Xtrac. Being one of motorsport's top component suppliers, it is crucial that everybody does not leave the office at once every time there is a major race. Development director Cliff Hawkins admits, though, that this rule is ignored for Le Mans week. "The office is empty then," he says. Even people who work in motorsport make sure that they take time off to go to Le Mans.

walked away "and he never gave me another penny." Chamberlain did win the C2 World Championship that year, but there was no Silk Cut money to come.

The following year the Chamberlain team easily won the C2 category with Richard Piper, Ferdinand de Lesseps and Olindo Iacobelli, although Hugh admits that there were few cars in the class that year. "You're not complete without a win at Le Mans, not outright but a class win will do."

In the early 1990s Chamberlain became a prime mover in bringing back the GT class to Le Mans. With Group C on the wane, this he felt was the way in which the race should be heading. In 1993 and 1994 he was team manager for the works Lotus Esprit GTs, but unfortunately the factory's heart was not in the project. In 1997 – the year he says he learnt how to change a valve spring with a ball of string – Chamberlain began four years of running Chrysler Vipers. Two years later his team came a creditable third in the GTS class behind the two ORECA Vipers. However, it nearly did not happen.

Driver Ni Amorim was so concerned that he could not bring the troubled car to the finish that he waited until he could be absolutely sure that the race was over before struggling round the final part of the lap. With the radio not working and the track being invaded by the spectators Chamberlain could only wait in the pits, aware that unless the car actually crossed the line it would not be qualified.

In 2000 Chamberlain ran the Team Goh Viper and a driver crew led by Walter Brun. During the morning the Swiss had a horrendous shunt when a tyre exploded on the run between Mulsanne and Indianapolis. Amazingly, although the car's bodywork was destroyed the chassis was found to be still true after the event.

Chamberlain then became involved late in MG's return to Le Mans. "The chassis was great but the engine was hopeless," he recalls, saying that engine builder AER was not given sufficient time to prepare it. "Before the race no engine had been tested for more than 45 minutes." During the two years that the Lola-MG EX 257s ran they were quick but troublesome. Mark Blundell told Chamberlain that they were the nearest thing to a Formula One car that he had driven, with more downforce than a Champ Car.

In 2004 Chamberlain joined with team owner Gareth Evans to manage the Chamberlain-Synergy operation. Their two cars were the TVR Tuscans that had raced the previous year in DeWalt Salisbury colours (with Chamberlain mechanics), both having undergone modifications to lose weight and improve reliability. For 24 hours the purple pair gave the impression of circulating in convoy and, indeed, finished in 21st and 22nd overall, albeit nine laps apart. For 2005 the team turned its attention to the LMP2 class with Evans winning his class in the year-long Le Mans Endurance Series. The car, an AER-engined B05/40, retired during the night with an oil leak. As mentioned, the similar Lola of the RML team won the class, the first of just four walking wounded to be classified. Almost anything can happen in the class battles at Le Mans… and invariably, almost anything *does* happen.

Overall victory in the early years of the 21st century fell to cars in one of two classes, either the LMP 900 category or the LM GTP. Most of the time it was one of the former that came first, thanks to the dominance of the Audis. A variety of British drivers competed in R8s, but none with success. So, what is an American-entered, foreign-crewed, German car like the one pictured here doing in a book like this? The answer is that Audi could not have achieved its success without the use of British transmission. A Ricardo six-speed gearbox was fitted to all the R8s. However, the new R10 uses a lighter 'box from rival British firm Xtrac. (Author)

Major British interest in 2005 centred round the two works Aston Martin DBR9s, the first factory entries from the company since 1989. Various maladies meant that they eventually lost out to the Chevrolet Corvettes after a mighty tussle. That they had made their mark could be seen when the entry for the 2006 race was published with DBR9s from Russian Age Racing and BMS Scuderia Italia joining the two works cars. (Original painting by Eddy Dodwell – reproduced by kind permission of BEN)

PART EIGHT
1999-2005

Bentley and Aston Return

"And gentlemen in England, now a-bed, Shall think themselves accurs'd, they were not here." Guy Smith and the victorious green Bentley EXP Speed 8 revive all that is British about Le Mans as they cross the line near the end of the 2003 race. *(Bentley Motors)*

CHAPTER 29

THE BRITISH AT LE MANS
1999-2005

"Once they were sure of victory the Britons sent on to Paris…"
(Geoffrey of Monmouth, *The History of the Kings of Britain*)

Let us be honest. If you were not British or were one of those cynics who said the Bentleys were merely green Audis, the 2003 Le Mans race was rather boring. However, if you were patriotic about these things then it was 24 hours of nail biting as the two Speed 8s swept round, seemingly impervious to anything else that was happening on the track.

There had been all kinds of comment beforehand. Some said that the Volkswagen Group had decreed the Bentleys would win, others that the national teams now running the Audi R8s were determined that they could ape the works' results of the previous three years. The Bentley was a better racing car, developed with just one aim in mind, to win Le Mans, but could the Audis trip them up with fewer pit stops? To some the result seemed a foregone conclusion but if, so to speak, you had waited 73 years for this day, the 24 hours ahead would be long ones.

The true patriot probably wanted the number '8' car with its predominately British crew to win, but whatever, there was going to be at least one Englishman at the wheel if a Bentley did win. A faint, if unsporting smile, may even have been raised when one of the Audis, baulked at the pits entrance, failed to refuel on time and stopped out on the track. Unfortunately, it was the Audi UK car, but every Audi out meant less pressure on the Bentleys.

At the end of the race one wondered why the concern. The Bentleys totally dominated and, if one beat the other, it was only because the number '7' car of Tom Kristensen, Rinaldo Capello and Englishman Guy Smith had experienced a trouble-free run. The car that Johnny Herbert and Mark Blundell shared with Australian David Brabham was victim to a number of niggling incidents and so was two laps down at the finish although Herbert had set the fastest lap.

The modern Bentleys first turned up at La Sarthe in 2001. The same year the MG Lolas also brought back a British flavour to the track. It was about time. Since Allan McNish's 1998 win there had been little

Oh, we of little faith. Was there ever any real doubt that the Bentleys would win in 2003? Here Guy Smith is almost at the end of the collective British nail biting. *(Author)*

to cheer about. The year 1999 had seen an excellent entry of works cars – none of them British unless you point to the fact that the BMWs and Audi R8Cs were built in England – and an exciting climax to the race, but that was between a German and a Japanese car. Steve Soper, who finished fifth in a privateer BMW, was the only British driver in the top 10. Having said that, if you had just watched or read the news in the following days you would have assumed that Scot Peter Dumbreck had been the star of the show, but more of his aviation exploits elsewhere.

The following year the Audis were well and truly upon us, but McNish was in the second-place car and took fastest lap. He also claimed the pole during practice. There was additionally victory for a Canadian-entered Lola B2K – driven by North Americans Greg Wilkins, Scott Maxwell and John Graham – in the newly introduced LMP 675 category. The team's manager, Brit Ian Dawson, was one of the few people in the team to have competed at Le Mans before. In recent seasons the 'second division' has often been a case of survival of the fittest and this year was no different, the only other surviving LMP 675 finishing eight laps back.

So to 2001 and the return of the green. The weather, one might say, was also somewhat British. It poured with rain, and the British were back in their droves to experience it. Two famous names were making a comeback. Bentley was present with two cars while MG also had a works team of what were called MG EX257s, but were in fact Lola B01/60s with AER engines. These were easily the fastest in the LMP 675 class but were deemed fragile. Lola's head of engineering Julian Cooper was to describe them as "a manufacturing project. We took more risks than we would have done with private customers". In this respect, although it was the spiritual predecessor to the B05/40 LMP2 that was to win its class in 2005, it was not initially seen as a customer car.

The rain dominated the race, but at one point Martin Brundle was able to take the Bentley he shared with Guy Smith and Stephane Ortelli into the lead for a short while. That car was to retire with gearbox maladies, but its sister, that of Andy Wallace, Eric

British representation was more obvious in 2001 and 2002. Here the sole Bentley leads one of the two MG Sport & Racing-entered cars. Although built by Lola, the latter were called MGs that year. (Bentley Motors)

van der Poele and Butch Leitzinger, went on to finish third behind the works Audis. The MGs also proved themselves quick, the Mark Blundell, Kevin McGarrity and Julian Bailey car briefly moving into third place during the first round of pit stops. But by midnight both the cars were out, one of them simply drowned. A British-built car did, though, survive to win the LMP 675 category, this being the French-entered and Volkswagen-powered Reynard of Pascal Fabre, Jordi Gene and Jean-Dennis Deletraz. Meanwhile, the performance of both the Bentleys and the MGs gave the British hope for the future.

Having said that, for the following year there was just the lone Bentley for Wallace, Leiztinger and van der Poele. MG had two cars again with an all-British line-up of Warren Hughes, Johnny Kane and Anthony Reid, and Bailey, McGarrity and Blundell. American team Knight Hawk Racing also had one of the MG-branded Lolas. In the GT class Morgan was back with a privateer Aero 8 entry that had factory support. One of those running the technical side of the project was Chris Lawrence, who in 1962 had finished first in the 2-litre class driving a Morgan. Drivers of the Aero 8 were another all-British trio of Richard Hay, Richard Stanton and Steve Hyde, all of them Le Mans virgins.

The lone Bentley made an excellent start and, despite turbocharger bothers which dropped it back to 18th at one point, it was able to hold off the rest of the field to finish the highest non-Audi in fourth place. Bentley again won the LM-GTP class but with no opposition this was somewhat meaningless. The void between the MGs and the rest of the LMP 675 class was obvious. However, rather than settle for a gentle category victory, the two works EX257s muscled with the big boys, one of them running as high as third after five hours. But they paid for their impudence, one or the other having led their class for 16 hours; one dropped out with a broken gearbox, the other with engine troubles. Again the LMP 675 victory went to a Reynard, with Deletraz partnered this time by Christophe Pillon and Walter Lechner.

On to 2003, and if the Audi teams thought they could compete on pit stops they were mistaken. The Bentleys were able to triple-stint their narrower tyres, also to make their 90-litre fuel tanks last for 14 laps, just one fewer than the Audis. The Capello, Kristensen and Smith car ran faultlessly; the Herbert, Brabham and Blundell car suffered minor niggles including a loose door headrest and the need for a battery change, which was why number '7' beat number '8' by those two laps. From a lead point of view it really was that simple.

In retrospect there never seemed any chance of an Audi win. However, the cause of the German cars received a knock when that Audi Sport UK entry retired early in the race having run out of fuel. Driver Frank Biela was in third spot when he missed his pit lane entry, having failed to negotiate a slower car. Another eight and a half miles were impossible and the British-run R8 ground to a halt at Indianapolis.

Elsewhere, though, it was a good year for the British, even if the MGs had not returned, at least not in works guise. Victory in the GTS class may have gone to a bright red Ferrari F 550 Maranello, but it has to be pointed out that this was developed into an endurance racer by Oxfordshire's Prodrive. Briton Jamie Davies was also one of its three drivers. The LMP 675 class fell to the previous year's victor, Noel de Bello's Reynard-Lehmann, driven this time by Jean Luc Maury-Laribiere, Didier Andre and Christophe Pillon. It seemed that a British chassis could win the category, just not a British entrant or driver. Easily the quickest in the class though was a new name to Le Mans, the DBA 03S, which unfortunately ran into problems early on. The car had started life as a Reynard design, a successor to the 2KQ that, while unloved, now seemed to be winning the class with regularity. With the demise of the Reynard company it became first an IRM and then, in deference to its sponsor, a Danish press group, the DBA. Significantly, in the wake of Reynard it was the go-ahead engineering group Zytek that took over, completing the car and fitting one of its engines. The DBA would be back at Le Mans – as would Zytek – having in 2003 at least shown its speed.

With Morgan having returned to La Sarthe the year before, this year it was the turn of TVR, an all-British line-up of Richard Stanton, Richard Hay and Rob Barff, and Tim Sugden, Mike Jordan and Michael Caine driving the two immaculate Tuscan 400Rs. However, one crashed early on, while the other suffered propshaft failure after 93 laps.

By the start of the 2004 season Bentley had been and gone, its task fulfilled. Practice, though, indicated plenty of reasons to wave the Union Jack as three cars fought for pole. True, two of them were Audis, but they came from the impressive Audi UK Team Veloqx. A bit of green, as had been witnessed on the previous year's entry, might have helped, but it could be said that their purple livery was the most attractive ever seen on an R8. Challenging them was a really British effort, both chassis and engine being built here. This was the Zytek 04S, successor to the DBA, driven by Andy Wallace as well as the rapid young Japanese Hayanari Shimoda, who had raced the 03S the year before, and David Brabham. Although the DBA was originally an LMP 675 design, the rules had been changed for 2004 and a number of the LMP 675s now found themselves in the new LMP1 class with the former LMP 900s.

For around an hour of practice the 04S held pole, and Zytek founder Bill Gibson could not hide his pride. "We've made them work for it. Audi has never been pushed like this before." He was optimistic, feeling that the gap in performance between the car's Michelin race and qualifying tyres was probably not as large as those on the Audis. As a former LMP 675 car the Zytek was expected to go a lot further on a set of tyres than the German cars.

"The ACO has done a good job of equating LMP 900s and LMP 675s. They have got it just about right," he said, then adding, "probably the LMP 900s have a slight advantage."

The British Audis, though, were having none of this. Coming through the last part of the Ford chicane on the pace lap, pole sitter Allan McNish was right up

on the kerb inches away from the green marker poles. Jamie Davies was right beside him, pushing hard. On the exit to the bend they rubbed flanks – the start line was still a few yards away, the race yet to start. It is said that the radio airwaves went blue. For the first hour Davies led the contest ahead of his team-mate while the Zytek gradually slipped back into the pack and was failing to fulfil its practice form. It was eventually to retire with a blown engine at about half-distance. The car, though, did appear a threat to the establishment and there were those who relished the thought of its return.

The second hour saw a pivotal point in the race. McNish was still running in second place just ahead of the American-entered Audi. Both cars then hit a patch of oil and water that had been laid down by the British-entered PK Sport Porsche GT3-RS in the Porsche curves. The Scot came off worse and it was some time before what looked like a pile of purple and black wreckage staggered down the pit lane. McNish jumped from the car and promptly collapsed. He was taken to hospital and advised not to race again that weekend. It seems amazing now that what looked like a pile of junk, with only two available drivers, Frank Biela and Pierre Kaffer, should even take any further part in the race let alone finish fifth.

The Herbert, Smith and Davies car was now well in the lead, but in the ninth hour the latter had to serve a stop-go penalty for passing under the yellow flags. The Japanese-entered Audi unlapped itself. The pendulum then swung each way before what was to be the only lead change in the whole of the 24 hours. Herbert brought the British Audi into the pits with a seized rose-joint in the left-hand rear suspension, the resulting pit stop losing them two laps. Now the Japanese car was a lap ahead. Davies, perhaps the star of the race (he also set fastest lap), set off after the leader with purpose. His verve and a few problems for the leader brought the Veloqx car back onto the lead lap. In the run up to the finish Herbert really pulled the rival R8 in. With an hour to go the gap was just 45 seconds. With the final pit stops over, it was down to 34 seconds. Time, though, was running out and following a trip across the gravel at the second Mulsanne chicane, the British driver had to settle for

In 2000 the only British-built representatives in the LMP 900 class were two Lolas and a Reynard, all foreign-entered. The Konrad Motorsport Lola B2K/10 retired during the evening after a wheel fell off at one of the Mulsanne chicanes. *(Author)*

Ray Mallock approaches Arnage in the privately entered Nimrod Aston Martin during the 1982 race. Note the protrusion above the windscreen that had to be installed to ensure the car passed scrutineering. *(Author)*

RAY MALLOCK

With only a short while to go in the 2005 race, the Ray Mallock-entered Lola was back in third place in the LMP2 class behind two French Courages. Then the car appeared to spin at the first part of the Ford chicane, hitting the gravel trap at speed and sending up a shower of tiny stones. It looked as if Mallock's quarter-century quest for a win at Le Mans was over for another year.

Disappointment at Le Mans is nothing new for Ray Mallock, yet he remains passionate about the place. Even the start of his first drive there in 1979, at the wheel of Martin Raymond's Lola T286, saw "a huge disappointment at the start. The car had run faultlessly during qualifying. We had the freshly rebuilt race engine fitted, and on the warm-up lap it started misfiring. (This was in the years before the race day warm-up.) I came straight in. We spent about two hours trying to identify the problem." It was subsequently found to be an ignition fault within the distributor. The engine ran fine up to half-throttle and then misfired after that. The weather

that year was particularly bad and Mallock's abiding memory of it is seeing the sky lit up by lightning as he drove down the Mulsanne straight. "It was like driving into a curtain of steel darts." In those conditions the fact that he only had use of about half-throttle was less of a penalty and, in fact, his was the fastest car on the track when it was at its wettest. However, at about 5.00am one of the rear calipers became detached from its mounting. Suddenly Mallock had no rear brakes heading for the Mulsanne corner. "I headed off down towards Tours." As the team had no spare third caliper, it plugged up the brake hose and the car carried on to finish 20th overall. "It was a challenging debut for me at Le Mans." It was Mallock's first ever sportscar event and he was captivated by the place. "It became my life's passion and still is."

Working closely with his father, the redoubtable Arthur Mallock, Ray was responsible for the chassis development of the Nimrod Aston Martins, initially on Viscount Downe's car which he raced himself in 1982 and 1983. Although the budget was "very low" and the car "too heavy to be competitive," Mallock "loved driving (it) at Le Mans." At one point the team ran as high as fourth. Work on the Nimrod took Mallock and his mechanic Willem Toet into the wind-tunnel (MIRA's) for the first time. Today Toet is chief aerodynamicist for the BMW Sauber team. The result was that the car, with three times the downforce and 10 per cent less drag, was 11 seconds faster at Le Mans the following year purely through changes to the bodywork. The 1982 seventh place, though, was the high spot of the Nimrod's three-year career there. However, powered by a turbocharged engine that was never used at La Sarthe, Mallock achieved the fastest ever lap of a closed circuit in the UK when he

PETER DUMBRECK

All was relatively quiet in the media centre when suddenly, on the monitors, a Mercedes-Benz CLR appeared to rear up into the sky and disappear towards the right of the screen. "The sequence," states Peter Dumbreck, the 'pilot' of said car, "must have made Eurosport a ton of money!" For the third time that week, one of the factory Mercedes has taken off like an airplane and, for a few days, its Scottish driver was to become world famous.

Quite how Dumbreck found himself in that Mercedes is a story in itself. In 1997 he was competing in the British Formula Three Championship and heard how one of the other drivers, Australian Mark Webber, had introduced himself to Mercedes' Norbert Haug at a Formula One race. "I thought that was a good idea and did the same at the British Grand Prix." For 18 months this fleeting moment was his sole contact with Mercedes.

The season ended with Dumbreck third in the championship. The following year he moved to Japan and won the F3 championship there outright. Driving through Tokyo at the end of the year he received a telephone call telling him that Norbert Haug would like a word with him. He pulled off to the side of the road to hear about the 1999 Le Mans project, which would require nine drivers. Would he like to be involved?

He first tested the previous year's car at the Italian track Vallelunga; "it was alien to me." Then he was introduced

to the new CLR LM-GTP machine for a 30-hour test at Fontana, in California. Thanks to a Formula Nippon deal that year, Dumbreck was certainly having to fly about the globe.

"We did a lot of miles in the car and nothing showed up at all. Nothing went wrong at pre-qualifying either. The problems only showed up in race week."

With the experienced Christophe Bouchut taking the lion's share of the driving, novice Dumbreck had a fairly uneventful practice with the exception of "a wee trip into the gravel at one point in the night. It's not good going back to a Mercedes pit after that kind of thing."

Then Webber, whose approach to Haug had also borne fruit, almost flipped one of the other CLRs halfway between Mulsanne and Indianapolis. "In my mind there was no reason why we should not continue." Then during the Saturday warm-up Webber again flew through the air, this time just before the Mulsanne corner. "We were now thinking what's that all about? From my point of view we were there to do a job. I was not concerned that it would happen to me. You never believe that you are the one that is going to crash."

Mercedes was down to two cars now, with three winglets fitted to either side of the nose to give more downforce. Dumbreck's car, with Bouchut at the wheel, started well. He and Nick Heidfeld shared the first three stints before handing the car over to him. The Scot admits

toured the Millbrook bowl at an average of just under 200mph.

In 1984 Mallock became responsible for the design and development of the Ecosse C2 cars that we have already met in Chapter 12. There is no doubt that he found creating these effective little machines very satisfying. Unfortunately their potential was not realized at Le Mans, although they did win the Manufacturers' Championship in 1986. Between 1982 and 1987 the whole year for Mallock and his company revolved around Le Mans. "There was huge anticipation, but frustration at not getting that elusive (class) win."

Mallock had one more year left at Le Mans as a driver, sharing an Aston Martin AMR1 with Davids Leslie and Sears. He feels that his driving suffered that year because of his responsibility for the technical development of the car. However, his involvement continued, including working with Nissan Performance Technology Inc in 1990. The Lola-chassised car run by the team traded the lead with the eventual race-winning Jaguar until a ruptured fuel cell put the car out at about 7.00am.

In the early 2000s Ray Mallock Ltd twice entered a Saleen SR7 – a competitive car designed from scratch at RML – in the GTS class, and then in 2004 a Lola B01/60, one of the former MG works cars. Still that elusive victory, even at class level, avoided Mallock's team. "We have come back from Le Mans a number of times with our balloons well and truly deflated."

In 2005, as so often before, it appeared a favourite to win its class, this time with one of the new Lola B05/40 LMP2 cars. But frustrating problems meant that a number of unscheduled pit stops kept putting the car back, but by 2.00pm it was third in class and running fast.

In 2005 it seemed that Ray Mallock's hopes had been dashed again. With less than two hours to go, suspension failure caused Thomas Erdos to spin into the gravel trap. The RML Lola was towed onto hard ground, enabling the Brazilian to three-wheel into the pits via the course vehicle entrance. Despite this drama, the team was able to snatch the LMP2 class in the dying minutes from an ailing Courage. *(Author)*

Tommy Erdos, Warren Hughes and Mike Newton were chasing the leading Courages hard. Then, as the race was seemingly coming to a close, Erdos appeared at the Ford chicane, charging backwards with suspension failure. As the car hit the gravel, Mallock thought "we've been here before."

This year, though, was to be different. A lightning corner change was carried out by the team. The two Courages were hardly healthy and, as they crawled towards 4.00pm so the Lola was able to catch and pass them.

"There was great relief that we had managed to beat the race at last. You begin to wonder whether it will ever happen. There was joy and lots of tears – we've shed those before for different reasons."

For 2006, Mallock was preparing to defend his LMP2 title, but now that he has at last tasted the victory that La Sarthe has surely owed him for so long, he has other plans for the more distant future. "Now we want to be able to put ourselves in a position where we can win outright."

that after "a lot of hanging around" and with his car ahead of its stablemate he was "dead nervous about letting the side down." However, his pace was good. "I was in control and happy." A red car appeared ahead in his sights, which he rightly assumed to be the second-place Toyota. Then, about to start his fifth lap, a GT Porsche turned into him in the Ford Chicane, making him angry. It may be that the Porsche knocked one of the winglets off at that point.

Dumbreck was now closing in on the Toyota under braking for the Mulsanne corner. However, it pulled away from him coming out of the bend. The Mercedes drivers had been warned about getting too close to the other cars for fear of disturbing the aerodynamics. However, there now seemed to be a sufficient gap to the car ahead for Dumbreck to feel it was safe to stay flat all the way down to Indianapolis.

"The rest is a bit of a blur. I remember the front of the car just coming up and seeing the blue sky and thinking 'it's a nice night tonight and I am going to have a crash.' I remember getting into a ball. It was like taking off in a 'plane. It happened really quickly but it was still, like slow motion. I don't remember any more."

Dumbreck has since heard various stories about how he got himself out of the car, although photographs show him being lifted out. However, his next flash of memory is of being held tight on a stretcher and trying to break free. Again, memory fails until he recalls being in a medical

centre or hospital and being visited by Mercedes reserve driver Darren Turner. He also recalls being asked to take a breath test, although "I could hardly breathe." The next memories are of returning to the track and meeting people "who thought I was dead." His wife Claire had gone up in a helicopter at the time and the first she knew of his accident was when *Autosport*'s Charles Bradley sent her a text to say he was "OK".

Dumbreck's Mercedes, in fact, had somersaulted several times in the air and landed on its wheels behind the guardrail. Luckily the trees had been cleared from this very spot the week before. However, a tree trunk still pierced the passenger's side of the car. Dumbreck ponders on the fact that he was not driving a British car, also that he landed backwards rather than forwards.

The next day he was flown by Mercedes to Paris and then on to England. By the Sunday night he was back in his own bed…and then at about 6.30am the phone started ringing. "For the next few days it never stopped." The name of Peter Dumbreck was broadcast in newspapers and on television across the world. A trip was made to London to appear on John Inverdale's sports show, although he was "still quite woozy."

Since 1999 Dumbreck has competed regularly at international level, in particular in the German DTM touring car series and in Japan. However, he still tends to be introduced as the man who flew at Le Mans.

The radio waves went blue as the two Audi UK R8s rubbed flanks even before the flag had fallen in 2004. (*Author*)

One year on and the first British-entered car is only seventh at the start. The leading GT car, currently in 15th place, is however an Aston Martin. (*Author*)

second. A repeat of 1969 was not on the cards.

Further back, the amazingly rebuilt second Audi UK car came home 29 laps behind the leaders. Briton Oliver Gavin was one of the drivers of the GTS-winning Corvette. The American team had turned the metaphorical tables on the Prodrive Ferraris. The first of these, third in class and ninth overall, had an intriguing driver line-up including Gavin's GT-class British rival Darren Turner and former World Rally Champion Colin McRae. The two Chamberlain-Synergy entered TVRs both finished. There seemed times in the race when they were inseperable. There was, indeed, only one lap between them at the finish. The sparsely entered second division, now the LMP2 class again, went to a British-built 'tortoise', this time the Lola B2K/40 entered by Intersport Racing but owned by Scot Bill Binnie and driven by Le Mans debutant Binnie, Rick Sutherland and Clint Field. A lone Morgan Aero 8, driven by teenager Adam Sharpe, Steve Hyde and Australian Neil Cunningham, was also still around at the finish, but following a troubled run which included some time stuck out at Indianapolis, failed to complete enough laps to be classified. Mention must also be made of the way in which the British were paving the way on the energy-efficient stakes, the Nasamax bio-ethanol team returning for a second year and Team Taurus running the first diesel to race at La Sarthe for over half a century. However, more of these anon.

After the potential of the Veloqx cars and the Zytek, there seemed to be no chance of a British entry winning overall at Le Mans in 2005. The French-entered Audi R8 was actually owned by Audi UK, not that this was

Having co-driven the Team Veloqx Ferrari to GTS victory the year before, Jamie Davies stayed with the squad when it moved up to the LMP1 class with an Audi R8. *(Author)*

THE MISSED PIT STOP

Le Mans 2003 was a disaster for the Audi UK team. It had entered its own Audi R8 with drivers Perry McCarthy, Mika Salo and Frank Biela. The latter was still on his first stint when, about two hours into the race, he missed the pit entrance and ran out of fuel. Team manager David Ingram explains:

"What we all think happened is that Frank was coming up to the pit entrance and there was a Panoz in front of him on the right-hand side of the track. He went to overtake him on the left and then pull into the pit entrance. As he got alongside the Panoz suddenly sped up. What he thinks happened was that the Panoz had missed a gear and was in neutral when he was closing on him. As he got alongside, the driver must have found the gear and spoilt Frank's trajectory into the pit entrance. He had to make the decision in a fraction of a second whether to have an accident or run out of fuel. That was it, game over.

"It just wasn't real, it wasn't happening. It hit me for six."

A film crew had been hired to make a 'fly on the wall' documentary about the race. Ingram recalls seeing the film crew. "The young lady producer was in floods of tears. It really got to me. I felt so sorry for the team . . ."

The film, it has to be said, is a triumph over adversity, a film about Le Mans with nearly all the action taking place at Sebring.

The Team Jota Zytek of Sam Hignett, Haruki Kurosawa and John Stack follows the Chamberlain-Synergy Lola onto the Mulsanne straight in 2005. Although not as developed as the absent works car, it was in fifth place when its transmission failed in the late morning. Unclassified, it still completed more laps than all but the first 11 finishers. *(Author)*

241

Despite being the only car to challenge the Audis in practice the year before, the works Zytek was declined an entry for 2005. However, by virtue of finishing second in the Le Mans Endurance Series, it was granted a place for the following year. Here it appears out of the mists at Spa to win the first 1000kms race of the year. *(Author)*

Although his R8 finished four laps behind the second-place Pescarolo, Allan McNish was still pressing during his final stint of the 2005 race. *(Author)*

obvious. And, what, no works Zytek? Amazingly the factory car, which had already won the Spa 1000kms that year and was to win again in Germany and the USA, was refused an entry. Gibson was mystified. Others muttered darkly about the Zytek's potential to beat the French Pescarolos. Almost ironically, the privately entered and far less developed Zytek 04S of Team Jota was allowed in, and came close to finishing, while the DBA, now British-run by Creation Autosportif and powered by a Judd V8, returned to Le Mans for a second time. British driver interest in the LMP1 class included McNish in an American-entered Audi, and Wallace and Jamie Campbell-Walter in the DBA. Martin Short was back, this time with two Dallaras, with himself driving the Judd-engined version.

As the race progressed, though, there was little British interest up front apart from McNish and a brief but magnificent run in second place, and maybe even first, by Short's Rollcentre Dallara. It was in the LMP2 and GT1 classes that we looked for glory and for some while it seemed as if the debuting Aston Martin DBR9s in the latter category would give the fans the chance to wave the Union Jacks vigorously. After success at Sebring and Silverstone hopes were running high despite the Corvette's record at Le Mans. It had to be remembered, though, that these were still early days for the DBR9 and to compete in the way that it did was pretty impressive. The yellow-identified car of David Brabham, Stéphane Sarrazin and Darren Turner eventually came a troubled third in class, but the orange-banded version of Tomas Enge, Peter Kox and Pedro Lamy, which had led for so long, retired with fuel problems.

With the Astons in problems and the leading British LMP2 car, the Lola B05/40 of RML (driven by Tommy Erdos, Mike Newton and Warren Hughes) back in third in class, it was beginning to look like a bleak year for the British. Then suspension failure caused the Lola to go off coming into the Ford chicane. It really did seem all over for another year. But amazingly the two Courages ahead of the Lola were in even greater trouble, and after a rapid corner change the car was back on the track to take a long deserved win for Ray Mallock's team. The British could still be victorious at Le Mans after all.

CHAPTER 30

RETURN OF THE GREEN CARS

"I would say that the British are amongst the most splendid soldiers in the world. Give them fair play and they are unconquerable." **(Private Benjamin Harris, 95th Rifle Regiment)**

The occasion was quintessentially British. All was green and the members of the press were being fed and watered with Pyms and cucumber sandwiches. Derek Bell was on hand to underline the illusion, for the event was taking place in the heart of France. The location was the Bentley hospitality complex on the inside of the Ford chicane, the date Friday, June 13, 2003.

In the next two days, the Bentleys had to win Le Mans, there was no question about it. "There was a tremendous pressure on everybody," recalls Bell.

The three private Audi teams, one of them Audi Sport UK, were talking up their chances, but there were many who felt that the Volkswagen Group would not be too amused if they rained on the final act of Bentley's three-year plan to recapture victory at its favourite race track.

The Bentley EXP Speed 8 certainly looked the part, purposeful when compared to the Audi R8's virtual non-styling. It was also solely built to win Le Mans while the Audi had a whole season to worry about. As Guy Smith, who raced both cars at Le Mans said, "they both do everything so well." However, he does point out that main and visually obvious difference between the two cars. "The big thing about the Bentley is that it has a roof and therefore it is amazingly quiet inside the car; very calm and very quiet, with none of the wind noise that you have in an Audi."

In late 2000 it was announced that Audi-owned and Norfolk-based rtn *(lower-case letters for racing team norfolk)* had been commissioned to build an LM-GTP car for Le Mans that was to carry the charismatic name of Bentley. Overseeing the project was South African Brian Gush, Bentley's director of chassis and powertrain engineering operations and motorsport director. rtn had already been responsible for the Tony Southgate-designed Audi R8C coupe that had appeared just the once in 1999. Consultant Southgate had now retired and rtn's chief designer, former Arrows, Lola, Nissan and TOM's man, Peter Elleray would take overall responsibility for the car. Veteran sportscar entrant Richard Lloyd, whose Porsche

956GTI had finished second overall in 1985, was to run the race team with Apex Motorsport.

The result was a fine chassis with an adapted version of Audi's turbocharged V8 engine mated to a new XTrac gearbox. If anything, it suffered from having originally been conceived to use the bulky Volkswagen W12 engine. Unusually it used Dunlop tyres. The rules stated that closed-top cars had to use 2-inch narrower tyres. Now the British really did have something to get excited about at Le Mans, particularly as MG was also returning with two EX257-badged Lola-AER LMP 675s.

The first 'EXP Speed 8' to be seen was, in fact, a test car that rtn had built to use the W12 unit, but had been converted to take a Nicholson McLaren-prepared Cosworth DFR V8. Painted green it was displayed at the 2001 Detroit Motor Show. The first genuine EXP Speed 8, chassis plate 002/2, which appeared some two

Bentley's return to Le Mans in 2001 was the beginning of a three-year project which involved intensive testing on other circuits between the cars' race appearances. For the Bentley EXP Speed 8 these included endurance tests at Paul Ricard, in the south of France, from February to May 2002. *(Bentley Motors)*

months later, really was new, with the exception of the engine.

The car complied with the LM-GTP regulations as opposed to the LMP 900 rules of most of its competitors. Indeed, in their victory year, 2003, the two Bentleys were the only LM-GTP cars entered. Apart from the closed cockpits of the GTP runners there was little that was different in the two sets of rules; the main dissimilarity was the maximum tyre width of 14 inches for the GTPs and 16 inches for the LMPs. Each had a maximum rim diameter of 18 inches. The larger tyres obviously gave better roadholding and acceleration in the lower gears and suffered less wear.

The Le Mans race conditions in 2001 were appalling. The screen's rain repellent spray-on film did not work as well as expected, while the Bentleys' wiper blades were only ever intended for pit lane use. *(Bentley Motors)*

Both Bentleys had gearshift problems in 2001 caused by the rain. The number '8' car was fitted with two new Megaline electronic control units during the night. *(Bentley Motors)*

Unlike the Audi R8C, which featured a monocoque plus roll-cage structure, the Speed 8 had a structural roof, having a 100 per cent advanced composite structure. It certainly looked different to anything else on the 2001 grid, although there was a hint of the Toyota GT-One car of the late 1990s. At the Le Mans test days 002/2 and its sister car 002/3 proved their worth with third and seventh fastest times. The driver line-ups were Andy Wallace, Butch Leitzinger and Eric van der Poele, and Martin Brundle, Guy Smith and Stephane Ortelli. As recorded, the latter were to retire, but the other car came home a most promising third in the rain, beaten by only two factory Audis.

At first, Team Bentley used the turbocharged 3.6-litre indirect fuel injection version of the Audi V8 that had been seen in the R8C. The size of the engine was increased to 4-litres for 2002, the year that the ACO restricted the maximum turbo boost for an LM-GTP engine to that of an open-top LMP. The EXP Speed 8 also now benefited from Audi's FSI direct injection system, first seen in the 2001 R8. The chassis remained basically unchanged for 2002, although the nose was shortened and the tail lengthened following a major wind-tunnel test programme in Switzerland. Elleray, though, was already working on a new design for 2003.

Only one car, chassis 002/6, was entered in 2002, driven by the third-place finishers of the previous year. The result was fourth place, the car again being the first non-Audi R8.

Everything was set for Bentley to win in 2003. There were no factory Audi R8s, only 2002-specification cars in private hands. The team changed to Michelin tyres, arguably an obvious move given that all the other front-runners used the French supplier, although of course these tyres would have to be of a different size to those of the LMP cars. The engines were the same, although restrictor size had been reduced under new regulations. Otherwise these were new cars. The team, though, was changed. Rather than use Apex Motorsport again, Bentley formed a new in-house team at rtn headed by John Wickham, who had been team manager for Apex. With no works Audis racing this year, personnel were also brought in from Joest Racing, who had been running the R8s. Audi Sport's Jo Hausner was to be race engineer on the winning car, 004/5, rtn's Paul Thomas on its sister, 004/3. Factory drivers Tom Kristensen and Rinaldo Capello were loaned to the team to partner Guy Smith. Mark Blundell, David Brabham and Johnny Herbert lined up in the other car. It was said that there were others who might have got a drive but were too tall for the low coupe.

The new car was built in one piece up to the level of the glass area, rather than the two halves of the 2001/2 car. The nose box was shorter and the tail cover extended further. Front wheel pods opened a route between the main fuselage and new wheel-covering fixtures, exposing the suspension linkages to the airflow. The EXP Speed 8's biographer Ian Bamsey says that this could almost be seen as a return to the outrigged cycle wings of the pre-war Bentleys. The frontal area of the cockpit was also reduced and

By the start of the 2003 race the Bentleys had been the subject of much media coverage and were probably the most photographed cars in the paddock and pit lane. With expectations running so high, a win was a 'must'. *(Author)*

the roof-mounted air intake of the 2001/2 cars was replaced by two side-mounted scoops to provide a greater, less perturbed airflow over the rear wing, thus increasing downforce. It was reckoned that no sportscar had borrowed so heavily from the then current single-seater aerodynamic thinking. The result, observed Smith, was a "meaner and more aggressive" looking car.

The 2003 EXP Speed 8s only raced twice. In practice for the Sebring 12-Hours the cars were quickest, only to be relegated to the rear of the grid because of the way in which the American scrutineers measured the diffuser height. The two cars carved their way up to third and fourth places from the back and that is where they stayed, ahead of them a pair of those Audi R8s. The annual Le Mans test event saw them first and third quickest. Again, an Audi was in the way. Life was not yet perfect and so Team Bentley travelled down to the Paul Ricard circuit in southern France for a 24-hour test. Pit stops at Sebring had not been as good as they should. That the team overcame this can be seen in the fact that the Bentley that was to win Le Mans spent less time in the pits than any other competitor, although the Audis were able to complete more laps between stops. The Bentleys were now quicker than the Audis virtually all the way round the circuit. Smith recalls that they were doing about 210-215mph down the Mulsanne straight. Interestingly, the two cars were not identical, the winning car running a higher downforce package, something that could be seen by the four, rather than two, stakes each side of the nose diffuser. Despite this, the laps times were almost identical and it was only because of a few niggling problems for the 'Grand Prix driver'-crewed

car that the two were not together at the end. A small consolation for the second-placed car was that fastest race lap by Herbert.

British Le Mans spectators may look back on 2003 with increasing nostalgia as the years go by. While it is conceivable that a car from a small English specialist manufacturer could win the race in the future, where is the mass-market vehicle manufacturer perceived as British that is likely to top the podium again? The Bentley, a green Audi? No way; the engine may have been an Audi but Bentley Motors headed the operation and rtn built the car. Even the multi-plate clutch was AP, as opposed to the Sachs clutch of the Audis, the brakes also by AP as opposed to Brembo (although the purist may point out, at this stage, that AP Racing

It was nearing the end of the 2003 race when this photograph was shot, which might explain the rather strange line taken by the second-placed car at the Ford chicane. *(Author)*

The DBR9s were built at Banbury by Aston Martin Racing, a joint venture between Aston and Prodrive. *(Ben Sayer)*

is now owned by the Italian Brembo concern). Both Bentley and Audi used British-built gearboxes, Xtrac in the case of the British car, Ricardo in the case of the German. Finally, for those who really do want an argument about the Britishness of the Bentley EXP Speed 8, was not the chassis of the Audi R8 made by the Italian racecar manufacturer, Dallara?

Aston Martin's motorsport business manager Sarah Durose pointed out how dissimilar her company's aim was to that of the Bentleys. "The reason our programme is different to the Bentley (Le Mans) programme is that, from the start, their objectives were clear in that it was only ever going to be a three-year programme whereas we would like motorsport to become an integral part of our strategy."

The Aston Martin DBR9s are built by Aston Martin Racing, a joint venture between the vehicle manufacturer and Banbury-based Prodrive. The latter, which had already created the 2003 GTS class-winning Ferrari F550 Maranellos, was given a five-year contract with Aston. Aston Martin Racing technical director George Howard-Chappell admits that the work carried out on developing the Ferraris "helped enormously." Twelve works and 20 customer DBR9s were ordered, the total of 32 harking back to the production of the DB3S.

Aston Martin Racing's technical director George Howard-Chappell (left) and Ian Ludgate ready for radio contact on the grid before the 2005 race. *(Author)*

Ian Ludgate, Aston Martin Racing drawing office manager, and his team started looking at how to convert a DB9 into a racecar during 2002. Ludgate had previously been working for Aston itself and for three years had been examining ways that the company could go racing. At one point there was even a possibility that a programme could be run in-house. However, a number of other companies were considered, and Prodrive "offered the best all-round experience and package."

In describing how his company approached developing the DB9 into a GT1 racecar, Howard-Chappell stated: "As with rallying and touring cars, you tend to look at the production car with a view to the parts you have to carry over and what it offers you as a donor car. What you get with the Aston Martin is a very nice V12 normally aspirated engine, and a very stiff, relatively light aluminium chassis. You get double-wishbone suspension and a shape that has some aerodynamic potential, although clearly it does not have the same aerodynamic potential as some other cars in its class. What you carry over essentially is the main structure of the car and the chassis, the castings of the cylinder head and the block, the shape of the car above wheel centre-line. Almost everything else is free."

In addition to the fact that the chassis has been modified in a number of ways that are allowed by the regulations, Ludgate points out that there have also been a couple of dispensations from the FIA and ACO to make it suitable. Thus, for example, the tunnel top has been modified so that a fuel cell can be fitted.

"Clearly it is a car running in the same class with a similar engine (as the Ferrari 550) so we knew the key things to look at and where the performance is derived from. That said, there are very few parts that are straight carry-over." He calculates that less than 20 components are the same on the two cars.

"However, there is certainly a theme there and in some areas the Aston Martin is essentially an evolution of the Ferrari. We learnt things that we needed to improve." As an example, Howard-Chappell cites the gearbox, which is basically the same Xtrac six-speed sequential unit as that run in the Ferrari but improved "in certain areas." The result is a lighter unit with a longer life.

The Ferrari was essentially a privateer programme with limited funds. Therefore, there was no opportunity to carry out an evolution of the car each year, as there might have been had it been a major manufacturer's project. The mechanical side of the Ferrari has been fixed since it first appeared. The Aston has given the Banbury operation the opportunity to evolve some of the ideas that had been started on the Ferrari.

A comprehensive aerodynamic programme was carried out. This was very different to the Ferrari, where there was no model programme, just a couple of full-scale wind-tunnel tests and then straight-line testing. However, the Ferrari was developed in 16 weeks; the DBR9 took around nine months. "If you put the two cars side-by-side you can really see that in the detail and the quality," says Howard-Chappell.

Work on the chassis was very different from a

The two Aston DBR9s in close formation as they exit the Esses early in the race. The different coloured nose bands distinguished the cars. *(Author)*

carbon car or a traditional steel monocoque. With the Ferrari, Prodrive had been used to working with a steel shell. "You weld your roll-cage into that and away you go." The Aston Martin features a bonded aluminium chassis. Howard-Chappell had some experience of this before as he was technically in charge of the Lotus Elise-based GT1 car in 1997. (Two Lotus GT1s were entered for Le Mans that year, one retiring after 121 laps, the other failing to qualify.) "So I knew a little bit about producing a competition chassis from a bonded aluminium structure." The challenge was that the roll-cage had to be made outside of the car as a single unit, it being impossible to weld the cage in place. The cage is thus dropped into the chassis while it is still on the jig and before the top assemblies are glued and riveted in place. Initially it is fitted in loose because of the different co-efficients of expansion, after which the chassis is placed in the oven with the roll-cage already inside. This means an extremely sound structure with the roll-cage integrating well with the chassis itself. "Essentially the chassis is a bit like an Airfix kit – a load of aluminium extrusion, glued and riveted but primarily glued together."

Ian Ludgate pays tribute to the co-operation of Aston Martin itself with regard to the roll-cage. "Obviously it had knowledge of the chassis and we wanted to make sure that the cage was well integrated. I gave Aston Martin my idea for the design of the cage and its integration into the chassis and it carried out analysis, making recommendations as to where it could be made lighter and stiffer."

The road car specification means that the DBR9 uses double-wishbone suspension – described by Howard-Chappell as "highly desirable" – all round. The pick-up points are free and here Prodrive relied heavily on its Ferrari experience with regard to geometry "with a few new ideas."

Between the axles the car features a flat bottom. Rearward of the rear axle the regulations permit a flat diffuser. There is a choice of where the break point is as long as it is not forward of the rear axle. It is not permitted to have more than 150mm change between the flat bottom and the top of the diffuser. The splitter forward of the front wheels is free. How the manufacturer blends the bumpers to the wheelarches is basically free as long as it is sympathetic to the road car. The sides of the cars below the doors are free as long as they do not encroach on where the original bodywork was. The rear wing is completely free as long as it fits within a 'box', and is not higher than the roof and further back than the rearmost part of the car. The majority of the cooling is essentially free. "It's definitely an aero formula. It's a key part of the performance of the car."

Howard-Chappell acknowledges the work done on the F550 as having an influence on the DBR9's engine. "We learnt a lot about making one of these engines go well from the Ferrari, but I don't think that there is a component in the engine that is the same. The Aston Martin is quite a different beast and gave us its own challenges."

The GT1 regulations state that the original cylinder block and head have to be retained. They also say that you can only move the engine as far back in the engine bay as possible without changing the internal dimensions of the cockpit. In other words you cannot move the engine bay bulkhead. Because of the way in which the engine bay is laid out, Aston Martin Racing

was able to move the engine further back and lower than in the Ferrari.

Jason Hill, Aston Martin Racing chief engineer – engines, points out that the engine was developed "with a cheque book rather than a rule book in hand." It was also designed so that it could be manufactured in reasonable numbers and to a consistent quality. It was additionally essential that the performance target should exceed that of the Ferrari. The design philosophy has been very different from the Ferrari for the Aston Martin has been developed to be made in numbers. As Hill points out, it is only when you intend manufacturing for as many engines as the DBR9 programme will use that you put down tooling for, for example, the sump.

"Clearly there will be people of different levels operating these cars," says Hill. His team used the robustness of the Porsche 996 GT3 as an inspiration in order to overcome this. "We tried to head further in that direction than we did with the Ferrari," adds Hill, who was in charge of both programmes. "The F550 needed a certain amount of attention all the time although it has proved to be a very successful customer

car. With the Aston we have gone further and created a car that can be operated without an awful lot of assistance. This comes down to details in the design."

The Aston Martin DBR9 brought a new dimension to the GT field in 2005. It is truly within the spirit of the regulations, being based on a genuine, existing road car and it brought a famed name back to the sport. Following its class win at Sebring and then overall victory at the Silverstone TT, hopes were high for Le Mans.

The GT1 class was extremely close, with the two Astons in hourly combat with a pair of Chevrolet Corvettes. Even when the lead car had dropped back with problems, Ian Ludgate was still optimistic, pointing out that the DBR9 was quicker than the American car. "Don't worry," he said to a concerned Brit. The fairy tale return was not to be, though, and with less than two hours to go, all hope of a happy ending was finally shattered as the quicker car of Tomas Enge, Peter Kox and Pedro Lamy succumbed to a fuel-related malady and that of David Brabham, Darren Turner and Stephane Sarrazin dropped back to third in class with a radiator problem.

DAVID INGRAM

Technical public relations manager David Ingram first made the journey to Le Mans in 1982, has never missed a year since, and has progressed from Page & Moy customer – sleeping in the coach – to team manager of the pre-race favourites.

As an Audi employee he already knew Porsche 924 entrant Richard Lloyd, so that first year he took advantage of this by visiting him in the paddock. Lloyd decided to buy a Porsche 956 for 1983 with sponsorship from Canon. He needed "a tall bloke" to help with refuelling and so he asked Ingram if he would be able to take a few long weekends off during the year. "That was when I fully appreciated the whole element (of Le Mans)."

Ingram stayed with Lloyd for a few years, but had to stop helping out when the latter embarked on the whole World Sports Car Championship and he was unable to take enough time off work. He could not miss Le Mans, though, so like so many others he piled in a car with a tent and some "mates" from work. That started a run of staying in the campsites, finding ways of getting to the inside of the circuit next to the Mulsanne straight or out to the famed restaurant on the other side. There was also the matter of a lap of the circuit on "push bikes."

He did say to himself that he would not go every year, and one year this nearly happened. In 1992 he was working for Audi in Germany, and it was late in pre-race week before he decided that he could not really miss out, so despite not having his tent with him he jumped in the car and set off for the track. He turned up late on the Friday and slept in the car. A year later, when he was back working in Milton Keynes, he discovered that there was already a group of Le Mans stalwarts that went from Audi's UK base.

"I love driving down there, I love staying at the circuit during the race and I love listening to Radio Le Mans."

Audi entered touring car racing in the UK in 1996, which gave Ingram the opportunity to meet the company's motorsport boss Dr Wolfgang Ullrich. "If there was a clash between a touring car race and Le Mans then my touring car responsibilities missed out." However, he had no indication at that time that Audi would move into sportscar racing. The first inkling came in 1997, and when the decision was made, for Ingram "it was like a dream come true." It soon transpired that the company would be entering two types of car, the roadster and the coupe, and that the construction and development of the latter would be carried out in the UK with Richard Lloyd running the car. This enabled Ingram to be close to the Audi sportscar programme from the very beginning.

It was, he recalls, "a fun year, almost a comedy routine from start to finish," thanks in particular to the crew of one of the R8Cs, Andy Wallace, James Weaver and Perry McCarthy. His does add, though, that when the trio were in the car they were "consummate professionals."

During the 'works' years, Ingram and Audi PR man Martyn Pass exploited Audi involvement with the British media and he even found himself on the end of a microphone with Radio Le Mans. "These were my heroes and here they were asking me questions." He admits to still listening to Radio Le Mans "with reverence" despite the fact that the broadcasters are now good friends.

In 2003 Audi decided not to field a works team, but Audi UK bought its own R8. Director Kevin Rose had asked the previous year why the British operation could not run its own car "and that was all the encouragement I needed," says Ingram. Mike Earle was contracted to run the car, starting at Sebring, where it finished sixth following a gearbox problem. Then Le Mans turned into a disaster when Frank Biela failed to pit and ran out of fuel, as recounted elsewhere. This meant that as far as Ingram was concerned Le Mans was unfinished business. He was determined to be back, but at the time not sure how. Then he received a call from Dr Ullrich asking if he knew Sam Li, who had a racing team based in Brackley, wanted to win Le Mans, and knew that the only way he could achieve this was with an Audi. So they put a programme together to run a two-car team in the 24-Hours and the Le Mans Endurance Series, one with an all-British line-up in one of the R8s. "We had a wonderful year," winning the LMES and finishing second at Le Mans by less than a minute. Ingram admits that the Le Mans result was also "disappointing." However, it was a long way from that Page & Moy coach 22 years previously. Now he dreams of possibly running an R10. Whatever his involvement, "I cannot consider a year when I do not go to Le Mans."

Never happier than when he is at Le Mans, David Ingram first visited the circuit for the 1982 race and has not missed a year since. *(Author)*

Can it be that Hawaiian Tropic girls are more attracted to refuellers than racing drivers? Jonathan Palmer (far right) wonders why; David Ingram (centre) is not complaining. *(David Ingram collection)*

It's inside the Audi A6 TDI diesels.

The Audi R10 V12 TDI - the world's most powerful diesel racing sports car - winner at Sebring, the opening race of the 2006 American Le Mans series. You too can discover the TDI power that helped the R10 to its maiden victory, because its technology is inside all Audi TDI diesel engines. For more information on the Audi A6 see the Audi channel on Sky Guide number 884 or visit www.audi.co.uk
Vorsprung durch Technik

Official fuel consumption figures for the Audi A6 diesel range in mpg (l/100km) from: Urban: 23.5 (12.0) - 32.1 (8.8), Extra Urban: 42.8 (6.6) - 56.5 (5.0), Combined: 33.2 (8.5) - 44.1 (6.4). CO_2 emissions 172 - 229g/km.

Chapter 31

GUY SMITH

"Perhaps even they will form a band of their own and revive the days of the 'Bentley Boys'." (**Sir Henry Birkin,** *Full Throttle*)

In theory, Guy Smith should not have been in Bentley number '7' for the final stint in 2003. "I thought my job had been done," he recalls; he looked forward to enjoying the final hours as his team-mates ensured the victory. But engineer Jo Hausner had different ideas. The whole spirit of this very BRG team was British, and it was appropriate that, being Yorkshire-born, Smith should take the chequered flag rather than a Dane or an Italian. Hausner accordingly shuffled the stints around.

For Smith this meant conflicting emotions. There was, of course, the glory. The new 'Bentley Boys' had

been told of their history, their heritage, just what it meant to be the successors of Barnato, Birkin and Benjafield. All being well, Smith would be the first British driver to take the winner's flag in a Bentley since 1930. Indeed, he would be the first British driver to carry out a victorious final stint in a British car for many a long year.

Then there was the downside. "I was extremely nervous. What if I crashed or the engine blew? I could feel a lot of pressure." The large Rolex clock at the start line grew even larger; it was in Smith's face every time he exited the Ford chicane. "I was sure it wasn't

Back in the car for the final driving stint and understandably Smith is grappling with mixed emotions as the Le Mans race draws to a close. *(Author)*

moving. It was the longest two hours of my life." This is a good point to bring in the cliché, uttered by so many at Le Mans, that there was still more than the length of a Grand Prix to go.

Many things were going through his mind. "You even start to write your own headlines." At the same time, he was intently listening to every sound the car made, anxious that none of them would herald a problem. He had heard of too many drivers who had lost Le Mans in the closing stages. Then came the final quarter of an hour and the realization that to all intents and purposes the team could not be beaten. There was talk of a formation finish with the second-placed Bentley, but Smith felt that this was courting danger. Driving slowly to let Johnny Herbert catch up, he was more likely to do something silly than if he continued to proceed at a reasonable speed. Smith decided to ignore that script.

However, for about the final lap and a half he was cruising, as should have been most of the field at that point, apart from a Panoz and a Courage that were almost trading paintwork in a frantic last-minute

battle for fifth. It was then that Smith began to hear the crowd and to see the waving flags. Sitting enclosed in the Bentley's cockpit, he found it "quite eerie, quite surreal."

He now thinks back on history. "It makes you realize how privileged you are to win Le Mans…and to do it in a Bentley." Initially, though, it did not sink in. Straight after the finish he saw his father Peter who, as the boss of Swift Caravans, had sponsored Dave Scott in Formula Three and Formula 3000. "I've won Le Mans, I thought. He's won Le Mans, he thought, but there was a kind of disbelief." On the podium there was pure elation, coupled to simple relief and a natural feeling of tiredness. Down below there was "a sea of people," many of them waving the green Bentley flags. "You could feel the emotion of everyone. I had just won one of the biggest races in the world…and in a Bentley, but it took a week to sink in."

Guy Smith was brought up in a motorsport environment. Father Peter had been a decent amateur rally driver as well as Dave Scott's sponsor. "I really used to idolize Dave," says Smith. Scott sourced a couple of karts for the young Smith and the boy learnt his craft out in the orchard, his father soaking the grass with a hosepipe. "At that age your reaction is to put on opposite lock…I would race anyone who came to the home."

Aged 10, Smith entered kart racing properly – with his father as mechanic – coming second in the senior World Championship in 1991. Later that year he competed in a Formula First winter series having just passed his driving test the week before the opening race. There followed a Formula Ford series in New Zealand and a tantalizing series of single-seater championships – second in Formula Vauxhall Junior, third in Formula Ford and third in Formula Vauxhall.

Then, in 1995, he became a champion, winning the British Formula Renault series.

Two years followed in Formula Three, the first as the team-mate at Fortec of future Grand Prix winner Juan-Pablo Montoya. Smith won his first F3 race, at Silverstone, but hampered by Mitsubishi engines, could only finish the season sixth, one place behind the Columbian. The following year he describes as "a disaster." Where to from there? As far as Smith was concerned, "Formula 3000 was too hit-and-miss and very expensive." His next move was to take him, ultimately, on the way to sportscars and to Le Mans.

Smith's first Le Mans 24-Hours was in 2000, driving the Johansson Matthews Racing Judd-engined Reynard 2KQ. (He was still to be driving with North Carolina food industrialist Jim Matthews in the North American Grand-Am series five years later.) Significantly for Smith's Le Mans future, the team manager was John Wickham. The car retired in the night with engine failure, but "John Wickham thought I'd done a good enough job." Obviously so, for Wickham was shortly to be appointed team manager of the exciting new Bentley project. The famed team was coming back to Le Mans for the first time since 1930 and a young British driver was sought. "John Wickham pushed my case," recalls Smith, acknowledging how much he owes the man.

Smith had first come to know the co-owner of the Reynard team, former Grand Prix driver Stefan Johansson, some two years previously when, despairing of Formula 3000, he had investigated the possibility of racing in the North American Indy Lights single-seater series. In the USA he had met Johansson ("typical Stefan, very friendly … European") and the

Swede had invited him to join a new team that he was building. Smith finished that year in second place in the championship – with two wins and three pole positions – behind Cristiano da Matta, who was to move up to become Champ Car Champion and then into Formula One. Smith stayed in Indy Lights the following year, moving to the championship-winning Tasman/Forsythe team and starting the season as favourite. Unfortunately, most of the mechanics who had run da Matta had moved up to Champ Car with him and it was the team's last and, sadly, lacklustre year in Indy Lights. Smith then wanted to move up to Champ Car himself, but there were no opportunities. Concerned with the way his career was going, he asked his former team boss for advice. The Swede was now looking to set up a sportscar team with Jim Matthews to race in the American Le Mans Series. "He said I could drive with him and I thought this might do me some good." At the time, though, he did not really see sportscars as a career path.

The Reynard proved very fragile. During the Daytona 24-Hours, the team had to change five gearboxes. "One missed shift and the gearbox was gone." However, the American race gave Smith his first taste of sportscars racing against the BMWs and Audis. "It was at Daytona that I got my love of sportscars, seeing the sun coming up at the start of the day."

Following the Daytona and Sebring races, Matthews, disappointed by the car's lack of speed, sent it back to the factory for modification. At Le Mans it lasted, running in the top 10, until the very early hours of the morning, when it retired with engine failure. Smith, though, had done enough to impress John Wickham.

Sitting waiting for Guy Smith's first Le Mans, the Johansson Matthews Racing Reynard 2KQ. From the start of the 2000 race it stayed in the top 10 until its Judd engine expired in the middle of the night. *(Author)*

The 'baby' of the Bentley team in 2001, Smith was teamed with Martin Brundle and Stèphane Ortelli. He believes one of the benefits of sportscar racing is that it brings young drivers into contact with experienced ones, not as competitors but as team-mates. "The way that Martin Brundle debriefs is amazing. If you are smart as a young driver you learn from these things."

Brundle started the Bentley at Le Mans, initially in changeable conditions. He led some of the early laps, but began to find the gearshift system was developing a mind of its own. By the time Smith took over the problem seemed to have solved itself, but the rain had begun to fall heavily. "We were running first or second and everyone was looking at me!" The rain became torrential; the inside of the cockpit began to fog up and the wiper blades to lift. Smith was even aquaplaning behind the pace car that had been sent out. Water was also getting inside the brake cooling ducts and onto the gear-shifting sensors.

In the fifth hour of the race the car became stuck in sixth gear going into Indianapolis. Despite slipping the clutch, he was unable to avoid stalling at Arnage. "In hindsight I should have gone straight across the grass." Smith then attempted to nurse the car back to the pits on the starter motor, but unlike team-mate Andy Wallace with his similar problem, only got as far as the exit of the Porsche curves. In trying to restart the car he had caused neat fuel to get into a turbocharger. This started a small fire, damaging the turbocharger, bodywork and wiring. None of this was terminal, but the clutch plates disintegrated and the clutch was welded solid. As the night closed in Smith abandoned the car.

He would not be back the following year, at least, not as a competitor. The Bentley master plan was to run one car in 2002 and two again the following season, with Smith promised races at Sebring and Le Mans that year. He was also retained as test driver.

Jim Matthews was now running a Riley & Scott Mk IIIC in America and invited Smith to race the next year at Daytona with Scott Sharp, Robbie Gordon and himself. The team led for most of the 24-Hours, but lighting problems intervened and they finished a close second. "Daytona is always good fun to do." Smith also went to Sebring, finishing third. Matthews would have liked him to be with the team for Le Mans, but Smith was down as reserve driver for Bentley and therefore unable to race there for anyone else. Matthews' team was to retire in the early hours of the morning with a broken engine.

The spectating Smith "became a fan" and went out on his own to find out what Le Mans was all about, including visiting the famous funfair; clearly, the track has a certain magic for him. He first went there in 1991 and to the little kart circuit inside the Porsche curves that was host to the World Karting Championship. "I remember just looking at the track and being amazed by the sheer size of it. One day, I said, I would be back to race there."

Nine years later he really was back. "I went to look at the kart track, curious to see it again. I had good memories of it, having so nearly won the World Championship. I could not believe how small it was."

Following the karting event he was not to return to the track again until he drove for the Johansson Matthews team. "There were more people at

Nervous tension turns to elation as Smith becomes the first Englishman to take victory at Le Mans in a Bentley since 1930. *(Bentley Motors)*

THE LADIES

The ladies at Le Mans have so far had scant mention in this book. Perhaps that is not surprising. It may be politically incorrect to point it out, but most regard their trip to Le Mans as something of a lad's event and only one British female driver has taken part in the race since the Second World War. Betty Haig shared a blue 2-litre Ferrari 166MM Berlina with France's Yvonne Simon in 1951, the car being, it was said, "driven fast and well". The pair finished 15th overall and won the *Coupe des Dames*.

Before the war matters were very different, as personified by the all-ladies MG team entered by George Eyston in 1935. Joan Richmond and Mrs Gordon Simpson, Doreen Evans and Barbara Skinner and Margaret Allan and Collen Eaton crossed the finishing line in eighth, ninth and tenth places respectively. Other British lady drivers from the period were Dorothy Champney, the Hon Mrs Chetwynd, Marjorie Eccles, Prudence Fawcett, Kay Petre and Joan Riddell. Only Petre and Richmond participated more than once, the former, who drove both Riley and Austin, coming 13th in her only finish in three starts. There has been talk of a ladies entry in recent times that would include a British element with Chamberlain-Synergy entering Amanda Stretton in a Lola B98/10 for the 2005 Silverstone 1000kms to indicate its viability.

Attitudes, of course, change. A magazine article in the 1950s reported Tony Rolt's wife, Loïs as waiting with "a flask of hot coffee and an encouraging smile" for every pit stop. "The greatest excitement is the twenty-four hour race at Le Mans," Mrs Rolt told the journal. "Then Mrs Hamilton, Mrs Walker and I do the catering – which means cooking bacon and eggs interminably through the night for a hungry works team of thirty men."

Guy Smith's wife Alicia reports that the race is "fun, and better if there are other drivers' wives and girl friends around that you can spend time with." At Le Mans in 2004 she was with Allan McNish's wife Kelly and Jamie Davies' girlfriend Andrea. "When the boys are busy doing their thing we have to say that they are in 'race mode'.

Alicia Smith, Guy's wife, proudly displays one of the victors' Le Mans trophies. *(Author)*

They will be completely focussed so we will keep out of the way. At Le Mans we all had our different motor homes but hung out together." During the night they would take turns sleeping and listening to the race, depending on whose partner was driving at the time. "You can't really have a good night's sleep while your other half is going round at a hundred and something miles an hour."

At 1.00am the trio went up in the famed Ferris wheel. As it reached its zenith so they could see the Audis below them. "I saw Guy at about 10 minutes before the race started and then 10 minutes after. The days of handing the driver the hot coffee as he jumps from the car are long over.

"Fantastic," says Alicia of the 2003 race. "When Guy brought the car over the finishing line I was in tears. I was so pent up with emotion." There was perhaps too much happening around the Bentley pit, so Alicia, along with Guy's father, Peter and sister Frances had chosen to watch the finish from the grandstand. "Trying to find Guy after the race was a nightmare. There were people everywhere. I saw him over a fence for, literally, five seconds before he was dashed off again."

Bentley repeated history with a victory dinner at the *Savoy Hotel* in London. From the left: Derek Bell joins the winners Kristensen, Capello and Smith as the second-place crew of Herbert, Blundell and Brabham strike a suitable pose beyond the car. *(Bentley Motors)*

scrutineering than I had seen in all my previous races put together. Why, I wondered, did people want my autograph? I remember really enjoying it as the atmosphere just builds and builds. It made me realize this is a really big race."

On behalf of Bentley he spent 2002 pounding round Snetterton and Paul Ricard helping to develop the 2003 car that was so different from its predecessors. Towards the end of the year he had the chance to try it on Michelin tyres for the first time, recalling that it was "incredibly quicker."

The following year he went into the record books. He was placed in what was regarded as the sportscar drivers' team, for the number '7' car; the number '8' car was regarded as for the Formula One drivers. "We didn't have the fastest car in 2003 but we had the best strategy." The number '7' was also recording a better fuel mileage. The car, however, lost ride height and seemed prone to porpoising. Smith will eagerly show you film of the race to illustrate this. However, as he says, "we just got on with it."

Smith recalls there was "a great atmosphere" in the team, especially in 2003. "There were no egos." Bentley encouraged its drivers to be 'Bentley Boys' and rewarded them afterwards with dinner at the Savoy, an echo of past glories. Smith remembers the menu for that event, a copy of the one from 1927 but with pictures of the 2003 winners.

There was to be one more foray into single-seaters. The inexperienced Nelson Philippe and Paul Gentilozzi's Rocketsports Racing team had parted ways halfway through the 2003 Champ Car season. Smith was drafted in to replace Philippe and came 10th in his first race. However, Rocketsports was not a front-running team and "the rest of the season was disappointing". Smith says that he enjoyed his time racing open-wheeled cars in North America, "but now my heart is concentrated on sportscars. They were not necessarily my first choice, but they proved to be the best thing that has happened in my career."

Smith's Le Mans story does not, of course, end with the Bentley win, although he muses: "I wish Bentley could have done a couple more years." He had been forging links with the Audi UK and Team Veloqx people and had driven one of the latter's Ferrari F550 Maranellos at Spa and Donington during 2003. Sam Li's operation moved up in 2004 to run two Audi R8s for the British importer and Smith was invited to join the team for Sebring and Le Mans, where three drivers would be required.

His team led early on at Le Mans, but into the second of a planned three driving shifts, Smith felt the left rear drop slightly. The problem caused the car to understeer and to make the front tyres work much harder. The car was by then a lap ahead of the Japanese Audi, but it was losing one or two seconds a lap. A third stint was ruled out and engineer Ed Turner decided that the problem, a seized rose-joint, had to be fixed if the following car was not to catch up. It took seven minutes, enough to drop the car a lap behind the new leader. Smith and his co-drivers Johnny Herbert and Jamie Davis raced hard to make up that deficit, but the Japanese team remained calm and the time ran out. "I really thought I was going for a second victory," says Smith.

Le Mans in 2005 was notable for the names that were missing, including the above trio. During that season Smith raced in the Grand-Am series for Matthews as well as at Sebring and Petit Le Mans with Dyson Racing, finishing second in the Atlanta event. "When Petite comes I hope to make an impact," he had said earlier in the season. That he undoubtedly did for his Lola, which had been running second, then fell back to 16th when a wastegate pod failed. In the eight hours that followed Smith and co-driver Chris Dyson hauled it back onto the podium. As a result, the 2006 season saw him with full-time drives in both the American Le Mans Series and Grand-Am championships for the Dyson team.

In November 2005 Smith joined the Chamberlain Synergy team to help it maintain its position at the top of the Le Mans Endurance Series LMP2 table. Driving

A year after his victory, Smith was back at Le Mans with an Audi Sport UK R8 in which he shared the driving with Jamie Davies and Johnny Herbert; they led the race for the first 15 hours. *(Gavin Ireland)*

its Lola B05/40 at Istanbul with regular pilots Gareth Evans and Peter Owen, he finished second in class behind RML's similar car, thus clinching the series for the team and the driver's championship for Evans. He certainly rang the neck of the Lola that day and there were those who described him as the star of the show.

Lola reckoned him to be the fastest driver to have sat in one of its LMP2 cars all year.

May be these results will have helped Smith again get a top drive at La Sarthe. "I cannot afford to miss Le Mans again," he said candidly, mid-way through the 2005 season.

MARTIN SHORT

Martin Short is not sure whether he did, or did not, briefly lead at Le Mans in 2005, although Radio Le Mans and Eurosport seemed to think so at the time. Whatever, given the great performances – with scant reward – that his independent Rollcentre team had put in over two years, it is fitting to think that he did, indeed, lead the field.

Former airforceman Short was first entered for Le Mans in 2002, but team-mate Sam Hancock had crashed their JMB Ferrari F360 Modena at the karting corner before he had a chance behind the wheel. Two years later Short was back with one of the two ex-Oreca Dallara prototypes that he now owned. His co-drivers were fellow countryman Rob Barff and Portuguese Joao Barbosa. At 7.20am Short hit the wall, also in the karting section, when his left-hand rear suspension collapsed. At that point an overall fourth place had looked on the cards. It had been an underdog performance the British fans could appreciate.

Rollcentre took both of its Dallaras to Le Mans in 2005. Short was teamed up with Barbosa and Vanina Ickx, daughter of six-times winner Jacky, in the Judd-engined car. Le Mans 'rookie' Bobby Vernon-Roe drove with Michael Krumm and Harold Primat in the now Nissan-powered version. During the early evening Barbosa had taken advantage of the problems besetting the pre-race favourites, the Pescarolos, and had hustled the car up

from ninth to second place. It was proof that the 2004 performance had not been a one-off. The team was triple-stinting and its pit stops were particularly slick. Short freely admits that he expected the car to slip back down to fifth once he took over. It did not help that this was the only stint when the radio was not functioning.

The safety car was out at this point to clean the track in the Mulsanne-Indianapolis section. With pit stops also taking place at this time and no radio, Short was unsure as to his race position. He could feel the power steering playing up and knew that it was only a matter of time, once the safety car had gone in, before he was overtaken. Sure enough, an Audi "came cruising up behind me. I thought he must have been lapping me. I obligingly let him through."

Was Short in the lead at that point? "Some people say I was, some people say I wasn't." It would seem almost churlish to check the ACO's records. In the hourly charts the car was officially as high as third at the end of the first four hours – a magnificent performance. Sadly the steering put paid to a decent result and the car soon dropped out of the top 10. Rollcentre's other Dallara retired at 11.00am with an oil leak and suspension breakage. Short's own car eventually finished 16th; however, he was later to win the inaugural Silverstone 24-hours race at the wheel of a Mosler.

Joao Barbosa, seen here towards the end of the 24 hours, enabled Martin Short to take over in second place early in the 2005 race. The Cambridgeshire entrant was aiming to return in 2006 with the first Radical LMP2 car. *(Author)*

Ed Morris, then only 17, practised the Tracsport Tampolli for the Silverstone 1000kms in 2005. For 2006 he planned to progress to Le Mans and claim the title of the youngest ever Englishman to compete there. (Author)

Having been the youngest Englishman to compete at Le Mans in 2004, Adam Sharpe moved on a year later to become the youngest to mount a class podium there driving a Courage C65 for Paul Belmondo's team. (Adam Sharpe)

THE YOUNGEST

When Adam Sharpe stood on the LMP2 podium in 2005 he was thought to have been the youngest Brit to reach this exalted position, having been born in 1984. He had, indeed, still been a teenager when he had made his Le Mans debut the year before at the wheel of the works Morgan. Now he had achieved second place in the LMP2 race of the 'walking wounded', driving one of Paul Belmondo's Gulf Courages.

At the beginning of 2006 it was announced that a contender had arisen for Sharpe's record as the youngest Brit to race at Le Mans. Teenager Ed Morris had been down the previous year to drive a Tampolli LMP2 in the Silverstone 1000kms. For 2006 he was to be entered for Le Mans in Franck Hahn's G-Force Racing Courage alongside Vanina Ickx. If he were to start it would make him the youngest ever Briton in the race at 18 years and one and a half months, just a few days older than the outright record-holder. Morris is no Formula One 'wanabee'. "I have set my heart on Le Mans," he says.

CHAPTER 32

THE GREEN GOES GREEN

"A warm welcome to the future of motorsport."
(Motorsport Industry Association brochure)

By the year 2005 interest had grown strong in the subject of what sounds like a contradiction in terms, namely environmentally friendly motor racing. In Britain, the pro-active Motorsports Industry Association was enthusiastically promoting what it called EEMS (Energy Efficient Motor Sport). In France, during the week prior to Le Mans, two significant announcements were made. The French manufacturer Peugeot announced that it would be returning to the race in 2007 with a diesel-engined LMP1 car. Then the ACO stated that it was introducing an award for the most environmentally friendly competitor, bringing back memories of its Index of Thermal Efficiency prize first run some four decades previously. The winner of the new award (announced some months later as the overall race-winning Audi) would be judged on a range of criteria including engine type, emissions and noise level.

At an Audi conference the day before the race it was former entrant and racer Alain de Cadenet who

was bold enough to repeat the question so many had already been asking over the previous months. Would the German car manufacturer also be entering a diesel car? Head of Audi Motorsport Wolfgang Ullrich again refused to confirm that there would even be a new car of any kind. Most believed, though, that Audi would replace its all-conquering R8 with a diesel contender, and sure enough, in the December it duly launched the R10, a twin-turbo TDI-engined car. It was like the midwife proclaiming "it's a boy," months after the parents had seen the scan. (It soon became apparent that one of the R10's drivers at Le Mans would be Scot, Allan McNish.)

Despite the French and German interest, it must be pointed out that in recent years it has been the British who have led the way at Le Mans on the subject of energy efficiency. Small, independent teams like Nasamax and Team Taurus took alternatively fuelled cars to Le Mans in the years immediately before either Peugeot or Audi made their announcements. Zytek

It was the British who led the way by being the first for 50 years to run a diesel-fuelled car at Le Mans. The Team Taurus Lola exits the Ford chicanes during the opening laps of the 2004 race. *(Author)*

has also stated that it may appear with something even more radical for 2007. However, none of this interest in fuel efficiency is new to the British. Nasamax, Taurus and Zytek had spiritual predecessors in the shape of the teams which contested the Index of Thermal Efficiency awards in the 1960s.

The Index of Thermal Efficiency may have been brought about, as Team Elite member John Wagstaff, who was the second winner of the prize, recalls, in order to give the French DB-Panhards something to win, but it did show the ACO's commitment to EEMS many decades before the term was coined.

In 1959, its first year, the Index had the ACO's desired effect in that it produced a French win, and the award had not even entered Team Elite's consciousness until about halfway through the following year's race. Wagstaff is not sure exactly when it began, but slowly it started to dawn on the team that it stood a chance of winning this strange new award. It was probably Lotus' Mike Costin, who was assisting the team at the time, who noticed it first. The sheer complexity of the prize formula made it difficult to grasp, but as Wagstaff happily recalls, it ranked second to an overall race win in terms of both prestige and prize money. Whilst the outright victory would be rewarded with approximately £3750, the winning team in the Index of Thermal Efficiency would take home a relatively generous £2250, whereas the Index of Performance victory was to be worth a mere £1875.

Derbyshire Lotus distributor David Buxton and solicitor Bill Allen, the father of ITV Formula One commentator James, had formed Team Elite the year before. The plan was to enter Lotus Elites into the classic endurance races, something that the factory lacked the capacity to do themselves; Colin Chapman was too busy with Formula One and Formula Junior to be able to handle a GT programme as well. However, works blessing was given and the cars were entered, in name at least, by Lotus Engineering, thus giving the fledgling operation the clout to gain entrance to Le Mans. Drivers contracted to Team Lotus were

also made available for the team to partner its regular pilots.

Two of the team's three cars were entered for the 1960 Le Mans race, one of a pair from Buxton's dealership, the other being Wagstaff's own car. The team manager was Stan Kennedy Chapman, father of the Lotus boss. That first year the cars were painted in British Racing Green; the white livery with a central broad green stripe flanked by two narrower stripes was yet to come (in later years, others were to copy this team's distinctive striping).

Wagstaff, a friend of Buxton, had begun racing a few years earlier with first a Triumph TR2 and then a Lotus Eleven. For the 1960 race Lotus teamed him with Tony Marsh, a driver arguably more used to events that lasted less than a minute rather than 24 hours. Having won the British RAC Hill Climb Championship in 1954, 1955 and 1956, he was to repeat the hat-trick just over 10 years later. He also knew how to circuit race, though, and he started in three German Grands Prix between 1957 and 1961 as well as the 1961 British Grand Prix. That latter year he was also the only person to win at the wheel of a BRM, coming first in the Climax-engined P48 ahead of Mike Spence's Emeryson in the Stuart Lewis-Evans Trophy, a low-key, non-championship Formula One race at Brands Hatch.

During practice, Le Mans novice Bill Allen in one of the other Elites had found an ideal braking marker on the approach to Indianapolis, a fluorescent green diamond attached to a tree. Then on one lap the marker had disappeared, and Allen only just managed to scramble round the banked left-hander. It was, he says, "a close shave." It subsequently transpired that a man had been standing in front of the diamond. "A valuable lesson had been learnt."

As the 1960 Le Mans race evolved, so Team Elite became increasingly interested in the regular bulletins that were being issued, statements that indicated that it was in with a real chance of the efficiency prize. That year, the Elites were very light even though fully trimmed. However, what probably made the most difference was the fact that the drivers could run four-hour stints without stopping. There were also no tyre changes, in fact Wagstaff recalls a set of tyres that lasted for both the 1962 and 1963 races.

He also remembers the car being very easy to drive thanks to its excellent roadholding, the only real problem resulting from those four-hour stints – four hours without a pit stop and, therefore, no chance of cleaning the windscreen. As the sun began to set over La Sarthe so it became increasingly difficult to see through the myriad of Gallic flies that had met their doom on the front of the Elites. Team Elite was to try a variety of bug deflectors over the years, but none of them proved really satisfactory.

The French, recalls Wagstaff, were "a little bit sniffy" when they found that one of the little British cars had won their Index of Thermal Efficiency with a fuel consumption of 21.87mpg. History tends to recall this result, although there was to be a postscript. It was claimed that a French-entered Elite had averaged 22.57mpg, rather than the 21.25mpg officially given. Seven days later the records were re-examined and, sure enough, the claim was found to be correct. The ACO decided that the best thing to do was award a second first prize, if that is not a contradiction in terms. They also had to award the French team an equal amount of prize money.

That first Index victory may have come as a surprise to Team Elite, but thereafter it was to arrive at the track determined to win it again. In 1961, though, it was to be another British car, the Sunbeam Alpine Harrington of Peter Harper and Peter Procter, that took the Index of Thermal Efficiency, mainly it has been said because it was 50 per cent heavier than the others competing for the award. Future fastback coupe Alpines would be known as Le Mans models.

Team Elite, though, remained serious about winning the trophy that had not even been on its radar at the start of the 1960 race. A conversion to 40 DCOE Weber carburettors, aerodynamic work on the nose, Girling large-diameter front discs and lightweight seats were all included in the changes made for 1961. Alterations were also made to the rear wheelarches to accommodate larger tyres. Ninety-litre fuel tanks, the maximum allowed for the class, were fitted. The frames of the windows were also removed, single-pane plexiglas now being taken right up to the door opening.

During scrutineering it seemed almost certain that the Elites would fail the clearance test during which the car had to be pushed over a wooden box without catching it. Somehow, some carefully selected local stones found their way into the front coil springs and with the ride height found to be within limits the cars were in the race.

Bill Allen had his own 'tweak' for his 1961 car. His mouth would go dry when racing, but drinks, he decided, were not the answer. Instead, his solution involved a certain brand of English sweets that came loose in tins, but were covered in powder so did not become sticky. However, he had forgotten to buy any in the UK prior to travelling to Le Mans, and having

failed to find a suitable replacement in France, he had to buy some wrapped ones. These he unwrapped and kept in a box on the propshaft tunnel, but this idea proved useless as the heat fused the sweets together. So for his second driving stint he placed wrapped sweets in the box, then proceeded to unwrap them on the Mulsanne straight with the steering wheel clasped between his knees. As he recalled recently: "What price Health & Safety?"

The team entered two cars again in both 1961 and 1962. In the latter year, David Hobbs, paired with Australian Frank Gardner, brought one of them home in eighth place overall, a magnificent achievement. The Index of Performance also returned to the team, the third year running that the British had won it. These results were achieved despite a series of generator and starter problems. The rules said that rotating electrics could not be replaced, only repaired. Accordingly, the mechanics had two buckets full of water ready, they said, to cool the removed component before working on it. Perhaps not surprisingly, at the bottom of each bucket were a new generator and starter, respectively. Even the drivers, let alone the pit lane officials, were unaware of what was happening.

In 1963 the Index of Thermal Efficiency was back in the hands of the French, and British success was not to be repeated, so as far as the remit of this tale is concerned, the trophy passes out of interest. Team Elite ran again in 1963 and 1964. Wagstaff, who had not driven during the previous two Le Mans races, returned, now paired with Pat Fergusson who, like Tony Rolt and Michael Burn, was a former inmate of Colditz Castle. On the first lap, Fergusson, trying to outbrake faster cars at the end of the Mulsanne straight, went off the road and into the dreaded sand at the exit; not a good idea given the number of photographers who always gathered there for the early stages of the race. "We wondered where he was," recalls Wagstaff. A spade miraculously appeared from somewhere, as usually one did under such circumstances, and after Fergusson had dug the Elite out, the pair recovered

More used to hill-climbing than endurance racing, Tony Marsh (seen here at Prescott in the 1960s) won the Index of Thermal Efficiency on his only visit to Le Mans. (Author)

A competitor at Le Mans in 1960, Tony Marsh was still attacking the speed hill-climbs in 2005. (Author)

to win the 1300cc class. The feat was repeated the following year, Wagstaff this time being paired with Clive Hunt, who was now a director of the team. This gave the Lotus Elite six consecutive class wins at Le Mans. The last of the Team Elite cars was sold to the USA, but Wagstaff was able to buy it back many years later, and it now sits, exactly as raced, in an outhouse on his Derbyshire estate.

The final chapter in the Team Elite tale occurred in 1967. Ownership of the team had already changed hands before Wagstaff and an old friend, David Preston, decided to revive it, and they were pleased to find that no one had registered the name before them. They entered a Lotus 47, the sole example of the twin-cam racing version of the Europa to run at Le Mans, only to retire in the fifth hour with brake problems and a blown head gasket. Earlier in the year Wagstaff had broken his back in a bobsleigh accident at St Moritz. He nevertheless drove at the Le Mans test day wearing a plaster cast, and was fit enough to drive the car in the race.

Fast-forward now to 2003 and the British were once again at the forefront of energy efficiency development. The ACO had stated that year that diesel cars would be permissible for the 24-Hours. As a result, Ricardo, the UK engineering concern responsible for the gearboxes of, among others, the Audi R8, announced that it had designed a 600bhp, 1400Nm, 5.5-litre all-aluminium diesel racing engine based on the Judd V10, which it would build if backing could be found. But none of the vehicle manufacturers – the only people with the appropriate amount of cash – came forward, although a small amount of funding was given by the Government-backed Motorsport Development UK late in 2005.

Instead it was Team Taurus that stepped forward in 2004 to run the first diesel car of the modern era at Le Mans. Audi's Dr Ullrich may have been critical of the smoke-belching progress of its Lola, but it has to be said that teams such as this operate on budgets the size of the loose change in Audi's back pocket. It was not a lack of technology that meant the Taurus diesel occasionally left a black trail behind it, it was a lack of sufficient funding; Taurus had to carry out its development in public. During the latter half of 2005 the car was redeveloped to run on a mix of regular diesel and biodiesel produced from vegetable oils.

A year before this Team Nasamax had set out to prove that even motor racing can have an environmentally friendly side with another alternative to petrol – bioethanol. The first year its specially converted Reynard 01Q, driven by Robbie Stirling with Romain Dumas and Werner Lupberger, ran for around three-quarters of the race before blowing its engine. It was a magnificent effort, which had brought the benefits of this initiative to a wider audience. In all, the car lasted 139 laps, and had it run the full distance it still would have required only an acre and a half of corn to produce its fuel; bioethanol is alcohol distilled from, in this case, corn mash. Virtually all of the carbon dioxide released when the alcohol is burned is reabsorbed by the next crop.

Team Nasamax was a consortium of parties interested in both motorsport and alternative energy. Included were 02 Empower and ASTEK, which specializes in technology for the manufacture of bioethanol and, importantly, ways to make production more economic.

The team was only given the go-ahead to enter a bioethanol-fuelled car in the race in December 2002.

The rapid development programme, combined with an engine that destroyed itself during the morning warm-up session, which led to a four-hour engine change and other consequential damage such as gear selector problems, meant that completing over 16 hours of the race was a major achievement. For eight of those hours the team reported that it ran "with no problems at all." Also, records could be claimed as this was the first time that wholly renewable fuel had been used at Le Mans.

Competitive lap times were achieved – the Nasamax car was 21st out of the 49 cars that practised – but the volumetric efficiency of the fuel compared to petrol meant that more pit stops were required (one more every two and a half to three hours); bioethanol has about 60 per cent of the calorific value of gasoline and therefore a greater volume needs to be burnt. Unfortunately, in 2003 the race regulations stated that the car had to have the same sized fuel tank as the others in the LMP900 class.

Bioethanol has to be purchased as a fuel in order to avoid alcohol tax. That means it has to be 'de-natured' with 5 per cent of additives. For the interest of the technically minded, the mix used at Le Mans included 3 per cent acetone and 1 per cent isopropylalcohol, as well as around 20 parts per million Bitterex to give it an unpalatable taste. One perhaps less obvious environmentally friendly result was that this car sounded quieter than all its competitors. Team Nasamax's technical consultant John McNeil, who heads up Sittingbourne Analytical Laboratories, a specialist in alternative fuels, was also at pains to point out that it also smelt a lot better.

For the first year, Cosworth Racing developed the car's 2.65-litre V8 turbocharged engine from its successful methanol-burning XD used in the American Champ Car single-seater series. The problems on the morning of the 2003 race and the resulting rapid engine change in order to make the grid were something from which the team never really recovered. Unhappy with its supplier, it changed to a Judd V10 engine for the following year. The car was also the first to be converted to the new hybrid LMP1 specification that could have allowed it to keep competing at Le Mans up to and including 2006, as well as to have a larger fuel tank. KW Motorsport's Kieron Salter, the engineer responsible for the original design, carried out the work. Nose, tail, sidepods and floor were all changed and the car was renamed after the team. With its new Judd engine and downforce reduced by 20 to 25 per cent, the Nasamax had one of the fastest straight-line speeds in the 2004 field.

A number of problems beset the Nasamax during the early part of that year's race and with just three hours completed it was 20 laps behind the leaders. However, despite ignition problems in the morning,

Ricardo's Le Mans diesel project received a small amount of Government funding to enable a test engine to be built. However, far more money will be needed if it is ever to become a reality. (Ricardo)

The Nasamax bioethanol-fuelled Reynard parked by the track, having retired during the 17th hour of the 2003 race. *(Tim Wagstaff)*

the team of Stirling, Lupberger and Kevin McGarrity pulled back 34 places, including six in the last three hours, to finish 17th.

For Team Nasamax, running a bioethanol-fuelled car was not so much a case of proving that the technology works but more of raising the profile of 'renewable' fuels. This it certainly did, with more seemingly to come when it was announced that a new LMP1 car would be built during 2005 to replace the hybrid, again using KW Motorsport. But sadly, the optimism apparent at the beginning of that year could not be matched with sufficient funding. The new car was never started and the original Nasamax was withdrawn from the entry for the 2005 race.

The other British energy-efficient flag carrier, Team Taurus, which entered the first diesel seen at Le Mans since the early 1950s, also ran into financial problems that saw it disappear from the grids for 2005. However, support from D1 Oils, a producer of biodiesel from renewable energy crops, was to make a return to the tracks likely for 2006.

The sound of the car was hardly warlike and it did belch out the occasional black smoke, but there were those who saw the future of endurance racing in the team's silver Lola. Where Peugeot and Audi may now tread, Team Taurus, a Norfolk-based team run by Le Mans stalwart Ian Dawson – he commissioned the Grid Group C car that ran in 1982 – has already been.

With Le Mans regulations allowing greater restrictor area and boost pressure for compression-ignition (CI) engines, Taurus removed a 5-litre TDI PD V10 from a Volkswagen Touareg, liased with another British firm, Mountune, as its engine partner and married it to a Lola B2K/10 chassis. Mountune had already carried out design studies on racing diesels.

In 2004 the car was to manage just short of three hours of racing at Le Mans. Throughout the whole of the week the engine ran troublefree and it was only the demands it placed on the clutch that caused it problems. The Lola eventually managed to run 16 laps without a pit stop; Dawson believes it could have gone 17. Compare this to the 11 of the front-running Audis that year.

After the race Dawson spoke of a plan, money permitting, to convert the car to comply with the then new LMP1 specifications, which would have enabled the team to replace its 80-litre tank with a 90-litre version. "If the car could run for 20 laps with sub-four-minute laps then we begin to make sense of what diesel can do," said Dawson. However, there was more to it. "You can build a vehicle that can go a long way between stops, but you need a tyre that can still double-stint and disciplined and fit drivers who can run more than two and a half hours at a certain pace."

And the black smoke? When the drivers came off the throttle and then back on again, some was certainly emitted. Dawson pointed out that the team was running with normal diesel fuel without additives. He reckoned that there were areas where diesel road

DRIVING THE DIESEL

According to Calum Lockie, one of only two British drivers to have competed at Le Mans in a diesel-engined car (the other being Phil Andrews), the main difference between this and a petrol-fuelled racer is the noise. Or lack of it. "The diesel was so quiet you had a different appreciation of what was happening. You had a muted roar behind you, but that was all. By far the loudest thing was the wind noise rattling your visor."

Lockie, a director of the Gold Track Driving Club, could even hear the crowd as he drove the Team Taurus Lola B2K/10 in 2004. Some of them nicknamed it the 'magic carpet'. Nowhere was the sensation of tranquility more apparent that in the corridor of trees between the two chicanes on the Mulsanne straight. "The car is so quiet that you are looking around and then you hear the other cars coming up to lap you. You don't get any sensation of speed from the noise of the car." Lockie reckons that driving it was more akin to an airplane than a car, using instruments more than the senses. With petrol-engined cars the driver can soon identify the sound of the engine at the point he needs to change gear. However, the sound of the diesel was almost entirely flat.

The other major difference was the narrow power band. "We had from 3300 to 4500rpm to use and that was it." That meant it was revving so quickly through the low gears that there was little time between gear changes. The drivers almost had to anticipate the change in the lower gears. "So we were much more busy on the gear stick. You really had to concentrate to avoid hitting the rev-limiter." The Lola used a manually operated sequential box, so the drivers had to take their hand off the wheel and pull the lever back in the time fashioned manner; the budget did not exist at that point to install a paddle shift system.

"This created some interesting side issues. Originally, the radio communication button was on the right-hand side of the steering wheel, making conversation impossible if you wanted to change gear, something that had to be modified before the race."

The other major difference was the weight of the "hefty" engine. This, in combination with the short tail that the Taurus Lola ran in 2004, and a relatively rudimentary rear wing and huge torque meant that the drivers had to be very careful with what they did with the throttle coming out of the slower corners. As the weight came off the wheels the car could snap away into oversteer or spin with no warning at all. Once it started to slide it was hard to stop it as the momentum built up so rapidly.

In the race Lockie "did a swift 360" at the first chicane and the car simply carried on. He also describes how the drivers felt the extra weight under braking, causing the car to move. "You had to be particularly careful with trail braking."

On a normal lap the Lola would be in fifth gear along the pit straight before braking and changing down for the Dunlop chicane. If the driver changed into second, the engine tended to be out of the usable power band coming out of this corner, "which made it feel rather sluggish," but going down to first put an extra strain on the transmission. Most of the time Lockie used second. He would then change up to fourth down the sweeps before the Esses, which would be taken in third; back to fourth before Tertre Rouge and then down to third. Along the Mulsanne the gearbox would be up to sixth and down to second for the chicanes. The ruts on Mulsanne had a major effect on the diesel car because of its weight and reduced downforce. "It moved around quite a lot."

The Mulsanne corner would be taken in first and then it would be back to sixth for the run up to the third-gear Indianapolis. Arnage would be taken in second and then it was only up to fifth before the fourth and third-gear Porsche curves. The big right-hander in the middle of these was particularly tricky for the diesel car. "You could really feel the back end wanting to swing round. You had to be incredibly careful."

On the run up to the Ford chicanes Lockie would be in fifth, then down to second for those bends, where he found he could "push on hard" and back up to fifth.

Calum Lockie (seen here) and Phil Andrews were the first two British drivers ever to have competed with a diesel car at Le Mans. *(Calum Lockie collection)*

Nasamax was back in 2004, its car being the only one in the race to have been converted into a hybrid LMP1. *(Author)*

car development could benefit from the project. He pointed to the use of the filters that are used to collect particulates at low rpm. He also mused on the fact that diesel road cars are no longer purchased simply for economy but can now been seen as performance vehicles that just happen to go longer on fuel. "So now is the time to race diesels," he declared.

Endurance racing is about finishing, and that means compromise. For example, during flat-shifting through the gearbox severe torque spikes were experienced. To overcome this the power had to be reduced. Following a clutch problem in practice the engine was also re-mapped to a much lower power figure – nearer to 400bhp than the 520bhp seen previously. This resulted in an improvement in throttle response and in getting the car out of the slower corners. However, this again increased stress on the clutch.

Had the team been able to use a carbon clutch – with a theoretical torque capacity of 1300Nm – as originally envisaged, Dawson felt that it could have run a lot longer. However, the team's only carbon clutch failed during practice; a mystery "even to (supplier) AP." A selector fork also broke during the warm-up to the race and the driver had to bring the car back on the replacement, lower torque capacity, sintered clutch. Driver Phil Andrews, therefore, started from the pit lane as a safety measure, but the knock-on effect was to prove the car's undoing.

Dawson was well aware that the big battalions would take up the diesel mantle, but he is proud of the fact that he was first to use a diesel engine in modern endurance racing. But being a pioneer can be an expensive business, and at the end of the season Team Taurus was unable to continue. An ill-conceived rescue plan appeared on the horizon for 2005, something from which Dawson was able to extricate the programme later in the year. With the major manufacturers having taken over diesel development, he still believes he can bring something new to Le Mans. In 2004 he was looking beyond the horizon and talking of a biodiesel. The partnership with D1 Oils meant that he was able to convert the Lola in late 2005 to run on this fuel with the hope, in vain, of an entry for Le Mans the following year.

Also looking ahead, Zytek is developing a hybrid-electric system to compete at Le Mans in 2007. The company was responsible for the electric motor and controls for the hybrid Panoz Q9 which finished second in class at Road Atlanta in 1998 but failed to qualify for Le Mans earlier in the year. However, this will be a totally different system and, says Trevor Foster, managing director of its chassis division, "will have to be very intelligent to gain maximum advantage." Bill Gibson, the founder of Zytek, is known to regard the Q9 as unfinished business. The ACO has issued an equivalency formula for hybrid-electrics that includes a significant weight penalty. However, Zytek, with its road vehicle interests, feels it worthwhile to go ahead to showcase the concept.

As Le Mans looks to a new era in which diesels, and perhaps other alternative energy sources, may take over at the head of the race, it is obvious that the British will still be in there playing their part. The race may take place in France, be run by the French and, in recent times at least, may often be won by a German car…but for the many thousands of devotees from the United Kingdom *Les Vingt-Quatre Heures du Mans* is, and hopefully will continue to be, a peculiarly British motor racing festival.

Cosworth is an example of a once very British company that is now in overseas ownership. Twice a winner at Le Mans with its DFV engine, it returned to the race in 2003 when an XD-derived engine was converted to run on bioethanol for the Nasamax team. Technical consultant John McNeil (right) had reason to be concerned in the hours before the race. *(Author)*

Ian Dawson's project was revived towards the end of 2005 to run on biodiesel. *(D1 Oils)*

British involvement in the Le Mans story continues. One of those listed to drive the new Audi R10 diesel at the 2006 race was Allan McNish. Earlier in the year, on March 18, he was one of the team that scored an historic first for a diesel in international sportscar racing, victory in the Sebring 12-Hours. Here the Scot secures pole position for the race. *(Audi)*

BRITISH DRIVERS AT LE MANS

Compiled by Gordon Creese

Abecassis	George	1950 5th, 1951 5th, 1952 DNS, 1953 DNF
Acheson	Kenny	1989 2nd, 1990 DNF, 1991 3rd, 1992 2nd, 1993 DNF, 1995 DNF
Adams	Nick	1985 NC, 1986 NC, 1987 NC, 1988 DNF, 1989 DNF, 1990 DNF, 1991, DNF, 1993 DNF, 1995 17th
Aldington	Harold John	1937 DNF, 1949 3rd, 1951 DNF
Allam	Jeff	1982 DNQ, 1983 18th
Allan	Miss Margaret	1935 26th
Allard	Sydney	1950 3rd, 1951 35th, 1952 DNF, 1953 DNF
Allen	Bill	1960 DNF, 1961 12th
Allison	Cliff	1956 DNF, 1957 14th, 1958 DNF, 1959 DNF, 1961 DNF
Andrews	David	1985 NC, 1986 DNF, 1987 DNF, 1988 23rd
Andrews	Phil	1994 NC, 2004 DNF
Anthony	C.M.	1939 18th
Appleton	John	1934 DNF
Ashdown	Peter	1960 DNF
Attwood	Richard	1963 DNF, 1964 DNF, 1966 DNF, 1967 DNF, 1968 7th, 1969 DNF, 1970 1st, 1971 2nd, 1984 DNF
Ayles	Gary	1995 18th, 1997 DNF, 1998 19th
Bailey	Julian	1989 DNF, 1990 DNF, 1997 DNF, 1998 DNQ, 2001 DNF, 2002 DNF
Baillie	Ian	1960 9th, 1962 DNF
Baillie	Sir Gawaine	1960 DNF
Bain	Duncan	1985 NC, 1986 DNF, 1987 DNF
Baker	Clive	1964 24th, 1965 DNF, 1966 DNF, 1967 15th, 1968 DNF, 1969 DNF, 1970 DNF
Baker	Jonathan	1994 NC
Baker	R.H.	1934 15th, 1935 DNF
Baker	Roy	1984 DNQ
Ballisat	Keith	1960 NC, 1961 9th, 1963 DNF, 1964 DNF
Barbour	John	1935 27th
Barff	Rob	2003 DNF, 2004 DNF
Barnato	Woolf	1928 1st , 1929 1st, 1930 1st
Barnes	John Donald	1934 18th, 1935 DNF, 1937 DNF, 1938 DNF
Bartlett	Jack	1931 DNF, 1949 13th
Baumer	Maurice	1932 DNF, 1933 6th, 1934 DNF, 1935 DNF
Beauman	Don	1955 DNF
Beckworth	Mike	1967 DNF
Bekaert	John	1961 DNF
Bell	Derek	1970 DNF, 1971 DNF, 1972 8th, 1973 DNF, 1974 4th, 1975 1st, 1976 5th, 1977 DNF, 1978 DNF, 1979 DNF, 1980 13th, 1981 1st, 1982 1st, 1983 2nd, 1985 3rd, 1986 1st, 1987 1st, 1988 2nd, 1989 DNF, 1990 4th, 1992 12th, 1993 10th, 1994 6th, 1995 3rd, 1996 6th
Bell	Justin	1992 12th, 1994 12th, 1995 3rd, 1998 11th, 1999 12th, 2000 11th
Bellm	Ray	1984 DNF, 1985 14th, 1986 19th, 1988 13th, 1989 DNF, 1994 DNF, 1995 4th, 1996 9th, 1997 DNF
Beloë	A.C.	1934 23rd, 1935 15th
Benjafield	Dr John	1925 DNF, 1926 DNF, 1927 1st, 1928 DNS, 1929 3rd, 1930 DNF, 1933 DNS, 1935 13th
Bennett	Phil	2005 24th
Berridge	Bob	2004 21st, 2005 DNF
Bertelli	Auguste Cesar	1928 DNF, 1931 5th, 1932 7th, 1933 7th, 1934 DNF, 1935 DNS
Bevan	Anthony	1931 DNF
Bezzant	Jack	1928 DNF, 1931 DNF, 1932 DNF
Bicknell	Reg	1956 7th
Bilney	M.K.H.	1937 14th
Birchenhough	Tony	1976 22nd, 1978 DNF, 1979 18th
Birkin	Sir Henry	1928 5th, 1929 1st, 1930 DNF, 1931 1st, 1932 DNF
Birrane	Martin	1972 DNQ, 1977 NC, 1978 DNF, 1980 22nd, 1981 DNF, 1982 DNF, 1983 DNF, 1985 15th, 1986 DNF, 1988 DNF
Birrell	Gerry	1972 10th, 1973 DNF
Black	Norman	1932 DNF, 1933 DNF, 1934 15th, 1935 DNF, 1937 DNF
Black	William	1954 DNF

Blond	Peter	1958 DNF
Blumer	Jimmy	1964 DNF
Blundell	Mark	1989 DNF, 1990 DNF, 1992 1st, 1995 4th, 2001 DNF, 2002 DNF, 2003 2nd
Bolton	Peter	1956 DQ/DNF, 1957 10th, 1958 8th, 1959 DNF, 1960 NC, 1961 9th, 1962 DNF, 1963 7th, 1964 DNF, 1965 DNF
Bond	Richard	1971 12th, 1972 8th, 1973 20th, 1974 DNF, 1975 DNQ, 1977 DNF, 1978 DNF
Boughton	G.H.	1937 DNF
Boulton	James	1934 DNF, 1935 19th
Bracey	Ian	1976 22nd, 1977 DNF, 1980 DNQ,
Brackenbury	Charles	1934 16th, 1935 3rd, 1937 DNF, 1939 3rd, 1949 DNF, 1950 6th
Bradley	Jim	1939 DNF
Bradley	Bill	1964 24th, 1965 DNF
Bridger	Tommy	1958 DNF
Brigham Metchim	H.	1933 DNF, 1934 DNF
Brindley	John	1980 DNQ
Bristow	Laurence	1989 DNF
Brodie	David	1994 DNF
Brooke	Leslie	1955 19th
Brooks	Tony	1955 DNF, 1956 NC, 1957 DNF, 1958 DNF
Brown	John	1954 15th, 1955 21st
Brown	Peter	1969 DNF
Bruce	Victor	1925 DNS
Brundle	Martin	1987 DNF, 1988 28th, 1990 1st, 1997 DNF, 1998 DNF, 1999 DNF, 2001 DNF
Buckley	Dennis	1937 DNF
Bueb	Ivor	1955 1st, 1956 6th, 1957 1st, 1958 DNF, 1959 DNF
Burt	Kelvin	2003 DNF
Burton	John	1969 DNF
Buxton	David	1960 DNF, 1961 DNF
Caine	Michael	2003 DNF, 2004 21st
Callingham	Leslie	1927 DNF, 1930 5th
Campbell-Walter	Jamie	2005 14th
Carnegie	Robin	1961 DNF
Carr	John	1935 27th
Carway	Warren	2001 DNF
Chambers	Marcus	1938 10th, 1939 14th
Champney	Miss Dorothy	1934 13th
Chapman	Colin	1955 DQ/DNF, 1956 DNF
Chappell	Dominic	1994 NC, 1995 DNF, 1996 DNF
Charles	Maurice	1958 DNF, 1962 DNF
Charnell	Tony	1977 DNF, 1978 DNF, 1979 17th
Chatham	John	1971 DNQ
Chetwynd	Hon Mrs	1931 DNF, 1932 DNA
Clark	David	1953 DNF
Clark	Jim	1959 10th, 1960 3rd, 1961 DNQ
Clark	Peter	1938 10th, 1939 14th, 1949 DNF, 1950 12th, 1951 13th,1952 7th, 1953 DNS
Clarke	Peter	1980 22nd,
Clarke	Tom	1935 8th, 1950 8th, 1951 22nd
Clarkson	Nigel	1975 29th
Cleare	Richard	1982 13th, 1983 DNF, 1986 14th
Clement	Frank	1923 4th, 1924 8th, 1925 DNF, 1926 DNF, 1927 DNF, 1928 DNF, 1924 4th, 1930 2nd
Clements	Evan	1986 8th, 1987 DNF, 1988 DNF, 1989 17th
Clifford	Freddy	1934 DNF, 1938 DNF
Collier	Michael	1935 DNF, 1939 DNF
Collins	Ben	2001 DNF
Collins	Peter	1952 DNF, 1953 DNF, 1954 DNF, 1955 2nd, 1956 2nd, 1957 DNF, 1958 DNF
Connell	Ian	1935 DNF, 1939 8th
Cook	Humphrey	1931 DNF
Coombe	Mike	1971 DNQ
Cooper	John	1975 6th, 1977 DNF, 1978 DNQ, 1979 DNF, 1980 DNF, 1981 4th, 1982 8th, 1983 11th, 1984 DNF, 1987 DNF
Corner	Neil	1973 DNF
Coulthard	David	1993 DQ
Coundley	John	1962 DNF, 1963 DNF
Couper	Mike	1931 DNF
Courage	Piers	1966 8th, 1967 DNF, 1968 4th, 1970 DNF
Crabb	Percy	1958 16th
Craft	Chris	1971 4th, 1972 12th, 1973 DNF, 1974 DNF, 1975 14th, 1976 3rd, 1977 5th, 1978 15th, 1979 DNF,1980 25th, 1981 DNF, 1982 DNF, 1983 DNF, 1984 DNF
Culpan	Norman	1949 3rd, 1950 20th, 1951 DNF
Cunningham	Neil	2004 NC
Cunningham-Reid	Noel	1957 DNF
Cushman	Leon	1929 DNS
Dalton	John	1957 13th, 1960 16th
Daniels	Paul	2004 DNF
Dashwood	John	1959 DNF
Davidson	Anthony	2003 DNF
Davies	Jamie	1998 7th, 2001 DNF, 2003 10th, 2004 2nd
Davies	Tim	1935 DNF
Davis	Colin	1958 11th, 1959 DNF, 1961 DNF, 1962 DNF, 1964 DNF, 1965 DNF, 1966 4th
Davis	S.C.H.	1924 2nd, 1926 DNF, 1927 1st, 1928 9th, 1929 DNS, 1930 DNF, 1933 7th
Day	Steven	2001 16th
de Cadenet	Alain	1971 DNF, 1972 12th, 1973 DNF, 1975 14th, 1976 3rd, 1977 5th, 1978 15th, 1979 DNF, 1980 7th, 1981 DNF, 1982 DNF, 1983 DNF 1985 20th, 1986 18th
de Clifford	Lord Freddie	1934 16th, 1937 DNF
de Lautour	Simon	1977 12th
Densham	P.L.	1928 DNA
Dewis	Norman	1953 DNS, 1955 DNF
Dibley	Hugh	1968 DQ/DNF
Dickson	Bob	1955 14th

Surname	First Name	Results
Dickson	Tom	1958 NC, 1961 DNF, 1962 DNF
Dixon	Freddie	1934 3rd, 1935 DNF
Dobson	Arthur	1938 DNF, 1939 3rd
Dodd-Noble	Tom	1986 8th, 1987 DNF, 1988 DNF, 1989 15th
Dodson	Charles	1935 28th, 1937 DNF
Don	Guy	1935 6th
Donaldson	Ian	2004 18th
Donkin	Peter	1935 11th
Donnelly	Martin	1989 DNF, 1990 DNF
Donovan	Robin	1986 NC, 1987 DNF, 1988 25th, 1989 DNF, 1990 DNF, 1991 11th, 1993 DNF, 1994 6th, 1995 11th, 1996 DNF, 1998 DNF, 1999 DNF, 2001 DNF
Down	Richard	1977 NC, 1978 DNF, 1980 23rd, 1982 DNF
Driscoll	Pat	1932 7th, 1933 5th, 1935 DNF
Dron	Tony	1980 12th, 1981 DNQ, 1982 13th, 1983 DNF
Dryden	Curly	1949 DQ/DNF
Duff	John	1923 4th, 1924 8th, 1925 DNF
Duffield	David	1984 DNF
Duller	George	1925 DNF, 1926 DNF, 1927 DNF
Dumbreck	Peter	1999 DNF
Dumfries	Johnny	1987 DNF, 1988 1st, 1989 DNF, 1990 DNF, 1991 DNF
Dunfee	Clive	1930 DNF
Dunfee	Jack	1929 2nd, 1930 DNS
Duret	Francois	1982 DNF, 1984 DNQ, 1985 NC
Eaton	Hugh	1930 3rd
Eaton	Mrs Coleen	1935 26th
Eccles	Mrs Marjorie Lindsay	1937 DNF
Eccles	Roy	1934 4th, 1937 DNS
Edwards	Guy	1971 DNF, 1977 DNF, 1978 DNF, 1979 DNQ, 1980 9th, 1981 15th, 1982 DNF, 1983 5th, 1984 DNF, 1985 4th
Elford	Vic	1967 8th, 1969 DNF, 1970 DNF, 1971 DNF, 1972 DNF, 1973 6th, 1974 DNF, 1983 DNF
Elwes	Jim	1934 DNF, 1935 12th
Enever	Roger	1968 15th, 1969 DNF, 1970 DNF, 1971 DNF
England	Gordon	1925 DNF
Epstein	Jackie	1968 DNF,
Escott	Colin	1959 DNF, 1960 12th
Essendon	The Lord	see Hon Brian Lewis
Evans	Bob	1978 DNF, 1979 DNF, 1980 25th, 1981 DNF, 1982 DNF
Evans	Gareth	2004 22nd, 2005 DNF
Evans	Miss Doreen	1935 25th
Eyston	George	1928 DNF, 1929 DNF, 1933 DNS,
Fairfield	Pat	1937 DNF fatal accident
Fairman	Jack	1949 8th, 1950 DNS, 1951 DNF, 1952 DNF, 1953 DNF, 1954 8th, 1955 9th, 1956 DNF, 1958 DNF, 1959 DNF, 1960 9th, 1961 DNF, 1962 DNF
Fane	A.F.P.	1935 DNF, 1937 DNF
Faulkner	Maurice	1934 10th 1935 8th
Faure	Nick	1975 6th, 1976 NC, 1977 DNF, 1978 DQ/DNF, 1979 12th, 1980 DNQ, 1981 DNF, 1982 DNF, 1983 17th, 1984 DNF, 1985 11th
Fawcett	Miss Prudence M.	1938 13th
Fenwick	Alistair	1990 28th
Ferguson	Pat	1963 10th
Fiennes	C.W.	1929 DNF
Firester	Piers	1969 DNF
Firman	Ralph	2004 NC
Fisken	Gregor	2004 18th, 2005 DNF
Fitzpatrick	John	1972 DNF, 1973 DNF, 1974 5th, 1976 DNF, 1977 DNF, 1978 DNF, 1979 DNF, 1980 5th, 1982 4th, 1983 5th
Flockhart	Ron	1955 DQ/DNF, 1956 1st, 1957 1st, 1959 DNF, 1960 DNF 1961 DNF, 1961 DNF
Folland	Dudley	1949 DNF
Fontès	Luis	1935 1st
Ford	John Ludovic	1932 DNF, 1933 6th, 1934 DNF, 1935 DNF
Fotheringham-Parker	Philip	1953 DNF
Fotheringham-Parker	Thomas	1934 DNF, 1935 DNF
Franchitti	Marino	2005 DNF
Franey	Mike	1978 DNF
Frost	Bill	1958 DNF
Gallop	Clive	1926 DNF, 1927 DNS, 1928 DNF
Galvin	Mark	1984 DNF
Gardner	R.P.	1934 23rd, 1935 15th
Gavin	Oliver	2001 18th, 2002 11th, 2003 11th, 2004 6th, 2005 5th
Gee	Neville	1949 DNF
Gerard	Bob	1953 DNF
Gibson	Ron	1933 DNF
Gilbert-Scott	Andrew	1989 4th, 1997 DNF
Goodacre	Charles	1935 DNF, 1937 DNF, 1951 DNF
Grant	Robert	1972 DNQ
Green	Willie	1973 DNF
Greene	Keith	1959 DNF
Greensall	Nigel	2004 22nd
Griffith	Pat	1952 DNF
Grob	Ian	1978 DNF, 1979 DNQ
Guest	H.B.	1935 20th
Gunter	Sir Ronald	1933 DNS, 1935 13th
Guthrie	Malcolm	1969 DNF
Hadley	Bert	1937 DNF, 1950 DNF, 1952 DNF, 1953 11th, 1955 15th
Haig	Miss Betty	1951 15th
Hailwood	Mike	1969 3rd, 1970 DNF, 1973 DNF, 1974 4th
Haines	Nick	1949 7th, 1950 12th
Halford	Bruce	1957 DNF, 1958 15th, 1959 DNF, 1960 DNF, 1961 DNF

Halford	Ted	1937 13th, 1939 DNF
Hall	Eddie	1950 8th, 1951 DNF
Hall	Keith	1956 DNF, 1957 14th
Hall	Mike	1986 DNF
Hamilton	Duncan	1950 4th, 1951 6th, 1952 DNF, 1953 1st, 1954 1st, 1955 DNF, 1957 6th, 1958 DNF
Hamilton	Hugh Charles	1933 DNS
Hamilton	Lord Malcolm Douglas	1935 11th
Hamilton	Robin	1977 17th, 1979 DNF
Hammond	Bert	1928 DNF
Hampshire	David	1951 7th
Hancock	Sam	2002 DNF, 2004 DNF
Handley	W.C.	1928 DNF
Harcourt Wood	Beris	1930 DNS
Hardman	Peter	1993 DNF, 1994 DNF
Harper	Peter	1961 16th, 1962 15th, 1963 DNF, 1965 DNF
Harris	Jeff	1969 DNF
Harrower	Ian	1977 NC, 1978 DNF, 1980 DNQ, 1982 DNF, 1983 NC, 1984 DNF, 1985 16th, 1986 8th, 1987 10th, 1988 18th, 1989 DNF, 1990 DNF
Hartshorne	John	2005 NC
Harvey	Maurice	1928 6th, 1931 5th
Harvey	Tim	1988 20th, 1989 DNF, 1990 18th, 1991 DNF
Hats	Richard	2002 DNF, 2003 DNF
Hawkes	Douglas	1928 11th, 1929 DNF
Hawthorn	Mike	1953 DQ/DNF, 1955 1st, 1956 6th, 1957 DNF, 1958 DNF
Hay	Jack	1949 6th, 1950 14th, 1951 22nd
Hay	Mrs	1949 DNS
Hays	E.J.	1928 DNF
Heal	Anthony	1949 DNF
Hedges	Andrew	1964 19th, 1965 11th, 1966 DNF, 1967 15th, 1968 DNF, 1970 DNF
Hendy	Gordon	1934 DNF, 1935 19th
Herbert	Johnny	1990 DNF, 1991 1st, 1992 4th, 2001 DNF, 2002 2nd, 2003 2nd, 2004 2nd
Hewland	William	1994 DNF
Hicks	Jack	1930 DNF
Hicks	Bob	1958 DNF
Hignett	Sam	2005 NC
Hill	Damon	1989 DNF
Hill	Graham	1957 DNS, 1958 DNF, 1959 DNF, 1960 DNF, 1961 DNF, 1962 DNF, 1963 13th, 1964 2nd, 1965 10th, 1966 DNF, 1972 1st
Hindmarsh	Johnny	1930 4th, 1931 DNF, 1934 7th, 1935 1st, 1937 DNF
Hine	John	1962 DNF
Hine	John	1970 DNF, 1972 DNF, 1977 DNF
Hitchens	Robert	1937 11th, 1939 12th
Hitchings	Alfred	1951 31st, 1954 DNF

Hobbs	David	1962 8th, 1963 DNF, 1964 21st, 1965 DNF, 1966 DNF, 1967 DNF, 1968 DNF, 1969 3rd, 1970 DNF, 1971 DNF, 1972 DNF, 1979 DNF, 1981 DNF, 1982 4th, 1984 3rd, 1985 4th, 1987 DNF, 1988 5th, 1989 DNF
Hodgetts	Chris	1988 20th, 1989 7th, 1990 18th, 1995 DNF
Holmes	Guy	1996 DNF
Hopkirk	Paddy	1961 DQ, 1962 DNF, 1963 12th, 1964 19th, 1965 11th, 1966 DNF
Howe	The Earl, Viscount Curzon	1929 DNF, 1930 5th, 1931 1st, 1932 DNF, 1933 DNS, 1934 DNF, 1935 DNF
Hoy	Will	1985 21st, 1987 DNF, 1988 19th, 1989 DNF, 1991 DNF
Hughes	Warren	2001 DNF, 2002 DNF, 2005 20th
Hunt	Clive	1962 8th, 1964 22nd
Hunter	Hugh Charles	1950 14th
Hurrell	Sydney	1959 DNF
Hutchinson	W.R.	1929 DNF
Hyde	Steve	2002 DNF, 2004 NC
Hyett	Ross	1989 16th, 1990 25th
Ireland	Innes	1958 DNF, 1959 DNF, 1962 DNF, 1963 DNF, 1964 6th, 1965 DNF, 1966 DNF
Irvine	Eddie	1992 9th, 1994 2nd
Irwin	Chris	1967 DNF
Isherwood	Ray	1952 DNF
Jacobs	Dick	1955 DNF
James	Ian	2005 DNF
Jason-Henry	Guy	1949 DNF
Jenvey	Richard	1979 18th, 1980 DNQ
Johnson	Leslie	1949 DNF, 1950 DNF, 1951 DNF, 1952 3rd, 1953 11th
Johnson	Piers	2005 NC
Jones	Arthur L.	1953 DNS
Jones	Arthur W.	1939 18th, 1949 7th
Jones	Richard	1978 DNF, 1979 17th, 1982 13th, 1983 DNF, 1984 DNF, 1985 DNF, 1986 NC, 1987 NC, 1988 DNF, 1989 DNF, 1990 27th, 1991 DNF, 1992 DNF, 1995 17th
Jopp	Peter	1956 7th, 1957 DNF, 1958 16th, 1959 DNF, 1961 DQ, 1961 DNF, 1963 DQ/DNF
Jordan	Mike	2003 DNF
Joscelyne	Brian	1976 22nd, 1977 DNF, 1978 DNF, 1979 18th
Joyce	John	1925 DNS
Kahn	Ian	2003 18th, 2004 23rd
Kane	Jonny	2001 DNF, 2002 DNF
Keegan	Rupert	1982 DNF, 1983 5th, 1984 DNF, 1995 DNF
Keen	Mike	1952 7th, 1954 9th, 1955 8th
Kempton	Steve	1984 DNF
Kensington-Moir	Herbert	1925 DNF
Kenyon	M.	1935 10th
Kidston	Glen	1929 2nd, 1930 1st
Kinch	Nathan	2004 DNF, 2005 DNF
Kindell	Freddy	1930 DNF, 1931 DQ/NC

King	Frank	1928 DNF
Kirkaldy	Andrew	2005 DNF
Knight	Mike	1975 30th
Knight	Richard	1975 30th
Konig	Mark	1969 DNF
Lalonde	Tim	1969 DNF
Lanfranchi	Tony	1965 DNF, 1969 DNF, 1985 NC
Langley	Alf	1933 13th, 1934 8th, 1935 16th, 1937 DNS
Langton	Soames	1996 DNF
Lawrence	Chris	1962 11th, 1963 DQ/DNF, 1964 DNF, 1967 DNF, 1968 DNF
Lawrence	John	1957 2nd, 1958 DNF, 1959 DNF
Lawrie	Robert	1949 11th, 1950 17th, 1951 11th, 1952 DNF
Lee-Davey	Tim	1985 NC, 1986 DNQ, 1987 DNF, 1988 DNF, 1989 15th
Lees	Geoff	1982 DNF, 1985 DNF, 1986 DNF, 1987 DNF, 1988 12th, 1989 DNF, 1990 6th, 1992 DNF, 1993 8th, 1995 DNF, 1996 19th, 1997 DNF, 1998 DNF, 2000 DNF
Leslie	David	1984 DNF, 1985 DNF, 1986 DQ, 1987 8th, 1988 17th, 1989 DNF, 1990 DNF, 1991 DNF, 1993 DNF, 1995 NC
Leston	Les	1955 DNF, 1957 DNF, 1960 NC, 1961 11th
Lewis	Hon Brian	1929 DNF, 1930 3rd, 1931 DNF, 1932 5th, 1933 3rd, 1934 5th, 1935 DNF
Lewis	Jack	1963 DNF
Lewis-Evans	Stuart	1957 5th, 1958 DNF
Liddell	Eric	1968 DNF,
Liddell	Robin	2002 DNF, 2003 24th, 2005 DNF
Line	John	1954 9th
Line	Tommy	1955 8th
Lloyd	Nevil	1935 DNF
Lloyd	Richard	1981 DNQ, 1982 DNF, 1983 8th, 1984 DNF, 1985 2nd
Lockett	Johnny	1953 12th, 1955 12th
Lockie	Calum	2004 DNF
Lockwood	W.P.	1931 DNF
Lovett	Peter	1977 DNF, 1978 DNQ, 1979 DNF, 1980 DNF, 1982 DNF
Lumsden	Peter	1959 8th, 1962 5th, 1963 DNF, 1964 DNF
Lund	Ted	1955 17th, 1959 DNF, 1960 12th, 1961 DNF
Lye	F.H.	1937 DNF
Macari	Joe	2005 DNF
Macklin	Lance	1950 5th, 1951 3rd, 1952 DNF, 1953 DNF, 1954 DQ/DNF, 1955 DNF
Maclure	Percy	1934 6th, 1935 DNF
MacQuillan	Gerard	1995 17th, 1998 DNQ
Mahony	Jerry	1990 DNF
Mallock	Ray	1979 20th, 1982 7th, 1983 DNF, 1984 DNF, 1985 DNF, 1986 DQ, 1987 8th, 1989 DNF
Mangan	G.	1937 DNF
Mann	Nigel	1949 13th, 1950 19th, 1951 10th, 1952 DNF

Marendaz	Donald	1928 DNA
Marsh	Arthur	1935 20th
Marsh	Chris	1995 NC
Marsh	Jem	1967 DNF, 1968 DNQ
Marsh	Tony	1960 14th
Marshall	John	1950 15th, 1951 14th
Martin	Charles	1934 4th, 1935 3rd
Martland	Digby	1968 DNF, 1970 DNF
Masarati	Piers	2002 DNF, 2003 24th
Mason	Nick	1979 18th, 1980 22nd, 1982 DNF, 1983 DNF, 1984 DNF
Masters	C.H.	1933 DNF, 1934 DNF
Mathieson	T.A.S.O.	1938 DNF, 1939 DNF, 1949 DNF, 1950 9th
Mayers	Jim	1954 7th, 1955 7th
McAlpine	Kenneth	1955 DNF
McCarthy	Perry	1996 DNF, 1997 DNF, 1999 DNF, 2002 DNF, 2003 DNF
McGarrity	Kevin	2001 DNF, 2002 DNF, 2004 17th, 2005 DNF
McKay	Bill	1961 DNF
McKee	Mike	1961 DNF
McKellar Jr.	Ian	2001 DNF, 2002 DNF,
McNish	Alan	1997 DNF, 1998 1st, 1999 DNF, 2000 2nd, 2004 5th, 2004 3rd
McRae	Colin	2004 9th
Mercer	David	1984 DNF, 1985 DNF, 1986 11th
Merrick	Bill	1955 DNF
Meyer	Thomas	1953 DNS
Miles	Ken	1955 12th
Miles	Ken	1965 DNF, 1966 2nd
Mitchell	Ian	2005 24th
Mitchell	Laurence	1953 13th
Mitchell-Thomson	Hon Peter	see Lord Selsdon
Monkhouse	Peter	1949 DNF
Morris-Goodall	Mortimer	1933 DNF, 1934 DNF, 1935 12th, 1937 11th, 1938 DNF, 1939 12th, 1949 DNF, 1950 19th, 1951 10th, 1955 19th
Morrison	Charles	1938 DNF
Morrison	John	1979 DNF
Moss	Sir Stirling	1951 DNF, 1952 DNF, 1953 2nd, 1954 DNF, 1956 2nd, 1957 DNF, 1958 DNF, 1959 DNF, 1961 DNF
Mountain	Frank	2004 19th
Mowlem	Johnny	2000 17th, 2001 DNF, 2003 DNF, 2005 DNF
Mullen	Tim	2005 24th
Murray	David	1937 DNF
Murton-Neale	R.C.	1930 DNF, 1937 5th
Musetti	Val	1986 DNF
Nathan	Roger	1967 DNF
Naylor	Brian	1958 15th, 1959 DNF
Nearn	Robert	1996 14th, 1997 DNF, 1998 17th, 2004 DNF

Needell	Tiff	1980 DNQ, 1981 DNF, 1982 DNF, 1983 17th, 1984 9th, 1985 11th, 1987 DNF, 1988 24th, 1989 DNF, 1990 3rd, 1991 DNF, 1992 12th, 1995 DNF, 1996, 19th, 1997 DNF, 1998 DNQ
Nelson	Edward	1968 DNF
Newman	George	1928 DNS
Newsome	Sammy	1929 8th, 1930 6th, 1931 DNF, 1931 5th, 1934 6th, 1935 DQ/DNF
Newton	Mike	2003 22nd, 2004 DNF, 2005 20th
Nicholson	Chuck	1982 DNF
Noël	John Cecil	1934 11th
North	Roy	1959 DNF
Nuttall	Harry	1994 DNF
Oats	R.F.	1933 DNS
O'Brien	Eugene	1995 11th
O'Connell	Martin	2001 DNF
Odlam	Dick	1955 DNF
Oliver	Jackie	1968 DNF, 1969 1st, 1971 DNF
O'Rourke	Steve	1979 12th, 1980 23rd, 1981 DNF, 1982 DNF, 1983 17th, 1985 11th, 1996 DNF, 1998 4th
Ovey	David	1983 11th, 1984 DNF
Owen	Peter	2002 DNF, 2005 DNF
Owen-Jones	Lindsay	1994 DNF, 1995 DNF, 1996 5th
Palmer	Jonathan	1983 8th, 1984 DNF, 1985 2nd, 1987 DNF, 1991 DNF
Parish	Don	1935 DNF
Parker	Robert	1949 11th, 1951 DNS
Parkes	Mike	1960 DNF, 1961 2nd, 1962 DNF, 1963 3rd, 1964 DNF, 1965 DNF, 1966 DNF, 1967 2nd, 1970 DNF, 1971 DNF, 1972 7th
Parnell	Reg	1950 6th, 1951 7th, 1952 DNF, 1953 DNF, 1954 DNF, 1955 DNF, 1956 NC
Paul	Cyril	1928 DNF, 1929 DNF, 1934 3rd, 1935 DNF
Peacock	Kenneth	1929 8th, 1930 6th, 1931 DNF, 1932 DNF, 1933 4th, 1934 5th
Peacock	Rodney	1952 10th, 1954 DNF
Penn-Hughes	Clifton	1933 5th, 1934 DNF, 1935 DNF
Percy	Win	1981 DNF, 1986 DNF, 1988 14th, 1993 DNF, 1995 DNF
Peters	Mark	1987 DNF
Petre	Mrs Kaye	1934 13th, 1935 DNF, 1937 DNF
Phillips	George	1949 DQ/DNF, 1950 18th
Phillips	Simon	1976 22nd, 1977 DNF, 1978 DQ/DNF, 1979 20th, 1980 23rd, 1982 7th
Pickering	Gavin	2002 23rd, 2003 29th, 2004 DNF, 2005 DNF
Piper	David	1963 6th, 1965 DNF, 1966 DNF, 1967 DNF, 1968 7th, 1969 DNF, 1970 DNF
Piper	Richard	1990 21st, 1991 NC, 1992 14th, 1993 DNF, 1994 DNF, 1995 DNF
Pool	Colin	1989 DNF
Poole	Alec	1968 15th, 1976 DNF
Postan	Alex	1990 28th
Preece	David	1977 17th, 1979 DNF
Preston	David	1967 DNF

Price	Hugh	1997 13th
Prior	Richard	1962 DNF
Procter	Peter	1961 16th, 1962 15th, 1964 DNF
Purdy	Harold John	1928 6th
Quick	John	1968 DNQ
Raby	Ian	1957 15th
Raymond	Martin	1978 DNF, 1979 20th
Redman	Brian	1967 DNF, 1968 DNF, 1970 DNF, 1973 DNF, 1976 DNF, 1978 5th, 1979 DQ/DNF, 1980 5th, 1981 DNF, 1982 DNF, 1984 DNF, 1985 DNF, 1986 DNF, 1988 10th, 1989 11th
Reece	Peter	1951 31st
Rees	Alan	1966 DNF
Reid	Anthony	1990 3rd, 1991 DNF, 1996 19th, 1998 DNQ, 2001 DNF, 2002 DNF, 2005 DNF
Rhodes	John	1965 12th, 1966 DNF
Richardson	Cliff	1935 4th
Richardson	Ken	1955 15th
Richardson	R.G.	1935 28th
Rickett	Charles	1991 DNF, 1992 11th, 1994 DNF
Riddell	Miss Joan	1937 16th
Riley	Peter	1959 8th, 1960 DNF
Rippon	Alan	1951 DNF, 1952 DNF, 1953 2nd, 1954 DNF, 1955 DNF
Riseley-Prichard	John	1955 DNF
Robinson	Barry	1984 DNF
Robinson	Brian	1972 DNF
Robinson	John	1997 13th, 1998 DNQ, 1999 DNF
Robinson	Stanley	1969 DNF
Rolt	Tony	1949 DNF, 1950 4th, 1951 6th , 1952 DNF, 1953 1st, 1954 1st, 1955 DNF
Rose-Richards	Tim	1929 DNF, 1930 4th, 1931 3rd, 1932 5th, 1933 3rd, 1934 DNF
Rossiter	Jeremy	1984 DNQ
Rothschild	Michael	1959 DNF
Rouse	Andy	1980 12th, 1981 11th, 1982 DNF
Rubin	Bernard	1928 1st, 1929 DNF, 1933 DNS
Rudd	Ken	1953 DNP/DNS, 1957 10th
Ruddock	Gerry	1952 10th, 1954 DNF
Russell	Jim	1957 DNF, 1959 DNF
Sadler	Peter	1969 DNF
Salmon	Mike	1962 DNF, 1962 5th, 1964 DQ/DNF, 1965 DNF, 1966 DNF, 1967 DNF, 1968 DNF, 1977 17th, 1979 DNF, 1981 DNF, 1982 7th, 1983 DNF, 1984 DNF
Salvadori	Roy	1953 DNF, 1054 DNF, 1955 DNF, 1956 DNF, 1957 DNF, 1958 DNF, 1959 1st, 1960 3rd, 1961 DNF, 1962 4th, 1963 DNF
Samuelson	Sir Francis	1925 DNF, 1928 DNF, 1930 DNF, 1931 NC/DQ, 1932 DNF
Sanderson	Ninian	1955 14th, 1956 1st, 1957 2nd, 1958 DNF, 1959 DNF, 1960 NC, 1961 DNF, 1962 DNF, 1963 7th
Sargent	Peter	1962 5th, 1963 DNF, 1964 DNF
Saunders-Davies	A.C.	1929 DNF

Saunders-Davies	Owen	1931 3rd, 1934 DNF
Schirle	Robin	1998 22nd
Scott	Archie	1937 13th, 1939 DNF
Scott	James	1953 DNS
Scott-Douglas	James	1949 DNF, 1951 13th
Sears	David	1989 DNF, 1990 3rd
Sears	Jack	1960 DNF, 1962 5th, 1964 DNF, 1965 8th
Segrave	Sir Henry	1925 DNF
Selsdon	The Lord	1935 DNF, 1939 4th, 1949 1st, 1950 DNF
Sharpe	Adam	2004 NC, 2005 21st
Shawe-Taylor	Brian	1951 5th
Shead	James	1989 16th, 1990 25th
Sheldon	John	1980 DNQ, 1982 DNF, 1983 NC, 1984 DNF, 1985 16th, 1986 DNF, 1987 10th, 1988 20th, 1989 DNF, 1990 DNF, 1991 DNF, 1992 DNF
Shepherd-Barron	Richard	1962 13th
Short	Martin	2004 DNF, 2005 16th
Sieff	Jonathan	1959 DNF
Simpson	Mrs Gordon	1935 24th
Skailes	Ian	1970 DNF
Skeffington	J.M.	1937 5th
Skinner	Miss Barbara	1935 25th
Slaughter	Miss Juliette	1978 DNF
Smith	Barrie	1972 14th
Smith	Guy	2000 DNF, 2001 DNF, 2003 1st, 2004 2nd
Smith	Nigel	2001 9th, 2003 18th, 2004 23rd
Smith	Paul	1982 8th, 1983 11th, 1984 DNF, 1985 21st
Smith	Robin	1977 DNF, 1978 DNF, 1979 17th, 1985 DNF, 1987 DNF, 1988 25th, 1989 DNF, 1994 DNF
Smithson	Mark	2002 DNF
Soper	Steve	1983 18th, 1996 11th, 1997 DNF, 1998 DNF, 1999 5th
Spence	Mike	1967 19th
Spender	Chris	1963 DQ/DNF
Spice	Gordon	1964 DNF, 1978 14th, 1979 DNF, 1980 3rd, 1981 3rd, 1982 DNF, 1984 DNF, 1985 14th, 1986 19th, 1987 6th, 1988 13th, 1989 DNF
Stacey	Alan	1958 NC, 1959 DNF
Stanley Barnes	Frank	1933 13th, 1934 8th, 1935 16th
Stanley-Turner	Miss Dorothy	1937 16th
Stanton	Richard	2002 DNF, 2003 DNF, 2005 NC
Stapleton	Ernest	1949 DNF
Stewart	Ian	1952 DNF, 1953 4th, 1954 DNF
Stewart	Mrs Gwenda	1934 DNF, 1935 DNF
Stewart	Sir Jackie	1965 10th
Stirling	Robbie	1989 16th
Stisted	Mrs H.H.	1931 DNF
Stoop	Dickie	1950 9th, 1951 19th , 1952 DNF, 1956 DNF, 1957 DNF, 1958 8th, 1959 DNF, 1960 DNF, 1961 DNF
Straight	Whitney	1934 DNS
Sugden	Tim	1998 4th, 2003 DNF, 2004 23rd
Surtees	John	1963 DNF, 1964 3rd, 1965 DNF, 1967 DNF
Sutcliffe	Peter	1964 DQ/DNF, 1965 DNF, 1966 DNF, 1967 17th
Sutherland	David	1984 9th
Taggart	Peter	1968 DNQ
Taylor	Dennis	1957 DNF
Taylor	Henry	1960 DNF
Taylor	Mike	1958 DNF, 1959 DNF
Taylor	Trevor	1961 12th
Thatcher	Mark	1980 DNF, 1981 DNF
Thackwell	Mike	1987 DNF
Thistlethwayte	Tommy	1926 DNF
Thomas	C.T.	1935 10th
Thompson	Eric	1949 8th, 1950 DNF, 1951 3rd, 1952 DNF, 1953 DNF, 1954 DNF, 1955 DNF
Titteringham	Desmond	1956 DNF, 1957 14th
Tomlinson	Lawrence	2004 22nd
Tongue	Reggie	1934 10th
Trimmer	Tony	1979 DNF, 1980 DNQ, 1981 DNF
Turner	Darren	2003 DNF, 2004 9th, 2005 9th
Turner	John	1959 7th
Turner	Jack	1962 DNF
Turner	R.F.	1929 DNF, 1935 DNF
Urquhart-Dykes	William	1928 9th, 1929 DNF
Van der Becke	Alex	1933 4th, 1934 5th, 1935 4th
Vann	Christian	1999 22nd, 2004 20th, 2005 8th
Verdon-Roe	Bobby	2005 DNF
Vesty	Paul	1968 DNF, 1969 DNF, 1971 12th
Wadsworth	Edgar	1954 15th, 1955 21st
Wagstaff	John	1960 14th, 1963 10th, 1964 22nd, 1967 DNF
Waleran	The Lord William	1939 4th, 1949 1st, 1950 DNF
Walker	Alistair	1970 5th
Walker	Peter	1951 1st, 1952 DNF, 1953 2nd, 1954 DNF, 1955 DNF, 1956 DNF
Walker	R.R.C.	1939 8th
Walkinshaw	Tom	1976 DNF, 1977 DNF, 1978 DNF, 1981 DNF, 1982 DNF
Wallace	Andy	1988 1st, 1989 DNF, 1990 2nd, 1991 4th, 1992 8th, 1993 DNF, 1995 3rd, 1996 6th, 1997 DNF, 1998 7th, 1999 DNF, 2000 21st, 2001 3rd, 2002 4th, 2003 6th, 2004 DNF, 2005 14th
Waller	Ivan	1951 11th
Walshaw	Robert	1956 DQ/DNF, 1957 13th,
Warnock	Dave	1997 DNF, 1998 22nd, 2001 16th, 2002 DNF, 2003 DNF, 2004 DNF
Warwick	Derek	1983 DNF, 1986 DNF, 1991 4th, 1992 1st, 1996 13th
Watney	Richard	1929 DNF, 1930 2nd
Watson	John	1973 DNF, 1984 DNF, 1985 DNF, 1987 DNF, 1988 DNF, 1989 DNF, 1990 11th

Watson	Neil	1938 DNF
Weaver	James	1983 18th, 1985 2nd, 1986 16th, 1987 DNF, 1989 DNF, 1990 DNF, 1991 13th, 1995 DNF, 1996 9th, 1997 DNF, 1998 DNF, 1999 DNF
Welch	Lewis	1939 DNF
Westbury	Peter	1972 DNF
Wharton	Ken	1953 13th, 1954 DNF, 1956 DNF
Wheeler	Jen	1934 11th
Whitcroft	C.R.	1933 7th
White	Geoffrey	1938 13th, 1939 15th
Whiteaway	Ted	1959 7th
Whitehead	Graham	1953 DNF, 1954 DNF, 1957 DNF, 1958 2nd, 1958 DNF, 1960 DNF
Whitehead	Peter	1950 15th, 1951 1st, 1952 DNF, 1953 4th, 1954 DNF, 1955 DNF, 1957 DNF, 1958 2nd
Whitmore	Sir John	1959 10th, 1962 DNF, 1963 DNF, 1965 DNF, 1966 DNF
Widdows	Robin	1969 7th
Wilds	Mike	1981 DNF, 1982 DNF, 1984 DNF, 1985 DNF, 1986 DQ, 1987 DNF, 1988 14th
Wilkins	Gordon	1939 18th, 1951 23rd, 1952 13th, 1953 14th, 1955 DNF
Wilks	William	1959 DNF
Williams	Jonathan	1968 DNF, 1970 NC
Wilson	Justin	2004 NC
Wilson	Peter	1950 20th, 1951 19th, 1952 DNF, 1954 7th, 1955 7th
Wingfield	John	1968 DNF
Winterbottom	Eric	1950 18th, 1951 14th
Wisdom	Mrs Elsie	1933 DNF, 1935 DNF, 1938 DNF
Wisdom	Tommy	1934 18th, 1935 DNF, 1938 DNF, 1939 DNF, 1949 6th, 1950 16th, 1951 DNF, 1952 3rd, 1953 DNF, 1954 8th, 1955 9th
Wise	Tommy	1950 16th, 1951 DNF, 1952 DNF
Wood	Dudley	1980 DNF, 1981 4th, 1983 DNF, 1984 DNF, 1986 5th, 1987 9th, 1988 11th, 1989 17th, 1990 27th
Woolfe	John	1968 DNF, 1969 DNF
Worth	Charles	1935 DNF
Worthington	Derek	1975 29th
Wrottesley	Richard	1965 DNF
Wyllie	John	1961 DNF, 1962 11th
Youles	Mike	1990 21st, 2001 16th

Abbreviations:
DNP=Did Not Practice;
DNS=Did Not Start;
DNQ=Did Not Qualify;
DNF=Did Not Finish;
DQ=Disqualified;
NC=Not Classified.

The British (not to mention a few Danes) gather to proclaim the Bentley victory of 2003. *(Author)*

BRITISH CARS AT LE MANS

Compiled by Gordon Creese

AC	1957	1958	1959	1960	1961
	1962	1963	1964	1965	
ADA	1984	1988	1989	1990	
Allard	1950	1951	1952	1953	
Alta	1932				
Alvis	1928	1929	1949		
Arnott	1957				
Argo	1986	1987	1988		
Ascari	2001	2002			
Aston Martin	1928	1931	1932	1933	1934
	1935	1937	1938	1939	1949
	1950	1951	1952	1953	1954
	1955	1956	1957	1958	1959
	1960	1961	1962	1963	1964
	1979	1989	2005		
Austin	1925	1933	1934	1935	1937
Austin-Healey	1953	1955	1960	1961	1962
	1963	1964	1965	1966	1967
	1968				
Bardon	1986	1987			
Bentley	1923	1924	1925	1926	1927
	1928	1929	1930	1931	1932
	1933	1949	1950	1951	2001
	2002	2003			
Bristol	1953	1954	1955		
BRM	1992	1997			
Chevron	1968	1969	1970	1972	1977
	1978	1979	1982	1985	
Cooper	1955	1956	1957	1959	1961
Costin Nathan	1967				
DBA	2003	2005			
De Cadenet*	1974	1975	1976	1977	1978

	1979	1980	1981	1982	1983
Deep Sanderson	1963	1964	1968		
Derby	1934	1935			
Duckhams Special	1972	1973			
Ecosse	1984	1985	1986	1987	
Elva	1965				
EMKA	1983	1985			
Ford	1937				
Frazer Nash	1935	1937	1949	1950	1951
	1952	1953	1954	1955	1956
	1957	1959			
GRID	1982	1983	1984		
Gulf	1974	1975			
Harrier	1993	1984			
Healey	1949	1950	1968	1969	1970
HRG	1937	1938	1939	1949	
IBEC	1978	1980	1981		
Invicta	1929				
Jaguar	1950	1951	1952	1953	1954
	1955	1956	1957	1958	1959
	1960	1962	1964	1986	1987
	1988	1989	1990	1991	1993
	1995				
Jowett	1950	1951	1952		
Kieft	1954	1955			
Lagonda	1928	1929	1934	1935	1937
	1939	1954	1955		
Lea Francis	1929	1930			
Lenham	1976				
Lister	1958	1959	1963	1995	1996
	1997	2004			
Lola	1960	1963	1967	1968	1971

	1975	1976	1977	1978	1979
	1980	1981	1982	1984	1999
	2000	2001	2002	2004	2005
Lotus	1955	1956	1957	1958	1959
	1960	1961	1962	1963	1964
	1993	1994			
McLaren	1981	1995	1996	1997	1998
March	1975	1982	1984	1985	1986
Marcos**	1962	1966	1967	1968	1996
	1997				
MG***	1930	1931	1932	1933	1934
	1935	1937	1938	1939	1949
	1950	1951	1955	1959	1960
	1961	1965	2001	2002	2003
	2005				
Mirage****	1967	1973	1976	1977	1978
	1982				
Morgan	1938	1939	1952	1962	2002
	2004				
Nasamax	2004				
Nash-Healey	1950	1951	1952	1953	
Nimrod	1982	1983	1984		
Nomad	1969				
Peerless	1958				
Pilbeam	2001	2003	2005		
Piper	1969				
Reynard	2000	2001	2002	2003	2004

	1933	1934	1935	1937	1938
Riley	1933	1934	1935	1937	1938
	1949	1950			
Royale	1987				
Rover-BRM	1963	1965			
Singer	1933	1934	1935	1937	1938
	1939	1949			
Spice	1985	1986	1987	1988	1989
	1990	1991	1992	1993	
Sunbeam	1925	1961	1962	1963	1964
Talbot (UK)	1930	1031	1932		
Tiga	1984	1985	1986	1987	1988
	1989	1990			
Tojeiro	1958	1959	1962		
Triumph	1954	1955	1959	1960	1961
	1964	1965	1980		
TVR	1962	2003	2004	2005	
Unipower	1969				
Zytek	2004	2005			

Notes:
* see also Duckhams Special
** includes Mini Marcos
*** includes MG Lola
**** see also Gulf

The above lists all British branded cars that either raced or attempted to qualify for the Le Mans 24-Hours. It does not include those cars assembled in Britain for foreign brands (e.g. Ford, Nissan and BMW)

Where a car has raced under two brands (e.g. the Nasamax was rebuilt from a Reynard that had raced the previous year) it is listed under the brand entered that year

Martin Short brought a new name to the Le Mans entry list in 2006 with his Radical LMP2 car seen here the month before at Spa-Francorchamps. *(Author)*

PERSONALITIES

Tailpiece: A Bristol 450 embarks for Le Mans in 1954. The works team finished seventh, eighth and ninth overall that year, just one more example of the many British successes at Le Mans. (L.J.K.Setright)

BENTLEY

FEDERAL MOGUL

The best brands in the business